LATIN EROTIC ELEGY AND THE SHAPING OF SIXTEENTH-CENTURY ENGLISH LOVE POETRY

How did Latin erotic elegy influence and shape sixteenth-century English love poetry? Using an interdisciplinary approach, this book offers detailed readings of poetry with close attention to the erotic, sometimes problematically 'pornographic', 'wanton' and 'lascivious' verse that exists in both periods. Moving beyond arguments that relate Renaissance eroticism more or less solely back to Ovid and Petrarch, Linda Grant breaks new ground by demonstrating the extent to which a broader sense of classical, specifically Latin, erotics underpins conceptions of sexual love, gender and desire in Renaissance literature. Methodologically sophisticated and moving away from static source study to the dynamism of intertextuality and reception, Grant shows the value of dialogic readings, exploring how elegy speaks to Renaissance poetry and how reading poems from both periods together illuminates both sets of verse.

LINDA GRANT has been a Teaching Fellow and Visiting Lecturer in Renaissance Literature at Royal Holloway, University of London. She has also previously taught at Birkbeck in both the English and Classics departments, and at Queen Mary, University of London. Her research focuses on Renaissance discourses of love and the erotic.

LATIN EROTIC ELEGY AND THE SHAPING OF SIXTEENTH-CENTURY ENGLISH LOVE POETRY

Lascivious Poets

LINDA GRANT

CAMBRIDGE
UNIVERSITY PRESS

CAMBRIDGE
UNIVERSITY PRESS

University Printing House, Cambridge CB2 8BS, United Kingdom

One Liberty Plaza, 20th Floor, New York, NY 10006, USA

477 Williamstown Road, Port Melbourne, VIC 3207, Australia

314–321, 3rd Floor, Plot 3, Splendor Forum, Jasola District Centre, New Delhi – 110025, India

79 Anson Road, #06-04/06, Singapore 079906

Cambridge University Press is part of the University of Cambridge.

It furthers the University's mission by disseminating knowledge in the pursuit of education, learning, and research at the highest international levels of excellence.

www.cambridge.org
Information on this title: www.cambridge.org/9781108493864
DOI: 10.1017/9781108663847

First published 2019

Printed in the United Kingdom by TJ International Ltd. Padstow Cornwall

A catalogue record for this publication is available from the British Library.

ISBN 978-1-108-49386-4 Hardback

Contents

Textual Note

As a general principle, quotations from classical Latin texts are from the Oxford Classical Text (OCT), with translations from the Loeb edition lightly adapted by the author unless otherwise stated. The few Greek quotations are given in translation only from either the Loeb or, in the case of Homer, from the Richmond Lattimore translations.

Early modern quotations are taken from standard editions as noted in the notes and bibliography, modernised here in terms of spelling and punctuation.

Abbreviations that appear in the notes are *OED* for the *Oxford English Dictionary* and *OLD* for the *Oxford Latin Dictionary*. Standard abbreviations for Latin texts are given in footnotes, but the texts are given their full name in the body of chapters to avoid confusion.

Introduction
'All That Rout of Lascivious Poets That Wrote Epistles and Ditties of Love'

'We Should Write Just as Bees Make Honey': *Imitatio*, Roman Love Elegy and the 'Petrarchan'

The opening sonnet of Philip Sidney's *Astrophil and Stella* gives a vivid picture of a sixteenth-century English poet struggling to write love poetry. Astrophil's first recourse is to previous poets: 'oft turning others' leaves, to see if thence would flow | some fresh and fruitful showers upon my sunburnt brain'.[1] Poetic inspiration is presupposed to come from reading prior writers, 'turning others' leaves'. But the practice of Renaissance literary *imitatio* is not a simple or unsophisticated one. 'Turning' certainly refers to the turning over of pages as Astrophil scours through what has already been written; but it also implies a metamorphic art, the 'turning' of one image, trope, text or even genre into something undoubtedly related and, yet, different.[2]

This book traces the imitation – a 'turning' – of Catullus and classical Latin love elegy (specifically Propertius, Ovid and Sulpicia) in, and into, the so-called 'Petrarchan' love poetry of four English writers of the sixteenth century: Thomas Wyatt, Philip Sidney, John Donne and Mary Sidney, with a brief foray into the seventeenth century via Mary Wroth at the end. While Catullus does not always write in elegiac metre and is not conventionally grouped with the elegists proper, this book reads him as a kind of proto-elegist who sets the erotic framework which elegy proper comes to adopt.[3] That Catullus was so presented by the elegists themselves as well as by Renaissance writers, including Petrarch, will be seen later.

The following chapters explore, through close and detailed readings, the complex dialogues set up by and between the selected Roman and English texts. By focusing on *imitatio* as a reciprocal textual dialogue, this project considers both what erotic elegy does to, and for, sixteenth-century love poetry, and what sixteenth-century poetry does with, and to, love elegy. In other words, eschewing a simplistic and one-directional model of classical influence or source study which implies a hierarchical and overly mechanistic approach to the Renaissance imitation of classical texts, this book instead investigates how placing these poems in juxtaposition leads to readings which mutually illuminate both the Roman and English texts.

Imitatio, as Thomas Greene points out, is a broad, loose and unstable critical term that encompasses appropriations of style, vocabulary, theme, topoi or form, as well as adaptation, paraphrase or translation.[4] It is also, as the *Astrophil and Stella* quotation above shows, a fundamental 'literary technique' of Renaissance poetics. The next section of this introduction problematises Greene's influential analysis of *imitatio*. For the moment, however, it can be said that the influence of Roman erotic elegy on sixteenth-century love poetry is a surprisingly under-explored topic.

Much has been written on the imitation of Ovid in the Renaissance generally, and there have been specific studies on the influence of the *Amores* as well as the *Heroides* and the *Metamorphoses*.[5] Catullus, too, has attracted some attention: both the way in which he was read in Renaissance Italy, as well as how his poetry might be situated against the Petrarchan.[6] But there has been no study, to date, of classical erotic elegy as a genre which serves to inform, organise and shape what is a dominant mode, for Renaissance poetry, of articulating literary love and erotic relationships.

Given this gap in the scholarly literature, the aim of this book is to investigate the following questions: how do sixteenth-century English texts participate in the discourses mapped out by Catullus and Roman elegy, and what work might classical love elegy do in cultural, social, political, literary and ideological terms for English Renaissance love poetry? What does elegy enable that Petrarchism and epic, say, do not, especially in terms of gender constructions and sexualised power relations? In pursuing this agenda, we will also consider what an identification with the sometimes problematic texts of Catullus and the Latin elegists might signify in sixteenth-century England; and what the cultural potential and hermeneutic possibilities of erotic poetics might be for our specific English poets. A subsidiary objective is to trace how varying practices of *imitatio* might work on an intimate, text-to-text level.

The practice of *imitatio* might be a fundamental principle of Renaissance poetics but, as Charles Martindale, amongst others, remarks, it functions more as 'creative assimilation' rather than as simple allusion or quotation, and tends to result in texts which are 'derived from, but independent of, the original'.[7] This can be seen clearly from Renaissance writers' own articulation of their practice of *imitatio*. Petrarch, in a letter to Giovanni

Boccaccio in 1366, says: 'the imitator must take care that what he writes is similar but not the same'.[8] In the same letter, Petrarch uses the analogy of bees making honey, drawing on Seneca's epistle on imitation, as a stimulus to creation:

> we should stick with Seneca's advice, which, before him, was that of Horace, to write as bees make honey, not preserving the flowers but converting them into honeycombs, so that from many assorted elements a single thing is created, different and better.[9]

Petrarch is not concerned here with straightforward allusion but with a more complex, almost alchemical, process by which a multiplicity of sources inform, and are themselves transformed into, something creative and original. Indeed, Renaissance writers positively reject the idea of the easy and unthinking lifting and re-use of past texts. In a letter from c.1485 Angelo Poliziano states:

> those who compose only on the basis of imitation strike me as parrots or magpies bringing out things they don't understand. Such writers lack strength and life; they lack energy, feeling, character ... there is nothing true in them, nothing solid, nothing efficacious ... to draw nothing from the self and to imitate always is the mark of the unhappy mind.[10]

John Donne is even more direct in his indictment of writers who simply regurgitate others' texts:

> But he is worst, who (beggarly) doth chaw
> Others' wits' fruits, and in his ravenous maw
> Rankly digested, doth those things out-spew,
> As his own things; and they are his own, 'tis true,
> For if one eat my meat, though it be known
> The meat was mine, th' excrement is his own.[11]

Ben Jonson, too, in epigram 81 'To Prowl the Plagiary' makes an implicit distinction between *imitatio* and plagiarism.

Petrarch's bees analogy is not just on the subject of *imitatio* but is itself a reproduction of Seneca's aesthetics of imitation. As the following chapters will show, Roman literature is itself acutely and self-consciously imitative as it negotiates its relationship to prior Greek and Latin texts. It thus provides, for sixteenth-century writers, not just a model of content to be reworked and renewed, but serves as a paradigm of creative and metamorphic *imitatio*.

One of the key points to be drawn from Renaissance texts on *imitatio* is the differentiation and prioritisation of the *res*, 'matter' from the *verba*, 'words'. Roger Ascham's *The Scholemaster* contains an extended discussion

of this point, that writers should be concerned with the matter or content
of the texts which they are imitating, not simply the words, literal liftings
or verbal echoes. This can be seen in practice when we consider the identification of 'Petrarchan' poetry in English: it is quite rare to find straightforward borrowings and literal translations of Petrarch's own texts, even
in quasi-translations such as Wyatt's 'Whoso List to Hunt'. Chapter 2,
which considers Wyatt's renewing of Catullan concerns in this poem, also
traces how Wyatt's text draws attention to Petrarch's 'Una candida cerva'
as a precedent while simultaneously transforming both it and Catullan
allusions into a text with a specifically Henrician context and relevance.
Imitations of elegy, as will be seen in detail throughout this book, operate
in a similarly sophisticated, hybridised manner, and the very absence of
direct quotations, bearing out Petrarch's 'similar but not the same', may
be one of the reasons why this relationship has not been explored in more
detail to date.

That is not to say that Roman elegy has been ignored completely
in the literature: some scholars have certainly acknowledged a more
complex genealogy for English 'Petrarchan' poetry than just Petrarch.
Jennifer Petrie, for example, discusses the way Petrarch, in the *canzoniere*,
appropriates themes and styles from what she calls 'the Augustans': while
she accepts Petrarch's knowledge of Propertius, she is more interested in
tracing the presence of Horace, Virgil and Ovid in his love poetry, as
well as the influence of the vernacular Italian tradition.[12] Stella Revard
argues for a Propertian influence in Donne's early love poetry but is
overwhelmingly concerned with the persona of the lover as represented
by both poets, and many of the arguments she makes about the character of the Propertian lover could equally be applied to the Catullan
and Ovidian lovers who precede and supersede him.[13] She draws particularly on Helen Gardner who herself sees echoes of *Amores* 1.9, Tibullus
1.10, Propertius 3.4 and 3.5 in Donne's 'Love's War', a testament to the
way the Latin elegiac genre influences Donne, rather than a single elegiac poet.[14]

Paul Allen Miller recognises what he calls a 'Petrarchan-Ovidian' tradition, as does Barbara Estrin; Arthur Marotti, however, sees the Ovidian
and the Petrarchan as opposed to each other since he associates the Ovidian
with 'the anti-feminist devaluation of women' versus Petrarchan devotion.[15]
Heather Dubrow cites the influence of classical poets on Petrarch, W.R.
Johnson reads Petrarch's lover as developing out of Catullus, and Gregory
Heyworth remarks that Petrarch's *canzoniere* play a critical role in 'advan-
cing the form of the elegiac sequence from its Augustan origins in Ovid,

Tibullus, Propertius and Catullus' – but these are all passing comments in books which have other concerns than the imitation of elegy.[16]

In a more focused study, Joseph Blevins argues for what he calls a 'Catullan consciousness' in Renaissance love lyric but sees this as an alternative to, and deviation from, the Petrarchan conventions, rather than as springing from one of the strands which informs the development of Petrarchism, as this project does.[17] At the same time, he reads Catullus' Lesbia poems as the first love sequence in Western literature, a premise which, surely, argues for a closer rather than more distant relationship between Catullus, Petrarch and their imitators, even though the Lesbia poems are, perhaps deliberately, not ordered as a sequence.[18]

It is certainly not new, then, to detect a relationship between Catullus, Latin erotic elegy and Renaissance 'Petrarchan' love lyric but the approach taken here, in contrast to past scholarship, is that of a sustained, focused and less fragmented view of Latin elegy allowing an examination of the way elegiac discourse as a whole informs the 'Petrarchan' mode of poetics. Petrarch, in this book, serves as a crucial mediator of love elegy into sixteenth-century England.

The elegiac 'plot' is a simple one, and can be mapped onto the Petrarchan with relative ease. In Catullus and elegy, the poet-narrator ('Catullus', 'Propertius', 'Ovid', 'Sulpicia') is obsessively in love with a sexually available though somehow still elusive mistress (Lesbia, Cynthia, Corinna) or, in the case of Sulpicia, the male Cerinthus, and the poems celebrate his or her erotic servitude. Many of the same tropes and conventions reappear in each poet's work: the *recusatio* where the narrator defends his writing of 'trifles' (*nugae*), rather than serious epic; the *paraclausithyron*, recited before the mistress's closed door; the birthday poem; the sickness poem; 'kiss' poems; poems which voyeuristically undress the mistress; and the repeated use of the conventions and imagery of *militia amoris*, 'the military campaign of love'.[19]

It is not hard to see how these tropes which help constitute the elegiac genre inform Petrarch and Petrarchan poetry: the depictions of obsessive love, the elusiveness of the mistress, the overwhelming concern with the poet-narrator's subjectivity, the translation of *militia amoris* into the bows and arrows of Cupid, the prevalence of kiss poems, and the re-emergence of the undressed mistress as the Renaissance blazon. Even the form of a 'cycle' of elegies may be linked to the Renaissance sonnet sequence, both modes displaying their fragmentation as much as their unity.

Petrarch's elegiac appropriations are many and his debt to Ovid has been especially well served by the literature, but it is also possible to identify more varied, intriguing and non-Ovidian elegiac echoes within Petrarch's texts.[20] *Canzoniere* 250, for example, portrays a scene where 'Petrarch' is visited by Laura's ghost, an event which also serves as the basis for his *Triumph of Death*, translated by Mary Sidney, both poems drawing on Propertius 4.7, where Cynthia's ghost comes back from the underworld. Laura's speech in c.250 draws on Propertius 4.7 but also Sulpicia's last poem, [Tibullus] 3.18; and Petrarch's c.224, written in a single sentence, also alludes to [Tibullus] 3.18, Sulpicia's poem notably written in one long, breathless sentence. We will return to these specific instances of *imitatio* in the relevant chapters on Propertius-Sidney and Sulpicia-Mary Sidney respectively, but for now the point to be made is that to trace the 'Petrarchan' solely back to Petrarch, or Petrarch's poetry only back to Ovid, is misleadingly narrow and distorts the literary framework through which sixteenth-century English love texts and sonnets may be read. Ovid is certainly central to this body of verse, and Petrarch operates as an important mediator and transmitter of elegy, but the relationship between elegy, Petrarch and English (indeed, European) 'Petrarchan' love lyric is a more convoluted, tangled and fascinating one than has been previously acknowledged in the literature.

As we will see in the following chapters, Petrarch's sonnets and the 'Petrarchan' mode are not simply elegy under a different name: while frustration may certainly be a keynote of elegy, the sexual relationships between Roman poet and mistress ('*puella*') are consummated in a way that is rare, though wholly possible, in the Renaissance texts under investigation.[21] Petrarch's own sonnets may be chaste but Donne, for example, returns to the more cavalier attitude to sexual relations shown in elegy. Tone, too, can be various: the instances of humour we find in Petrarch's sonnets tend to be gentle and wry; elegy may offer a more erotically playful mood, irreverent wit, and even a robust model for a vigorous extension of the possibilities of love verse, especially in the case of Ovid, that proves productive in terms of Renaissance poetry. Rather than merely conflating the Petrarchan with the elegiac, this study explores what elegy offers as a model for imitative practice that Petrarch's poetry does not.

So why does this expansion of literary precedents matter? The labelling of poems as 'Petrarchan' settles an interpretative framework on them which foregrounds the undoubted debt owed to the *canzoniere*, but which also tends to obscure elements which do not fit the Petrarchan model.[22] Poetic deviations from Petrarch are overwhelmingly defined as 'anti-Petrarchan' so that they remain located within the contours of Petrarchan discourse.[23] One significant transformation which Petrarch makes in his re-writing of Roman love elegy is the neo-Platonic moralisation of Laura. As will be seen in Chapter 2, Catullus' Lesbia is conspicuous for her immorality: the texts show her lying and cheating, and make much of her monstrous sexual appetite and lack of chastity. Propertius' Cynthia, Ovid's Corinna and Sulpicia's Cerinthus might not be represented with quite the level of invective and obscenity that is found in Catullus, but they, too, are, according to their narrators, unfaithful and deceitful. Petrarch's chaste, virtuous, muted and untouchable Laura is none of these things, and his editing out of the sexual explicitness and debauched morality of elegiac women is hugely influential on sixteenth-century sonnet sequences and love poetry. Sidney's Stella certainly owes much to Petrarch's Laura but more problematic facets of the elegiac mistress re-emerge in Donne's erotic poetry, in the 'betrayal' poems of Robert Sidney to be looked at presently in Chapter 1, and in Wyatt's women who, as shown in Chapter 2, are neither untouchable nor silent.

The recognition of Catullan and elegiac erotics as a source of *imitatio* for so-called 'Petrarchan' love poetry thus becomes critical because it shifts and refocuses the interpretative framework through which this body of verse may be read. As is the case with genre, identifying an imitative model sets certain expectations, concentrates and 'signposts' the reader's attention towards particular elements in the imitating text. This does not, of course, mean that imitations cannot interrogate, resist or dismantle the sources from which they spring – Petrarch does precisely that by moralising the elegiac mistress in his creation of Laura. A failure to recognise and acknowledge a model in the first place, however, prevents us from comprehending what might have been done with it in its imitative transformation. As John Frow asserts, 'the prehistory of the text is not a given but is relative to an interpretative grid'.[24]

An example of the kind of mis-readings this failure of recognition can give rise to may be found in an essay by Gordon Braden on Petrarch and Ovid. Braden reads what he sees as Petrarch's appropriation of the last lines of the *Metamorphoses* into the *canzoniere* as 'one of the most innovative and influential twists' Petrarch gives to love poetry as 'his lady is … all but indistinguishable from his literary ambition'.[25] Propertian scholars, however, had been exploring the way in which the elegiac 'mistress' (*puella*), operates as an embodiment of the literary project and elegiac text well before 2000.[26] Rather than Petrarch being an originator of this 'twist', his poetry is adopting what becomes a conventional elegiac trope from Propertius onwards. The metapoetic nature of the elegiac beloved is made especially prominent by Sulpicia when her beloved is named Cerinthus, 'wax-man', an allusion to the wax-tablets on which her elegies are written.[27] Petrarch's 'innovation' comes from the application of this trope to the chaste Laura, rather than the sexually active mistress (or male beloved) of elegy, and thus reveals something important about his resistance to, and re-writing of, elegiac erotics. What this example demonstrates is how recognising the source of *imitatio* as, in this case, Roman love elegy, reconfigures our understanding of the relationship between Petrarch's sonnets, sixteenth-century English Petrarchan poetry, and the classical precedents with which they engage.

Imitatio and Intertextuality: 'What Gives Us Permission to Connect One Text to Another'?

In his influential *The Light in Troy*, published in 1982, Thomas Greene asked how can we 'discuss imitative works *as* imitations' (his emphasis) and account for the 'dynamic presence' of classical texts in Renaissance poetry.[28] He goes on to define four strategies of Renaissance *imitatio* but, for all his precision, his analysis prompts reservations.[29] The chief of these concerns his quest to uncover and articulate a single and unifying theory of Renaissance *imitatio* at a macro level. He reads *imitatio* as designating the broad cultural relationship between a classical past and a Renaissance present, and thus allocates to humanism a coherent and monolithic agenda. In his schema, *imitatio* is nothing less than a grand and all-embracing system for negotiating a relationship with the lost classical past, an attempt 'to heal that estrangement which humanism had constantly to face'.[30] Greene's narrative is one of loss and a conscious sense of anachronism, but does this vast, comprehensive and all-embracing approach help us to understand the relationships on a microcosmic level between two (or more) texts?

Malcolm Bull contests Greene's unifying narrative and suggests that the humanist engagement with classical culture was less coherent and consistent, more fragmentary and arbitrary than Greene proposes.[31] Charles Martindale also expresses some discontent with his analysis: discussing Shakespeare's 'free and relaxed' use of classical texts, he fails to discern the sense of melancholic loss and cultural disjunction at the heart of Greene's narrative.[32]

So does Greene's analysis really help to explain all that is happening when Donne, for example, writes erotic elegies in London in the 1590s – is Donne confronting an entire lost classical civilisation, or is he working on a far smaller scale; do his elegies really enact a wholesale cultural clash, or construct a far more intimate relationship with one or more individual poetic texts? The explorations in the following chapters take account of these questions and consider whether, and where, anxieties might be located as sixteenth-century poets engage with Catullus and Roman elegy.

What is productive from Greene's analysis is his positioning of *imitatio* as a form of intertextuality.[33] This is, of course, like *imitatio*, a baggy and capacious term. For Greene, intertextuality is a means by which Renaissance texts register a sense of 'cultural discontinuity', a way of structuring their estranged relationship from a lost classical past.[34] What this model fails to allow for are mediations, such as Petrarch's re-writing of elegy, that insert themselves between the classical 'originals' and Renaissance 'imitations', and the way in which Renaissance verse may be engaging with near-contemporary texts at the same time as it is imitating classical poetics.

This book builds, then, on Greene's siting of *imitatio* as a form of intertextuality, but complicates the intertextual function. Instead of understanding intertextuality in Renaissance texts as a marker of cultural loss, here it is read in positive terms as a means of intensifying our sensitivity to the presence of other textual voices – both classical and 'contemporary' (to sixteenth-century readers) – and of expanding the relational complex against, and within, which poems site themselves. Two important elements of this nexus are Catullus and Roman elegy, but the following chapters also read Wyatt, for example, not just with Catullus but in relation to Petrarch and Henry VIII's love letters; and Donne with Thomas Nashe as well as Ovid. Latin elegy, too, frequently defines itself against other earlier and contemporary texts, and some of its own revealing allusions and intertexts are discussed throughout this book. A central critical assumption underpinning this project is that if *imitatio* is a crucial praxis of sixteenth-century, and Roman, poetics, then the resultant texts have to be read relationally, against preceding, contemporary, and possibly even later, writing.

One of the methodological dissimilarities between reception and intertextuality, as these terms are commonly used, is the move from a form of objective stability to something more subjective and, possibly, uncertain. Shakespeare's use of Ovid's Pyramus and Thisbe story, for example, in *A Midsummer Night's Dream*, or John Marston's re-writing of Ovid's Pygmalion as *The Metamorphosis of Pigmalion's Image* are both clear and upfront about their uses of the prior poet's texts: it would be a perverse reader who claimed that these were not receptions of Ovid. The intertexts with which this book is largely concerned are, frequently, less fixed and fixable: they have a postmodern indeterminacy about them. There is no clinching argument on offer that 'proves' Wyatt's intended and straightforward reception of Catullus, or Sidney's of Propertius, for example – all the same, the detailed readings of a few carefully selected and juxtaposed texts highlight the interpretational value of reading these chosen poems together. After all, one of the freedoms that the praxis of intertextuality allows is the renewing of a text's relations. If the author is 'dead', to use Barthes' term, then intertexts or points of textual connections are themselves subjective and in the consciousness of the individual reader. In other words, while the readings that follow have been hedged by the facts of the Latin texts being printed and available, being read and commentated on, even being introduced to the relevant early modern writers at school (apart, perhaps, from the female authors in Chapter 5), there is no 'smoking gun' to clinch an argument of proven intentional reception.

That said, some conventional and established receptions such as Donne's debt to Ovid in his songs, sonnets and elegies are no more proven in strict terms: we do not generally find Donne quoting or paraphrasing Ovid.[35] What has been read as his reception of the elegist might more accurately fit with the idea of intertextuality being discussed here where the textual connections are based on a situational and attitudinal likeness (witty sexual encounters with a mistress) as well as engagements with the politics of gender.

This raises, then, a fundamental question, one not often asked: as Jeffrey Wills puts it, 'what gives us permission to connect one text to another?'.[36] Wills is working specifically on Latin poetry with some attention to Latin allusions (his term) to prior Greek texts, but his interrogation can be productively applied to other literatures. Indeed, given the role played by Latin texts in the early modern period as paradigms of *imitatio*, it might be especially pertinent here.

For Wills, an 'allusion' or intertext might be identified and understood on the basis of diction (reused words, syntax, length of sentence, the line position of a word); narrative similarities such as those just noted between Ovid and Donne; or allusion through form. The first, allusion through diction, is problematic in most of the cases looked at here since we are generally concerned with intertextual relations in different languages, Latin and English. We will, though, see some examples of allusion through word repetition in Sannazaro's neo-Latin, and Petrarch's Italian, re-writings of Catullus in Chapters 1 and 2. Wills' identification of parenthesis as a basis for recognising an allusion through diction is also noted in Chapter 5 where Mary Sidney recalls a sonnet of her brother, Philip Sidney. Allusion through form might also be helpful since many, though certainly not all, re-writings of elegy are in the sonnet or sonnet sequence form (Petrarch, Wyatt, Philip Sidney, Donne, Wroth). The majority of intertexts explored here, however, are what Wills categorises as narrative similarities: poems are linked through themes such as perfidious speech, settings like the bedroom, or motifs such as the female muse.

Wills is useful, therefore, for what he defines as technical 'permissions' to connect texts and we will see these at work in the chapters to come. He does also acknowledge, though he does not discuss, the role of a reader's interpretation in identifying an intertext, and this looser, more subjective, even speculative approach will also be in evidence. To put it simply, as readers, we bring differing and various literary memories to our current reading and this helps to shape our hermeneutics. At the most basic level, a scholar in an English department is almost certain to meet Wyatt, Sidney, Donne and others before encountering Catullus and the elegists – historical chronology becomes subordinate to a personal reading history, and elegy may be read as containing traces of Renaissance love poetry rather than the other way around. This project is driven overall by an understanding of intertextuality as always anachronistic in a positive sense, of literary interpretation as moving across and between texts, and of necessarily implicating the reader – a historically situated figure who is always working to make texts 'readable' in the present moment.

One effect of self-consciously reading texts in this historicised relational mode is to collapse the hierarchy which Greene's model maintains of classical texts as always being originary and prior to later 'imitations'. In *Redeeming the Text*, Charles Martindale suggests that insights into classical texts might be 'locked up' in later receptions.[37] Martindale's contention is a valuable one. However, the terminology ('locked up') might be taken to imply that meaning is static and dormant within a text, always there but somehow invisible until a later text provides a key to release it. Chapter 4 draws explicitly on Martindale's theoretical insight but explores a less linear (in whichever direction) and more contingent, reciprocal or relational reading strategy. It considers how moving between texts results in mutual illumination that complicates ideas of which text is elucidating which. As John Frow remarks, 'the identification of an intertext is an act of interpretation. The intertext is not a real and causative source but a theoretical construct formed by and serving the purpose of a reading ... the prehistory of the text is not a given but is relative to an interpretative grid'.[38]

The following chapters have been built on these theoretical principles of positive anachronism and intertext as construct, and highlight the way Renaissance intertextual connections to Catullus and elegy may bring previously unseen elements of elegiac meaning into startling focus. The concern here is not just what elegy does to its sixteenth-century imitations, but what they do to our reading of elegy.

Reading the Erotic: 'To Teach and Delight'?

'Erotic' is a notoriously difficult term to pin down whether as a description or a critical term. The *Oxford English Dictionary* gives 'of or pertaining to the passion of love; concerned with or treating of love; amatory'. What is deemed 'erotic' in literature (as in life) is relative and subjective. It is also shaped by, and understood through, historicised cultural and aesthetic norms. Distinctions between what is defined as 'erotic', 'pornographic' or sexually explicit are difficult to delineate and tricky to enforce. The following chapters unpack some of the complexities of these categorisations. They also explore the tensions set up by the studied texts between the erotic and the transgressive, and the way literary eroticism may be used to interrogate, contest, possibly even subvert, social and cultural hierarchies. It is helpful, then, to consider the use of the term 'erotic' as it applies to the Latin and early modern texts under consideration here.

The only use of the term erotic elegy (*elegeia … erotica*) in the classical period is in Aulus Gellius' *Noctes Atticae*.[39] In book 19, there is a dinner party at which the guests are entertained by a group of young singers: 'they sang in a most charming way several odes of Anacreon and Sappho, as well as some erotic elegies of more recent poets that were sweet and graceful' (19.9.4.2–4).[40] One of the Greek guests suggests that Latin literature does not have such 'exquisite, charming, or erotic poems' (*carminum delicias*, 19.9.7.11–12) 'except Catullus' (*nisi Catullus*, 19.9.7.12), but another guest, the Roman rhetorician Antonius Julianus, defends Latin literature claiming that it, too, has poetry about 'lovers and Venus' (*amasios ac venerios*, 19.9.9.7). In this debate, erotic verse is associated with cultural refinement and sophistication, and Catullus is deemed to be at least the equal of, if not superior to, Anacreon and Sappho. The erotic is thus used in this instance to negotiate the relationship between Greek and Roman culture.

Prefacing the *editio princeps* of Catullus published in Venice in 1472 was a biography of the Roman poet:

> He loved Clodia, a girl of the first rank, whom he called Lesbia in his poems … No-one was his superior. In wit he was delightful, to the highest degree, and in serious matters, most truly grave. He wrote erotic verse.[41]

This extract from the biography of Catullus is discussed in more detail in Chapter 2 but for now we should note the way in which Catullus is presented to his early modern readers: 'he wrote erotic poems' (*erotica scripsit*). This is especially striking since the word 'erotica' did not come into English usage until 1854, and its first use was as the title for the elegies of Propertius. Even the word 'erotic' is not used in English until 1668, although the derivative 'eroticall' is used slightly earlier in 1621.[42] Instead, as we will see in a moment, terms such as 'lascivious', 'wanton', even 'scurrilous' are used by early modern writers to indicate the presence of problematic erotic material.

The 'erotic' takes, and may be found in, many literary forms in sixteenth-century England: 'Ovidian' epyllion such as Shakespeare's *Venus and Adonis* or Marlowe's *Hero and Leander*; the 'Petrarchan' poetry with which we are concerned here; bawdy and lewd ballads such as Nashe's *Choice of Valentines* which we will read in Chapter 4. One of the concerns of this project is, therefore, to consider the hermeneutic and cultural possibilities of reading and writing the erotic. For the guests at Aulus Gellius' dinner party listening to recitations of erotic elegy is a way in which to mark their taste, style and civility. But the cultural presence of erotic poetry in Latin literature has a broader significance in this text: beyond the personal, it is also used as a symbol for the equality, at least, of Roman culture with Greek. What, then, and how might the erotic be made to mean in early modern England?

It has become a critical commonplace, even an orthodoxy, of Renaissance literary scholarship that the underlying principle of poetry in the period was that it should 'teach and delight'.[43] Certainly this is what many English Renaissance writers themselves tell us. For example, Elyot praises Homer for showing us 'not only the documents martial and discipline of arms, but also incomparable wisdoms and instructions for politic governance of people'.[44] Spenser's often-quoted letter to Walter Raleigh which prefaced the 1590 edition of the *Faerie Queene* openly states that 'the general end therefore of all the book is to fashion a gentleman or noble person in virtuous and gentle discipline'.[45] As we have seen, Sidney's *Defence* gives poetry a didactic aim; and Puttenham also defines the subject matter of poetry as 'the praise of virtue and reproof of vice; the instruction of moral doctrine'.[46]

This more or less general consensus derived from the literature of the period has led Brian Vickers, for example, to assert that a 'coherent theory of literature' existed in the Renaissance, which was derived from an epideictic commendation of virtue and condemnation of vice.[47] Literature, he asserts, has a role not just in the moral education of the individual, but also in creating a morally good society: 'that writers as diverse as Sidney and Heywood, Milton and Hobbes, should celebrate the power of poetry and drama to arouse a love of virtue and a desire to emulate it is further proof that Renaissance literary theory was perfectly coherent, being based on the union of rhetoric and ethics'.[48]

But if this is true, how do we account for the presence of so much erotic poetry in the English literature of the sixteenth century? Why is Roman love elegy such a prominent model for imitation given the way in which it is described as wanton and lascivious even at the same time as it is learned? There is certainly evidence that Petrarch 'cleaned up' elegy, turning the promiscuous mistress of the Latin genre into the chaste and virtuous Laura – but English 'Petrarchan' poets such as Wyatt, Robert Sidney and Donne revert to something much closer to Roman elegy in their depictions of faithless (Wyatt, Robert Sidney) and sexually active (Wyatt, Donne) mistresses.

It is significant, too, that so much of this erotic verse is not written by marginal poets, but by the canonical: Wyatt, Sidney, Donne, Marlowe, Shakespeare. If a central function of literature in the sixteenth century is to stimulate the reader to emulate its morals, then what are we to learn from erotic verse and love sonnets? It is certainly not as simple as saying that imitations of elegy provide a negative example, that they reverse the moral direction and demonstrate bad behaviour which we should avoid – the excellence of the poetry partly takes issue with that argument – so there do seem to be more complex premises which make sense of this antithetical relationship between erotic love sonnets and the supposedly ethical role given to poetry in general.

This question of reading the erotic and exploring its hermeneutic possibilities in sixteenth-century love poetry is one of the concerns here. Renaissance *imitatio* may be a transformative process, and one which concerns itself with the body or matter of a text, rather than with literal borrowings – but what is at stake when the concerns of the 'source' text are explicitly, perhaps even uncomfortably, sexual? How might English Renaissance poets, concerned with the precept or defence of poetry that it exists to 'teach and delight', negotiate a relationship with literary eroticism? David Franz and, more recently, Bette Talvacchia, Ian Frederick Moulton and Georgia Brown have argued for rescuing the erotic, even the 'pornographic', from the margins of early modern studies and replacing it at the centre of Renaissance literary culture.[49] So one strand of this project is to read the texts under investigation not just as Catullan and elegiac imitations, but as self-consciously erotic imitations of a genre which is intensely sexualised: what, this book asks, is the cultural potential of the erotic in sixteenth-century England; what – and how – might it be made to mean?

Sir John Harington's 'Preface' to his translation of the *Orlando Furioso* is a rich source for framing this investigation as Harington navigates his way through the tricky, and sometimes contradictory, issues surrounding the erotic in literature.[50] In responding to poetry's detractors he remarks:

> The last reproof is lightness and wantonness. This is indeed an objection of some importance since as Sir Philip Sidney confesseth, Cupido is crept even into the heroical poems, and consequently maketh that also subject to that reproof. I promised in the beginning not partially to praise poesy but plainly and honestly to confess that that might truly be objected against it, and if anything may be, sure it is this lasciviousness … As for the pastoral, with the sonnet or epigram, though many times they savour of wantonness and love and toying, and now and then, breaking the rules of poetry go into plain scurrility, yet even the worst of them may not be ill-applied and are, I must confess, too delightful.[51]

Firstly, it is worth noting Harington's language here – lightness, wantonness, lasciviousness – all terms which are associated with Roman love elegy, a genre which might almost be said to self-consciously embody these characteristics. The sonnet and epigram, the most prevalent forms for the Renaissance imitation of Catullus and erotic elegy, are openly associated by Harington with 'wantonness and love and toying', and, interestingly, in 'breaking the rules of poetry' as they embrace the scurrilous. Yet, even though they might transgress these implied moral rules, these poetic forms may still be 'too delightful' – where the excess expressed in that 'too' may even be attributed precisely to their illicit 'scurrility'.

Harington's 'delightful' seems deliberately chosen both for its more usual utilisation in the frequently quoted formula 'to teach and delight', and also for the way in which it possibly contests this very axiom by pointing back to its provenance in Horace's *Ars Poetica*. Horace's text does not couple these two concepts, but opposes them: 'poets want *either* to profit *or* to delight' (my emphasis).[52] Harington's text thus foregrounds a complicated, even contradictory, response to the erotic in poetry: on one hand, it is frivolous, wanton, lascivious and scurrilous, qualities apparently to be disapproved of; on the other, it is the site for an eager and, perhaps, unruly readers' (and writers'?) pleasure.

Going on to talk specifically about the *Orlando Furioso* and the 'lascivious' in Ariosto, Harington says:

> yea methinks I see some of you searching already for these places on the book, and you are half-offended that I have not made some directions that you might find and read them immediately.[53]

This is a potent testament to the popularity and appeal of the erotic in literature which counters the idea of readers solely perusing texts for moral instruction: indeed, according to Harington, some readers would prefer to skim through the serious parts and go straight to the 'lascivious' bits. Harington might here be deliberately echoing Ovid in *Tristia* 2 talking about *Aeneid* 4:

> and yet the blessed author of your *Aeneid* brought his 'arms and the man' to a Tyrian couch, and no part of the whole work is more read than that union of illicit love. (*Tristia* 2.533–6)[54]

Even taking into account the ironic tone and deliberately selective reading of the Ovidian narrator throughout the *Tristia*, both Harington and 'Ovid' draw attention to the appeal of the erotic in supposedly virtuous heroic poetry. It appears that both periods under consideration have a self-consciousness about the popularity of erotic episodes which co-exists with, and possibly undermines, a more morally focused discourse on the practice of reading. On Ariosto's 'lascivious' episodes, Harington does, perhaps disingenuously, suggest that we should 'read them as my author meant them, to breed detestation and not delectation', a retreat to the didactic rhetoric that surrounds poetry. These terms, however, seem to define categories that are unnervingly close: Harington's preface seems to advertise the possibilities of detestation and delectation overlapping, or even being exchanged.

One of the defences that Harington uses to support and excuse Ariosto's eroticism is, unsurprisingly, the authority of classical models. Strikingly, however, he does not depend on Ovid, but on Virgil:

> but as I say, if this be a fault, then Virgil committed the same fault in Dido and Aeneas's entertainment [manner of behaviour], and if some will say he tells that mannerly and covertly, how will they excuse that when Vulcan was entreated by Venus to make an armour for Aeneas?[55]

We will return to this use of Virgil as the legitimator of the erotic when we look at Renaissance receptions of Ovid in the next chapter. For now, we can say that Renaissance readers do not necessarily interpret Ovid and Virgil as two extremes on an erotic–moral continuum: Virgil's texts can support and authorise the erotic in poetry just as much as the elegiac might.

The reason why Harington's preface is so pertinent to the concerns of this project is that he foregrounds the spaces that open up between what is said about poetry and its moral aim, and the actual practices adopted by writers and readers. There might certainly exist a prescriptive moral view of literature, that it should 'teach and delight', but in practice that delight may well be sited not in the virtuous, but in the wanton, the frivolous and the lascivious. A quotation from Martial appropriated by Harington in his preface articulates some of the complexity that Renaissance readers and writers experience around literary eroticism: *laudant illa, sed ista legunt*, 'they praise those, but they read these'.[56] The treatises, commentaries, prefaces and defences of poetry tell a story, but not a complete one: poetry may masquerade beneath a mask of morality but its true delight may come from the way in which it opposes and undermines the ethical stance which allows it to exist and to be culturally valorised. One locus of this tension between the prescriptive and the actual practice of writing and reading is erotic love poetry.

The next chapter looks at the transmission history of Catullus and the elegists, their surprising presence on the English humanist school curriculum, and offers a general overview of their Renaissance receptions as context for the readings which follow. The next four chapters are constructed around close and detailed readings of one or two elegiac texts which are then read with one or two Renaissance poems which renew and revitalise the concerns of elegy for a sixteenth-century English audience. The concern here is with reading deeply into a few texts rather than broadly and, arguably, more superficially across many. Chapter 2 concentrates on how the concerns of Catullus' proto-elegiac texts from the mid-50s BCE inform the erotic and cultural dynamics of Wyatt's love poetry. Focusing on gendered images of speech – the impotent or unreliable tongue, verbal duplicity, broken oaths and overt lies – it examines how issues of speaking are turned into ethical markers which can be mapped onto the spectrum of gender. Contextualising the poetry from the two periods against, respectively, one of Cicero's forensic speeches, and Henry VIII's love letters, it especially investigates how modes of speaking are used to contest or uphold the idea of masculinity as a moral state, not just a gender position: what it might mean to speak 'like a man' in Republican Rome and Henrician England.

The third chapter turns to Propertius and Philip Sidney and, taking its cue from Cynthia as the eroticised muse of Propertian poetry, and the scornful muse of *Astrophil and Stella* 1, explores metaliterary themes of poetic practice. Reading the muse as a figure for ideas of inspiration and creativity, for authority and canonicity, we will consider how the selected texts negotiate, articulate and configure ideas about the nature, identity and cultural function of poetry in Augustan Rome and Elizabethan England.

Chapter 4 investigates how Donne's 'To His Mistress Going to Bed' and Thomas Nashe's *Choice of Valentines* make cultural use of *Amores* 1.5 and 3.7. Framing the analysis through articulations of power and impotence, we will see how literary representations of sexual performance or failure reveal covert engagements with questions of politicised myth-making and story-telling. Sex will be read as a vocabulary which has a potent place in the support and subversion of the Augustan and Elizabethan regimes.

The fifth chapter is concerned with Sulpicia's female authored elegies, Mary Sidney's translations of Petrarch's *Triumph of Death*, and of Robert Garnier's *Antonie*, both texts which make prominent use of a female voice of desire, and Mary Wroth's first sonnet from her *Pamphilia to Amphilanthus*. The argument here is not so much that Sulpicia is a model for Mary Sidney and Wroth as an exploration, in each period, of what happens when a female author/narrator inserts herself into a discourse which is primarily gendered masculine. It analyses how previous instances of ventriloquised female voices in male authored elegy and Renaissance love poetry open up a space into which it is possible for a female author to insert herself. Of special interest will be the question of what happens when the female beloved speaks up, speaks back, speaks for herself. The chapter thus investigates the way in which female voices serve to weaken, overturn or even undo dominant master-narratives of elegy and the Petrarchan, sparking moments of crisis and revelation within the texts which have not received due critical attention to date.

The poets and texts read here are canonical ones, and the very familiarity of them serves to foreground the overarching argument of this project: that by changing the intertextual framework through and against which these texts are read, we also open up the texts themselves, allowing new ways of reading and understanding them to emerge into focus.

CHAPTER I

'Ovid Was There and with Him Were Catullus, Propertius and Tibullus'

Transmission, Teaching and Receptions of Roman Love Elegy in the Renaissance

The Transmission of Catullus, Propertius, Tibullus/Sulpicia and Ovid

Ovid travelled successfully through late antiquity and the medieval period to arrive in the sixteenth century with his place in early modern culture assured, but Catullus, Propertius and Sulpicia had more effortful journeys. After the collapse of the Roman empire in the west, the texts of Catullus, Propertius and Tibullus/Sulpicia were almost lost: traces of them can be found at the Carolingian court and through the medieval period, and, eventually, they resurfaced in fourteenth-century Italy.[1] Their transmission remains somewhat confused as manuscripts appear and disappear from the record, but what is certain is that Petrarch came to own manuscripts of all three poets in the last quarter of the fourteenth century.

The Propertian text has been described as 'one of the worst transmitted' of classical Latin texts.[2] The two earliest extant manuscripts (A and N) have been traced to northern France in the twelfth or thirteenth centuries. N found its way to Italy and was owned by Poggio Bracciolini: in a 1427 letter written to Niccolò Niccoli in Florence, Poggio asserts triumphantly 'Propertius has returned to us'.[3] N appears to be the source for some of the fifteenth-century manuscript copies which circulated in Milan; and also, interestingly for our concerns, may have travelled to England with Poggio in the fifteenth century.[4]

The manuscript designated A seems to have remained in France, found its way to Richard de Fournival, chancellor of the cathedral of Amiens, and is noted in the 1338 catalogue of the Sorbonne library to which his personal collection of manuscripts was transferred.[5] This is the manuscript that was copied by or for Petrarch in c.1333.[6] At this point scholarly opinion diverges: Heyworth, following Butrica, asserts that Petrarch's manuscript was copied for Coluccio Salutati in c.1380; Fedeli more recently suggests that Salutati's copy descended separately from Petrarch's.[7] The relationship between these Propertian manuscripts is a complicated one and cannot be worked out precisely. What is important for us is that Petrarch owned an early copy of Propertius, and, crucially, that many of the descendants from A and N contained not only Propertius but also Catullus and Tibullus, including Sulpicia.

P, probably descending from Petrarch's manuscript and copied in Florence c.1423, contains Catullus, Tibullus and Ovid's 'Epistula Sapphus'.[8] B, produced in Milan c.1460, contains Propertius and Tibullus.[9] Q, from southern Italy sometime in the second half of the fifteenth century, contains Catullus and Tibullus alongside Propertius, as do U and C.[10] Butrica speculates that Propertius and Tibullus, possibly with Catullus too, were transmitted in a single codex from late antiquity and were only separated in the Carolingian period, perhaps by Richard de Fournival.[11] This could be a reason why the *editio princeps* of 1472 to which we will turn presently published Catullus, Propertius and Tibullus/Sulpicia in a single volume: the printed edition was drawing on the codex and manuscript tradition in publishing Catullus and the Latin love elegists together. This joint transmission in both manuscript and print is important for our concerns here since it means that readers of Catullus, Propertius or Tibullus from about the late fourteenth century onwards would have had access to all three poets in one volume.

We continue to see this attention to Catullus, Propertius and Tibullus as a group of poets: in 1485, for example, Angelo Poliziano (1454–94), a tutor in the Medici household, commented on his textual work and emendations: 'I, Angelo Poliziano, from my youth began to discuss the books of Catullus, Tibullus and Propertius, and from my judgement at that time either to correct or interpret them.'[12] Poliziano is perhaps best remembered by classicists today for his infamous 1489 'obscene' reading of Catullus' *passer* or sparrow poems (cc.2 and 3), an important component of Catullus' receptions as we shall see presently.

Catullus, Propertius and Tibullus were first printed by the Aldine press in Venice in 1472, together in one volume, with Statius appended. This edition was reprinted in Venice in 1475 and in the same year the first commentaries on Catullus, Propertius and Tibullus/Sulpicia were published in Rome by Beroaldo. Between 1481 and 1553 an additional six editions of a combined Catullus, Tibullus and Propertius (no longer with Statius appended) were published in Europe. That they were published together in a single volume may certainly have been due to the relative slightness of their *oeuvre* (in terms of size), but is also evidence that they were read together in this period and that the generic alliances between them were well recognised. If we accept that they were transmitted in a single codex from late antiquity, then even before their first appearance in print the relationship between Catullus, Propertius and Tibullus seems to have been well established. A particularly important commentary, the *Castigationes in Catullum, Tibullum, Propertium*, by Joseph Scaliger, published in Paris in 1577, continues this tradition late in the sixteenth century. We will look more closely at what this commentary has to say about the reception of female authorship in the Sulpicia poems below.

Ovid has a separate transmission history from the other extant elegists. He had served as an author studied in the church schools from the fifth century CE, although most commentators discuss the *Metamorphoses, Ars Amatoria, Heroides* and the exile poems rather than the *Amores* which might not have been widely known as an educational text at this time.[13] The text of the three-book *Amores* exists in complete form in four manuscripts dated between 800 and 1100 CE, and M.L. Stapleton argues for their influence on troubadour poetry and Dante's *Vita Nuova*.[14] Certainly Dante places Ovid in his neutral first circle of hell along with other virtuous but unbaptised heathens, and his poetic companions there are Homer, Horace, Lucan and Virgil.[15]

The Renaissance *editio princeps* of Ovid was published in Bologna in 1471, the year before Catullus, Propertius and Tibullus, with another edition in Rome of the same year, and the Aldine edition in Venice in 1516–17.[16] A striking aspect of Ovid's transmission and circulation which differs from that of Catullus and the other elegists is that his works were translated into English during the sixteenth century. This has the effect of widening Ovid's English readership beyond a Latin-educated elite. Golding's translation of the whole of the *Metamorphoses* was completed in 1567 and, in the same year, George Turbeville translated the *Heroides* as *The Heroicall Epistles of Publius Ovidius Naso in English Verse*.[17] Marlowe's translation of *All Ovids Elegies* was possibly written in the 1580s while he was at Cambridge though not published until c.1595–9 and was the first English translation of the complete *Amores*.[18] The *Remedia Amoris* was translated into English in 1600 and titled *Ovidius Naso his Remedies of Love. Translated and Intituled to the Youth of England*.[19]

An additional point about Ovid's *Metamorphoses* worth noting here is that it was sometimes printed with engravings: the first illustrated edition of the *Metamorphoses* was produced in Bruges in 1484 by Colard Mansion, one of the city's pioneers of printing, and was followed in 1497 by a Venetian edition.[20] In England, George Sandys printed his *Ovid's Metamorphoses Englished, Mythologiz'd, and Represented in Figures* in 1632, the 'figures' being full-page engravings that summarised the stories of each book in minute and engrossing detail. This association of Ovid with the visual will be picked up later when we explore the complicated Renaissance receptions of our poets – but first we will see how Catullus and the elegists were introduced to schoolboys (and some girls) in the humanist classroom.

'Hig, Hag, Hog': Elegy in the Humanist Classroom

WILLIAM: Articles are borrowed of the pronoun, and be
 thus declined. *Singulariter nominativo: 'hic, haec, hoc'.*
EVANS: *Nominativo: 'hig, hag, hog.'* Pray you mark:
 genitivo: 'huius'. Well, what is your accusative case?
WILLIAM: *Accusativo: 'hinc'-*
EVANS: I pray you have your remembrance, child.
 Accusativo: 'hing, hang, hog'.
MISTRESS QUICKLY: 'Hang-hog' is Latin for bacon, I warrant you.
        (*The Merry Wives of Windsor* 4.1.36–44)[21]

This short, comic scene of a Latin lesson takes place in the Page household in Windsor and shows us William, the young son of the household, being taught the basics of Latin grammar by the parson, Sir Hugh Evans. With his Welsh accent, Evans is made the butt of the joke here as he declaims 'hig, hag, hog … hing, hang, hog' – perhaps revenge taken on behalf of generations of schoolboys persecuted by Latin declensions, as Shakespeare himself must have been at Stratford grammar school.[22] Not only is Evans mocked for his pronunciation, but Mistress Quickly, the housekeeper, makes an amusing intervention built on his accent: ' "Hang-hog" is Latin for bacon, I warrant you.' The humour of this scene derives from the common experience of Renaissance schoolboys (and some girls) whose education centred on the learning of Latin language and literature. William, in this scene, is being taught privately at home, but the concentration on Latin grammar and the rote learning method was also central to humanist schools in England and Europe. In this section, we will look briefly at medieval education, then trace the development of secular schools and explore the surprising presences of Catullus, Ovid, Propertius and Tibullus/Sulpicia in the humanist schoolroom.

During the medieval period, schooling in England was associated with the church. From around the twelfth to fourteenth century onward, secular schools start to develop and there is an increasing move towards the establishment of free endowed grammar schools. This development was encouraged by the church, especially as the funds or endowments came from non-church sources: local nobility, merchants, trade guilds, even villagers who clubbed together to finance a local school.[23] The impetus for this was the increasing need for educated and numerate men to take up positions outside of the church: in commerce, in government, at court and in the burgeoning civil service. At first the methods of learning and the books studied were the same as at the church schools, but from the mid-fifteenth century the curricula, teaching methods and schoolbooks used in England were adopted from the Italian humanist education establishments.

This new humanist programme of study was promoted and supported by prominent Tudor scholars, educators and administrators, men such as Thomas Linacre, one of the first Englishmen to study Greek in Italy, and tutor to Erasmus; William Lily, scholar and master at St Paul's school, whose Latin grammar we will meet presently; John Colet, Dean of St Paul's Cathedral, friend of Erasmus and educational pioneer; Thomas Elyot, diplomat and government official; Roger Ascham, who served as an administrator in the governments of Mary I, Edward VI and Elizabeth I, as well as being the young Elizabeth's Latin and Greek tutor; John Cheke, the first Regius Professor of Greek at Cambridge who did much to revive Greek learning in Renaissance England; and Erasmus himself who more or less set a school agenda for Northern Europe. In order to understand the presence of love elegy on the humanist school curriculum, it is helpful to go back briefly to the medieval schooling system and the subsequent development of humanist education in Italy, the source of English curricula.

Catullus, Propertius and Tibullus/Sulpicia were absent from medieval school programmes due to the problematic transmission of their texts, but Ovid was central to the curriculum. The most popular Ovidian texts were the *Metamorphoses*, the *Fasti*, the *Tristia* and the *Heroides* (usually under the title *Epistolae Heroidum*).[24] These texts were first met via the florilegium: a manuscript collection of poetic extracts, *sententiae*, fables and rhetorical figures which were sourced from both classical and biblical authors. In terms of our interests, Ovid and Virgil were central to medieval school florilegia such as the *Flores Poetarum* which was composed at about c.1300 and remained on the curriculum for hundreds of years.[25] It is noteworthy that both Latin poets kept company with authors such as Jerome and Augustine, as well as the Bible, and were given a kind of moral parity in the florilegia.

We find a similar easy confluence between 'pagan' and Christian authors in Peter Abelard's twelfth-century *Historia Calamitatum*, a kind of auto-biographical letter which recounts his scholastic and philosophical career, his love affair with his pupil, Heloise, and his castration by her irate uncle.

Written in Latin, it is sprinkled with quotations to support its own rhetoric. When speaking of how his own brilliance brought about the malign
jealousy of his rivals, for example, Abelard quotes from Ovid's *Remedia
Amoris*, 1.369: 'Envy aims at the summits, the winds blow over the highest
places.'[26] Later in the letter, when describing how he and Heloise were
caught *in flagrante*, he says 'and so we were caught in the act as the poet says
happened to Venus and Mars' – a story that is told in *Odyssey* book 8, but
which was best known in the medieval period from Ovid's *Metamorphoses*
4.169–89 and *Ars Amatoria* 2.561–74. It seems that it is unproblematic in
the period to mingle references to Ovid alongside quotations from the
Bible, from Jerome's letters, and from Eusebius' *Historia Ecclesiae*. A similar
fusion of secular Latin poetry and Christian texts is found in the florilegia
that underpin medieval and, later, Renaissance schooling. This complicates
how we read the receptions of Ovid, something to which we will turn in
the next section.

While Ovid had a crucial role in the medieval schoolroom, readings
and interpretations of his amatory works were somewhat slanted in order
to make them morally acceptable. In some cases they were read allegor-
ically, as was the *Aeneid*; in others there was a narrowed focus on what
might be read as exemplary in them. The *Heroides*, for example, were
used as models of superlative letter-writing and rhetorical skill, and the
ethical lessons that schoolboys were encouraged to take from them were
the praise of chastity, the importance of married love and the rejection
of foolish sexual infatuations.[27] This form of selective reading on the part
of schoolmasters seems typical of pedagogical approaches to our poets
and we will meet it again when we turn to the Renaissance schoolroom.
The question seems to be how to balance an acknowledgement of, in
this case, Ovid's eloquence, elegance, wit and style with a possible per-
ception of his moral trifling and wanton nature. The solution appears to
be to refocus schoolboys' attention away from the latter – though how
successful this form of redirection might be is open to opinion. What is
notable is that erotic passages were not necessarily censored in the florilegia and were available for schoolboys to read both inside and outside
the classroom.

The private school started to develop in Italy in the fifteenth century.
Gasparinus Barzizza (1360–1430), for example, an academic at the university at Padua, combined his official post with teaching pupils privately in
his home between 1407 and 1421. We also find private schools run by, for
example, Guarino Guarini (1374–1460) at Verona and Ferrara, and Vittorino
da Feltre (c.1373–c.1446) at Mantua.[28] These schools taught aristocratic

children classical languages and literature, and went on to influence the establishment of humanist schools across Europe and in England. The florilegium was still the basis of teaching in these private schools, though they were sometimes compiled by the teacher as was the case with Barzizzi. This allowed some expansion of the medieval educational 'canon' though it is difficult to pin down exactly what was on each curriculum apart from the standard medieval authors including Ovid and Virgil.

The advent of the printing press in the mid-fifteenth century changes things. Firstly, manuscript florilegia start to be printed, making them an economical option for school use. In addition, printed copies of what start to be called commonplace books from the sixteenth century onwards, begin to standardise the pedagogical curriculum across Europe. For example, the fourteenth-century manuscript *Manipulus Florium* composed by Thomas Hibernicus in Paris in 1306, was printed in Piacenza in 1483, Venice c.1493, Venice again in 1550 and was reprinted at least twenty-five times until the seventeenth century. Although this book contained no poetry, it comprised c.6000 extracts from 366 different classical prose works including those by Cicero, Seneca and Valerius Maximus.[29]

More important for our investigations are the *Margarita Poetica* and the *Ex Elegiacis trium illustrium poetarum Tibulli Propertii ac Ovidii carminibus selecti versus magis memorabiles atque puerorum institutioni aptiores*. The *Margarita Poetica* was composed by Albertus de Eyb (1420–75) in 1459, first printed in 1472 in Nuremburg, and reprinted at least thirteen times before 1503 in various European cities including Strasbourg, Paris, Rome, Venice and Basle.[30] The first edition included extensive extracts from Virgil, Tibullus and Ovid, including a large selection from the *Amores* in addition to the other Ovidian texts. Eyb later revised the book so that the editions printed between 1495 and 1503 enlarged these selections and added in extracts from Propertius and Catullus. What is notable about the *Margarita* is that, firstly, it confirms the presence of Catullus and the elegists in the humanist schoolroom from the last quarter of the fifteenth century; and secondly, it is a testament to how rapidly Catullus and Propertius become school texts given that the Aldine first edition, as we have seen, was only printed in 1472. Since the English printing trade was relatively slow to realise the potential of the school market, the majority of books used for pedagogical purposes in England before the seventeenth century were imported texts from Europe. The *Margarita* was certainly used in English humanist schools throughout the sixteenth century as were other printed commonplace books from Italy, France and Germany which became institutionalised on school programmes.[31]

Catullus was attractive to pedagogues because of his relatively straight-forward vocabulary and diction, at least in the short poems, and thus appears in an elementary commonplace book, *De Poetica Virtute*. Regarded as an introduction to poetic eloquence, it was compiled by Antonius Mancinellus (1452–1505), was first printed in 1486 in Venice, reprinted there in 1493 and went through repeated reprintings by both Italian and French presses until 1510. There was also an exclusively Ovidian common-place book, the *Sylva sententiarum ex Ovidio*, also aimed at the youngest pupils, which was first printed in Leipzig in 1515. Roger Ascham, in his *The Schoolmaster*, recommended that English teachers would do well to follow German educational programmes, especially those from Lutheran territories.

The *Ex Elegiacis trium illustrium poetarum Tibulli Propertii ac Ovidii carminibus selecti versus magis memorabiles atque puerorum institutioni aptiores* was compiled by Johannes Murmellius (1480–1517) and printed in 1500 in Cologne.[32] It is worth pausing on the title: that Tibullus, Propertius and Ovid are 'three famous poets' (*trium illustrium poetarum*), thus linking them together as a group, and that their texts as given here are 'more suit-able' (*aptiores*), presumably, in this case, excerpted for boys in school. The preface to this first edition draws attention to the poetic trio as 'pagan and hazardous poets' (*gentiles et lubrici poetae*), and advises schoolmasters to choose extracts carefully for the schoolroom. Note, though, that, as we have previously observed, Murmellius does not simply expurgate or exclude the so-called morally dangerous poetry, and we have to wonder to what extent schoolmasters were able to police the boys' reading of these 'hazardous' texts. From 1537 even this moralising preface was dropped, the texts were updated from the Aldine editions and the book was retitled *Loci communes sententiosorum versum ex elegiis Tibulli, Propertii, Ovidii* ('General passages of sententious verses from the elegies of Tibullus, Propertius, Ovid').[33] The ambivalent moral position towards these poets is notable: they may be dangerous, but they are still worth studying at school.

By the 1530s printed commonplace books from European presses were entrenched in English schools. Two popular textbooks were the *Sententiae et proverbia ex Plauto, Terentio, Virgilio, Ovidio etc.* printed by Robert Estienne in Paris, 1534; and the *De re poetica* compiled by Georgius Fabricius (1516–71), a textual editor and neo-Latin poet: he based his book on Ovid, Tibullus and Propertius, and later extended it into the *Descriptiones variae* which comprised poetic 'set pieces' from the same elegists. The latter was first printed in Antwerp in 1564, with later editions in Paris and Leipzig.[34]

Humanists, then, extended the medieval school curriculum and placed Catullus and Latin elegy in the classroom. Its presence, though, was not unproblematic and we find evidence of concerns, both moral and pedagogical, about the teaching of erotic poetry. In 1436, for example, Ugolini Pisani, a courtier at Ferrara and owner of a laurel crown, tried to dissuade teachers from promoting study of Catullus, Propertius, Tibullus, the *Ars Amatoria* and the *Priapea*, as well as selected verses by Juvenal and Martial: reading these poets, he suggested, should take place only in the home.[35] Eneas Silvius Piccolomini (later Pope Pius II) in his 1450 *De liberorum educatione*, a treatise on the education of boys, wrote: 'all the writers of elegy should be withheld from a boy. Tibullus, Propertius, Catullus and the bits of Sappho that we have in translation are too soft and effeminate. Their writings are almost all about love, and they are continually bemoaning their lost loves.'[36] Strikingly, Ovid is not on this proscribed list from Piccolomini. Jacobus Wimpheling, on the other hand, when compiling his commonplace book, says 'the young cannot be permitted to read the work of Ovid in its entirety, but excerpts will be profitable to them'.[37] In 1560, a dialogue written by Thomas Becon, an English schoolmaster, was printed which condemned Catullus, Propertius, Tibullus, Martial and the *Ars Amatoria* as 'wanton … filthy … ungodly … more wickedness than godliness, more sin than virtue' and asserted that they should not be read by the young.[38] In 1579, too, John Stockward, another schoolmaster, gave a sermon attacking the English school curriculum and complaining about the reading of 'Tibullus, Catullus and Propertius, Gallus, Martial … and a great parte of Ovid'.[39] He goes on in the same speech to condemn the *Priapea* poems, at the time generally attributed to Virgil:[40] 'the most horrible beastliness of Priapus … joined to the end of every Virgil', where the accusation is itself built around sodomitical imagery applied to the single-volume *Opera*, though whether this is intentional or not is hard to know. Nevertheless, Catullus and the elegists maintained their place in the commonplace books and, thus, in the English classroom. Remarking on early Latin practice sentences, Ian Green amusingly relates 'there were many references to falling in and out of love and the wiles of Cupid and some frank remarks about naked lovers'.[41] As late as 1582, the Privy Council made an attempt to curb the teaching of morally questionable texts, citing 'Ovid *de arte amandi, de tristibus* or such like'.[42]

It is difficult to be sure why Catullus and the elegists remained in the commonplace books and on the curriculum in defiance of some of the attacks on them. Certainly the first generation of humanist teachers concentrated on what was understood as the inherent value of classical texts as models of supreme culture and exemplary eloquence, but later generations, from the last quarter of the fifteenth century onwards, focused increasingly on authors whose complexity of interpretation allowed them to showcase their own scholarly competences. Propertius, in particular, seems to have entered the school 'canon' at least partially because of the textual and hermeneutic difficulties he carried with him.[43] Whatever the reasons, humanist schools continued to study a wide range of verse genres, including love elegy, and pupils were required to memorise extracts and show the ability to imitate them in their own compositions from the third form upwards.

The commonplace book, then, was a fundamental tool of humanist pedagogy in England as well as in Europe, and was a part of every schoolboy's intellectual practice – an experience which included an early acquaintance with Catullus, Propertius, Tibullus/Sulpicia and Ovid. Looking more deeply at sixteenth-century English education, the great majority of schoolteachers were educated to at least BA standard with degrees from Oxford or Cambridge.[44] Teaching Latin in England started with *Lily's Grammar*, a text which was later known as 'the King's Grammar' since it was used in all English schools by the royal command of Henry VIII. After being introduced to the basics, pupils moved quickly to construing and parsing sentences from *Lily*, though these were hardly neutral, e.g. *lego Virgilium, prae quo caeteri poetae sordent*, 'I read Virgil beside whom other poets seem unworthy'. Despite this explicit prioritising of Virgil, *Lily* included short sentences from Ovid, too, and boys were encouraged to start compiling their own commonplace book as an aid to language learning and vocabulary development. In moving on from *Lily*, most pupils were introduced first to Ovid, Virgil and Horace both to continue their mastering of Latin, and as models for imitative composition.

Following the European schools, the prime texts for English study were those of the late Republic and early Empire but other Latin texts were also introduced via the commonplace books: the comedies of Terence, those of Plautus who was regarded as old-fashioned but a good source of colloquial Latin, Seneca's tragedies, Juvenal, Lucan and Statius. Martial was read but was not thought suitable for schoolboy imitation. Cicero's *Ad Familiares* were considered polished models of informal letter-writing. Poetry was fundamental and even small, local schools made Ovid and Virgil central to their teaching. Again, anxiety over immorality was channelled into slanted, edifying readings: the plots of Terence and Plautus, for example, were treated as exhortations to fidelity in marriage, obedience to parents and sexual continence. Catullus was especially problematic and his 'obscenities' were expurgated from some books, left in others. Virgil's *Eclogues*, too, were the subject of some concern, especially with regard to the homo-eroticism of *Eclogue* 2. Erasmus, in his *De Ratione Studii*, his 1512 treatise on education, suggests that instead of suppressing or censoring sexually freighted content, it can be quoted in full but that the schoolteacher should guide the pupils' attention from immorality by allegorical readings and by drawing attention to alternative themes such as the importance of mas-culine friendship. This Renaissance sense of Virgil as, in places, an erotic poet, as someone whose texts need to be worked around in the schoolroom is another point we will pick up presently when we look at the reception of the elegists. The important point here is that there was little outright censorship in the commonplace books used in English schools, and even Ovid and, sometimes, Catullus were presented unexpurgated.

As we have already noted, commercial printing developed far more slowly in England than in Europe so that school and university books (common-place books, full Latin and Greek texts) were imported during much of the sixteenth century. It was not until the 1570s that London printers realised the opportunity and started to exploit what was a large and stable market. At first patents were granted for a monopoly on printing set texts: Thomas Vautrollier, for example, a Huguenot immigrant in London, owned the patent on all editions of Ovid from 1573 to 1583.[45] Soon, though, the Stationers' Company in London developed a joint stock venture known as the 'English stock' which printed all schoolbooks, English as well as Greek and Latin. This was as much a means of preventing pirating as it was of safeguarding a regular, easy and profitable business.

We can see from the catalogues of the 'English stock' that as well as commonplace books, they printed full, unexpurgated texts of Ovid's *Metamorphoses, Tristia, Fasti, Epistolae Heroidum*, and Virgil's *Opera* for the average grammar school.[46] 'Stock' texts were generally bare of marginal notes, glosses or other pedagogical apparatus, and were thus open to teachers' and schoolboys' own readings. Even the most used single-volume edition of Virgil's works, edited by Paolo Manuzio, contained only occasional mar-ginal notes on vocabulary and allusions with an added argument at the head of each book of the *Aeneid*.[47] Editions of school commonplace books that had previously been printed in Europe were adopted into the 'English stock' where possible: Octavius Mirandula's *Illustrium Poetarum Flores*, for example, which had been printed in Venice in 1507, Lyons in 1512, Strasbourg in 1538, became part of the 'English stock' at the end of the sixteenth century.

So, what was the purpose of the commonplace book and how was it used in the classroom? The medieval florilegium, the ancestor of the commonplace book, makes clear its status as a form of compilation literature: the 'collected flowers' of the name gestures back to the imagery of bees making honey from many flowers that we have already examined. Johannes Murmellius (who, we will remember, compiled the *Ex Elegiacis trium illustrium poetarum* ...) also wrote a number of educational treatises: in his *Opusculum*, a guide to student learning which was printed in Cologne in 1505, he discusses the use of commonplace books as part of the directed activity of the classroom; and Erasmus, in his *De Ratione Studii*, agrees that the commonplace book is the primary working tool of the schoolmaster.

Schoolboys were introduced to Latin literature via this concept of excerpting: the aim was to teach them firstly how to analyse and appreciate how Latin worked grammatically, and then to write and express themselves with eloquence and elegance. According to Erasmus, pupils being trained in composition can read fables, *sententiae*, historical events, and rhetorical figures in commonplace books which serve as models for their own writing. He also recommends that teachers should compile their own commonplace book to be used alongside the printed texts available on the market, and that boys should be taught to do the same thing, copying out extracts to be reused later in their own written exercises. Diversity of selection was emphasised by Erasmus, indicating a need for wide reading across the Latin corpus, and he also suggested that excerpts might be usefully organised by topic, such as friendship (*amicitia*), or rhetorical device to enable easy comparison. The commonplace book was thus an aid to composition via intertextual imitation, institutionalising that practice from a boy's earliest experience of education.

Girls, too, might be educated via the Latin commonplace book. Erasmus offers a picture of Thomas More's daughters, renowned even to contemporaries for their classical learning, compiling excerpts: 'they flit like so many little bees between Greek and Latin authors of every species, here noting down something to imitate ... there getting by heart some witty anecdote to relate among their friends.'[48] We can see here that the bees metaphor is applied directly to the young women themselves, and may note the range of their reading ('Greek and Latin authors of every species'). The aim, too, of their activity is defined: 'noting down something to imitate' in their own writing, even if that is domestic and private, and enhancing their social capital through 'some witty anecdote'. The 'getting by heart', something which also happened in the classroom, seems to be a way of internalising classical tropes, images, vocabulary and quotations which might emerge later, intentionally or not, in imitative writing.

This shared educational curriculum across humanist Europe means, then, that intertextual practise is institutionalised from an early age, shaping a way of thinking about, consuming and producing literature which is both formative and programmatic. In addition, the printed commonplace book serves as a mediator of a sophisticated urbanity centred on Latin literature. It transmits a common language, a way of acculturating pupils from an early age and creating an educated elite with shared cultural codes. At the heart of both the commonplace book itself and the pedagogical system centred on it is the concept of *imitatio*: the collection of 'flowers' from wide and various sources to make a new form of 'honey'. As we have seen, Catullus and the elegists are part of that field of 'flowers' first introduced to English school pupils in the classroom. This practice of imitation extended beyond education, too: in a preface to his *Protrepticus studiosorum poetica* dated 1517, Murmellius advises 'if you intend to write elegy, lay your hands on Tibullus or Propertius!'[49] It is to this reading, re-writing and reception of Catullus and the elegists that we will now turn.

Renaissance Receptions of Catullus and the Latin Elegists

A review of modern Renaissance scholarship on erotic love poetry will reveal an extensive attention to the influence of Ovid and the vaguely defined term of the 'Ovidian'.[50] But this quotation from Petrarch's *Triumph of Love* (4.22–4) is evidence that Petrarch himself placed Ovid firmly within the elegiac love tradition, even if he does give him prime position, indicating a canon of classical love poets upon whom he draws:

> Ovid was there, and with him were Catullus,
> Propertius and Tibullus, and they all
> Were fervid singers of the power of love.[51]

By depicting himself as a fellow victim of love paraded in this triumph alongside Catullus, Propertius, Ovid and Tibullus, Petrarch inserts himself into this roll-call of love elegists. As Chapter 5 discusses in more detail, Petrarch's *Triumphs* were frequently appended to his *canzoniere*, and were read as a kind of appendix to the sonnets.[52] Positioning himself here as following in the footsteps of Catullus and the Roman elegists would therefore have a spill-over effect into the sonnets themselves which draw quite explicitly on elegiac conventions.

Petrarch's overt acknowledgement of his debt to elegy is one example of where a distorting gap has opened up between modern Renaissance scholarship which subsumes elegy under the umbrella term of the 'Ovidian', and the way Renaissance poets themselves constructed a wider Roman poetic love tradition. Before reviewing some of the other evidence for this, and without wishing to downplay the undoubted importance of Ovid, it is worth a reminder here that Ovid was not working at the start of what might loosely be called the elegiac tradition, short as it is, but right at the end. As such, his texts pick up on, and respond to, the work of Catullus, Propertius, Tibullus and Sulpicia.[53]

Ovid himself makes clear his debt to his predecessors, and acknowledging an elegiac 'tradition' becomes itself a shadowy convention within elegy. In *Tristia* 4, for example, speaking of Tibullus, 'Ovid' states 'he was your successor, Gallus, Propertius his; I was the fourth in time's order' (4.10.53–4).[54] Gallus here refers to Cornelius Gallus, the apparent originator of love elegy whose work now exists only in fragments.[55] [Tibullus] 3.6.41 makes reference to 'learned Catullus' when discussing his c.64 about the love of Ariadne for Theseus; and Propertius 2.34, a poem about Roman poetry, ends with a genealogy of elegy leading up to Propertius' own work:

> Such themes the verse of wanton Catullus also sang, which made Lesbia better known than Helen herself … and in these recent days of how many wounds has Gallus, dead for love of fair Lycoris, laved in the waters of the world below! Yea, Cynthia glorified in the pages of Propertius shall live, if Fame consent to rank me with poets like these. (2.34.87–94)[56]

Amores 3.9 is Ovid's funeral elegy for Tibullus which ends with an imagining of Tibullus in Elysium where he will be met by Gallus and 'learned Catullus' (3.9.62). Ovid's *Remedia Amoris* asks 'Who could read the poems of Tibullus safely, or yours, whose sole theme was Cynthia?'[57]

Re-reading Petrarch's *Triumph of Love* in the light of these references proves it to be not only an acknowledgement of the power of Catullus and the elegists as poets, but also an intertext in its own right, an instance of Petrarch re-using a trope already made conventional by the elegists who have preceded him. As both Propertius and Ovid had previously delineated a tradition which had culminated in their own work, so Petrarch implicitly does the same. To trace Petrarch and the Petrarchan solely back to Ovid is clearly too contracted a history.

'Wanton Catullus … Learned Catullus'

Catullus, as we have seen, was first printed in 1472.[58] Before that date, though, we can find references to, and imitations of, his texts that help us piece together the ways in which he was read and thought about in the early modern period. Antonio Beccadelli's (1394–1471) *Hermaphroditus* of 1425, for example, contains the lines:

> I burn, my Galeaz, to bring back wanton Catullus, so that I am able to please my mistress. Lascivious she repeatedly reads the tender poets, and prefers, learned Catullus, your lines.[59]

The keynote of Beccadelli's Catullus is the potent combination of eroticism and erudition. The narrator wishes to lay his hands on Catullus in order to gratify the desires of his mistress who, we learn, prefers him to other 'tender' or 'soft' poets, possibly Propertius, Tibullus and Ovid. Certainly the term *mollis* and the idea of being learned (*doctus*) are drawn from the ways in which Tibullus, Propertius and Ovid described Catullus, and are important elements of Catullan receptions. The mistress herself follows Lesbia, Cynthia and Sulpicia in her concern with the reading of poetry, and the connection is explicitly made between the reading of wanton verse and the lascivious nature of the mistress herself. However fictional this portrait might be, it indicates that elegy was potentially available to female readers and writers in the early modern period, and that women might respond to the learned Catullus as well as to the wanton nature of the poet. Already in 1425 we can see the Catullan text being used as a vehicle to articulate a different vision of erotic love from that conveyed in Petrarch's sonnets, one that is bound up with a languorous sexuality and textuality, and which offers a more active role to the mistress than that of Petrarch's passive, elusive and chaste Laura.

Beccadelli established the *accademia* in Naples, and was succeeded in 1471 by Giovanni Pontano (1429–1503) who also worked references and homages to Catullus into his verse.[60] Michael Marullus, associated with the *accademia* under Pontano, wrote 'Love to Tibullus, Mars to Virgil is indebted ... hendecasyllables to learned Catullus'; and also composed an epigram on the death of his brother which makes clear references to Catullus' poem on the same subject: 'and forever brother, my tears, farewell!'[61] These allusions widen the role of Catullus who serves as a model for epigrammatic poetry and also a more conventional death elegy written in mourning for a male relation. His association with the erotic, however, is always prominent.

We can find this presentation of Catullus as a supreme erotic poet being pressed upon readers of the 1472 *editio princeps*. It was a large quarto printed by Aldus Manutius in Venice and, as already noted, published Catullus in a single volume with Propertius and Tibullus/Sulpicia. Opposite the first page was a biography of Catullus which situated his birth a year before that of Sallust and which then continues as follows:

> He loved Clodia, a girl of the first rank, whom he called Lesbia in his poems … No-one was his superior. In wit he was delightful, to the highest degree, and in serious matters, most truly grave. He wrote erotic verse.[62]

This paratext frames the Catullan poems for his Renaissance readers in deliberate ways: it foregrounds the Lesbia texts as central to the work of Catullus, and categorises them as erotic poems (*erotica*). It also identifies Lesbia as Clodia, who would have been known to readers from Cicero. It gives a cultural judgement on Catullus' work: that he had no poetic superiors; and, finally, it gives a sense of the tone of his texts – that they are full of wit and charm (*lepidus*, itself a Catullan term), but that they also speak of more sombre and sober concerns. This latter aspect is important because Catullus' Renaissance receptions have previously been read by modern scholars primarily via the mediations of Martial.[63] The racy, amusing, untroubled Catullus of Martial certainly has a presence in the Renaissance, but we should also be attentive to the more passionate aspects of the poet which helped shape concepts of Renaissance love poetry. In the next chapter, it is Catullus the anguished, urban love poet who will be traced in detail through the poetry of Thomas Wyatt.

To return, though, to 1489, when we find Poliziano causing a furore over his reading of two Catullan poems, cc.2 and 3. Now infamous amongst classicists, Poliziano was the first to suggest that 'sparrow' (*passer*) was Latin slang for 'penis', and that therefore the antics of Lesbia's pet bird which she kissed and stroked and which lay between her breasts was a coded, witty and mischievous way of representing a far more explicitly sexualised scenario than might at first appear.[64] Whether we agree with Poliziano's interpretation or not (and I do) his reading foregrounded two important things: firstly, that there were places where Catullan wit and eroticism might tip over into the 'obscene'; and, secondly, that a surface reading of the texts might hide other meanings. While moralists might cavil, other poets embraced the playful ambiguities of Catullus' sparrow, notably John Skelton in late fifteenth-century England.

The generally accepted position on Catullan reception in England admits that Catullus was probably known from the late fifteenth century but cites Nicholas Udall's 1533 *Floures for Latine Spekyng* as the first direct allusions to his work; and Philip Sidney's translation of c.70, and Walter Ralegh's adaptation of c.5.4–6 as the first English imitations.[65] While scholars have noted John Skelton's *The Book of Phyllyp Sparrow*, the consensus is that since there are no obscene overtones in the poem, it is a response not directly to Catullus, but to European imitations of his sparrow poems.[66] Despite Skelton claiming the title of the 'British Catullus', scholars to date have dismissed this as vague and imprecise self-aggrandisement rather than as an acknowledgement from Skelton of a specific imitative model for his verse.[67] Certainly there is an accumulation of sparrow poems from the fifteenth to seventeenth centuries, with the sparrow sometimes being turned into Martial's dove, but textual evidence discussed here suggests that it is possible to tie Skelton's *Phyllyp Sparrow* more closely to Catullus with specific and precise allusions. Skelton's *Garlande of Laurell* which incorporates *Phyllyp Sparrow* was not printed until 1523, but the poems of which it consists seem to have been composed between the 1480s and early 1500s and circulated amongst readers at, and attached to, the English court such as the Howard family.[68] Skelton was himself closely associated with the Henrician court: he was tutor to the young Prince Henry between c.1496 and 1502, and wrote an advice book for him, the *Speculum Principis*, in 1501. He went on to write verses for Anne Boleyn's coronation in 1533, possibly commissioned by Thomas Howard and Cardinal Wolsey.

Skelton's *Phyllyp Sparrow* was composed in c.1505 and is a curious, long, rambling, sometimes satiric poem written in the voice of Jane Scrope for her dead bird. Although McPeek and Gaisser have dismissed the possibility of this poem as a direct response to Catullus' sparrow poems, there are counter arguments to be made. Gaisser, for example, denies that there are erotic or obscene overtones to be read in Skelton's verse. A consideration, however, of these lines describing the sparrow and its interactions with its mourning mistress, might belie that position:

> It had a velvet cap,
> And would sit upon my lap
> And seek after small worms
> And sometimes white breadcrumbs;
> And many times and oft
> Between my breasts soft
> It would lie and rest
> [...]
> It was proper and prest
> [...]
> Then he would leap and skip
> And take me by the lip.
> (120–7, 139–40)

The 'velvet cap', 'lap', 'breasts', 'lip' certainly impart a distinctly eroticised air to this text, replaying the scenes with Lesbia's sparrow whom she holds in her lap or breast (*quem in sinu tenere*, where '*sinu*' can mean both, 2.2; also 'nor would he stir from her lap', *nec sese a gremio illius movebat*, c.3.8). 'Prest', meaning quick, is perhaps also a witty nod to the phallic reading of Catullus where c.3 is positioned as a post-coital poem of temporary sexual incapacity, especially when combined with 'lie and rest' ... 'between my breasts soft'.

Even more persuasive is the concern for the sparrow's journey after death. C.3 makes reference to the dark road, presided over by Orcus, which the dead sparrow must travel, from which no one returns – unless the *passer* has the recuperative powers of the male sexual organ.[69] Skelton's poem expands this figure as the narrator prays that the sparrow's soul will be kept from 'the mares [marsh] deep | of Acherontes well' (67–9) and depicts a distinctively classical underworld inhabited by Pluto (72), 'foul Alecto' (74), Proserpina (83) and Cerberus (85) 'whom Theseus did afray | whom Hercules did outrage' (86–7). Skelton takes Catullus' lines and expands them to display his classical learning. His poem about the dead sparrow draws on Catullus in two ways: in giving a mischievously eroticised edge to the trope of the dead pet bird, and in incorporating a vision of the bird's journey after death. The Catullan influence is strong, especially when placed alongside Skelton's self-identification as the 'British Catullus'.

Skelton's Catullus is, then, an explicitly sexualised poet whose bold, edgy eroticism might be hidden in plain view. For Johannes Secundus, a Dutch neo-Latin poet, it is specifically Catullus' 'kiss' poems (cc.5 and 7) which offer him a route to a whole volume, *Basia* (The Kisses), of gently sensual and seductive verse. Born in The Hague in 1511, Secundus' father was a friend of Erasmus and ensured that all his sons had a humanist education.[70] Secundus himself studied law at university and went on to hold positions in various European courts as well as serving as secretary to the Bishop of Utrecht before dying in 1536 at the untimely age of just twenty-four. His *Basia*, his *Amores* and his *Elegies* were published post-humously in a 'pirated' edition in 1539, then in an edition authorised by his brothers in 1541. From the titles alone of these volumes we can infer the influence of Catullus and the elegists, and one of the notable aspects of Secundus' poetry is the extent to which he mingles receptions of all these poets in his own verse – an example of taking his pollen from many flowers. Nevertheless, he shows an acute affinity with Catullus not just in expanding the two kiss poems into a whole volume, but also in his 'Epithalamium' drawing on cc.61 and 62.

While some of the *Basia* are relatively straightforward imitations of Catullus, the volume allows Secundus to stretch the trope so that Catullus' own verse becomes a kind of launch-pad for further meditations on erotic love. *Basium* 9, for example, contests the countless kisses of Catullus and suggests that a mistress who withholds her kisses will always keep her lover from satiety, prolonging his desire: 'When I demand three times three kisses | subtract the seven and only give me two.'[71] It is as if the narrator has taken account of the behaviour of Lesbia and turned it into a quasi-Machiavellian strategy which he passes on as advice to his own mistress. If he can turn her into Lesbia, can he become 'Catullus'?

Basium 12 confronts the blatant sexuality of Catullus and claims that, in contrast, there is no need for chaste girls and matrons to turn away from the poet's own pages, as he sings of only harmless kisses. Strikingly, though, when the narrator catalogues what will be expunged from his verse, he seems to be recalling Ovid's *Metamorphoses* more than Catullus or elegy: 'I do not sing here of the furtive frolics of gods or of figures of monstrous desire.'[72] The multiple intertexts certainly showcase Secundus' breadth of source texts and the connections he is drawing between Catullus and Ovid here, but also point to the way in which receptions in this period are easily 'contaminated'. Joint print transmissions (Catullus, Propertius, Tibullus/ Sulpicia) as well as the excerpted nature of commonplace books might work systematically against 'pure' receptions of just, say, Catullus.

Returning to sixteenth-century England, some lines from one of Henry VIII's songs may attest to a Catullan source though, admittedly, the parallels are not particularly close: 'for idleness | is chief mistress | of vices all' may be drawing on Catullus' 'idleness, Catullus, does you harm, you riot in your idleness and wanton too much' (c.51.13–14).[73] C.51, the re-writing of Sappho 31, also stands behind Wyatt's sonnet about the 'unkind tongue' (16.3), his 'What Means This'.[74] Peter Herman, questioning the literary history which has Wyatt as one of the earliest importers of 'Petrarchism' to English verse, suggests that Henry VIII's early poetry from c.1508–15 is already using Petrarchan tropes before Wyatt.[75] The argument here is that what has been identified as 'Petrarchan' draws directly and explicitly on Catullus and his elegiac successors, and that it is possibly Catullus who is being imitated by Henry VIII here as much as mediated versions of the Catullan in Petrarch.

Further evidence for a clear Catullan presence in the poetry of the early Henrician court can be found in John Leland's epigrams, many of which are written in elegiac couplets or are hendecasyllabic, metres which are associated with Catullus. Scholars have not been able to date them accurately but Leland was clearly recognised as a poet by the time he contributed to Udall's *Floures* and Anne Boleyn's coronation, both in 1533, and so it can be assumed with some confidence that some of his epigrams, of which there were 282 printed in the 1589 edition, were written before that date, a period also tentatively ascribed to the Wyatt love poems considered in the next chapter.[76]

It is certainly possible to place Leland, like John Skelton, within the first generation of English humanists, and to get a sense of where his poems circulated and by whom they were read. Leland spent some years in Paris during the 1520s, studying and writing Latin verse. From his reputation amongst French classicists such as Guillaume Budé and Jacques Lefèvre d'Etaples, the royal librarian to Francis I, his poems certainly were in cir- culation with a scholarly, courtly French audience.[77] One of his poems was addressed to Jean Salmon Macrin, whose own *Carminum Libellus* of 1528 draws on Catullus, and both Macrin and Leland wrote in sapphic metre, as does Catullus in cc.11 and 51. Leland's associations with the English humanist circles of Erasmus and Thomas More, and his later role in establishing a royal library for Henry VIII suggest that his poetry was also known and read in these English courtly and intellectual settings. Leland's epigrams circulated only in manuscript and were not printed until 1589, almost forty years after his death, but his *Naenia*, elegies on the death of Thomas Wyatt, were published in 1542. According to one of these poems, Leland was a student with Wyatt at Cambridge, 'the dearest Granta joined me to you as your companion'.[78]

Epigram 17, *Natale Solum*, 'My Native Soil', gives us an idea of how Leland placed himself poetically:

> Mantua gave birth to Virgil, and Verona to Catullus. The noble city of London is my home.[79]

Written in an elegiac couplet, Leland's poetic tradition, albeit one which is sharply abbreviated, leads from Virgil, via Catullus, to Leland himself. It is difficult to tell whether the order of Virgil then Catullus is important here or not: certainly it inverts the chronological order so perhaps it is a marker of poetic hierarchy. It is notable that it is Catullus who is used here not, for example, Ovid. Place is also central: London becomes the cultural birthplace of poetic genius (however wishful, in the case of Leland, this might be), and specifically London as *urbs*, the modern city. We will see in the next chapter the extent to which Catullus' poetry is grounded in Rome amongst elite, cultured 'sets' in the city: the poetic equivalent for the six- teenth century will be the court centred in London.

Leland's elegy 237 is titled *Castos esse decet poetas*, 'poets should be chaste', a direct allusion to Catullus' c.16, *castum esse decet pium poetam*, and serves as a testament to knowledge of the elegiac 'tradition'. Again the chronology is skewed, starting with Catullus, moving back to Gallus, then proceeding to Ovid and Propertius:

> Beautiful Lesbia pleased wanton Catullus
> [...]
> [Lycoris was] the delight of Gallus, the learned and famous poet
> [...]
> The milk-white mistress of Ovid of Pelignum flourished,
> Corynna was accustomed to give matter for his verses:
> Cynthia is praised nymph of the newly-cleaned Propertius.
>
> (237.1–11)[80]

There are a number of noteworthy points here apart from the delineation of love elegy as a genre. Lesbia is given prime position as the archetypical mistress, and Catullus is 'wanton', an epithet which goes back to the Italian humanists of the fourteenth and fifteenth centuries, as well as Roman elegy itself. The foregrounding of Catullus as an erotic poet and his relationship to the beautiful Lesbia is central. Striking, too, is the positioning of Corinna as 'subject matter, material' for and of Ovid's verse. This concept of the elegiac woman as a figure for the elegiac text itself is a prominent one in modern readings of Propertius and Ovid, so this very early and sophisticated recognition of the mistress as 'a written woman' (*scripta puella*) is remarkable.[81] 'Newly-cleaned' in relation to Propertius seems to be a comment on the quality of the Propertian, and other elegiac, texts only recently having been 'cleaned up' in philological terms, and still subject to scholarly emendations and commentaries to make them comprehensible to a Renaissance readership. Written early in the Tudor period, this epigram gives us firm evidence for the presence of certainly Catullus, but also love elegy as a genre, at the Henrician court. Once again, as with Secundus, we find an easy, relaxed cross-contamination of our poets in a single verse.

These are not the only references that Leland's epigrams make to Catullus: in epigram 30, *Ad Catullum*, Leland addresses the dead poet directly:

> There are those who admire, there are those who revere and look up to your poems, learned Catullus.[82]

This is notable for its ambiguity about the status of Catullus' poems: *suspiciunt*, from *suspicio*, means to admire, to esteem, but also to be suspicious of, a revealing choice of terms that gives us a sense of Catullus' edginess as a poet to be imitated. Leland's own stance is clear: in *Ad Famam*, epigram 32, he calls on Fame to imbue his own verses with the colour of those of Catullus:

> If you [Fame] grant this now, they [his Muses] will strive for new beauty and take on a bright hue, so that they might come to closely resemble those of Catullus. (7–9)[83]

In *Communis Dolor*, one of a series of elegies written by Leland on the death of Wyatt in 1542, this ambivalence towards Catullus emerges once again:

> Wanton Catullus used a sad poem to complain of his dead sparrow. Stella, that soft degenerate little bugger of a poet, mourns the misfortune of his dove. But we, who attend to more serious things and are in the service of more pious Muses, are employing a just sorrow to complain that Wyatt, that light of good judgement, has been taken from us.[84]

This is a somewhat surprising response to Catullus, as it might have been expected that Leland would draw on Catullus' poems on the death of his brother for this funeral elegy (c.101, for example, with its haunting ending of 'and forever, o my brother, hail and farewell!', *atque in perpetuum, frater, ave atque vale*). Instead, Leland returns to the sparrow poems, and this time contrasts himself to Catullus rather than taking him as a direct model for imitation. The frivolity of Catullus' mourning for a pet bird (however that 'bird' may be read) is contrasted with Leland's own more sombre grief, and Leland sets a distance between himself and the Latin poet. Catullus is 'barely chaste or virtuous', (*parum pudicus*) itself a Catullan phrase, while Leland follows 'more hallowed or sacred' muses (*sacratiores*). At the same time, this poem ties together Catullus and Wyatt: it questions the moral status of Catullus, in this poem at least, but also makes an explicit link between his works and Wyatt, the subject of the next chapter.

Another notable imitator of Catullus is Jacopo Sannazaro (1458–1530). He is best known now for his *Arcadia*, possibly the first Renaissance pastoral work in imitation of both Greek and Latin models, which was hugely popular and influential throughout Europe: after circulating in manuscript from 1481, it was printed in 1504, and its mix of prose and eclogues was a direct influence on Sidney's *Arcadia*. Less well known are Sannazaro's three books of elegies and epigrams, collected and published posthumously in 1535. Ralph Nash identifies references to Tibullus and Propertius in them; Michael Putnam also highlights the influence of Ovid and Catullus.[85] The Catullan intertexts are particularly striking.

Ad amicam alludes to Catullus 5 and 7: 'my light, grant me in my desire as many kisses snatched from you as charming Lesbia had given to her poet' (1.57.1–2).[86] Sannazaro's elegy 1.3 reworks c.70 (incidentally, the first Catullan text to be translated into English by Philip Sidney in his *Certain Sonnets*): the Catullan original has 'the woman I love says that there is no-one whom she would rather marry than me, not if Jupiter himself were to woo her' (c.70.1–2);[87] Sannazaro's imitation appears to switch the gender of the constant partner so we have 'no woman will be able to draw away my affection, though Venus herself depart from the heavens and stars' (1.3.1–2).[88] But the Catullan epigram has a bitter twist to it which is also encompassed in Sannazaro's re-writing – it ends 'she says – but what a woman says to her ardent lover should be written in wind and running water' (Catullus 70.3–4).[89] Sannazaro's text captures the trope of male constancy upon which elegy is built.

This Catullan epigram is of special interest to the discussion of Chapter 2 as is Catullus' arresting use of *foedus*, 'contract, treaty, tie of friendship', within the context of his adulterous relationship with Lesbia. This term is echoed in Sannazaro's same elegy, 1.3, when he says 'once, then, the gods ratified the compact between us, a compact not to be broken until the concluding funeral pyre'.[90] That repetition of 'compact' (*foedera*) within three words seems deliberate, and we will see why it becomes such a potent yet contested term in Catullus' verse, and what it might be doing, in the next chapter.

As well as imitating Catullus himself, Sannazaro also comments on the philological project undertaken by Italian humanists on Catullus' texts. In epigram 1.13 *De emendatione Catulli ad Iovianum* addressed to Giovanni Pontano, he writes:

> if learned Catullus were to return from the vale of Elysium, and Lesbia alone were to lead behind her her thankless throngs, he will not so much bewail the losses in his blemished little book as he will exult in your service, Giovanni. (1.13.1–4)[91]

The imagery of Catullus returning from Elysium, where he had been left in Ovid's *Amores* 3.9, makes a tacit gesture linking Catullus to Ovid; and the idiom throughout Sannazaro's poems echoes that of Catullus himself (*da mi basia, mea lux, foedera, libelli*) as well as using the most common epithet, *doctus*, which both Ovid and Tibullus allocate to Catullus and which, as we have seen, becomes a defining quality of his Renaissance receptions.

Before turning to receptions of Propertius, it is worth briefly touching on two poets whose imitations of elegy are not much discussed, those

of Robert Sidney, brother to Philip and Mary, and Ben Jonson. Robert
Sidney's poems are not always written in sonnet form and certainly rely on
intertextual relations with his brother's *Astrophil and Stella* as well as other
non-elegiac 'classical and continental models'.[92] It is worth noting, though,
the way in which his depiction of love betrayed, and the perfidy of the
beloved, owes a debt to erotic elegy and is quite different from the more
usual neo-Platonic or Petrarchan model, or his brother's sequence where
Astrophil is disappointed by Stella's chastity, not her duplicity.

Robert Sidney's so-called 'betrayal poems' (song 3, sonnets 16, 27, 29) are
especially Catullan in mood and tone:

> But I in searching out your truth did prove
> My true mishaps in your betraying love.
> Cruel, I love you still though thus betrayed.
> (Sonnet 16, 10–12)

>   ... and all too late
> I learn, when help is past, my sickness state.
> (Sonnet 27, 13–14)

> When you confessing faults, remission sought
> And for amends, large promises did make,
> But soon as I to my old bonds was brought,
> Trusting on so fair words, your word you brake.
> See then your purchase, your rich conquest see:
> You poison your own faith, to infect me.
> (Sonnet 29, 9–14)

These texts of Robert Sidney might not present verbal echoes or explicit
allusions to Catullus or erotic elegy but the idiom of unfaithfulness and
deception, the bitter articulation of love as a form of sickness or infection
which cannot be shaken off, the resigned acceptance of the insincerity
and unreliability of female words of love are typical of the Catullan Lesbia
texts: 'now I know you; and therefore, though I burn more ardently, yet
you are in my sight much less worthy and lighter' (c.72.5–6);[93] 'to this
point is my mind reduced by your perfidy, Lesbia, and has so ruined itself
by its own devotion' (c.75.1–2);[94] 'take away this plague and ruin from me
... I would myself be well again and put away this baleful sickness' (c.76.20
and 25).[95] In sonnet 26, too, Robert Sidney writes 'my love more dear to
me than hands or eyes' (9), an echo of Catullus 104.2 'of her who is dearer
to me than both my eyes'.[96]

These texts can thus be read as evidence of a parallel erotic model alongside the Petrarchan which exists in the sixteenth century. It is one which

takes its nature and identity from Catullus and the elegists, and which erases Petrarch's moralising reconfiguration of the wayward and morally corrupt elegiac mistress. As Chapter 2 argues, this model of elegiac gendered relations is crucial to Wyatt's erotics, and gives love elegy a central position in the depiction of Henrician love politics.

The second poet worth mentioning briefly here is Ben Jonson whose work sits just outside the sixteenth century. Not usually considered a 'love' poet, Jonson yet wrote in a tradition which might be identified as 'elegiac', sometimes even naming his poems elegies. His *A Celebration of Charis in Ten Lyric Pieces* is notable for its 'kiss' poems deriving from Catullus 5 and 7, and his Celia poems advertise themselves as imitations of the same Catullan texts:

> Suns, that set, may rise again:
> But if once we lose this light,
> 'Tis, with us, perpetual night.
>   (Song: To Celia 6–8)[97]

> Suns may set and rise again. For us, when the short light has once set, remains to be slept the sleep of one unbroken night.
>   (Catullus 5.4–6)[98]

Although fitting the *carpe diem* form, the debt to Catullus is unmistakeable. 'To the Same' is a translation, a fusion and an 'Englishing' of Catullus 5 and 7:

> ... First give a hundred,
> Then a thousand, then another
> Hundred, then unto the tother
> Add a thousand, and so more:
> Till you equal with the store,
> All the grass that Romney yields,
> Or the sands in Chelsea fields,
> Or the drops of silver Thames,
> Or the stars that gild his streams,
> In the silent summer nights,
> When youths ply their stol'n delights.
> How to tell them as they flow,
> And the envious, when they find,
> What their number is, be pined.
>   (8–22)[99]

> Give me a thousand kisses, then a hundred, then another thousand then a second hundred, then yet another thousand, then a hundred.
>   (Catullus 5.7–9)[100]

> As great as is the number of the Libyan sand that lies on silphium-bearing
> Cyrene, between the oracle of sultry Jove and the sacred tomb of old Battus; or
> as many as are the stars, when night is silent, that see the stolen loves of men ...
> kisses, which neither curious eyes shall count up nor an evil tongue bewitch.
>
> (Catullus 7.3–8, 11–12)[101]

Romney in Kent is close to Penshurst, the Sidney family home, and Chelsea
was the home of the Dudleys, Mary Sidney's natal family and the source
of Robert Sidney's title of Earl of Leicester after his uncle, Robert Dudley,
died childless. The 'Celia' poems appear in Jonson's *The Forest* just after his
country-house poem 'To Penshurst'. Jonson, then, adapts the more general
similes of Catullus in order to slip in flattering personal nods to an aristocratic family whose friendship he is keen to hold and celebrate. We also
find him dedicating and exchanging verse with Mary Wroth, the daughter
of Robert Sidney, whose poetry we will examine in Chapter 5.

So what can be said about these various references to, and appropriations
of, Catullus? Firstly, Catullus proves popular across humanist Europe and
we have seen his verse being commented on and re-written in Italy, the
Netherlands and England. The most prominent qualities attributed to
Catullus are his eroticism and his learned erudition – the two, perhaps,
balancing each other so that the latter compensates, possibly acts as a cover,
for the former. More importantly for the arguments of this book, they serve
as witness to a Catullan presence in English poetic culture earlier than has
been traditionally ascribed. These poems may not be direct translations of
Catullus into English but they certainly engage explicitly with Catullan
texts and the narratorial persona of the verses. Indeed, the very fact that
these are sometimes loose intertexts, echoes and resonances rather than
direct quotations, tells us something important about the relaxed nature of
imitatio in the period. Importantly, too, these appropriations tie a knowledge of Catullus specifically to the Henrician court, and even suggest,
given Skelton's role as Henry VIII's boyhood tutor, that the future king
encountered Catullus in his youth.

Strikingly, however, in terms of English receptions, Skelton's Catullus
is not necessarily the same as Leland's – or, as the next chapter discusses,
Wyatt's. Skelton's verse makes use of the wanton, frivolous Catullus whose
sparrow poems appear playful and tender on the surface but which may
hide a more slyly obscene edge. Leland's Catullus is more ambivalent: he is
primarily an epigrammatist, rather than a love poet, and one whom Leland
appears to esteem and yet also find unsettling. These Tudor receptions of
Catullus are thus shown to be multiple and contingent, drawing on different
aspects of the classical poet. Chapter 2 considers Wyatt's Catullus and argues

that for Wyatt he is a love poet, one concerned acutely with the trope of an unworthy love. Before that, we will turn to the reception of Propertius.

Propertius: 'Cynthia First'

Cynthia appears to be central to Renaissance receptions of Propertius, as if the period takes the poet's opening line quite literally: 'Cynthia first'.[102] Eneas Silvius Piccolomini, who we met earlier objecting to elegy on the school curriculum ('all the writers of elegy should be withheld from a boy. Tibullus, Propertius, Catullus ... are too soft and effeminate. Their writings are almost all about love, and they are continually bemoaning their lost loves') had no such qualms when writing for an adult audience. His *Cinthia* was written c.1426–31 and consists of nineteen poems, six of which are in elegiac couplets and addressed to his beautiful mistress, Cinthia. Drawing closely on Propertius, he depicts an unsatisfactory love with an elusive young woman who yet serves as the muse of his poetry:

> Cinthia, if any fame is due to my work, it is from you I shall receive what-ever honour there will be. It is you who give me strength for writing poetry, you who create my talent, you who create my eloquence.
>
> (1.1–4)[103]

This sense of Cinthia as almost a collaborator in the text re-writes Propertius 2.1 where it is neither Calliope nor Apollo who inspire the poet but 'my mistress herself who creates my talent' (2.1.4).[104] This placing of Cynthia as muse and potential poet in her own right will be the subject of our readings in Chapter 3 where we will see how Philip Sidney uses Propertius to engage with questions of inspiration and poetics.

Johannes Secundus imitated Propertius as well as Catullus and Ovid, and called his first book of elegies the 'Julia Monobiblos', a tribute to Propertius' first book, the 'Cynthia Monobiblos'. The name continues to draw attention to an important element of Renaissance elegiac recep-tion: the mingling of influences from the elegists, and sometimes Catullus, as a group. Secundus' Julia alludes to the biographical understanding in the period that Ovid had a love affair with Julia, Augustus' daughter – an element of Ovid's own reception to which we will return presently.[105] Secundus' later elegiac books move away from Julia as prime object of desire and take first Lydia and then Venerilla as their subjects, perhaps drawing from the multiple mistresses of Tibullus.

In any case, the important point is that many neo-Latin imitators of elegy such as Beccadelli, Piccolomini, Sannazaro, Secundus and Cristoforo

Landini (who wrote a three-book collection of elegies called the *Xandra*), drew components from the genre as a whole, rather than choosing to imitate, in many cases, a specific poet. We can find an example of this quite late in the sixteenth century in the verses of Thomas Campion. His epigram 2.60 takes the scenario of Propertius 1.3 where the narrator comes to the sleeping Cynthia and tries to place a gift of apples in her hands only to have her wake up and castigate him for arriving late, tired and possibly drunk, and mingles it with the triumphant outcome of Ovid's *Amores* 1.5 which details an assignation between the narrator and Corinna: Campion's poem has his hero Lycius furtively kissing the sleeping Clytha, only it turns out the girl is merely pretending to sleep and is secretly enjoying what turns out to be an illicit sexual encounter. Campion likes this merging of Propertius and Ovid so much that he writes an English version in his *Book of Ayres*, 1.8.[106] In fact, when his first book comprising 129 epigrams and sixteen elegies was first published in 1595, Campion claimed the title of 'the first poet from the name of Brutus [i.e. the first British poet] to sing sweet elegies and his own love affairs'.[107] His friend, Charles Fitzgeffrey, agreed with this statement in an epigram of his own written in 1601: 'you to whose genius Roman Elegy is indebted to the same extent to which it was earlier indebted to her Naso'.[108] This is startlingly erroneous, both because John Donne's Elegies had been circulating in manuscript since the early 1590s, and because, of course, Ovid was the last of the elegists and acknowledged his debts to Catullus and his predecessors, something which Fitzgeffrey either did not know or chose not to admit.

One of the reasons why it is difficult to find appropriations of just Propertius in the period might well be due to continued problems with the text. In 1557 the Accademia della Fama in Venice published their programme of proposed scholarly and philological projects to be undertaken by their members. They planned an examination of classical genres specifically prioritising the consideration of erotic elegy, and their intention was not just to study elegy, but also to translate it into the vernacular and to publish the best textual editions together with commentaries. For Propertius they proposed a complete edition of his elegies coupled with 'a brief and accurate interpretation by which all the difficult passages of this poet will be made easy'.[109] Hermeneutic uncertainties might well have combined with textual ambiguities, as well as a systematic inclination to combine multiple influences as learnt at school, to result in Propertius appearing as one elegiac element in Renaissance re-writings alongside Catullus and Ovid.

The interest evinced in Venice in elegy as a literary genre can be found, too, in England and it is worth pausing on George Puttenham's discussion in his *The Arte of English Poesy* (1589). In chapter 11 of the first book he mentions Catullus as a lyric poet like Anacreon and Callimachus among the Greeks and Horace among Latin poets, then goes on: 'there were another sort, who sought the favour of fair ladies, and coveted to bemoan their estates at large and the perplexities of love in a certain piteous verse called elegy, and thence were called elegiac: such among the Latins were Ovid, Tibullus and Propertius.' He continues in chapter 24 of book 1 'the third sorrowing was of loves, by long lamentation in elegy (so was their song called), and it was in a piteous manner of metre, placing a limping pentameter after a lusty hexameter, which made it go dolorously more than any other metre'.[110] Puttenham here separates erotic elegy from mourning elegy with its associations of death, loss, departure. He also recognises the intersection between form and content, identifying the classical elegiac metre which for the Latin poets was frequently a marker of genre affili-ation.[111] Notably, he separates Catullus from the Augustan elegists, and groups Propertius together with Ovid and Tibullus, not differentiating between them. While Puttenham is, in strict terms, justified as Catullus does not always write in elegiac metre, the Renaissance period, as we have seen, frequently reads Catullus more laxly as a kind of proto-elegist who sets the erotic framework which elegy proper comes to adopt.

It may be difficult to separate Propertian receptions textually, but there is one amusing instance in England of Propertius appearing as a character in a play. Ben Jonson's satire *Poetaster* was first performed in 1600–1 and is set in Augustan Rome. Jonson parades his knowledge of the elegists by making Propertius, Ovid and Tibullus characters in his drama alongside Horace, Gallus and Virgil.[112] In Act 1, scene 3 Ovid and Tibullus discuss their long-absent friend Sextus (Propertius) and agree that his social with-drawal is caused by the death of his beloved Cynthia. The joke, of course, is not just that Cynthia is Propertius' creation, but that she comes alive again in the poetry after her death. Later in the play, Ovid and Julia, Augustus' daughter, re-enact the balcony scene from *Romeo and Juliet* (first printed 1597). While the play is generally agreed to be a satirical weapon against Marston and Dekker with whom Jonson had an ongoing literary quarrel, it also reveals an acute knowledge of the Latin elegists and assumes that this is shared by his audience: the comedy, indeed, partly depends on us enjoying the spectacle of such earnest concern on the parts of Ovid and Tibullus for Propertius' mourning of Cynthia, his fictional mistress. By pretending to take elegy at face value, where Propertius, for example, is in love with a real mistress named Cynthia, Jonson succeeds in drawing attention to its artifice and fictional status.

In 'An Ode' Jonson also speaks of the elegists:

> Was Lesbia sung by learned Catullus?
> Or Delia's graces, by Tibullus?
> Doth Cynthia, in Propertius' song
> Shine more, than she the stars among?
> … Or hath Corinna, by the name
> Her Ovid gave her, dimmed the fame
> Of Caesar's daughter.
>
> (9–19)[113]

He goes on to place Petrarch's Laura, Ronsard's Cassandra, Sidney's Stella, and his own Celia into the same literary love mode, thus linking them all explicitly to Roman love elegy, and extending the tradition to his own verse.

An important reception of Propertius can be found in Petrarch's *Triumph of Death*. This poem draws on 4.7, the poem where Cynthia comes back from the underworld to haunt the narrator, and serves to highlight Petrarch's Christianised deviations from, as well as debt to, elegy. As it is discussed in detail in Chapter 5, it is merely mentioned here in passing.

It is, then, generally less easy to identify definitively Propertian allusions in early modern texts where they are more usually tangled up with generic influences and echoes of elegy as a whole. One of the keys, though, to the period's reception of Propertius is Cynthia, whether the muse figure and source of poetry that we find adopted into Piccolomini's *Cinthia*, the shade returned from the dead that we will see later in Petrarch, or the absent mistress leading to the comic representation of Propertius in Jonson's play where his whole persona is bound up in mourning Cynthia's death. The political poetry of Propertius' fourth book does not seem to find a purchase on the early modern imagination. For elegy as a potentially politicised mode of writing, we have to turn to Ovid.

'All Those Salacious Works Which Were Written by Ovid'

Ovid, as we have seen, was never lost as Catullus, Propertius and Tibullus/ Sulpicia were. During the medieval period, he was considered one of the three great Augustan poets along with Virgil and Horace, and all three were important stylistic models. His reception coalesces around three ideas: Ovid as lover and teacher of erotic skills; Ovid as mythographer; and Ovid as exile.[114]

In terms of love, John Fyler remarks that Ovid was, for medieval readers, 'the supreme authority on the psychology of the lover's mind', an important concern given the cultural position of love as part of the chivalric ideal.[115] We can find this aspect of Ovid's reception celebrated in Chaucer's dream-vision, *The House of Fame* (c.1379–80), which names Ovid, 'Venus' clerk' (3.1487) and places him on a literal pedestal next to Virgil: 'And next him on a pillar was, | of copper, Venus' clerk, Ovid, | that hath sown wonder wide | the great god of Love's name' (3.1486–9). While Virgil is on a pillar of 'tinned iron' (3.1482), possibly because iron was a metal associated with weaponry and Mars as god of war, Ovid is standing on a pillar of copper, a metal understood at this time to be sacred to Venus, the goddess of love. This facet of Ovid's reception continues to be central to Ovid's place in the Renaissance and has been well documented in the literature.[116]

The sense of Ovid as a transmitter of classical myths, especially in the *Metamorphoses* and *Fasti*, is also strong in both the medieval and Renaissance periods. Both texts, as we have seen, retain their place on the humanist school curriculum for this reason, despite the numerous sexual scenes and episodes of rape. In early modern England, the so-called 'Ovidianism' of the 1590s manifested in a fashion for epyllion drawing largely on erotic mythic episodes taken from the *Metamorphoses*: prime examples include Thomas Lodge's *Scillaes Metamorphosis* (1589), Shakespeare's *Venus and Adonis* (1593), Marlowe's *Hero and Leander* which draws also on the *Heroides* (published 1598, written before 1593 when Marlowe was killed) and Marston's *The Metamorphosis of Pigmalions Image* (1598).[117]

Ovid's exile has been seen as a key fact of his medieval and Renaissance biography and a clue to the way he was being read. Despite, or, rather, because of, Ovid's own notorious refusal to say anything more precise than to attribute his fault to 'a poem and a mistake' (*carmen et error*) medieval and Renaissance writers were quite happy to pad out Ovid's own reticence.[118] Medieval theories, as evidenced in twelfth-century commentaries used in cathedral schools, were that he was the lover of Livia, Augustus' wife, and a rival to Virgil for her erotic favours; or that he had witnessed Augustus himself having sex with a male lover.[119] In comparison, Renaissance musings about the cause of Ovid's exile are relatively tame: 'For abusing Julia, daughter of the emperor Augustus, although the pretence of the emperor was for the making of the book of the craft of love, whereby young minds might be stirred to wantonness' is the way Ovid's punishment is explained in one source, and variations of this story were frequently appended to volumes of Ovid in English and Latin.[120] Spenser, too, in his 'glosse' to January in *The Shepheardes Calender* (1579) comments 'so as Ovid shadoweth his love under the name of Corynna, which of some is supposed to be Julia, the emperor Augustus his daughter, and wife to Agrippa'.[121]

What is notable is that even Ovid's exile is underpinned in these stories by a sense of erotic indiscretion so that ideas of political, literary and sexual transgression are closely intertwined. This is certainly the way some modern scholars have interpreted his influence and reception. Georgia Brown, for example, discussing the way Ovid was read in the 1590s, states that his texts were used to 'sanction' the erotic, that he was seen as the alternative to 'the authoritative Virgilian cultural archetype'.[122] Syrithe Pugh agrees: in discussing the 'Ovidian' as opposed to the 'Virgilian' influence in Spenser's texts, she claims that Ovidian aspects encompass 'individualism, eroticism, playful irony and exilic discontent' while the Virgilian manifests as 'public-minded values, imperialist politics and serious political stance'.[123] For her, Virgil and Ovid are thus at extreme ends of a continuum and Ovid's textual voice is always a subversive one. On their relative responses to the erotic, for example, she argues that Virgil in the *Aeneid* condemns love while Ovid 'praise[s] love as a noble instinct'.[124]

This polarised way of reading Virgil and Ovid seems unproductive since it renders each author's texts flat, simple, univocal and uncomplicated, rather than acknowledging the richness and openness of texts which still elude a single definitive reading today. Instead, we might prefer to focus on the dialogue which takes place between the Virgilian and Ovidian texts (as well as between those of the other poets studied here) and the way they engage with, and expose, common themes, motifs, treatments and ideas that are already present, thus drawing the texts closer together in a fluid and pliable relationship rather than seeing one as undermining or opposing the other. After all, Chaucer, as we have just seen, placed Ovid and Virgil on pillars of fame beside each other, and by selecting, respectively, the metals associated with Venus (copper) and Mars (iron), might be subtly drawing attention to the close, though unsanctioned, relationship between them. Even the *Amores*, as we shall see in Chapter 4, is, at times, surprisingly close in erotic and political register to the *Aeneid*.

So should we assume that Renaissance readers and writers saw Ovid and Virgil as critically opposed and thus offering divergent and conflicting models of thought which could be integrated into their own works to add complexity as Pugh, for example, does? Or are Renaissance readers sophisticated enough to identify and distinguish what we might call 'further voices' that contest, compete and struggle to be heard from within a single text?[125] In other words, does a Renaissance textual concern with public, political values have to be 'Virgilian' or can it be a response to something which also exists in Ovid's texts? And, conversely, does a submersion in the erotic have to be 'Ovidian' (or, more accurately, perhaps, elegiac) or can it also be a deliberate engagement with Virgil's own uses of the erotic in the *Aeneid*?

Certainly Virgil's life, as understood in the Renaissance, and some of the texts attributed to him could be seen as being as potentially indiscreet and morally provocative as Ovid's. His biography was best known through the 'Life' by Donatus, the fourth-century tutor to Jerome, and was probably based on Suetonius' now-lost *Vita*. In this, Virgil was described as being 'somewhat inclined to pederasty', and this brief biography was frequently appended to his texts, especially the *Opera*, or complete works. His *oeuvre* was also understood to include the poems of the Appendix Vergiliana, so named by Joseph Scaliger in 1572 as questionable works attributed to Virgil since antiquity, including the erotic epyllion *Ciris*, and the *Priapea* poems narrated through the mouth of Priapus, the phallic god.[126] One of these is an impotence poem addressed to the narrator's 'accursed penis' (*sceleste penis*, 4.19) whose lack of performance will now deter both the delicate boy (*tener puer*, 21) and playful girl (*puella ... iocosa*, 24) and confine him to the sexual attentions of ugly old women. Possibly alluding to both Catullus 2 and *Amores* 3.7, this is clearly quite a different Virgil from the authoritative writer of the *Aeneid*, but one who was current in the Renaissance.

Despite Scaliger's questioning of the Virgilian attribution of the Appendix in 1572, Spenser wrote a translation called *Vergil's Gnat* based on the *Culex* from the Appendix in 1591. Aretino, too, a writer to whom we will return presently, defended his 'licentious speech ... by mentioning in its behalf Virgil's *Prispea* [*sic*] and all those salacious works which were written by Ovid, Juvenal and Martial'.[127] Virgil, it seems, could be seen during the Renaissance as surprisingly close to Ovid and associated with a similar sense of sexual transgression rather than as always morally authoritative. There is, in addition, at least some evidence of Renaissance readers being as discomfited by Virgil's last lines of the *Aeneid* as more modern readers. A hand-written Florentine commentary, for example, to the *Aeneid* and dated to 1587 expresses concern about Aeneas' killing of Turnus despite his pleading for clemency: 'and having been robbed of his wife by Aeneas, he was not spared: which the victor was accustomed to grant'.[128]

Ariosto's close imitation, too, of Virgil's last lines at the end of his *Orlando Furioso* (1532) problematise his reading of the *Aeneid*:

> So two or three times he raised his arm to its full height and plunged the dagger to the hilt in Rodomont's forehead, thus assuring his own safety. Released from its body, now ice-cold, the angry spirit, which among the living, had been so proud and insolent, fled cursing down to the dismal shores of Acheron.
>
> (*Orlando Furioso* 46.140)[129]

These comments and re-writings raise important questions of how Ovid and Virgil were being read in the Renaissance and highlight the extent to which a poet like Ariosto might be recognising and reflecting upon the instabilities we modern readers attribute to the *Aeneid*. We will return to this issue of reading Ovid and Virgil in greater detail in Chapter 4 but it is worth stating here that Renaissance readers appear to be perceptive, sophisticated and creative readers of classical texts, alive to the nuances, possibilities and traces which they contain.

Much of the literature on Renaissance poetry almost seems to equate eroticism with Ovid thus coining the term 'Ovidian' which is used loosely in a number of different contexts. But, while 'Ovidianism' was being replicated in epyllion as well as, for example, Marlowe's and Donne's elegies during the 1580s and 1590s, Ovid's actual texts were continuing to be taught in schools. This seems a testament to the fact that multiple ways of reading Ovid's texts existed in this period and were actively promoted, and that while the eroticised reading was one constructive mode utilised by writers, it was not the sole or even the most prominent method of interpretation.

Golding's prefatory epistle to his 1567 translation of the *Metamorphoses* reveals an anxiety about precisely this multitude of interpretative possibilities and works very hard to shape the reader's own understanding of this text. On the title-page there is an epitaph: 'with skill, heede, and judgement, this worke must be read | for else to the Reader it standes in small stead'.[130] This text, it implies, is simultaneously useful and useless and the differentiator is the reader's own ability to read: the skilful reader will render the text morally productive; the untrained student, on the other hand, will achieve nothing from it. The text itself is not characterised as dangerous, scandalous or subversive in any way but shifts its didactic status according to the mind of the reader.

This shading of the work continues throughout the epistle as Golding moralises Ovid's stories for a Christian audience. Indeed, he goes so far as to claim Ovid learned himself from Moses: 'what man is he but would suppose the author of this book | the first foundation of his work from Moses' writings took?' (342–3) and goes on to draw comparisons between Ovid's depiction of the Creation in *Metamorphoses* 1 and the Bible (379ff.). Christianising classical authors was commonplace, of course, to accommodate them to a post-pagan culture, but recognising Golding's placing of Ovid into this tradition works against the image of the 'subversive' Ovid who is frequently invoked when discussing Renaissance receptions of his texts. This moral version of Ovid as the proto-Christian is far closer to the Renaissance Christianising of Virgil and his 'messianic' *Eclogue* 4, or Sidney's reading of Aeneas as 'so excellent a man in every way' (*Defence of Poesie* 190), thus bringing these supposedly oppositional authors into a nearer relationship than is sometimes assumed.

Golding overlays a political as well as a religious and moral reading of the *Metamorphoses* in his prefatory letter: the Phaëthon episode, for example, is interpreted as a story about 'the disobedience of the child; and in the child is meant | the disobedient subject that against his prince is bent' (83–4). This is particularly interesting given the Renaissance biography of Ovid, since Golding remakes the poet, turning him from someone rebellious against political authority and exiled for his sexual behaviour as well as his sexually infectious texts into someone whose writings might be used to promote political and moral obedience and orthodoxy.

Although Golding moralises possible interpretations of the *Metamorphoses* in his prefatory epistle, he does not censor, edit or suppress the text itself which is surprisingly close to the original Latin. The epitaph and the epistle may alert the reader to the fact that s/he should read 'with skill, heed, and judgement' if s/he is to decipher the poem and comprehend it in a morally useful and virtuous way, but the text itself is not forced to foreclose or predetermine the reader's response to it, and reception is left ultimately in the mind of the reader.

This is itself a strikingly Ovidian way of thinking about reading which is put forward in the *Tristia* 2, a Renaissance school text as we have seen, and a work which has itself been called 'a document of literary criticism' concerned with reading and reception.[131] In answering an implicit question about the immorality of his poetry, in particular the *Ars*, the Ovidian narrator claims 'for from every song she can gain wisdom for sin' (255–6), 'from whatever she touches, be she inclined to wrongdoing, she will equip her character for vice' (257–8).[132] He goes on to give satirically selective misreadings of Latin texts such as Ennius' *Annals* ('naught is ruder than they' (259))[133] and even Homer's *Iliad* ('the very *Iliad* – what is it but an adulteress over whom her lover and her husband fought' (371–2))[134] and

Odyssey ('What is the *Odyssey* except the story of one woman wooed in her husband's absence for love's sake by many suitors?' (374–6))[135] to prove his point before asserting 'it is possible for the soul to be injured by every kind of poem' (264),[136] and that 'nothing is useful which cannot at the same time be injurious' (266).[137] He culminates with the claim that 'all things can corrupt perverted minds' (301), a back-handed insult to Augustus' readers who had caused Ovid's own text to be removed from the libraries precisely for its supposed ability to corrupt minds and morals.[138] Any poem, however, if read with a right mind (*recta si mente legatur*, 275) can harm no one (*nulli posse nocere*, 276). This idea of right or incorrupt reading reappears, it seems, in the epitaph to Golding's *Metamorphoses*, re-articulated as reading 'with skill, heed and judgement'. Ovid is critically concerned with both the politics of reading as well as the relationship between politics and poetry and, for him, texts are always open and able to be appropriated, or misappropriated, to the mind and reading practices of their audience. *Tristia* 2 separates the text from authorial intentionality and also makes a distinction between the moral status of text, author and reader: 'I assure you, my character differs from my verse – my life is moral, my muse is gay' (2.353–4);[139] 'chaste women may read much that they should not do' (2.308).[140]

This image of women reading Ovid is worth pausing on. The *Heroides*, in particular, seems to have legitimated the idea of women writing, however fictional Ovid's letters are, and we find Renaissance female writers such as Isabella Whitney using Ovid as a model in epistolary texts such as 'To her inconstant lover'. In 1643, too, Lady Anne Clifford finally came into a long-disputed inheritance and took possession of her family estates. One of the first things she did was to commission a portrait of herself in her house, surrounded by her family and her prized books – one of which, with its title clear to see, is the *Metamorphoses*. Ovid, it seems, can be associated with cultural prestige and claimed by women as well as men.

The important point to be highlighted here is the numerous versions of 'Ovid' which were available during the Renaissance: the schoolroom Ovid nurtured for his educational value; the moral Ovid who espoused Christian values; the politically orthodox Ovid; Ovid the literary critic who forces the idea of open audience reception; as well as the more familiar dissident, sexually seditious and morally rebellious Ovid. To reduce the possible Renaissance Ovids to just one of these – usually the last – narrows the scope of his texts and renders them thin, single-dimensional models to be used by later poets. But by restoring the variations of readings that were made possible by Ovid's texts in this period, we equally re-open the ways in which his works might serve as precedents to Renaissance poets.

There might have been numerous and various Ovids available to Renaissance writers but, however important the less familiar versions of the poet might be, we should not downplay the importance of Ovid as a poet who produced blatantly sexual texts. The *Metamorphoses*, especially, might have provided both an exemplar and a legitimising authority for the fashion for erotic mythological paintings and other visual art in Europe during the fifteenth and sixteenth centuries. The first illustrated edition of the *Metamorphoses*, as we have seen, was produced in Bruges in 1484 and was followed in 1497 by a Venetian edition which is thought to have influenced Italian artists.[141] While there is no firm evidence that Ovid's text was the source for erotic mythic scenes which appeared not just in paintings but also on tapestries and bridal chests, we know that one aspect of both the medieval and Renaissance view of Ovid was as a transmitter of classical myth.

The number of mythological paintings which appeared following the illustrated editions of the *Metamorphoses* is striking: Botticelli's *The Birth of Venus* (c.1485), Piero di Cosimo's *Venus and Mars* (c.1498) and *Death of Procis* (c.1510), Palma Vecchio's *Diana Discovers Callisto's Misdemeanor* (c.1525), Titian's *Venus of Urbino* (c.1538) and *Danaë* (c.1544), and Tintoretto's *Vulcan Surprises Venus and Mars* (c.1555) offer just a few examples.[142] The Villa Farnesina in Rome, built in 1509–11, was filled with mythological paintings, frescoes, statues and tapestries including depictions of Orpheus, Scylla cutting off her father's lock of hair, Philomela and Procne, Bacchus and Ariadne, and Ganymede, many of which appeared in the *Metamorphoses*.[143] When Francis I was preparing for Henry VIII's state visit to France, he had one of the chambers prepared for him hung with green velvet tapestries on which were embroidered 'fables from Ovid' in expensive gold and silver thread.[144] The point being made here is not just about the prevalence of Ovid's mythological influence in the Renaissance but, specifically, the visual nature of his texts which inspired artists and craftsmen as well as writers.

The *Metamorphoses* and the visual art it inspired might be erotic but is not usually deemed obscene or graphically sexual. There is one set of Renaissance appropriations, though, which do cross that line as it was drawn at the time, and which also derive from Ovid's texts though, in this case, the *Ars Amatoria* and *Amores*: Pietro Aretino's *sonnetti lussuriosi* and the obscene engravings that accompanied them, together known as *I Modi*, 'the postures or positions'. Giulio Romano created the original drawings of men and women in a variety of explicit and detailed sexual positions in Rome in 1524 and they were engraved that year by Marcantonio Raimondi.[145] They circulated amongst the Roman elite until Pope Clement VII ordered this first edition to be burned. Raimondi was imprisoned, distribution of the book was forbidden and a death sentence was imposed on anyone who reprinted the collection. Despite this, a second edition was produced in 1527 in Venice, and Aretino added sixteen sonnets to accompany each of the engravings. One of the notable things about this collection was that all of the perpetrators were well educated and known artists. Romano had been apprenticed to Raphael, had studied classical art and architecture, and had worked on projects at the Vatican and, interestingly, the Villa Farnesina which, as we have already seen, was filled with visual representations of Ovid's stories. Raimondi was a renowned engraver who had also worked for Raphael, and had been influenced by Michelangelo and ideas of classical Rome. He also made an engraving of a Hellenistic statue of Laocoön, for example, derived from the scene in the *Aeneid* (2.199–227).[146] He appears in Vasari's *Lives* where this story is recounted:

> Guilio Romano had Marcantonio engrave in twenty sheets the same number of different positions, attitudes and postures in which immoral men lie with women; and what was worse, for each position messer Pietro Aretino created a most obscene sonnet.[147]

Aretino himself was already known as a writer of satirical poems and lampoons before his *sonnetti* were published and had particularly been associated with *pasquinatte*, political satires especially aimed at the papal court.[148] His 'obscene' *sonnetti*, through their form and crude street language, place themselves into a deliberately antagonistic relationship to Petrarch and the fashion for writing refined and elegant sonnets about an elusive beloved. It is interesting to note, too, that Vasari's greatest objection is to the poetry that accompanies the engravings: 'what was worse, for each position messer Pietro Aretino created a most obscene sonnet'.

Classical sources for Aretino's sexual verses have been put forward: both Lynne Lawner and Bette Talvacchia have discussed Aretino's deliberate debt to ancient 'sex manuals', the idea of which fascinated Renaissance readers, and which they had heard about from Suetonius' life of Tiberius, and Martial's epigrams.[149] Ariosto, writing in 1529, both defended his own erotic work and drew attention to the relationship between classical 'erotica' and Aretino when he claimed 'my *Suppositions* are entirely different from those ancient ones Elephantis painted which have recently been revived in our city of Holy Rome, beautifully but shamefully printed up so that the whole world can get a copy of them'.[150] Aretino phrased his own defence in classical terms: 'the ancient, as well as modern poets and sculptors, sometimes engaged in writing and sculpting lascivious works as a pastime for their genius'; and in the preface to his *Ragionamenti* (1534) justified his 'licentious speech … by mentioning in its behalf Virgil's *Prispea*, and all those salacious works which were written by Ovid, Juvenal and Martial.'[151]

The engravings and Aretino's sonnets deliberately eschew the mythological 'loves of the gods' typology which served to give a veneer of classicising respectability to erotic paintings, and instead are frank and straightforward depictions of 'normal' men and women, possibly courtesans, having sex in a number of imaginative, adventurous and acrobatic positions in the private rooms of either their homes or, possibly, brothels.[152] While there is unlikely to be a single precedent for Aretino's texts, the role of Ovid's *Ars* and *Amores* as examples should not be ignored. Holt Parker suggests that Ovid himself drew on sexual handbooks as sources for the *Ars*, especially in book three where women are instructed to choose their sexual positions carefully in order to display themselves around their most attractive sexual features.[153] Ovid's text itself describes these positions as *mille modi veneris*, 'a thousand modes of love' (3.787).

One aspect, then, of Ovid to which Aretino is both attentive and to which he draws attention is the intense visuality of his texts which makes them such vibrant sources for artists as well as writers. The other Ovidian strand which Aretino foregrounds is the slippage between the erotic and the political. Aretino was known in his time not just as a writer of obscene verse but also as a political satirist, and his nickname was the 'scourge of Princes'.[154] In his preface to the *Ragionamenti*, he wrote: 'I hope my book will be like the scalpel, at once cruel and merciful, with which the good doctor cuts off the sick limb so that the others remain healthy.'[155] His *sonnetti* have been read as a provocative commentary on contemporary Rome, and 'an arrogant challenge to papal censorship': sonnet 12, for example, features Rangone, a soldier in the service of the Este family, and he also mentions the courtesans Lorenzina and Ciabattina in sonnet 7, who were both active in Roman Papal and political circles.[156] All of Aretino's works were placed on the Papal Index of forbidden books but perhaps as much for their free-thinking and rebellious approach towards the use of the erotic in literature as for the freedom of expression which they endorse.[157] Aretino is important to Renaissance receptions of Ovid because his texts recognise the way in which the erotic itself may serve, in Ovid's texts, as a form of political commentary. The cause of Ovid's exile, we remember, was figured in the Renaissance as resulting from a combination of sexual intrigue and a rebellion against imperial power. Ovid's boldness in standing up to Augustus, at least in his texts, provided a model for Aretino's own satirical take on papal and aristocratic sexual politics, and animated a submerged debate about authority and subversion.

Aretino has been called 'the most notorious figure of Italianate eroticism in Tudor-Stuart England', but while his sonnets and accompanying engravings were widely known to English readers and writers, there is no extant evidence of an Englishmen actually owning a copy of *I Modi*.[158] Spenser in his 'glosse' to January in *The Shepheardes Calendar* (1579) sets a distance between himself and Aretino: 'but yet let no man think that herein I stand with Lucian or his devilish disciple unico Aretino, in defence of execrable and horrible sins of forbidden and unlawful fleshliness', thus proving his knowledge of Aretino even while denying an association with him. Donne's Satire 4 mentions that 'Aretine's pictures have made few chaste' (70), and in a letter to Henry Wotton, Donne mentions reading Aretino.[159] The *I Modi* was not published in England but Aretino's *Ragionamenti*, a set of dialogues between an ageing prostitute and her daughter which might itself have drawn initial inspiration from Ovid's *Amores* 1.8, was printed by J. Wolfe in London in 1584 and was followed by four comedies, adapted from Plautus and Terence, produced by Wolfe again in 1588.

Day five of the *Ragionamenti* is particularly interesting for the light it throws on a Renaissance reading of Virgil's *Aeneid* and the perceived relationship between Ovid and Virgil. The focus of this day's stories is on the treachery of men, and the first story, told by Nanna to her daughter Pippa who wants to follow her in her career as a prostitute, becomes increasingly familiar. A baron, escaped from the 1526 sack of Rome, comes to 'the shore of a great city ruled by a lady whose name cannot be uttered' (233).[160] The pair fall in love and consummate their relationship, she considers them married, he does not, and, when he is forced to leave her for a greater destiny, her feelings are articulated in a series of extended speeches. The lady fails to move the baron and ends by committing suicide on his bed. Pippa asks her mother what the baron said when he heard about her death, and her mother replies laconically, 'that she was crazy' (244). Later, Pippa has a dream and in it a group of Romans shout 'your thieving mother has snitched Virgil's fourth book and is showing off in stolen raiment' (245). She tells her dream to her mother who replies 'ha, ha, ha! … but who the devil is this fellow? Even from the little I know about him, he must surely be a cretin to let a fourth of himself be stolen; and if that's how it is, the rest can certainly be thrown to the dogs' (245).

On one hand, of course, this is vastly comic as Aretino's readers very quickly recognise the story which Pippa has never heard before. But, on the other, it proposes a radical and almost shocking use of the Virgilian text which becomes subordinate to the lessons an ageing Roman prostitute wants to teach her young prostitute daughter. Like Ovid's own *Heroides*, Aretino remakes this part of a canonical text and, even more than Ovid, completely takes Dido's side: 'if it moves you hearing it told by me, who have torn it all apart, mixing it up pitifully as I tell it, what would it have done to you if you had heard it from her [Dido's] own mouth?' (243). The idea that Dido has her own story which perhaps, despite the *Heroides*, has not yet been adequately told is prompted by Aretino's text. The cutting out, too, of book 4 from the rest of the poem offers an alternative reading of the *Aeneid* where the hero's divine mission and the founding of Rome become irrelevant. The association between Virgil as originating poet and Nanna as his current mouthpiece also suggests a correlation between author or poet working under the patronage of the emperor and the prostitute who sells herself for sex. Aretino himself, we remember, survived without patronage in order to be able to write freely.

Aretino's deliberate appropriation of the *Aeneid* thus owes as much to his reading of Ovid as it does to the Virgilian text itself, and it turns a canonical text into a bawdy one, through the persona of the woman telling the story as well as through the story itself. Virgil's text becomes subordinate to an Ovidian mode of re-telling which itself draws attention to the possibilities for subversion which already exist in the *Aeneid*. By turning Virgil's great national epic into a counter-text which may challenge and overturn its own ostensible ideology, Aretino reveals a sophisticated and liberated way of reading which may itself owe a debt to both Ovid and Virgil's own texts.

In summary, then, Renaissance readings of Ovid (and Virgil) are more diverse, and sometimes more 'modern', than they are sometimes assumed to be. While the eroticism of Ovid's texts is one prominent element of his reception, the erotic also has the potential to spill over into the obscene or quasi-pornographic. Aretino's sonnets are important for this strand of Ovidian reception and we will also return to issues of visuality, eroticised looking, and the slippage between the erotic and the political in Chapter 4.

Sulpicia: 'Eruditus Poeta'

There are many places where we can find Ovid in the Renaissance but the same is not true of Sulpicia.[161] We can be sure, though, that her poetry is transmitted in the Tibullan corpus because of the commentaries. The first

Tibullan commentary was in 1475 by Cyllenius in Rome: *Albii Tibulli Elegiarum libri IV cum commentario Bernardini Cillenii Veronensis*, and this was frequently reprinted alongside more recent commentaries on Catullus and Propertius. Cyllenius, oddly, makes no comment on Sulpicia's gender and in his commentary treats her poems as if there is nothing noteworthy about love elegy being written by a woman. This makes it impossible to tell whether he is reading Sulpicia as a persona adopted by a male author, most probably Tibullus, perhaps in line with Ovid's *Heroides* voiced through female characters, or as an authentic female author, like Sappho. If the latter, his refusal to comment on her gender can be read in different ways: either he found nothing strange about a young Roman woman writing love elegy, or he was so scandalised or confused by the phenomenon that he refused to confront it and normalised it as unworthy of comment.[162]

Later commentaries followed Cyllenius in avoiding comment on Sulpicia as a female author. The first to engage with her problematic gender was Joseph Scaliger. In 1577 Scaliger re-organised the Tibullan corpus and created the Appendix Tibulliana, just as he had previously created the Appendix Vergiliana, and wrote a new commentary on Catullus, Propertius and Tibullus: *Castigationes in Catullum, Tibullum, Propertium*, printed in Paris. From this commentary it is still not easy to understand precisely what Scaliger thought about the authorship of the Sulpicia elegies. He does not explicitly contest Tibullan authorship but, by placing the poems in an Appendix, something he had previously done with the Virgilian poems of dubious provenance, he is clearly problematising their authorial status. In the commentary itself he writes of Sulpicia as a woman: 'she pretends that there are other lovers for her, who suffer because she is devoted to Cerinthus only. She pretends, I say, in order that she may inflame the love of the boy which is now lukewarm'.[163] *Alios amatores* makes the other lovers masculine, and *addicta* confirms the feminine gender of 'Sulpicia' but we cannot tell with certainty whether Scaliger is reading Sulpicia as author or as male-authored narrative persona, in line with Propertius' Cynthia, or Ovid's heroines.

He goes on to comment on how skilfully the 'learned poet' (*erudito poeta*) constructs the verse: 'it is really difficult to express how charmingly this is devised by the erudite poet'.[164] *Poeta* is a masculine noun in Latin so we have to wonder whether Scaliger uses it because he believes Sulpicia to be the construct of a male poet, or whether it is in itself a compliment, calling her a poet rather than a poetess. Certainly Scaliger would have been familiar with the noun *poetria*: Ovid's Sappho is made to describe herself as 'Sappho the poetess' (*poetria Sappho*) in *Heroides* 15.183; and in the *Pro Caelio*, Cicero describes Clodia as 'a poetess of experience who had already composed many comedies' (*veteris et plurimarum fabularum poetriae*, 64). Since both women are depicted in these texts in derogatory, even hostile, terms, the use of *poetria* seems to be deliberately belittling, and might be another reason why it is not a term Scaliger might choose to use of Sulpicia. So, like so much about Sulpicia and her work, there is an obliquity surrounding what we can know about Scaliger's own understanding of her gender and authorial status.

The question, then, of whether Sulpicia was recognised and read as a female author in the Renaissance or as a persona adopted and ventriloquised by a male poet, most probably Tibullus, remains a vexed one. Like so many Renaissance heroines, she may well have slipped into the period disguised as a man. There is, though, one poetic text which reads Sulpicia unambiguously as a female poet. In John Skelton's *Phyllyp Sparrow* we find these lines:

> Dame Sulpicia at Rome
> Whose name registered was
> Forever in tables of brass
> Because that she did pass
> In poesy to endite
> And eloquently to write.
> (148–53)

This verse might conceivably refer to the Sulpicia written about in Martial: 'let all girls who wish to please one man read Sulpicia; let all husbands who wish to please one bride read Sulpicia' (10.35.1–4).[165] Given, though, that if Martial's Sulpicia was an authentic female poet, her works have not survived, and that Sulpicia's elegies were published alongside the text of Catullus with whom Skelton explicitly compares himself ('the British Catullus'), it is more plausible that these lines should be referring to Sulpicia the elegist who can, then, be placed amongst English readers at the Henrician court. Skelton's description of her eloquence resonates with Scaliger's later judgement of her as a charming and skilled poet, and he attributes to her a fame which we cannot find explicitly elsewhere in sixteenth-century England. The mention of the 'tables of brass' possibly echo Sulpicia's own unsealed tablets (of wax, of course, problematically temporary in comparison with brass) which are so central to her opening poem. Alternatively, Skelton may be thinking of Chaucer's 'table of bras' in *The House of Fame* (1.142) on which is engraved a reference to the opening lines of the *Aeneid*. Comparing Sulpicia to Virgil is a bold judgement, indeed, on Skelton's part, perhaps more a case of him showing off his knowledge of Sulpicia than a considered critical response.[166]

So the problem of Renaissance readings and receptions of Sulpicia remains unresolved as far as her authorial gender is concerned. Her texts were, though, certainly read, known and discussed across humanist Europe, and seem to have been established in England from at least the start of the sixteenth century. In some ways, it is precisely this lack of critical probing into the question of her gender which might be significant. It seems to be evidence of a ready acceptance on the part of Renaissance readers of elegy as a genre which may easily be appropriated by a female voice – be it a fictional or authentic authorial one. Sulpicia's vocal presence is clearly not perceived as being anomalous to elegy, and fits neatly alongside the ventriloquised voices of Lesbia, Cynthia, Petrarch's Laura and, later, Philip Sidney's Stella amongst others. This tolerance for, even approval of, the voicing of female desire within this set of literary conventions thus opens the genre – elegy, the Petrarchan – to women poets. In Chapter 5 we will explore in detail how Mary Sidney and Mary Wroth, like Sulpicia, appropriate male-authored conventions and insert themselves into a poetic discourse more usually gendered masculine.

CHAPTER 2

'For Truth and Faith in Her Is Laid Apart'
Women's Words and the Construction of Masculinity in Catullus' Lesbia Poems and Thomas Wyatt

> But I perceive I lacked discretion
> To fashion faith to words mutable;
> Thy thought is too light and variable.
>
> (6.11–13)[1]

The error to which the narrator confesses in this poem by Wyatt is that he has been faithful to a woman whose own words of love are fickle, changeable and unreliable: 'words mutable'. The moral worthlessness of his mistress is one of the keynotes of Wyatt's love poetry: 'for truth and faith in her is laid apart', 3.11; and 'the holy oath whereof she taketh no cure | broken she hath', 1.3–4. That the 'holy oath' is a vow of love is made clear from the context as the poem is addressed to 'Love' in the form of Cupid with his weapons (6) and bow (11). This depiction of a mistress who is tainted and duplicitous marks a divergence of Wyatt's texts from the Petrarchan model with which they are usually read.[2] Petrarch's Laura may be cool and aloof but she is also positioned as a laudable object of the narrator's desire – indeed, her very remoteness is itself a symbol of her chastity and virtue. It is striking that Wyatt articulates the moral defects of his women in specifically verbal terms as faulty acts of speech: their words are 'mutable', their vows 'broken'. The combination of 'mutable' and 'variable' in the quotation above recalls the words of Mercury about Dido in *Aeneid* 4 ('a fickle and changeful thing is woman ever', *varium et mutabile semper | femina*, *Aeneid* 4.569–70) – a verdict perhaps contested by the *Aeneid* itself – but also evokes the flawed yet fascinating Lesbia of Catullus upon whose vows and promises the narrator can never depend. Catullus 70, for example, puts female verbal duplicity at its heart:

> My woman says that there is no one whom she would rather marry than me, not if Jupiter himself were to woo her. She says this – but what a woman says to her ardent lover should be written in wind and running water.[3]

63

Nulli se dicit mulier mea nubere malle
quam mihi, non si se Iuppiter ipse petat.
dicit: sed mulier cupido quod dicit amanti
in vento et rapida scribere oportet aqua.

(70.1–4)

The conspicuous repetition of *dicit*, 'she says', is striking in this epigram: used three times in just four lines, including twice in line 3, it reverberates throughout this short text, drawing insistent attention to the importance of the act of speaking. The syntax of the third line with the stop after that first *dicit* accentuates the word further, before the last two lines pronounce their stinging indictment on the reliability and trustworthiness of 'her' words.

By not naming Lesbia, by calling her 'my woman' (*mulier mea*), this text assumes an aphoristic status – that it is not just Lesbia's words which cannot be trusted but those of all women: that 'woman' is a cultural category tainted, mythically and proverbially, with the charge of verbal unreliability and deviousness. This is not, of course, an original position: there are many literary texts which assert the duplicity of women prior to Catullus – Clytemnestra, Helen, Medea, Phaedra are just a few examples of female characters from Greek literature who epitomise this cultural notion. What this chapter is concerned with is, firstly, how this trope of female verbal unreliability is used by Catullan texts and given a resonance specific to the context in which the poems were first written; and, secondly, how this concept is renewed in Wyatt's texts for an audience at the Henrician court. In tracing a discourse of speech-acts in Wyatt's poetry, this chapter builds on what Greene has described as Wyatt's concern with 'linguistic disarray' and 'truth' but, taking its lead from Catullus, analyses these in specifically gendered terms.[4] If the words attributed to women are shown to be deceptive, untrustworthy and essentially meaningless, then what might it mean to speak like a man?

The next section of this chapter explores Catullus' Lesbia poems and looks at how her acts of speaking are represented. It is especially concerned with the idea of female verbal corruption and considers how this is put to work to calibrate and authenticate the masculine status of the narrator. Wyatt's own Catullan intertexts are the subject of the fourth section, which examines how the terms through which speech acts are gendered are reworked and revitalised to have specific resonance and applicability to the politics of love in the Henrician court.

The poetry of both Catullus and Wyatt has been read biographically as texts which document their respective love affairs with Clodia Metelli and

Anne Boleyn.[5] Given Catullus' own warning from c.16 that we should not confuse the poetry with the poet, this biographical approach is certainly unsustainable and is a position from which modern scholars have generally moved. However, the striking resemblances between Catullus' Lesbia and the Clodia Metelli of Cicero's *Pro Caelio*, as well as the more generalised parallels between the women in Wyatt's poetry and textual representations of the historical Anne Boleyn do still need to be accounted for, and without recourse to simplistic readings of the poems as autobiographical documents akin to the diary entries of love-struck young men. The approach taken here is to explore the way the literary, the political and the personal might project into each other; the way poetry, forensic oratory and personal letters might draw on similar rhetorical, cultural and ideological models, in this case on the question of the reliability of female words – words attached or attributed to female characters – to make their points.

To consider this argument more fully, Catullus' verse is here contextualised against the *Pro Caelio*, and Wyatt's against the love letters written by Henry VIII to Anne Boleyn. Through detailed readings we will uncover how both sets of texts are linked via their positioning of female words as unreliable, sometimes opaque, and ultimately untrustworthy. Literary love narratives are thus shown in this chapter to be productive interpretative frameworks for reading what are supposedly non-fictional texts, in this case a legal speech and a set of letters. The representation of female speech-acts, as will be seen, can be put to use by male writers across a range of genres to interrogate and construct what it means, in late Republican Rome and the early Tudor period, to speak like a man.

'Written in Wind and Running Water': The Problematics of Female Speech in Catullus 70, 83, 76, 109

C.70, quoted in full above, is itself an imitation and re-writing of epigram 11 by Callimachus, and a comparison of the two underlines the changes that the Catullan text makes to foreground its own concerns.[6]

> Kallignotos swore to Ionis that he would never love
>   anyone, male or female, more than her.
> he swore, but it's true, what they say: the vows
>   of lovers never reach the ears of the gods.
> now he burns for a boy, and the poor girl
>   (as they say) is out in the cold.[7]

The most obvious alteration is that of gender: Callimachus' text exposes a male lover's broken vows to a girl. Julia Gaisser, discussing the relationship between this poem and c.70, concentrates on the way in which 'Catullus' is cast in the female role, the 'poor girl' betrayed by her male lover.[8] However, the representation of gender in Catullus' version is more nuanced and complex than a simple inversion, as will be seen shortly. Secondly, the Callimachean generalised notion of 'the gods' as guarantors of lovers' vows is made particular in c.70 where it is specifically Jupiter who is brought into the text: a problematic figure to invoke in this context, given his rather chequered erotic history in classical mythology. Thirdly, while Kallignotos swears love, he does not explicitly mention marriage, a cultural ritual which shifts the idea of love from the personal and individual to the social and public.

Written in elegiac couplets, the same metre used by Callimachus, Catullus' text forces itself into a dynamic relationship with Callimachus' poem, one as concerned with the differences between the epigrams as the similarities. Epigram 11 confirms the implied outcome of c.70 and assures us that Lesbia's words will not hold, that she will maintain her infidelity whatever she says. However, notable additions in the Catullan poem give emphasis to the ephemeral nature not just of Lesbia's words but of speech articulated by a woman, and give the notion of oaths and vows a broader social context in which to operate by explicitly associating Lesbia's words with the bonds of marriage.

Turning back to c.70 with the Callimachean epigram in mind foregrounds the way in which the Catullan poem is constructed from a cluster of implied voices attached to various characters and texts: the reported speech of Kallignotos and of Lesbia; the reminder of mythic, if unspoken, words of Jupiter; the words of Callimachus and the Callimachean narrator; and the direct words of the narrator himself, 'Catullus', which comprise the text of the poem. This issue of voice, and the clash of voices that emerge from and within the texts under consideration is one to which we will return throughout this book: for now, it is worth noting that c.70 is itself a text which is self-consciously constructed from a blend of voices.

Lesbia's reported claim that she would marry no one other than 'Catullus', not even Jupiter himself, is an easy one for her to make, at least if, as c.83 tells us, she is already married. So, of course, is Jupiter. From classical myth, we know Jupiter to be an infamously unfaithful husband whose notorious wooings cannot end in marriage because he already has a wife in Juno. Lesbia's reported speech places her in the potential position of one of the numerous mythic characters who are the objects of Jupiter's lustful desire ('if Jupiter himself were to woo her'), but, critically, also turns her into a female analogue of Jupiter himself, at least in terms of sexual fidelity. Like the god's, Lesbia's promises of love are themselves indicators of deceit, serving to violate her prior vows of marriage. While Jupiter's masculinity, however, is not compromised by – may even be valorised through – his extra-marital affairs, the correlation between Lesbia's sexuality and gender is more problematic. Her infidelity confirms her status alongside mythically unfaithful women (Clytemnestra, Helen), and separates her from authoritative exemplars of femininity built on chastity and virtue: Penelope, Andromache. Lesbia's words to 'Catullus' ('no one whom she would rather marry than me') are themselves a transgressive form of wooing, traditionally a male act, a way of binding her lover closer to her as she invokes an idea of marriage to which she cannot, in truth, be bound. Her statement of commitment is a devious one which she cannot uphold and, importantly, one to which he cannot hold her. Already we can see a complex discourse emerging which centres on questions of gender, sexuality, speech and broken vows.

Lesbia's words in this poem foreground a treacherous separation between word and action. It is not just that her words of love are potentially deceptive, but that they deliberately bring into play social and cultural rituals and obligations, such as those of marriage negotiations and contracts, more typically discussed and settled between men. By negating the efficacy and reliability of words upon and through which social relationships are built and sustained, Lesbia threatens to undermine the very structure of Roman elite society.

Lesbia's words, the narrator comments bitterly, 'should be written in wind and running water' (*vento, rapida ... aqua*, 4) thus emphasising the ephemeral nature of her verbal commitment and matching it to the most evanescent of media. The implicit contrast is with the narrator's own words fixed, even if only temporarily, on 'writing tablets' (*codicillos*) in c.42, or in the 'pretty new book, freshly smoothed off with dry pumice-stone' (*lepidum novum libellum | arida modo pumice expolitum*) in c.1 which the narrator prays will 'live and last for more than one century' (*plus uno maneat perenne saeclo*, 1.10). The hoped-for permanence of the narrator's textual words is thus made to signify a quality of reliability and trustworthiness in the emotional tenor of his speech, a verbal integrity which is conspicuously missing from Lesbia's words which are associated with the fleeting, the momentary and the impermanent.

This epigram ends on a cutting and embittered note of rebuke, exposing the capricious nature of Lesbia's words. So if Lesbia, or 'woman' as a category, can be at least partially defined by the transient and temporary nature of her sayings, then what of Catullan masculinity? The rest of this section goes on to explore in detail the discourse of speech and gender identified in c.70 and considers how it is used to negotiate and construct a version of Roman masculinity. William Fitzgerald and, especially, David Wray have also discussed the extent to which Catullan texts operate as a performance of Roman manhood; this chapter expands on that work by focusing on the role played by the representation of acts of speaking in forging and confirming gender.[9] On occasion, to be powerless might itself be an indicator of a kind of masculinity which depends on speaking with truth and candour.

C.83 sets up a triangular relationship between Lesbia, her husband, and 'Catullus', and evaluates love according to what is said, and the hermeneutic ability of the listeners:

> Lesbia says many wicked things of me in the presence of her husband, a great joy to the fool. Dull mule, do you understand nothing? If she forgot me and were silent, she would be heart-whole. But, as it is, her snarling and railing means this: she not only remembers, but – a much more serious thing – she is angry; that is, she burns, and so she talks.

> Lesbia mi praesente viro mala plurima dicit:
>   haec illi fatuo maxima laetitia est.
> mule, nihil sentis? Si nostri oblita taceret,
>   sana esset: nunc quod gannit et obloquitur,
> non solum meminit, sed, quae multo acrior est res,
>   irata est. Hoc est, uritur et loquitur.
>   (83.1–6)

It is worth noting, first, the emphasis on verbs associated with speech located prominently at the ends of the lines: *dicit*, 'she says' (1), *taceret*, 'she would be silent' (3), *gannit et obloquitur*, 'she snarls and interrupts' (4), *loquitur*, 'she speaks' (6). *Mala* (1) 'wicked, ugly, even evil things', indicate, on a symbolic level, the tainting of Lesbia's mouth through her speech. The Catullan narrator accuses her husband of being foolish (*fatuo*, 1; *mule*, 2) for accepting her words at face value, for giving them the meaning they seem to imply. He, 'Catullus', in contrast, reads beneath and between her words, sees through to an assumed truth that is indicated not by what she says, but only by twisting her words to mean the opposite of what they appear to articulate. 'Catullus' interprets Lesbia's angry words as displaced words of love, while he positions her husband as hermeneutically dense (*nihil sentis?*, 'do you understand nothing?', 3). This position is complicated by the reader's response to the poem, our own interpretative stance, where we might question or reject 'Catullus'' attribution of meaning. The wicked things that Lesbia says about her lover in front of her husband might indeed be a cover for an adulterous passion about which she cannot keep quiet; equally, however, they may be the words of a woman angry with her lover, frustrated that he insists on haunting her when she does not want him around. What is important here is the emphasis this text gives to questions of Lesbia's speech and the problematic interpretation of a woman's words.

What Lesbia says, in other poems as well as this one, is slippery in the extreme: what are the 'wicked things' that she says to 'Catullus'? Do they mean one thing if spoken in front of her husband, and another if her husband is absent? If her words can only be interpreted according to their context then, this poem seems to imply, her speech is contingent, not stable or reliable, free-floating and able to be appropriated to differing interpretations. The drama performed in this text is not just a love triangle, but a hermeneutic crisis which is enacted before our eyes. Lesbia's husband accepts her words as they appear: 'wicked things' are, to him, bad things spoken about 'Catullus' which he takes pleasure in hearing (*maxima laetitia est*, 2). To 'Catullus', however, they are covert words of passion, words which indicate Lesbia's emotional commitment to him. To be silent, he argues, would be an indicator of indifference; to speak is to be passionately engaged (*uritur et loquitur*, 6), even if what is spoken is 'wicked'.

So what we witness in this poem are two instances of interpretation in action, on the part of the husband and of the lover – while Lesbia's words and any intended meaning remain opaque. The two men in the poem each tie these words down to a single, defined sense, though 'Catullus' perhaps has to work quite hard to defend his reading. Neither interpretation, however, succeeds in taking precedence over the other, and the text itself, as well as Lesbia's words, remains tantalisingly full of possibilities. It is not so much that Lesbia's speech is incomprehensible, rather that it can be heard in varying ways: either that she is sincere in maligning 'Catullus', or that she is being deceptive in appearing to criticise him in front of her husband. The two male characters settle on their meanings, but as readers we cannot: the question of who is the foolish one (*fatuo*, 2), who understands nothing (*nihil sentis*, 3), is left finally unresolved, and the positions of the husband and the lover become interchangeable in hermeneutic terms. The text, like Lesbia herself, remains ultimately elusive and enigmatic.

C.83 aligns Lesbia's slippery and untrustworthy speech with her corrupt sexual morals so that the multiple meanings which can be attributed to her words reflect, to some extent, the numerous men with whom she has sexual liaisons. In this way, words and speech become moral emblems. If Lesbia's utterances serve to condemn her out of her own mouth, some of the other poems are more concerned with delineating the contours of Catullan masculinity through the form of speech. C.76, one of the most disillusioned poems in the Lesbia 'cycle' does precisely this. The poem opens by giving us a 'checklist' of Catullan virtues:

> If a man can take any pleasure in recalling the thought of kindness done, when he thinks that he has been conscientious and righteous; and that he has not broken sacred faith, nor in any compact has used the majesty of the gods in order to deceive men.

> Siqua recordanti benefacta priora voluptas
>   est homini, cum se cogitat esse pium,
> nec sanctam violasse fidem, nec foedere nullo
>   divum ad fallendos numine abusum homines.
>
> (76.1–4)

Esse pium, translated here as being 'conscientious and righteous', also encompasses qualities of uprightness, fidelity, patriotism, loyalty, piety and devoutness. *Fidem*, too, from *fides*, 'faith, loyalty, honesty, honour', is a resonant word in Roman culture, a 'cardinal virtue' which has religious associations linking it to the idea of a sacred trust which underpins oaths, contracts and treaties.[10] Scholars have noted that Catullus is the first writer to shift the concept of *fides* from the legitimate trust that supports political, social and commercial transactions and relationships to the semantic field of sexual fidelity: particularly, the socially dissonant context of 'Catullus'' relationship with Lesbia, one which is adulterous and dangerously erotic.[11] The third highly freighted term used in this text is *foedere*, 'contract, compact, promise, even marriage-bond', again transformed in Catullan usage to a specifically extra-marital, eroticised context: as Marilyn Skinner remarks, *foedus amicitiae* becomes the 'central elegiac trope' of Catullus' verse.[12] The reference to not using the power of the gods to abuse or deceive should also be noted, a comment which speaks to the Jupiter reference in c.70 discussed earlier. Both William Fitzgerald and Marilyn Skinner have documented Catullus' use of what Fitzgerald calls 'the language of aristocratic obligation': what we are concerned with is how these terms are made to intersect with the discourse of speech and gender being traced here.[13]

All of the aspects of virtuous conduct listed by this text are summarised as being performed by word or deed (*aut dicere … aut facere*, 7–8), and, in a self-addressed speech, 'Catullus' confirms that he has said as well as done what is required of him: 'these things have been said and done by you' (*haec a te dictaque factaque sunt*, 8). That repetition of *dicere* and *dicta* emphasise that what is spoken is at least as crucial as what is done. What this poem stages is a vocal performance of moral uprightness and integrity.

If 'Catullus' claims his words to be reliable and trustworthy, then the foil against which he measures them are Lesbia's broken vows. She is the unnamed exemplar who has, unlike the Catullan narrator, 'broken sacred faith' (*sanctam violasse fidem*, 3), she is the source of the 'ungrateful love' (*ingrate ... amore*, 6) who has refused to reciprocate, to uphold the compact of love that he has sought to build between them. The poem ends with an acknowledgement that to expect fidelity from Lesbia is impossible:

> No longer is this my prayer, that she should love me in return, or, for that is impossible, that she should consent to be chaste.

> non iam illud quaero, contra me ut diligat illa,
> aut, quod non potis est, esse pudica velit.
>
> (76.23–4)

In positioning Lesbia as refusing to enact the qualities of fidelity and trustworthiness, to acknowledge the compact that 'Catullus' wants to generate in words between them, Lesbia serves to throw the verbal integrity of 'Catullus' into relief. While certainly these terms – *fides, pietas, foedus* – are being used in a transgressive way in being applied to an extra-marital erotic relationship, the Catullan texts re-orient them so that they can reclaim some of the moral standing that they would have in more customary use. As words which are routinely deployed to uphold and venerate social and political relationships typically, though not exclusively, between men, these terms serve to recuperate and even define a Catullan masculinity. Even in the face of what could be an effeminising obsession with the promiscuous and deceiving Lesbia, 'Catullus' recovers a masculinity which is based on a model of speaking like a man.

Before considering the use of 'compact' (*foedus*) in c.109, it is worth noting the extent to which the emotional tone, register and even imagery of c.76 informs depictions of 'Petrarchan' love in sixteenth-century English poetry. This is perhaps one of the most disenchanted poems in the elegiac corpus, and the sense of 'Catullus'' exhaustion, both physical and moral, is strongly articulated. The quiet despair of 'it is difficult suddenly to lay aside a long-cherished love' (*difficile est longum subito deponere amorem*, 13) for example, might be usefully compared to Wyatt's 'the long love that in my thought doth harbour' (sonnet 10.1), a poem which ends in the word 'faithfully', derived from *fides*. The depictions of 'Catullus'' love as a 'plague' (*pestem*, 20), and as a 'baleful sickness' (*taetrum ... morbum*, 25) seem to inform Renaissance depictions of love-sickness such as that in

Robert Sidney's 'bitter' love sonnets noted in the previous chapter. Most pressing, however, is the emotional weariness of the Catullan narrator as he acknowledges the unworthiness of Lesbia as the object of his love, yet cannot escape from her thrall: 'what a lethargy creeps into my inmost joints, and has cast out all joys from my heart!' (*mihi subrepens imos ut torpor in artus | expulit ex omni pectore laetitias*, 20–1). While there are no direct verbal allusions, this aura of fatigue, of stasis and near-collapse is typical of Wyatt's love poetry and very prominent in the texts considered later in this chapter.

But to return to Catullus' use of *foedus*:

> No woman can truly say that she has been loved as much as my Lesbia was loved by me. No faithfulness in any bond was ever such as has been found on my part in my love for you.

> > Nulla potest mulier tantum se dicere amatam
> > vere, quantum a me Lesbia amata mea est.
> > nulla fides ullo fuit umquam foedere tanta,
> > in amore tuo ex parte reperta mea est.

> > > (87.1–4)

Lesbia can say (*dicere*) that she has been loved, while 'Catullus' loves; Lesbia is the object of a love-bond to which only one party adheres, and the repetition of *mea est* at the ends of lines 2 and 4 puts the emphasis on 'Catullus'' emotions, and the opaqueness of Lesbia's. If Catullan love can be articulated via the semantics of a compact or verbal bond then it also serves as a way of defining and differentiating Lesbia from 'Catullus'. The Catullan lover has often been read as effeminised, rendered emotionally impotent by his overwhelming and unrequited love for Lesbia.[14] By utilising the idiom of Roman elite masculinity, however – *fides, foedus, pietas* – these texts redefine a form of masculinity which may certainly be compromised but which is based around verbal honour and fidelity as opposed to the vocal deceptiveness and unreliability of Lesbia's words.[15] The association between the concept of a contract (*foedus*) and masculinity can be seen in c.72 and c.109, the last poem in the loosely defined Lesbia 'cycle'.

C.109 is built around a final burst of hope that Lesbia's promise of faithful and lasting love will hold true: 'ye great gods, grant that she may be able to keep this promise truly, and that she may say it sincerely and from her heart' (*di magni, facite ut vere promittere possit | atque id sincere dicat et ex animo*, 3–4). *Promittere*, 'to promise' and *dicat*, 'she may say' foreground the verbal nature of what is at stake here, and the final line articulates the goal to which the Catullan narrator aspires: 'this eternal compact of hallowed friendship' (*aeternum hoc sanctae foedus amicitiae*, 6). *Amicitia* may seem, to modern eyes, a rather tame aspiration for the passionate Catullan lover, but it serves to contextualise his expectations of Lesbia in a precise manner. *Amicitia*, loosely translatable as 'friendship', summarises a whole series of social bonds, predominantly between men, upon which Roman society is built.[16] By using this as the defining term of his love, 'Catullus' invokes a host of associations which are also tied to ideas of Roman masculinity. C.72 makes this very clear: in a poem which alludes to c.70 with which this chapter started ('you once used to say that you know only Catullus, Lesbia, and that you would not prefer Jupiter himself to me', 72.1–2), the contours of Catullan love are delineated:[17]

> I loved you then, not only as the common sort love a mistress, but as a father loves his sons and sons-in-law.

> Dilexi tum te non tantum ut vulgus amicam
> sed pater ut gnatos diligit et generos.
>
> (72.3–4)

This form of love encompasses, for 'Catullus', both erotic love for a mistress and a more generalised love that binds specifically male relationships. It is notably not just applied to a genetic relationship, the way a father loves his sons (*gnatos*), but also identifies a socially constructed relationship, that between a man and his sons-in-law (*generos*), men brought into the family through the marriage of his daughters who, significantly, are not mentioned here. That Lesbia fails to participate in this type of love is a marker of her femininity; but her gender is also a reason for her exclusion. Because her words are transient, untrustworthy and treacherous, she cannot be a party to the kind of social contract upon which masculinity is built.

'Catullus', on the other hand, consistently reiterates the steadfast and true nature of his verbal acts. Whatever the love narrative of the poetry tells us of the romantic anguish suffered by 'Catullus', the subtext is one acutely concerned with the dynamics of gender. The construction of Lesbia as the epitome of female verbal corruption and duplicity serves as a touchstone against which the negotiation of Catullan masculinity takes place. The love which is foregrounded in c.72 is 'this eternal compact of hallowed friendship' of c.109, and we know that Lesbia will not be a party to it because she can never speak 'like a man'.

Catullus' poetry is not the only Latin text from this period which concerns itself with the gendered dynamics of speech-acts. Cicero's *Pro*

Caelio is a defence speech given on 4 April 56 BCE and is of particular interest to readings of Catullus because of the parallels traditionally drawn between Cicero's Clodia Metelli and Lesbia.[18] The precise relationship between the historical Clodia Metelli, Cicero's depiction of her in the *Pro Caelio*, and Lesbia is problematic to pin down.[19] Certainly the mentions of Clodia in Cicero's letters after this trial indicate a different relationship between them than the antagonistic one of the defence speech, and show that they maintained some kind of social connection despite the court case.[20] A number of scholars have explicitly read Cicero's Clodia as a construction which draws on established literary traditions and tropes.[21] C.16, too, as noted above, is a helpful reminder of the highly crafted literary nature of Catullan poetry, however spontaneous, emotionally authentic and sincere it might appear to be. So how, then, can we read the undoubted correspondences between the representations of Cicero's Clodia and Catullus' Lesbia?

The date of Cicero's oration, 56 BCE, falls easily within the dateable period of Catullus' verse, 57–54 BCE, and there are intriguing mentions in the Catullan texts of a Caelius (e.g. c.58), and a Rufus (e.g. cc.69, 77) who has betrayed the narrator's friendship and appears to have stolen his girl, as well as a poem written about Cicero himself (c.49). Skinner suggests that Catullus drew on Cicero's portrait of Clodia Metelli to create his Lesbia but, as we shall see, the complex of references set up between the two texts seems to operate in both directions.[22] Whichever was first, what can be said is that the oration and the poetry are testament to the way a certain archetype of elite Roman womanhood might be put into circulation and prove valuable to male constructors of different genres of discourse. Cicero is performing a defence speech designed with the intention, which was achieved, of getting M. Caelius Rufus off a charge of 'violence';[23] Catullus is writing what might be called social poetry, concerned with the lives and values of certain 'sets' in Rome – young, urban, urbane, cultured, literary – and yet, despite their differences, both make rhetorical and ideological use of the portraits of Clodia Metelli and Lesbia which sit at their heart.

It is possible to add to this pair Sallust's well-known portrait of Sempronia in his *de coniuratione Catilinae* which was written sometime after 53 BCE though set in 63 BCE, and which seems to draw on some of the same characteristics for Sempronia as we see in Cicero's Clodia Metelli and Lesbia. Pertinent here is Sallust's commentary on Sempronia's verbal fluency: 'she could compose poetry ... tell jokes, and use language which was modest or tender or wanton; in fine, she possessed a high degree of wit and charm'.[24] Given that Sempronia is a shameless, wanton figure who epitomises the moral corruption of those associated with Catiline's 'conspiracy', her verbal dexterity is no more salubrious than is Lesbia's or, indeed, that of Clodia Metelli.

When Cicero says of Caelius' accusers: 'the only object of slander ... is to insult; if it has a strain of coarseness, it is called abuse; if one of wit, it is called elegance' (*si facetius urbanitas nominatur* (3.6)), he uses an idiom familiar to Catullus' verse.[25] There are other resemblances, too, between the Catullan persona and M. Caelius Rufus: Cicero describes the defendant as 'a man who never refused a dinner ... who has used unguents' (27). This portrait of youthful male pleasures in a man-about-town has its parallels in Catullan poetry: for example, the dinner party poems like cc.12 and 13, the latter of which promises that the divine perfume (*unguentum*, 13.11) of the unnamed Lesbia will make Fabullus want to be 'all nose' (*totum ... nasum*, 13.14).

If we can read resemblances between Caelius and 'Catullus', then the same can be done between Clodia and Lesbia: especially damning, perhaps, is Cicero's indictment of Clodia's flaunting sexuality. At the start of the speech he describes his client as being attacked by the 'wealth of a courtesan' (*opibus meretriciis*, 1.1) and, later, more maliciously, says of Clodia: 'she revels in her degraded lusts amid the most open publicity and in the broadest daylight' (*sed in turpissimis rebus frequentissima celebritate et clarissima luce laetetur*, 20.47). This recalls the lurid depictions of Lesbia taking her seat in the 'whore-house tavern' (*salax taberna*, 37.1); in c.11 taking on three hundred lovers at once; and in c.58 on the street-corners and alleyways of Rome where she 'serves the filthy lusts' of passing men.[26]

So what can be made of these salacious, even obscene, portraits of Clodia and Lesbia? Firstly, it is worth noting that invective itself, 'an accepted mode of discourse' in Republican Rome, is a marker of masculinity.[27] Having already noted the way in which Lesbia's slippery speech is mapped onto her sexual promiscuity, it is possible to trace a similar synthesis of concepts being activated in Cicero's oration. The *Pro Caelio* turns on issues of who is lying, who telling the truth, whose words we can – and should – believe. It is a speech about verbal deception, and the integrity of words, and it is this aspect which ties it to the dynamics of speech in Catullus. Very early in the oration Cicero makes it clear that he is positioning this case as one which is about what Caelius' detractors have said of him (*dixerunt*, 2.3) and, later, argues that his accusers have made 'not criminal charges but abuse and slander' (*non criminibus, sed vocibus maledictisque*, 3.6). *Maledictis*, from *maledicere*, 'to speak ill of, literally to say bad things', reminds us of c.83.1 where Lesbia abuses 'Catullus' (*mala*

plurima dicit) in front of her husband.[28] One of Caelius' accusers is, significantly, Clodia Metelli, so parallel accusations are made against Clodia and
Lesbia through the disparaging, even defamatory, things they are made to
say about Caelius and 'Catullus', the male targets of their maligning female
speech.

Cicero's defence strategy in this speech is clever: he does not deny Caelius'
affair with Clodia, but writes it off as the expected, even normalised, behaviour of an elite youth who should be allowed some indulgence before he
takes on the serious mantle of Roman manhood. This accepted period of
youthful extravagance is legitimated both by social custom and an appeal
to nature: 'for by common consent a young man is allowed some dalliance,
and nature herself is prodigal of youthful passions' (*datur enim concessu
omnium huic aliqui ludus aetati, et ipsa natura profundit adulescentiae
cupiditates*, 12.28). In a speech made in the public court by a man, about a
man and to other men, both of the jury and as spectators, there is accord
here: Clodia's sexuality may be aberrant, deviant and reprehensible, but
Caelius' can be seen as a legitimate expression of Roman manhood.

By a slippage in the semantic field being traced here, sexual behaviour
and verbal integrity are implicated in and against each other: Clodia's sexual
promiscuity becomes equated with a looseness in her speech, a wanton
disregard for both verbal and sexual probity. Caelius, on the other hand,
despite his own licentious behaviour, can be recuperated to a normalised
standard of masculinity: not only is his sexual affair with Clodia rendered
conventional and regular, its adherence to the customary expressions of
young Roman manhood serves to guarantee the truth of what he says.
Caelius is acquitted in this case because Clodia's accusations against him
are positioned as false (*falsa*, 15.35), the forged allegations of a reckless,
unruly and angry woman (*temeraria, procax, irata mulier finxisse crimen*,
22.55) against a man who has given 'conscientious evidence' (*vir religiose
testimonium dixisse videatur*, 22.55). In this final indictment, the potent
alignment of gender – *mulier, vir* – with verbal integrity (her 'forged,
invented, counterfeit accusation or slander'; his 'reverent, scrupulous even
pious testimony') is made transparent.

Cicero's debt to literary models – primarily 'new' comedy, but also a
mocking response to tragedy – has been much discussed, but the relationship between the *Pro Caelio* and Catullus' poems has tended to be
read differently.[29] Either both Cicero and Catullus have been seen to be
responding to the authentic historical figure of Clodia Metelli or, more
recently, Catullus has been read as drawing on Cicero's representation of
Clodia.[30] This chapter suggests that it is also possible to read Cicero as

drawing on Catullus' Lesbia in creating his own fictive Clodia Metelli; and that both texts exploit the already existing stereotypes of 'bad' women which revolve around sex, betrayal and lies.

Moving beyond a generalised misogynistic portrait, however, Cicero's Clodia and Catullus' Lesbia are put to very specific use in the service of negotiating an oppositional position of Roman masculinity. By foregrounding the treachery, deceit and duplicity of female words, these texts use Clodia and Lesbia to highlight the concomitant truthfulness and integrity of male speech as put into the mouths of Caelius and 'Catullus'. *Fides*, already a marker of elite Roman masculinity, is upheld in these texts and, in the case of the Catullan poems, serves to recuperate a sense of masculinity for the narrator despite his compromising sexual obsession with the faithless Lesbia. By dramatising moral integrity as something which can reside in the act of speaking, both the *Pro Caelio* and Catullus' Lesbia poems delineate powerfully what it means, in Republican Rome, to speak like a man.

'Graven with Diamonds': Wyatt's 'Lesbia' in 'They Flee from Me' and 'Whoso List to Hunt'

On the evening of Shrovetide 1522, a court pageant was performed in York Place in Westminster in honour of a visit by ambassadors from Charles V, the Holy Roman Emperor, to Henry VIII.[31] The revel took the form of an elaborate allegorical masque built around the theme of love, and is usually referred to as the assault on the *château vert*.[32] Eight ladies, representing the virtues of the perfect courtly mistress, were sequestered in a tower of a castle, and were protected by another eight ladies, the vices of love, who held position at the bottom of the tower. The castle was then assailed by a company of courtly gentlemen, led by Henry himself, whose names encapsulated the qualities of the ideal courtly lover: Amorousness, Nobleness, Youth, Attendance, Loyalty, Pleasure, Gentleness, Liberty. The male company of knights attacked the castle with dates and oranges and the ladies, though they defended themselves valiantly with rose-water and 'comfittes', were, of course, overcome. The vices of love were defeated and fled, the knights entered the tower to claim their ladies 'as prisoners by the hands', and the company danced together 'very pleasantly' before adjourning for a banquet.

The revel is significant to this chapter for the way in which it delineates the qualities of male and female love as constructed at the Henrician court, and, especially, in how it differentiates the idealised characteristics of the courtly mistress from the contrary female 'vices' which deter, under-mine and prevent the accomplishment of love.[33] The 'virtues' of love were emblazoned on the costumes of the ladies who personified them, and were pronounced to be Beauty, Honour, Perseverance, Kindness, Constancy, Bounty, Mercy, Pity. 'Beauty' was played by Mary Tudor, Henry's sister; 'Kindness' by Mary Boleyn, who had been, and possibly still was, Henry's mistress; and 'Perseverance' by the young Anne Boleyn, recently arrived at court and already, it seems, making her presence felt.[34] The female 'vices', played by male choristers and costumed 'like to women of Inde', that is, explicitly 'foreign' as well as compromised in their gender, were named as Danger, Disdain, Jealousy, Unkindness, Scorn, Strangeness (off-handedness) and – significantly for the discourse of speech and gender being traced here – Malebouche.

Malebouche, literally 'bad mouth', is translated by Ives as 'Sharp Tongue' but it seems to be a richer and more resonant term than that.[35] The pageant of *château vert* draws on the idea of an assault of love which is a staple of medieval love allegories epitomised by the *Roman de la Rose*. In that poem, Malebouche is associated with lying, as well as with gossip and rumour (e.g. 3017–19, 3493–51). Chaucer, in his *The Romaunt of the Rose*, translates Malebouche as 'Wicked-Tongue': 'Wicked-Tongue, that false espy, | which is so glad to feign and lie'.[36] The figure of Malebouche is not always transparently female so it is striking that in the Henrician masque, her gender is foregrounded by the way she is aligned with the female 'vices' or obstructers of love, even while it is also compromised by being played by a male chorister. The association being made between contrary female sexuality and a broadly defined form of verbal deception or dishonesty is a robust one.

The *château vert* entertainment thus provides important insights into early Tudor constructions of the gendered qualities of speech in love dis-course, and offers a suggestive frame for reading Wyatt's love poetry. The women in Wyatt's verse conspicuously refuse to conform to the 'virtues' defined by the court performance: they might be beautiful but they repudiate constancy, and are instead aligned to the 'vices' in their disdain, scorn, unkindness and, especially, the slipperiness of their words. The idea of love at the Tudor court is organised, regulated and articulated via lit-erary constructions and conventions. How a Catullan narrative might be activated by Wyatt is what this chapter turns to next.

There are various poems by Wyatt which might be read as drawing on Catullus: 'What Means This?', for example, with its depiction of the narrator's failed tongue whenever he sits near his mistress re-writes c.51;

epigram 38 about the narrator's stealing of a kiss and consequent punishment replays c.99, though the male Juventius is changed for a female mistress;[37] poem 106 with its stark acknowledgement of the cruelty and moral failings of the mistress from whom the narrator still cannot withdraw his love may be homage to c.76.[38] This section focuses on 'They Flee from Me' and 'Whoso List to Hunt', two of the most discussed of Wyatt's poems.[39] The latter, especially, frequently cited as 'evidence' of Wyatt's love for Anne Boleyn and his consequent competition with Henry VIII ('Caesar'), has been read as offering an authentic insight into the politics, both erotic and otherwise, of the Tudor court.[40] Both texts are revisited here because they include direct representations of ventriloquised female speech. In terms of this chapter's interests, the two poems stage a dialogic performance of gendered voices which, it is argued, draws on Catullus. A secondary concern is with Wyatt's practice of *imitatio*: 'Whoso List to Hunt' foregrounds a hybridised form of intertextuality as it negotiates a relationship with Catullus, Ovid and Petrarch. In untangling the way in which this poem maps out its own literary and creative space, we also consider the way in which *imitatio* is made to work in this instance.

'They Flee from Me' is one of Wyatt's enigmatic texts where 'they' shifts to 'she', where a past which 'hath been otherwise' (8) is set in contrast to the bleak present, and where gendered qualities in the protagonists are both oppositional and contradictory. There is a strange, alien quality to the women in this poem who are likened to deer or birds, and the imagery of hunting – flee, stalk (1, 2) – is clear.[41] Comparisons have been made with Ovid's elegies: 1.5 where Corinna arrives in the narrator's chamber 'veiled in an unfastened tunic' (*tunica velata recincta*, *Amores* 1.5.9), and 3.7 where she flounces out of their bed in her bare feet (*nudos ... pedes*) again 'veiled in an unbound tunic' (*tunica velata soluta*, *Amores* 3.7.81–2).[42] Ovid's descriptions of Corinna can be compared with Wyatt's women 'with naked foot stalking in my chamber' (2), and 'in thin array after a pleasant guise | when her loose gown from her shoulder did fall' (10–11). We can note, too, the dreamlike nature of Ovid's 1.5, and the narrator's response in Wyatt that 'it was no dream: I lay broad waking' (15). *Amores* 3.7 is a provocative intertext for 'They Flee' since the elegy depicts 'Ovid's' impotence, but while the failure is literal and physical in Ovid, in Wyatt's text it is turned to a more generalised powerlessness. So a debt to Ovid is clear in terms of setting and visual detail, but the emotional register of this poem is very far from the playfulness of Ovid's elegies. The erotic satisfaction of *Amores* 1.5 and the rueful, self-deprecating tone of 3.7 are replaced by the raw and anguished emotionalism of Catullan texts as Wyatt's narrator rehearses his own betrayal by a fickle and untrustworthy woman. Especially telling is the emphasis on her unreliable speech.

The opening stanza is built on contrasts which foreground the shifting nature of 'they': flee/seek, tame/wild. They 'do not remember' (4) while the narrator can do nothing but replay the past; they 'range | busily seeking with a continual change' (6–7) while the narrator is a still centre, steadfast, fixed. The second stanza, a rehearsal of an assignation that 'once' (9) took place, builds up the remembered details and culminates, significantly, not in the unclothing of the woman ('when her loose gown from her shoulders did fall', 11), or her kiss ('therewithal sweetly did me kiss', 13) but in an act of speech: 'and softly said, "Dear heart, how like you this?"' (14). These words spoken by the mistress positioned at the end of the stanza, and at the point at which past turns into present, place interpretative weight on this instance of female speech: her words become the central motif upon which the poem turns, an image of the discontinuity which haunts the poem and which is itself gendered feminine.

'It was no dream' (15) following straight after this instance of female speech thus seems to refer to the occurrence of the words themselves, not just to the occasion of them. The narrator reads them as indicative of a compact between him and his lover, parallel to the contract which Catullus strives to construct with Lesbia, but, as is the case in the Catullan precedent, the woman's words prove impermanent:

> But all is turned thorough my gentleness
> Into a strange fashion of forsaking.
> And I have leave to go of her goodness
> And she also to use newfangleness.
>
> (16–19)

'Gentleness' here is a loaded, even overloaded, term: it encompasses the narrator's mild temper and conduct, but also his social status, the idea of good breeding and courtesy – the notion of the courtly gentleman. Gentleness, too, as seen in the *château vert*, is one of the ideal qualities of the courtly male lover. In contrast, the woman displays 'strangeness', a quality of the female 'vices' from the *château vert*, meaning off-handedness, carelessness. Wyatt's woman certainly deserts her lover ('a strange fashion of forsaking') but he also positions her as disowning her own words. Her speech, as the Catullan narrator realised before, is always ephemeral, never stable. Wyatt's narrator wishes to read her specific words of seduction, tied to a single occasion, as a generalised contract of love between them – and is proved fatally mistaken.

But since that I so kindly am served
I would fain know what she hath deserved.
(20–1)

'Kindly' is an ironic and bitter reference to the quality of Kindness as one of the 'virtues' of the courtly mistress, but also shifts his specific mistress into the sphere of 'woman' as category, or 'kind'. It has the sense of being congruent with nature, so that the verbal transience exposed by the poem is positioned as innately female, a quality of the feminine against which masculinity may be defined. The changeability, unpredictability and 'newfangleness' (19) of the mistress thus serve to delineate and construct an oppositional masculinity which is steady, steadfast and true – even if those qualities lead to loss and pain.

The final words of the poem, 'what she hath deserved', return to the question of how the woman should be requited for her betrayal – and, in a Catullan sense, the poem itself serves as an exposure of her perfidy. This text is certainly far more restrained in terms of invective, in line with Tudor rather than Roman cultural mores, but still serves as a potent indictment of female duplicitous sexuality, lying and betrayal.

It can be seen that Wyatt's renewal of a Catullan discourse is a stealthy one: it may not be traceable in easily attributable quotations, but terms such as faith (*fides*) and oath (loosely attached to the idea of *foedus*) recur with notable frequency. Most markedly, we can trace Wyatt's response to Catullus in a comprehensive erotic narrative built around the idea of a haunting obsession with a fickle, unfaithful and deceitful mistress.

We looked earlier at how Cicero's oration draws on a discourse of gendered speech shared with Catullus: Wyatt's concern with female words can also be traced in texts drawn, supposedly, from 'life' rather than literature – Henry VIII's love letters to Anne Boleyn.[43] Seth Lerer has also read Henry's letters as being 'shaped by literary figures', but while he positions them against Chaucer's *Troilus and Criseyde* (another text concerned with female inconstancy), they can also be read productively alongside Catullus and Wyatt.[44] In switching between 'I' and a royal 'we', often in a single missive, Henry's letters oscillate between being the utterances of a man and a monarch – they thus serve as witness to the way in which a discourse of female vocal unreliability circulates in both private and public contexts.[45] Only one side of the correspondence has survived so Anne's historical 'voice' is missing: it is possible, however, to reconstruct a vocal presence for her based on Henry's responses to her missing words so that, on one level, she is as ventriloquised as are Lesbia and Wyatt's women.

Letter 1, provisionally dated to 1526, situates itself relatively early in Henry's courtship.[46] In it, he articulates his anxiety about Anne's constancy: 'and that by absence your affection for them [him and his heart] may not be lessened' ('et que par absens vostre affection ne leur soit diminué'). He contrasts this fear of her fickleness with his own fidelity: 'and so it is with my love for through absence we are far apart and yet it retains its fervour at least on my side, having the hope that it is the same on yours' ('ainsi fait-il de nostre amoure, car per absence nous sûmes eloinés, etneumoins elle garde sa farveur on moins de nostre chosté, aiant en enspoire la parayll du vostre'). In order to shore up his 'hope', rather than confidence in her love, Henry sends Anne a present, 'something the most connected to that [his physical presence] as is possible … that is my picture set in a bracelet' ('chose le plus appertiant à cella qui m'est possible … c'est à dire ma picture myse en braselette'). This piece of jewellery containing the king's picture is made to embody his presence, a vivid reminder of him as lover but also sovereign which acts to police her possible infidelity – a kind of eroticised handcuff worn on her person, which may remind us of the collar 'graven with diamonds' worn by the hind in Wyatt's 'Whoso List to Hunt'.

Letter 2 makes reference to a rumour that has reached the ears of the king: 'I have been told that the opinion [of me] in which I left you has utterly changed' ('on m'a averty que l'opinion en quoy je vous laissoye est de toute asture changé'), and that Anne is deliberately staying away from court. He claims that her behaviour is unwarranted and that he has done nothing to offend her ('je m'assure n'avoire jamès faite faute'), positioning her as a capricious mistress, subject to what Wyatt terms 'newfangleness'. He continues with the more ominous assertion 'if I heard for truth that you voluntarily desired this [her absence from him], I could do no less than to complain of my ill fortune while abating little by little my great folly' ('si je entendoy pur verité que volunterement vous la desiriés, je n'en pouis moins fere sinon plaindre ma mauvais fortune en rebatant peu à peu ma grande folie'). The trope of the mistress who is inconstant when away from the physical presence of her lover (as is the case in Chaucer's Criseyde) is certainly present here, and this letter also stresses the arbitrary nature of her fickleness which is not, he claims, a response to something he has done. The rhetorical pose of the lover who discovers some fault in his mistress replays Catullan rhetoric, though the narrators in Catullus and Wyatt are never able to draw back from their 'great folly'.

One final example here from letter 4 alludes directly to Anne's letters of reply, putting the emphasis firmly on the complexity of interpreting female words and the hermeneutic crisis to which they give rise:[47]

In debating with myself the contents of your letters, I am placed in a great agony not knowing how to hear them, whether to my disadvantage as shown in some places, or to my advantage as I hear in some others, begging you with all my heart that you will let me know expressly your whole intention with regard to the love between us two.

En debatant d'apper moy le continu de vous letter, me suis mis en grande agonye, non shachant commant les entendres, ou à mon desavantages come en aucune lieu le munstrés, ou à mon avantage comme en des aucunes aultres je les entende, vous suppliant de bien ceur me valoire certyffyere expressément vostre intention entire tochant l'amoure entre nous deux.

Anne's words are here positioned as opaque, dense and difficult, able to be read (heard, in this letter) in different ways, evading a single and defined meaning no matter how many times the reader (listener) pores over them. They become open texts, artful, devious, even possibly deceitful. The reader is forced to demand clarity in requesting another letter to decipher and make plain what is hidden in this one: 'begging you to make me a full [also clear] response to this my rude letter, so that I may know on what and how far I am able to trust' ('vous suppliant me faire entire responce de ceste ma rude letter, a quoy et en quoy me puis fiere'). Her tricky letter is contrasted to his 'rude' one, a dichotomy seen again in the opposition of Wyatt's blunt speech against that of his women.

There is a particularly notable Catullan moment in this letter where Henry compares the different kinds of love that Anne might have for him: 'if you only love me with the other sort of common love, this name [of 'mistress'] is hardly appropriate: for it denotes a singular love, which is a long way from the common sort' ('si vous ne me aimés de aultres sorte que d'amoure commune, c'est nome ne vous est point appropriée: car il denote ung singularis, lequel est bien longné de la commune'). C.73.3, discussed earlier, contains the line 'I loved you then, not only as the common sort love a mistress'. Henry certainly inverts the subject, but a Catullan allusion is possible.

What can be seen, then, is the way in which Henry VIII's letters draw on familiar literary discourses that meld those of 'courtly' love, the Petrarchan, and the Catullan. Themes of constancy versus fickleness become gendered, and the very medium of words spoken or written by Anne is rendered doubtful and complex in comparison to the 'rude' or unsophisticated transparency and forthrightness of Henry's own letters. The depiction of a capricious, variable woman throws Henry's own masculinity into relief: he may be the beseeching wooer, but his words are true, direct, candid and honest.

The second Wyatt text to be considered, 'Whoso List to Hunt', is clearly a re-writing of Petrarch's sonnet 190, 'Una candida cerva'. Wyatt's abandonment of the neo-Platonic scheme which structures Petrarch's poem (and sequence) is, however, particularly stark and it is worth paying attention to the ways in which the two texts diverge. Petrarch's hind is a figure for the Christianised idealisation of Laura whose virtue makes her inviolable and untouchable. The drama of the poem resides in the tension between the narrator's desires which are caught between the spiritual, invested in the hind, and the more earthly. The final fall of the narrator into the water, and the consequent disappearance of the hind serves as a marker of his inability to raise his mind above her flesh. So the poem is, in a way, one of failure, but it is a wry, self-deprecating, even gently humorous failure, one which speaks potently of physical desire as a very human, however troublesome, quality. Elements within the Catullan verse which underpin Roman ethical and civic concepts such as fidelity, piety, and moral worth become Christianised in Petrarch's verse, and the setting of the sonnet is that of a rarefied landscape quite unlike the specificity of Catullus' Rome. Lesbia's ultimate unattainability by 'Catullus', despite the fact that theirs is, the texts imply, a consummated sexual relationship, becomes transmuted into a spiritual allegory, and 'Petrarch's' betrayal is that of his own bodily nature, rather than any treachery on the part of Laura.

Wyatt's sonnet reshapes Petrarch's in multiple ways and it is possible to trace the way in which it situates itself in relation to Petrarch, Catullus, elegy and contemporary Tudor culture. The classical trope of the erotic hunt draws on Ovid, especially, and erotic elegy more generally, though it is not a figure associated with Catullus.[48] Sonnet 190, of course, is not a hunt so much – despite the presence of a hind – as a hallucinatory vision. Wyatt's setting is shifted from the almost surreal Petrarchan landscape to the specific backdrop of a Tudor hunt, a typical pastime at the Henrician court, and one acutely associated with a public display of virility.[49] The competitive nature of the chase where the narrator is ranked against his peers ('I am of them that farthest cometh behind', 4) gives the text a social dimension absent from Petrarch's poem which is inhabited solely by the narrator and the hind. This social consciousness relates the poem to Catullan verse situated in a recognisably detailed Rome where 'Catullus'' own status – as lover, but also as Roman man – is always at stake, always being negotiated. Two of Henry VIII's love letters to Anne Boleyn, tentatively dated to 1527 and 1528 respectively, show the king, too, drawing on this literary motif of the erotic hunt.

In letter 10 Henry names himself a hunter: 'I send you by this bearer a buck I killed late yesterday evening by my own hand, hoping that when you eat of it, it will remind you of the hunter' ('je vous envoye per ce porteur ung bouke je tué hersoire bien terde de ma main, esperant que quant vous en mangerés, il vous sovendra du chaseur').[50] In letter 9, too, Henry utilises the idiom and imagery of the hunt: 'and seeing my darling is absent I can do no less than to send her some flesh, representing my name, which is hart flesh for Henry'.[51] These letters are notable for a number of reasons: firstly, they are testament to a shared erotic discourse that circulates between the literary and 'life', just as we saw was the case between Catullus' Lesbia and Cicero's Clodia Metelli. Literary erotics, such as those which inform Wyatt's poetry, offer Henry a script or series of rhetorical postures which he can adopt to portray himself as a lover. Strikingly, the position of the lover is a fluctuating one in his case: he is the successful hunter in the first letter given here, but is the hart in the second where, as he points out, 'hart' also means 'heart'. Henry transforms himself from the subject of the hunt, the *chaseur*, to the object, the hart, which he then bestows upon his mistress. Letter 10, with its visceral emphasis on the killing having been done by the king's own hand ('je tué ... de ma main'), and his hope that the dead deer will recall its hunter to Anne's mind ('il vous sovendra du chaseur') has a potentially menacing subtext, reminding the recipient of this gift that she, too, is the object of the king's powerful pursuit – a courtship which ends, literally in the case of Anne, with her dead body.

These letters demonstrate how the qualities of the courtly lover are prescribed by literary discourse (as we also saw earlier in the *château vert*) and enacted in apparently non-literary texts – though letters, as scholars have pointed out, can never be read as innocent or transparent documents.[52] Courtly masculinity, when part of a lover's discourse, may be fluid and, to some extent, unfixed, even contradictory. Masculinity may reside in other qualities quite separate from the obvious 'manly' ones, and to assume the posture of the victim of the hunt may not be as emasculating, or as permanent, as might be assumed – an important consideration when it comes to reading the gendered status of Wyatt's narrators. The displayed qualities of the courtly lover, it seems, do not always align with normalised standards of political masculinity. Henry may be, metaphorically, bending his knee to Anne Boleyn when he sends her his 'hart', but he is still always the king and retains the power of his monarchical authority (as letter 10 reminds the reader) even as he seems to abdicate it in his role of the lover. The myth of Actaeon seems to underpin Henry's stance and he changes from being the aggressive Apollo of letter 10, to channelling the dismembered Actaeon in letter 9, in the process turning Anne from Daphne to Diana.[53]

Reading the Diana and Actaeon myth into 'Whoso List to Hunt' foregrounds the way this text situates itself against Petrarch's 190 and Catullus' Lesbia. Diana is a virgin huntress, and both qualities – her chastity and her status as a hunter – place her, symbolically, outside the *domus* or 'house': she is unfettered by marriage, and is most usually figured freely roaming the woods with her band of maidens. One of the signifiers of the disruptive nature of both Lesbia and Clodia Metelli is their propensity to be seen operating outside of the Roman household, an ideological space to which 'good' women are usually bound.[54] One way of interpreting the Actaeon narrative is as an encounter between mortality and divinity, specifically gendered as a mortal man and a goddess. Diana is sacrosanct and Actaeon's crime, however unintentional, is to have violated her sacred nature by seeing her bathing. Unravelling the complex re-use of Diana motifs that reside in 'Una cerva candida', 'Whoso List to Hunt', Henry VIII's letters and Catullus focuses the way these texts are implicated in and against each other.

Laura as a neo-Platonic image of eternal beauty and truth is well established: we might even be tempted to read her as a Christianised rendering of the virgin Diana, supported by the hunting associations activated by the hind. Her unassailable nature is inscribed on the hind's collar: 'nessun mi tocchi' ('let no one touch me'); and the lack of specificity in the landscape locates her metaphorically in a spiritual rather than earthly realm.[55] Yet the adjective 'candida' in Petrarch's first line, translated as 'purest white', might draw disturbing associations with the profane Lesbia of Catullus. In c.68.70 Lesbia is described as *mea ... candida diva*, 'my shining or bright, goddess'. The epithet draws inverse comparisons between the divine purity of Laura encoded through the unadulterated whiteness of the hind, and Lesbia. Lesbia may well be dazzling in her beauty, but *candida* is applied to her at the point at which she arrives for a clandestine and adulterous sexual assignation with 'Catullus' at the house of Allius: her brightness in c.68 is all physical, and her glittering appearance here is set in opposition to the corruption of her morals depicted in other poems. Nevertheless, the word *candida* in itself creates an intertextual conduit which connects Petrarch's Laura in an unsettling fashion with Lesbia – indeed, it draws attention to Petrarch's neo-Platonic scheme which moralises Lesbia (as well as later elegiac mistresses). The speech attributed to Wyatt's hind positions itself within this discourse in an acutely problematic fashion, creating a complex cluster of allusions built around notions of the divine, the sexual and the undomesticated.

Wyatt's sonnet ends with the words of his hind: '*Noli me tangere*, for Caesar's I am | and wild for to hold, though I seem tame' (12–14). The translation of Petrarch's 'nessun mi tocchi' into *noli me tangere* foregrounds the text's shift away from a Petrarchan model towards a Latin elegiac one. The Latin diction, however familiar to a courtly audience, also sits in contrast to the frank and blunt Englishness of the previous lines with their use of homely proverbs ('sithens in a net I seek to hold the wind', 8) and the alliteration associated with a middle English poetic tradition ('as she fleeth afore | fainting I follow', 6–7). Female words, as positioned in this text, may be described as being written in 'letters plain' (11) but are shown to be ornate, decorative ('graven with diamonds', 11), and fraught with ambiguity. *Noli me tangere*, of course, is taken from the Vulgate when the newly resurrected Christ speaks to Mary Magdalene: *Dicit ei Jesus: noli me tangere*, 'Jesus saith unto her, Touch me not', John, 20.17. An apocryphal story also existed that Julius Caesar had had deer in England marked with the words *Noli me tangere quia Caesaris sum*, 'do not touch me for I am Caesar's'.[56] Placing these words into the mouth of Wyatt's hind thus initiates a set of complex, sometimes contradictory intertexts: the blasphemous re-use of Christ's words to Mary Magdalene; the evocation of England's Roman past; Petrarch's prior poem; and the contemporary context of England's own 'Caesar'. Attributing Christ's words to the hind highlights further her distance from the sanctity of Petrarch's Laura and a return to the profane model of Lesbia: 'do not touch me' serves as a command but also, in the hind's mouth, as an invitation, evoking the seductive allure of the forbidden – a disconcerting, even shocking, re-use of speech taken from the mouth of Christ. What was an encounter with a mysterious divinity in the Vulgate and Petrarch, becomes something sensuous and erotic, teasing, taunting in Wyatt. In recalling Actaeon's forbidden vision of Diana it is also perilous – and Danger, we remember, is one of the female vices in the *château vert*. The weary exhaustion of the narrator ('the vain travail hath wearied me so sore', 3; 'my wearied mind', 5; 'fainting I follow', 7) foreshadows the fate of Actaeon torn apart by his own hounds, here serving as figures for the narrator's self-wounding, even self-destructive, desire, itself a reminder of the Catullan narrative.

The hind's words are 'graven with diamonds', stones associated with chastity and protection from lust. Diamonds are precious and brilliant, but they are also known as the hardest of substances, and are used metaphorically in this way in the *Roman de la Rose*: 'heart as hard as diamond'

(4385). To be marked with diamonds thus has the contrary implications that the hind needs to be policed against her own lust, yet is also hard-hearted, or, in the terms used in the *château vert*, displays Disdain, Scorn, Unkindness. The recollection of Lesbia is strong in the combination of an unruly sexual appetite, combined with a refusal to comply with culturally prescribed gendered qualities: the hind is aligned with the 'vices' of love which serve as obstacles to the (male) lover, rather than the 'virtues' which define the ideal courtly mistress.

The second half of the hind's 'speech' in Wyatt is a clear deviation from, and addition to, Petrarch's sonnet, and expresses powerfully the nature of the hind and the contrary language in which it is conveyed: 'and wild for to hold, though I seem tame' (14). The distance between surface and substance is explicit, the differential between what the woman seems, and what she is. The dichotomy of 'wild' and 'tame' feels particularly gendered, drawing on the paradigm of the uncontrollable nature of women who therefore need to be ruled, mastered and domesticated by men. The hind roams free, seemingly at her will, and though she gestures towards courtly allegiances ('for Caesar's I am', 13), she seems to have made 'outside' into her own territory: she claims uncivil wildness to herself.

'Wild for to hold' also has overt sexual overtones, conjuring up an image of unmanageable, ferocious, almost feral, female sexuality, a reminder of the monstrous image of Lesbia with her three hundred lovers in c.11. The hind's earlier fleeing ('as she fleeth before', 6) now becomes a form of delib-erately crafted and provocative foreplay since she, as seen from her confi-dent and commanding tone here, is in no danger. Indeed, as Chaucer's Pandarus makes clear, to seem to run in order to be chased is a standard move in the game of courtly seduction: 'so some times it is craft to seem flee | from thing which in effect men hunt fast' (*Troilus and Criseyde* 1.747–8). What initially seems to be a form of subversion on the part of the hind, turns out to be an acceptance of the female role in the practice of this form of courtly love. By seeming to flee, she enables the male role of hunter and pursuer; by declaring her own sexual wildness, she justifies his taming and domesticating of her. The role of Actaeon becomes a ritual posture adopted by the male lover but, while he expresses his weariness with the pursuit, his abject failure to possess, even his metaphorical dismemberment when Henry VIII offers his 'hart' to Anne Boleyn, it is the deer, in Henry's letter 10, who ends up dead.

What can be seen, then, from Wyatt's texts are the ways in which ventriloquised female speech is put to work in constructing and maintaining what it means to be gendered masculine and feminine in this discourse of love. Gender difference, in these texts, is constructed as oppositional: that is, masculinity is portrayed, by implication, to be what femininity is not. The construction of the feminine serves to affirm and legitimate both the status of masculinity, and also the powers and privileges that accrue to it. The power in 'Whoso List to Hunt' seems to reside with the hind, as it does in Petrarch's sonnet, but the abbreviated and unfinished chase has its end in Henry's letter. There the internal logic of the hunt reaches its approved end and the deer is *tué ... de ma main*, literally killed by the authoritative, and eloquent, hand of the king. The role of the male hunter slips seamlessly from that of Actaeon back into Apollo, and the hind is turned from Diana into Daphne, known forever as the possession of Apollo. Even the boasted wildness of the hind is shown to conceal a ritualised obedience to an overarching rhetorical scheme – wild, in the mouth of the hind, is a form of tameness.

The hind's voice in this poem thus blends with the prior voices of Lesbia and Laura. She appropriates Laura's words directly but translates them into Latin, in doing so turning them into something sacrilegious, as are Lesbia's broken oaths. The words themselves become unstable in her mouth, foregrounding the shifting nature of language, how words are calibrated by the person speaking them. Words that might be 'plain', truthful, even holy, in one context, become slippery, distorted, sexualised, impious, when spoken by this woman. So what of masculinity in Wyatt's poem? Catullus 76 seems to be a prime model for the exhausted weariness, disappointment and disillusion which marks this text. The inability of the narrator to leave off his pursuit ('yet may I by no means my wearied mind | draw from the deer', 5–6), may rework 'Catullus'' self-exhortation, 'why do you not settle your mind firmly and draw back' (76.11), and the later 'what a lethargy creeps into my inmost joints' (76.21–2).[57]

It is certainly possible to read Wyatt's poem as depicting a compromised, deficient form of masculinity, revealing an abject inability to master and overcome one's own weakness. However, by shifting our focus onto the discourse of speech, the narrator's masculinity may be seen to be recuperated as is that of 'Catullus'. The characteristics of the narratorial voice are those of honesty, forthrightness, even bluntness. His thoughts are couched in simple and straightforward language, a contrast to the Latinate diction of the hind. The very depiction of the narrator's own impotency and failure ('I am of them that farthest cometh behind', 4) serves as a testament to the veracity of his words. This poem may provisionally position the hind as powerful in her serene indifference to the pursuit of the narrator, even taunting him with his own impotence – and yet the representation of powerlessness can itself be read as a construction of a form of masculinity, one which depends on speaking with truth and candour.

Wyatt's Catullus, then, is different again from the Catullus of Skelton and Leland discussed earlier. Central to Wyatt's love poetry is the concept of the unworthy mistress, epitomised by the Catullan notion of *odi et amo*, 'I hate and I love'. She turns her back on the chaste virtue of Petrarch's Laura and, instead, flaunts her relationship to the profane, yet endlessly fascinating, Lesbia. Wyatt proves himself a sophisticated reader of Catullus as he reworks the Catullan anxiety about speech and masculinity, and gives it a resonance complicit with Tudor concerns. Importantly, while both sets of texts certainly draw on generalised misogynistic ideas of women as fickle, unreliable and untrustworthy, they also put these portraits to specific use. It is not just that women's words in their poems are demonstrated to be unruly, deceitful and betraying, but that these qualities of speech are themselves gendered feminine. By contrast, an idea of masculinity is actively constructed within these texts, one which has its basis in vocal integrity and literally 'speaking like a man'.

As well as staging a dialogue between gendered voices within the poem, 'Whoso List to Hunt' also seems to be self-conscious of its own status as an imitation, so that the poet's voice is always straining to be heard against the prior utterances of Catullus, Ovid and Petrarch. 'I know where is an hind' (1) speaks of a pre-existing awareness ('I know'), a return to an earlier intelligence, in literary terms to an earlier poem (Petrarch's sonnet 190), as well as an earlier genre and poetics (Catullus, Ovid, elegy). References to drawing from, following, of coming behind (ll.4, 6, 7) can all be read in metapoetic terms as the poem's acknowledgement of its own belated, imitative status; and the announcement 'I leave off therefore' (7) as an attempt to wrench the text into new territory. The poem both fails and succeeds: the models upon which it draws are not erased (and even the assertion of an attempt is a disingenuous one given the status of *imitatio* as literary praxis), but maintain a critical presence within the new text. Much of the complexity of Wyatt's sonnet comes from the interrelationships set up with the other texts upon which it draws, and the echoes of Catullus, Ovid, Petrarch, the Vulgate, even Henry VIII's courtship of Anne Boleyn sustain the idea of this text as the site of a convergence of multiplicitous, sometimes contradictory, voices.

It is worth noting that the female deer in this reading, can also be read as representing prior texts ('I know where is an hind'), can act as an embodiment of a previous literary tradition which this poem is pursuing and rewriting. The elegiac mistress as the embodiment of elegy itself is hardly new – Ovid's *Amores* 3.1 even personifies *Elegia*, with one lame foot to signify the elegiac couplet, a hexameter followed by a pentameter – and Petrarch's pursuit of Laura as a figure for poetic laurels is embedded in the scholarly literature. Nevertheless, the presence of this trope in Wyatt – the mistress as text – is another gesture towards Latin love elegy as a precedent, and an acknowledgement of elegy's intense concern with metapoetics. The next chapter turns to this topic in detail and considers how Propertius' figuring of Cynthia as inspiration and embodiment of his texts is read and re-written in Philip Sidney's *Astrophil and Stella*.

CHAPTER 3

' "Fool," Said My Muse to Me'
Reading Metapoetics in Propertius 2.1 and 4.7, and Astrophil and Stella 1

The opening poem of Philip Sidney's *Astrophil and Stella* is as much a text about the writing of love poetry as it is a love poem.[1] Astrophil struggles to articulate his desire for Stella but 'words came halting forth' (9), and previous poetry, 'others' feet' (11), serves only as an obstruction. Thwarted and frustrated ('biting my truant pen, beating myself for spite', 13), Astrophil's literary impasse is resolved in a surprising manner: ' "Fool," said my muse to me; "look in thy heart, and write" ' (14).[2]

Although the centrality of *imitatio* to Renaissance poetics is widely recognised, a modern valorisation of originality and emotional honesty seems to have obscured quite how provocative a moment this is. Astrophil's self-conscious striving for literary uniqueness, and his muse's sponsoring of apparent emotional authenticity as the basis for love poetry (' "look in thy heart, and write" ', 14) both mark a move away from imitative orthodoxy and towards something more transgressive. This turn, by Astrophil, towards what this chapter goes on to read as a narcissistic poetics, is one which deserves more critical attention than it has so far attracted: what are the implications of Astrophil's rejection of *imitatio* and how are we to interpret what is happening in this sequence presided over by such a muse?

The presence of a muse in sixteenth-century English love poetry as opposed to epic is itself surprising. *Tottel's Miscellany*, for example, primarily a collection of lyrics, many on the subject of love, contains no invocations to any of the muses. Even Petrarch in the *canzoniere* addresses Apollo in sonnet 34 but does not call upon him for inspiration. This contrasts with Petrarch's evocation of an epic muse at the start of his *Africa* (c.1337), a nine-book poem written in Latin hexameter with Scipio Africanus as its hero: 'Muse, you will tell me of the man renowned for his great deeds, redoubtable in war, on whom first noble Africa, subdued by Roman arms, bestowed a lasting name' (*Africa* 1–4).[3] Tasso's later *Gerusalemme Liberata* (1581) also invokes a muse but draws attention to his resistance to the classical muse and her replacement by Christ: 'O Muse, not you who upon

Helicon | garland your brow with long-since-faded bays, | but you who among heavenly choirs don | your golden crown of deathless stars always' (1.2.1–4).[4]

In the *Faerie Queene* Spenser invokes various muses: the most conventional is at the opening to book 1 when she is called upon, in an allusion to Virgil's *Eclogue* 6, to help make the transition from pastoral to epic poetry: 'for trumpets sterne to change mine Oaten reeds, | and sing of Knights and Ladies gentle deeds' (1.1.1.4–5).[5] In book 3 the narrator calls on Clio, the muse of history, as he traces the future offspring of Britomart and Artegall ending in the Tudors and Elizabeth (3.3.4.49). A conscious imitation of Anchises' speech in *Aeneid* 6 when Aeneas is shown a vision of the famous Romans who will spring from his bloodline (6.765–886), Spenser's muse functions here as political authenticator of the Tudor line, bridging both historical and literary time as the Tudor lineage intersects with the Roman: 'for from thy womb a famous Progenie | shall spring, out of the auncient Trojan blood' (3.3.22.5–6).

In sixteenth-century love poetry Astrophil's muse is an anomaly, and her behaviour is startling. Rather than waiting to be called upon by the poet as is traditionally the case, here she inserts herself into Astrophil's vacillations and bluntly cuts through his hesitancies. Irreverent and familiar (' "Fool," said my muse to me'), she serves as a personification of a wayward creative inspiration and a problematic mode of poetic production that is provocatively at odds with the prevailing literary orthodoxies of Sidney's time. What she is doing here and how she orients our reading of the sequence are two of the questions investigated in this chapter.

The figure of a muse may generally be absent from Renaissance love poetry but she is a significant presence in Roman love elegy. Ovid's *Amores* 1.1 ends with an appeal to what we might think of as a specifically elegiac muse who presides over the eleven feet of the elegiac couplet.[6] In Sulpicia's opening poem, too, it is her muse who has won over Venus and thus enabled 'Sulpicia' to attain the love of Cerinthus.[7] Propertius, the first of the elegists proper, engages perhaps most explicitly with a muse figure:

> You ask how it is that my love songs are written so often, how it is that my book sounds so soft upon the lips. It is not Calliope, not Apollo that puts these songs in my mind: my sweetheart herself creates the inspiration.

> Quaeritis, unde mihi totiens scribantur amores,
>   unde meus veniat mollis in ora liber.
> non haec Calliope, non haec mihi cantat Apollo:
>   ingenium nobis ipsa puella facit.
>
>   (2.1.1–4)[8]

That passive *scribantur*, 'are written', is surprising: 'Propertius' seems to be disavowing his own active role as writer of the poem and owner of the poetic imagination which informs it, and instead attributes the inspiration to Cynthia who becomes a form of muse.[9] It is she who 'creates' his 'talent, inspiration' (*ingenium*), and she does this through an active verb (*facit*) in opposition to the passivity of his composition. The repetition of *unde*, 'from where' (1, 2), and *mihi*, 'to me' (1, 3) reinforces this sense of the source of creation being external to the poet, to poetry as originating from somewhere beyond the poet's own imagination. And yet it is not Calliope, the leader of the muses, nor Apollo, the god of music and poetry, who sings (*cantat*) to or through 'Propertius', but only a mistress (*puella*) who creates his inspiration.

The figure of a muse serves, as is well understood, as a 'projection of the creative process' and a 'personification of literary practice'.[10] But the muse is, not surprisingly, a far from static metaphor. In the archaic Greek poetry of Hesiod and Homer the muses positioned poetry as a kind of divine epiphany, though certainly not in an unnuanced or unproblematic fashion.[11] Hellenistic poets such as Apollonius of Rhodes and Callimachus, both of whom are significant models for Roman elegy, complicate ideas of inspiration, creativity and the relationships between literary tradition and innovation.[12] Their texts reflect changing assumptions and ideas about poetry through their engagement with, and manipulation of, programmatic muse encounters.

So when Propertius writes of Cynthia as the source of his inspiration, and when Sidney's Astrophil later finds his attempts at writing love poetry hijacked by a condescending and scornful muse, both texts are responding to a complex language of muse figures as carriers of literary discourse. The next section goes on to read Cynthia not just as *materia* or the Callimachean embodiment of the Propertian text, but as a slippery figure who shifts between being a source of inspiration, possibly negative as well as positive, and taking on the role of a poet in her own right. The implications of a muse figure attaining a voice and story of her own are explored through Propertius 4.7, and are contextualised by two short episodes from Ovid's *Metamorphoses*: the muses' story to Minerva in book 5, and the story of the sibyl in book 14. By reading Cynthia with Ovid's vulnerable and increasingly compromised muses, as well as with the sibyl figures in the *Aeneid* and *Metamorphoses*, we will trace how these Augustan muse figures work intertextually, and how they prompt and foreground questions of literary orthodoxy, poetic authority and reception.

Returning to Astrophil's muse, the subsequent section considers how *Astrophil and Stella* makes productive use of Propertian, as well as Ovidian and Virgilian, metapoetics to inscribe questions about the right use of the human imagination, and sixteenth-century anxieties about the moral status of poetry within the sonnet sequence.[13] Astrophil's muse in the opening sonnet is, evidently, not Stella and so is not positioned as a simple counterpart to Cynthia. To make sense of how the muse encounter is made to work in this text, *Astrophil and Stella* 1 is framed by readings of two literary essays: Stephen Gosson's 1579 anti-poetic treatise, *The Schoole of Abuse*, and Sidney's own *Defence of Poesie* written some time after December 1579.

The readings of muse figures in this chapter thus build on previous literature which situates them as complex constructs which encode literary preoccupations, and which can be used to interrogate how a culture expresses its own concerns, anxieties and beliefs about the nature of imagination and the role of poetry.[14] In reading Astrophil's muse as a self-conscious, critical and revisionary response to Propertius's Cynthia, we get an insight into the way Sidney's texts locate themselves in terms of metaliterary discourse, and how they use an engagement with Propertian elegy as well as Ovid and Virgil to respond to, and extend, debates about poetry in the latter part of the sixteenth century in England.

'My Sweetheart Herself Creates the Inspiration': Cynthia, Inspiration and Poetic Authority in Propertius 2.1 and 4.7

Propertius 2.1 is a programmatic poem foregrounding a concern with questions of inspiration and poetic practice.[15] It is Cynthia, as we have seen, who is the source of the narrator's verse, and she explicitly replaces Calliope or Apollo, the more orthodox sponsors of poetry. The production of elegy inspired by Cynthia is articulated, not surprisingly, in eroticised terms: 'if I have seen her step forth dazzling in Coan silks, a whole book will emerge from the Coan garment' (*sive illam Cois fulgentem incedere vidi | totum de Coa veste volumen erit*, 2.1.5–6). The elegiac muse and the text she inspires, as has been frequently discussed, become proxies of each other.

But what does it mean that the source of Propertian elegy is a mistress (*puella*): irredeemably human rather than divine, and with an overt sexuality? It is not that elegy is simply defining itself as 'anti-epic' and counter to everything that epic stands for in cultural and literary terms since, as the poem goes on to contend, however playfully, 'if, her dress torn off, she struggles naked with me, then, be sure of it, I compose long Iliads' (*seu nuda erepto mecum luctatur amictu | tum vero longas condimus Iliadas*, 2.1.13–14). An intimate encounter with Cynthia does not deliver a mere 'volume' (*volumen*, 2.1.6) but something more specific, already imbued with cultural value and significance. The text continues: 'whatever she has said, whatever she has done, from absolutely nothing is born a great legend' (*seu quidquid fecit sivest quodcumque locuta* | *maxima de nihilo nascitur historia*, 2.1.15–16).

Nascitur, 'is born, is given birth to', is the same word used in Propertius 2.34 in relation to Virgil's composition of the *Aeneid*: 'something greater than the Iliad is coming to birth' (*nescio quid maius nascitur Iliade*, 2.34.66). In generic terms, 2.1 thus re-defines epic and elegy in terms of each other, foreshadowing Ovid's mischievous definition of the *Iliad* as 'an adultress battled over by husband and lover'.[16] Propertius' 'grand legend' of love (*maxima ... historia*, 2.1.16), situates itself in relation to Virgil's great Roman epic and reminds us that the *Aeneid* embeds two erotic stories at its heart: that of Dido and Aeneas, and the battle between Aeneas and Turnus for marriage to Lavinia. At the end of book 12, for example, when Turnus cedes the duel as well as the war to Aeneas, he admits 'Lavinia is your wife' (*tua est Lavinia coniunx*, 12.937). For Turnus, at least, the erotic is central to his struggle with Aeneas.[17]

More pertinently to our concerns, by drawing attention to parallels between elegy inspired by Cynthia and Virgil's epic, 2.1 forces questions about the sources and creation of poetic authority. Propertius' 'grand legend' is born 'from nothing' (*de nihilo*, 2.1.16) and so epitomises the mysterious alchemy of poetry that can take the most quotidian of things ('whatever she has said, whatever she has done') and turn them into something with cultural status and artistic potency. The unspoken concern is with the question of how this authority is accrued by a text given that it is always created from nothing but the imagination and poetic skill of the writer. The *Aeneid*, being composed more or less contemporaneously with Propertius' elegiac books, is a particularly pressing case since it seems, from the evidence of 2.34, to have already achieved prominence and amassed a reputation: 'greater than the Iliad' (*maius ... Iliade*, 2.34.66).

The figure of a muse is thus a marker in what we might think of as a 'discourse of inspiration' that operates in these Roman texts to negotiate questions of literary practices and poetic authority.[18] The *Aeneid* invokes muses at various points in the text and it is worth examining the book 1 invocation briefly for the way in which it can illuminate what Cynthia is doing in her muse role in the Propertian text:[19] 'Tell me, O Muse, the cause [of Juno's anger] ... can fury so fierce dwell in heavenly breasts?' (*Musa, mihi causas memora ... tantaene animis caelestibus irae?*, 1.8–11). The muse's overt role is that of a mediator between man and the gods but the invocation itself 'quotes' previous calls for inspiration so that her presence also bridges Greek and Roman literary culture, thus linking Virgil to his literary predecessors. The authority of this muse derives not just from her divine status within the mythic system of the text, but also from her inter-textual condition. By recalling other muses, such as those of Homer, the Virgilian text succeeds in appropriating the cultural respect and literary eminence of previous epic to itself.

Virgil's muse is asked not just to relate (*memora*) the story of Aeneas' travails driven by Juno's anger, but also to help us understand such a human and earthly emotion in a divine being: *tantaene animis caelestibus irae?* (1.11). She thus serves partially as an interpreter, intervening between story and meaning, and opens up the possibility that a muse could tell a story of her own. We will return to this notion presently in relation to Propertius 4.7 and Ovid's muses, but the important point for the moment is that the muse is part of a literary structure which is inherently inter-textual, and that the sanction which she bestows derives from her previous incarnations within a constructed literary 'tradition'. Insofar as the power of the muse depends on her intertextuality rather than her divinity, the muse can become human as in the case of Cynthia, and interrogate other issues of metaliterary import – such as who controls the narrative, and who gives it meaning.

In 2.1 Cynthia's Coan silks inspire 'a whole book' (*totum ... volumen*, 2.1.6), but they elicit quite a different response in 1.2. In the book 1 poem, Cynthia's exotic dress and elaborate hair, the precise attributes which inspire the poet of 2.1, are castigated for being artificial, unnatural and indicative of a lack of chastity:

> What avails it, my love, to step out with coiffured hair and flutter the sheer folds of a Coan dress? ... Believe me, there's no improving your appearance: Love is naked, and loves not beauty gained by artifice.

> Quid iuvat ornato procedere, vita, capillo
> et tenues Coa veste movere sinus [...]
> crede mihi, non ulla tuae est medicina figurae;
> nudus Amor formae non amat artificem.
>
> (1.2.1–2, 7–8)

Cynthia's erotic ornamentation in 1.2 is represented as specifically 'foreign' (*peregrinis*): silks from the Greek island of Cos, Orontean perfumes from Antioch, implying that imported luxuries are antithetical to the 'Roman' virtues of chastity and naturalness.[20] Yet the examples that the text goes on to give as female exemplars of virtuous chastity are all taken from Greek myth and art: Phoebe, Hilaira, Hippodamia. The text undermines its own

purported ideology of Roman artlessness by using examples that are themselves taken from Greek myth. The literary language of this poem draws
on other art forms, a stance at odds with its elevation and valorisation of
artlessness. This irony is foregrounded when the chaste beauty of these
mythic women is described as 'pure as the hues in paintings by Apelles'
(*qualis Apelleis est color in tabulis*, 1.2.22), drawing attention to their status
as constructed art objects. Cynthia, by covering herself in expensive clothes,
only serves to conceal her naked beauty which the narrator would prefer to
see displayed: 'preventing your figure from displaying its own true merits'
(*nec sinere in propriis membra nitere bonis*, 1.2.6), so that even the apparent
chastity of rejecting artifice is itself articulated in the language of nudity.

The import of reading 1.2 in the light of 2.1 is the way in which the
juxtaposition captures the instability of individual poetic responses to the
same source, revealing a poetic inconsistency between these two texts. One
reaction to Cynthia in her Coan silks is a moralising one that castigates
eroticised luxury; the other is a delighted one which elevates the *puella* to
the source of Iliadic poetry. Cynthia as a human muse thus serves as both a
negative inspiration (1.2) and a positive one (2.1), and emphasises the role
of the poet: not as mouthpiece for a divinely sanctioned muse, but as a
creative artist working from his imaginative response to the manifestations
of the world around him. By drawing attention to the unstable production
of poetry and its capricious responses to Cynthia as poetic source material,
the Propertian text stresses its status as a human art rather than a divine
one, putting the poet at the centre of the work and positioning literature
as the product of skilled artistry.

A secondary concern here is with the complex response of Roman poetry
to prior Greek cultural models. On one hand, 1.2 evinces a purported
desire not to follow the ornamental models of Greek poetry, and art more
generally, which are implied to be 'foreign' to Roman ideas of unaffected-
ness and a lack of artifice. On the other, supposedly Roman ideals such as
that of chastity in the text cannot be constructed without recourse to previous Greek paradigms. This cultural self-exploration and the struggle to
negotiate and express a sense of a Roman poetic identity will return later
in this chapter.

Propertius 1.2 is also a poem which puts forward the idea of Cynthia
not as a muse or source of inspiration but as a poet in her own right: 'all
the more since Phoebus endows you with his songs, and Calliope, nothing
loth, with Aonia's lyre' (*cum tibi praesertim Phoebus sua carmina donet* |
Aoniamque libens Calliopea lyram, 1.2.27–8). 'Propertius' claims he loves her
for her skills in singing, her playing of the lyre, her 'happy talk' (*iucundis*

... *verbis*, 29) but though her voice is referred to, it is suppressed within this poem. In 4.7, however, Cynthia speaks for herself, creating her own narrative when she returns, in macabre fashion, from the grave.[21]

In some respects 4.7 is a re-visiting of, and response to, 1.19 in which the narrator foretells his own death and fears that Cynthia will abandon his funeral: 'this fear is more cruel than the funeral rites themselves' (*hic timor est ipsis durior exsequiis*, 1.19.4). He claims that he will continue to love her beyond death and will always be known as 'your shade' (*tua ... imago*, 1.19.11). In 4.7 the situation is reversed: it is Cynthia who is dead and it is her shade which haunts 'Propertius'. In an inversion of 1.3 where the narrator steals into the bedroom to contemplate the sleeping Cynthia, Cynthia's ghost now visits the narrator's bed. The text carefully foregrounds the eerie contrast between Cynthia with her dress charred from the funeral pyre (*lateri vestis adusta fuit*, 4.7.8) and lips withered from drinking the waters of the Lethe (*Lethaeus triverat ora liquor*, 4.7.10), and the living voice (*spirantes*, 4.7.11) which emerges from her mouth and which gives her a greater speaking presence than in other poems when she was alive.

As soon as she begins to speak Cynthia starts to contest the idea of 1.19 that it is she who would abandon the dead poet, turning the accusation back against him: 'Treacherous one, from whom no girl can expect better, can sleep so soon have power over you?' (*perfide, nec cuiquam melior sperande puellae,* | *in te iam vires somnus habere potest?*, 4.7.13–14). In 2.20 the narrator had sworn on the bones of his mother and father that he would remain faithful 'to my dying hour', and that his parents' ghosts would haunt him if he lied (2.20.15–18). Here Cynthia accuses him of an instant and easy forgetfulness and turns his own curse against him when she returns from death to trouble him.

The appropriation of her accusatory opening words from those spoken by the ghost of Patroclus to Achilles in *Iliad* 23 is clear: 'You sleep, Achilleus; you have forgotten me; but you were not | careless of me when I lived, but only in death' (*Iliad* 23.69–70). The night visitation to a sleeping man also recalls Hector's ghost coming to the sleeping Aeneas in *Aeneid* 2 (2.268–98), as well as the return of Creusa's shade later in the same book (2.771–94). On these models, the Propertian narrator is figured as the epic hero – Achilles, Aeneas – while Cynthia plays the part of the dead and defeated Patroclus and Hector, and the 'wretched, unfortunate' (*infelix*, 2.772) lost wife. *Infelix* also links Creusa to Dido as it is an epithet repeatedly associated with the queen: *uritur infelix Dido*, 'unhappy Dido burns' (4.68) when she first falls in love with Aeneas; and when Aeneas encounters her shade in the underworld his first words to her are '*infelix*

Dido' (6.456). Although the term is not attached to Cynthia in this poem, there are possible connections to be drawn between her and Dido: when she learns of Aeneas' plan to leave Carthage, Dido promises that her shade will follow and haunt him (4.384–6) – Dido fails to enact her threat, but it is partially fulfilled on her behalf by Cynthia.

As was the case with Virgil's muse, Cynthia's shade – and, through her, Propertius' poem – becomes invested with literary authority derived from previous texts, specifically the *Iliad* and the *Aeneid*. The intertext is a layered one: Cynthia 'quotes' from the prior speeches of Patroclus, Hector and Dido, while her creator, Propertius, re-writes scenes from canonical Greek and, now, Roman epic. Cynthia's status as elegiac *puella* is over-written, though never replaced, by the roles of epic hero, wife and lover, so that in this poem, at least, she is a complicated figure who channels and unites, temporarily, various characters and the sometimes contradictory values they encode.

As Cynthia's ghost continues to speak, she persists in dismantling the foundations upon which 'Propertius'' fantasy of erotic love is built. She describes the way she used to climb secretly out of her window at night in order to be with 'Propertius', and their passionate nights spent making love outside at the crossroads (4.7.15–20). This is a quite different story from that which we have been told in the earlier three books: 'Propertius'' version is that of the archetypical *dura puella*, 'an unrelenting girl' (2.1.78) who, 'iron-hearted … never said "I love you"' (*illa tamen numquam ferrea dixit 'amo'*, 2.8.12). In other poems we have witnessed 'Propertius'' easy entry into Cynthia's home at night (1.3), and have heard his numerous references to making love in her bed (1.3, 2.15). He has frequently declared his constancy and contrasted it with her lack of fidelity (1.19, 2.5, 2.9a, 3.24), and her very openness about other lovers (1.9, 2.5) has led to the critical ambiguity over whether Cynthia is a courtesan.[22]

Now she, speaking for herself, claims constancy and represents herself as the abandoned lover: 'alas for the troth you plighted, whose deceitful words the South Wind, unwilling to hear, has swept away' (*foederis heu pacti, cuius fallacia verba | non audituri diripuere Noti*, 4.7.21–2). Her use of *foederis* here is notable in relation to the Catullan texts discussed in the previous chapter, supported by the notion of unreliable words as being 'written on the wind' as in Catullus 70. Cynthia, appropriating the role of 'Catullus', accuses 'Propertius' of the oath-breaking associated with Lesbia thus inverting the erotic gender dynamic upon which elegy is supposedly built.

Cynthia's voice is thus used within the text to contest not just the Propertian narrator's story but the 'master-narrative' of elegy itself. By refusing the trope of the *dura puella* and disputing the constancy of her lover, Cynthia unsettles the character and structure of elegiac love, and puts pressure on the contours that bound and define Propertian erotics. There is space, of course, within the narrative, not to believe her, but there have been earlier intimations of the narrator's infidelities (2.22, 3.20, 4.8), and Cynthia herself has declared her constancy in 1.3 and 2.29: 'do you think I am like you men in behaviour? I am not so fickle: enough for me to know one man' (*me similem vestris moribus esse putas? | non ego tam facilis: sat erit mihi cognitus unus*, 2.29b.32–3) – even if she does immediately undercut her own indignation somewhat by specifying that the one does not necessarily have to be 'Propertius': 'yourself or somebody more faithful' (*vel tu, vel si quis verior esse potest*, 2.29b.34).

Cynthia's voice thus clashes with that of 'Propertius' and enacts a struggle for control of the narrative as her story decentres and interrogates his. This interest in writing conflicting voices, frequently opposed through gender, and using them to draw attention to questions of narrative unity and authority underpins Ovid's *Heroides*, too, which picks up on these issues and makes them the focal point of the later text.[23] The competing voices of the *Aeneid*, also, are further evidence of an Augustan preoccupation with this dialogic mode of poetics: opposing textual voices serve as devices which mark out ideological and ethical systems, multiply meanings, complicate and enrich the texts which contain them.[24]

While Cynthia can be seen to contest the Propertian master-narrative, at the same time she uses 'Propertius'' own narrative strategies: the extended mythical exemplars in lines 55–70, the engagement with the *Aeneid*, so that their voices blend and merge as much as they separate. Cynthia's may be a contestatory voice but it is also a collaborative one: she both competes with the main narrative voice of 'Propertius' and yet is also aligned with it.

Cynthia's story in 4.7 is, of course, itself a partial re-telling of, and response to, *Aeneid* 6 and re-writes the religious and moral centre of that poem from a specifically gendered and eroticised position. Like Aeneas, Cynthia travels through the topography of the underworld and observes its inhabitants, but the images she brings back are very different from those of the *Aeneid*.[25] Most strikingly, Cynthia's underworld is peopled exclusively by women whom she divides into the good (Andromeda, Hypermnestra) and the bad (Clytemnestra, Pasiphaë), and who are located in the equivalents of Virgil's Elysium or Tartarus according to their sexual conduct (4.7.55–70). Virgil, for comparison, places people in Tartarus for political crimes and crimes of power, such as the Titans who tried to overthrow the Olympians (*Aeneid* 6.580–1). When Cynthia meets Andromeda and Hypermnestra, she specifies that 'they tell their stories' (*narrant historias ... suas*, 4.7.63–4). Hypermnestra also appears in *Heroides* 14, Hypermnestra to Lynceus.[26] Although the relationship between the Propertian and Ovidian texts is uncertain and the question of precedence unresolved, the existence of these elegiac texts concerned with mythic women speaking back to established narratives is evidence of a common interest in challenging canonicity.

By accusing 'Propertius' of infidelity and claiming sexual constancy for herself, Cynthia associates herself with the 'good' women of the under-world so that patriarchal codes become reinforced by a ventriloquised female voice. This reassertion of conventional Roman sexual values inverts the subversive moralities of Propertius' poetry and so temporarily aligns it with the moral register of Virgilian epic. Virgil, however, locates his Pasiphaë in the *Lugentes Campi*, 'the Mourning Fields', the place reserved for the victims of *durus amor*, 'stern love' (*Aeneid* 6.442) where Dido her-self wanders. Where Cynthia's underworld is split on gendered and moral lines, parts of Virgil's, as is the case with Pasiphaë, are more ambiguous, just as the precise nature of Dido's 'crime' which aligns her with Pasiphaë is left unvoiced. Certainly the mourning fields seem to be on the outskirts of the underworld and quite separate from Tartarus where the wicked are punished (*Aeneid* 6.539–43). Cynthia's underworld, then, judges women more harshly than does Virgil's. Thus in 4.7 it is the female voice of the sometime muse who reasserts the conventional patriarchal morality which Propertian poetics partially and at least superficially eschew, so that Cynthia celebrates her submission and sexual constancy in the face of infidelity just as, elsewhere, the Propertian narrator does his own.

In *Aeneid* 6, Aeneas and the sibyl leave the underworld in problematic fashion via the ivory gate, the gate of 'false dreams' (*falsa ... insomnia*), rather than through the true gate of horn (*Aeneid.* 6.893–8).[27] Cynthia, in contrast, claims she has come through the 'righteous gate' (*piis ... portis*) and that she is one of the 'righteous dreams' (*pia ... somnia*). The deliberate repetition of forms of *pius*, 'faithful, devout, religious, dutiful' draws fur-ther comparisons with Aeneas, as it is the epithet that is most consistently associated with him. Cynthia, by appropriating the language of the *Aeneid*, provides a partial commentary on that text. She draws attention to the enigmatic departure of Aeneas through the ivory gate and the questions that raises about the status of what he has seen and been told about the future of Rome. She also unsettles the meaning of *pius*: it is difficult to see how the same word can be applied to an elegiac mistress and a Roman epic hero without the term becoming loose and unfixed. The *Aeneid* itself, of course, problematises the term in relation to Aeneas, particularly at the end of book 12 when Aeneas' refusal of clemency and brutal killing of Turnus decisively reject the 'Roman' values that Anchises proclaims in book 6.

Cynthia's shade requests that 'Propertius' burn his poems about her just as her body has been charred by the funeral fire, reiterating a correlation between female body and poetic text (4.7.77–8). An extra-literary intertext also exists in the story that Virgil on his death-bed requested that the unfinished *Aeneid* be burnt, making Cynthia a bold proxy for Virgil himself.[28] She then goes on to dictate her own epitaph, a statement of permanence which replaces 'Propertius'' words about her with her own: 'here in Tibur's soil lies golden Cynthia: fresh glory, Anio, is added to thy banks' (*hic sita tiburtina iacet aurea Cynthia terra: accessit ripae laus, Aniene, tuae*, 4.7.85–6). Here, again, Cynthia is following Dido who also attempts to 'write' her own epitaph, and both fictional women strive to memorialise themselves in a way that is different from the way the texts in which they appear generally portray them: 'a noble city I have built; my own walls I have seen' (*urbem praeclaram statui, mea moenia vidi*, *Aeneid* 4.655). Cynthia appropriates something of epic heroism to herself (*laus*, 'glory') just as Dido claims she has completed a task that Aeneas has been set but not yet achieved.

So Cynthia in 4.7 takes on shifting roles within a system of poetic production and circulation. She is an early reader of, and commentator on, the *Aeneid* and foregrounds some of its fractures and inconsistencies. It is precisely these moments, highlighted by Cynthia, where the ideological systems at work in the text are shown to break down and the poem becomes imbued with its provocative density and richness. Cynthia is also a counterpart to Aeneas, as well as taking on some of the shades of other characters, notably Dido and, to a lesser extent, Creusa. In this sense, she becomes a participant in the *Aeneid*, albeit by creating an elegiac surrogate. When she asks that Propertius burn his poems about her, she signals her desire to 'be' Virgil, to move from being the subject of poetry to being a poet in her own right – and all that that implies in terms of having control over the narrative which contains her. By placing 4.7 with 2.1 we can see how Cynthia is moved from being a muse figure, a source of poetic inspiration, to something with greater agency, at least within the fictional boundaries of the Propertian narrative.

To frame these readings of Cynthia and to illuminate further what is at stake in her shifting metapoetic incarnations, it is worth turning to Ovid's *Metamorphoses*. Though it was written after Propertius, many of the questions with which we are concerned, especially issues of art and authority, are central to Ovid's epic and can help to make sense of what is happening in the Propertian text. We will start by looking at what happens when Minerva visits the muses in *Metamorphoses* 5.[29]

When Minerva arrives on Helicon, the muses are described as 'learned sisters' (*doctas … sorores*, 5.255), and it is worth remembering that *docta* is an epithet of Cynthia's (e.g. 1.7.11, 2.11.6, 2.13.11), prompting comparisons between them. Minerva comments on how fortunate the muses are in having their home on Helicon and at this point one of the muses, who remains anonymous, designated simply as 'one of the sisters' (*una sororum*, 5.268), intervenes. Firstly she implicates Minerva herself in the role of the muses: 'you, Tritonia, who would so fitly join our band' (*in partem ventura chori Tritonia nostri*, 5.270), and then reveals that their fate is endangered, that they are no longer safe on Helicon (*tutae modo simus*, 'if only we were safe', 5.272), which is no longer the sanctuary that it once was. These muses are ill at ease in the world, and have become alienated from it: 'to such an extent has nothing been forbidden to crime' (*vetitum est adeo sceleri nihil*, 5.273). The unnamed muse goes on to elaborate why 'all things frighten our virgin souls' (*omnia terrent | virgineas mentes*, 5.273–4), and tells the story of Pyreneus, a king of Thrace, who intercepted the muses on their journey to Parnassus, offering them shelter from a storm – and we should note that these muses are inconvenienced by bad weather, not an idea associated with the dignified and grave muses of Homer or Virgil. When the rain had passed and the muses tried to leave 'Pyreneus shut his doors, and offered us violence' (*claudit sua tecta Pyreneus | vimque parat*, 5.287–8). Given the emphasis on the virginity of the muses, and the framework of sexual violence which organises the *Metamorphoses*, the implication is that Pyreneus' violence is an attempt at rape. The muses escape but this short episode is instructive for the way in which it recalibrates ideas of the muses and what they represent as metaphors for inspiration and poetic practices.

Ovid's muses are vulnerable (to rain – as well as rape), and are no longer serene and impersonal. The muses themselves now have a story of their own to tell and this makes them partial, subjective and involved rather than disinterested. Their authority, previously represented as stemming, at least in part, from their detachment has been dissipated, and they are now shown to have an agenda of their own.

This story shows how the unnamed muse re-configures the authority of her narrative. With her divinity no longer unassailable, her words no longer carry the mandate of theocracy. Instead she is forced to re-locate the power of her story and she does this by relating it to her audience: Minerva, an Olympian, sister to Apollo, the patron of poetry, and a virgin goddess. By emphasising their common attributes – virginity, the way that Minerva herself could almost be one of the muses – the goddess is made partisan to the muse's story and, by extension, the fear that now haunts the muses: she, too, could be the object of sexualised violence.

Tales of pursuit, rape and other forms of eroticised brutality make up a significant portion, of course, of the *Metamorphoses*.[30] The muse's story of intended violence might turn her into just another narrator in a text interwoven through narrative voices, compromising, even eradicating, her privileged status. The muse attempts to reclaim her previous prerogative by shaping her story to have special resonance to her prime audience: Minerva, the virgin patron of poetry.

The tale told to Minerva of the poetic competition between the muses and the Pierides, and the embedded story of the rape of Proserpina, extend these concerns. The daughters of Pierus challenge the authority of the muses and attack their tenure as the guarantors of poetry: 'cease to deceive the unsophisticated rabble with your pretence of song' (*desinite indoctum vana dulcedine vulgus | fallere*, 5.308–9). *Fallere* also means 'to beguile' so another way of reading this accusation is that the muses have been beguiling the unlearned (*indoctum*) with false sweetness (*dulcedine*) – telling people what they want to hear. The connection, again, between the reputation and authority of a text and audience reception is foregrounded. The contest is set up with Helicon itself as the prize and, significantly, the judges are the nymphs who live there ('the nymphs were chosen judges and took oath by their streams', *electae iurant per flumina nymphae*, 5.316). So this is a compromised competition from the outset, and one which foregrounds the relationships between story, story-teller, audience and literary reputation.

The Pierides' song of the revolt against the Olympians is summarised dismissively in twelve lines (5.319–31), and the muse's abbreviated retelling to Minerva puts the emphasis on the way in which it humiliates the Olympians who fled from battle and hid themselves in 'lying shapes' (*mentitis ... figuris*, 5.326). Slyly slipped in amongst these shameful disguises is that of 'the sister of Apollo' (*soror Phoebi*), possibly Minerva herself, as a cat (5.330), a nice touch that must surely, as the muse intends, consolidate Minerva's prejudice against the Pierides whose narrative challenges Olympian status and power as surely as did the giants' revolt.

In contrast to this contingent and deliberately truncated version of the Pierides' story, the muse quotes her fellow muse Calliope's song of the rape of Proserpina verbatim (5.341–661). Included are two inset stories of Cyane and Arethusa, two water nymphs who courageously tried to prevent the abduction of the girl – figures who are bound to be prime objects of sympathy amongst the water nymphs who are judging the contest. Calliope, and the unnamed muse who quotes her, shapes her narrative to her audience, inscribing her hearers within the text as a way of aligning their interests with those of the story-teller. Nymphs, as we know, are particularly vulnerable to rape in the *Metamorphoses* and so Calliope's tale is one which cannot fail to speak to the interests and potential fears of the judges of this contest. Similarly, it and the prior story of Pyreneus are especially appropriate to be told to Minerva, the virgin, female Olympian.

This episode has been read as an Ovidian engagement with questions of political patronage and literary censorship, not least because of the textual associations between the Olympians and the Augustan regime within the text.[31] Pyreneus' attempt to kidnap the muses suggests that poetry may be attacked, that external powers may try to curb and constrain it, appropriate it for their own usage. But in terms of our concerns here, it is also a story which deals with the way poetic authority, no longer under the divine benefaction of the archaic Greek muses, has to be re-negotiated and established afresh. For Ovid's muses, it is the audience who confers authority and sanctions a poetic text – here symbolised as the winning of a poetic contest and the retaining of Helicon. Poetic authority is represented as a function of reception, but the audience is never unbiased or dispassionate. The Pierides, in losing, become marginal voices whose song is almost wholly suppressed but which still maintains a presence at the boundary of what becomes, according to the judgement of the internal audience, an orthodox, 'winning' text. What is symbolised – and problematised – in this episode is the establishment of literary and cultural canonicity.

There is further insight to be gained from an analysis of the sibyl episode in *Aeneid* 6 and Ovid's brief poetic rejoinder in *Metamorphoses* 14.[32] The sibyl is described as 'chaste, sacred, pure' (*casta*, *Aeneid* 5.735) and her role is to lead Aeneas through the underworld to Elysium where he will meet Anchises. She is thus a mediator, conducting Aeneas to the place of prophecy although she is also a direct source of divination and foresight for him. In book 6, we are taken into the sibyl's cave (6.10) and witness her possession by Apollo. Especially disturbing is the violence of the encounter, her frenzied resistance, and the extent to which the god has to mute her own voice in order to bend her to his will: 'so much the more he tires her raving mouth, tames her wild heart, and moulds her by restraint' (*tanto magis ille fatigat | os rabidum, fera corda domans, fingitque premendo*, 6.79–80).

An important reading of this episode interprets the sibyl as a proxy for the poet being possessed by the divine *furor* of inspiration.[33] In this model, the individual, personal voice of the poet is suppressed against his will as his words are pressed into shape by forces beyond him. This might also be read figuratively so that these forces may be understood to be not only the mysterious power of inspiration personified here by Apollo, but more widely those of genre and literary orthodoxy, of cultural obligations and political constraints. This is not necessarily a wholly negative transaction despite the violence of the sibyl–Apollo encounter in *Aeneid* 6. It is the sacrifice of the individual voice which gives the sibyl-poet access to something beyond: in the *Aeneid* it is a privileged contact with divinity and destiny.

So the sibyl in the *Aeneid* is imbued with authority as a seer through her submission to Apollo, and she has to suspend her own voice in order to channel his, the voice of divine and poetic power. Virgil's sibyl barely has a voice or history of her own outside of her prophetic and guide role, and the public and civic nature of her utterances is foregrounded in the text when Aeneas promises a temple to Apollo. This was built in 28 BCE on the Capitoline and housed the Sibylline books, so that the sibyl's prophecies in the poem match the Roman reality of Virgil's original readers.

Turning now to *Metamorphoses* 14, we can investigate how Ovid's sibyl episode speaks back to the *Aeneid*. Book 14 compresses much of *Aeneid* 6 into eighteen lines (*Metamorphoses* 14.101–19) but at the end of this epitome, the narrative suddenly expands. As Aeneas is following the sibyl out of the underworld, he starts a conversation which prompts her to tell her own story. Like so many other tales narrated in the poem through female characters it is a narrative of pursuit though not, in this case, of rape. Apollo courted her with gifts but when the sibyl requested a long life, she forgot to ask for eternal youth and is now aged and weary. Her description of the loss of physical presence reminds us of the vulnerability of the muses in book 4: 'the time will come when the length of days will shrivel me from my full form to but a tiny thing, and my limbs, consumed by age, will shrink to a feather's weight' (*tempus erit, cum de tanto me corpora parvam | longa dies faciet, consumptaque membra senecta | ad minimum redigentur onus, Metamorphoses* 14.147–9).

The sibyl's words can partly be read as evidence of the Callimachean influence in Ovidian poetry (*parva, minimum*) but also speak to the diminution of the divine authority of the sibyl as a literary figure. In the *Metamorphoses* she becomes, like the unnamed muse of book 4, another voice, another narrator in a text which is built from a plethora of voices, and hers has no special privilege or weight (*minimum … onus*).

So there are two things going on here: one is the dismantling of the established authority of the sibyl, a process which has implications for the status of the poet since neither can be unproblematically shored up by the conventional status of *vates* with access to divine inspiration. Yet the liberation of the sibyl from the governance of Apollo frees her to tell her own story, a story excluded from the *Aeneid* but which emerges in the *Metamorphoses* as a small, intimate moment of the personal, the usually marginalised, taking centre stage – if only briefly.

Ovid's sibyl can thus be read as a symbol for poetry which is self-interested and subjective; of a poet who cannot stand outside the text which she is creating or beyond the wider textual and literary system. A divine mandate has been dispensed with and the only authority that can take its place is a poetic one, one created by the potency of the text itself as superb poetry and splendid story-telling.

Taking these figures together – Cynthia as muse and poet, Virgil's sibyl, Ovid's muses and sibyl – provides evidence for the way in which Augustan poetry is fascinated by questions of metapoetic import. These muse and sibyl figures operate as metaphors which enable questions about inspiration, the creative process, literary practices and reception to play out within and between these texts. Especially potent seem to be issues of canonicity and conformism as we see figures who are more usually somehow muted – Cynthia, the sibyl, even, in some ways, the muse – emerge as story-tellers in their own right. The invested relationship between poet, story and audience is especially foregrounded and raises questions about poetry's political valences and issues of censorship, the latter especially prevalent in the *Metamorphoses*.

Common factors to all these Augustan incarnations of metapoetic figures is the perceived inadequacy of, and move away from, previous embodiments of creativity and inspiration. The divinely sanctioned muses of Hesiod and Homer can barely find a place in these Roman texts: they are threatened, imprisoned, almost violated and now fearful in *Metamorphoses* book 4, and in Propertius' texts have been replaced by the eroticised Cynthia. Even the *Aeneid*, which still has recourse to the 'traditional' muses, problematises the canonical representation of the poetic process in the unsettling scene between Apollo and the sibyl. Ovid's sibyl articulates her own decline and diminution as she lives through her designated thousand years, and his muses on Helicon find themselves at odds with the world they currently live in.

All of these texts reflect self-consciously on their own production, their status and their authority, and participate in a discourse acutely concerned with negotiating a sense of Roman poetic self-identity within Augustan culture. Propertius' Cynthia is an early indicator of this metaliterary turn in elegy but framing her representation as shifting between muse figure and poet with the *Aeneid* and the later *Metamorphoses* foregrounds the productive dialogue which may be initiated in Propertius but which continues beyond the classical period.

Especially notable is the way in which this dialogue manifests itself as a cross-genre phenomenon: rather than separating elegy and epic, it reveals their common literary concerns. Ovid's texts, which also refuse any easy differentiation between genres, continue to concern themselves with questions of poetic inspiration and authority, and how texts might situate themselves in relation to a literary 'tradition'. These Roman texts seem to be preoccupied with how canonicity is produced and upheld, and the relationships between poetry and the culture which produces it. Most of all they exhibit an interest in situating themselves against archaic Greek models in order to foreground the inadequacy of, and move away from, divine and theocratic authority towards an alternative poetics. Cynthia as a human muse encodes the subjective, the compromised, and the individual voice which is able to relocate itself from the margins of a text to its centre.

'Loving in Truth and Fain in Verse': Astrophil's Subversive Muse and the Abuse of Poetry in *Astrophil and Stella* 1

Astrophil and Stella 74 serves as a re-voicing of the questions about poetic inspiration raised in Propertius 2.1 and also asserts, in different words, that 'my sweetheart herself creates the inspiration'. In this sonnet, Astrophil rejects the tradition of the classical muses: 'I never drank of Aganippe's well, | nor ever did in shade of Tempe sit; and muses scorn' (74.1–3). The redundant geography of inspiration invokes revealing intertexts since Aganippe is a fountain of the muses on Mount Helicon and is specifically mentioned in the challenge of the Pierides in *Metamorphoses* 5 where it is one of the prizes which will go to the victors: 'if you are conquered, yield us Medusa's spring and Boetian Aganippe' (*vel cedite victae | fonte Medusaeo et Hyantea Aganippe, Metamorphoses* 5.311–12). Tempe is a vale in Thessaly through which the river Peneus flows (*Metamorphoses* 1.568–73): as Peneus is the father of Daphne, it turns out to be the site of Apollo's pursuit of Daphne, and thus links Astrophil, via Petrarch's Laura, back to a founding myth of elegy.[34] Astrophil goes on to deny any divine *furor* as the source of his verse: 'Some do I hear of poet's fury tell, | but (God wot) wot not what they mean by it' (74.5–6), and claims, in line with the opening sonnet, 'I am no pick-purse of another's wit' (74.8) – that *imitatio* is not, supposedly, the basis of his poetic practice. The irony of a poem which asserts its lack of imitation through poetic intertexts will be explored later in this chapter.

The next lines rework the questions of the Propertian narrator in 2.1: 'How falls it then, that with so smooth an ease | my thoughts I speak, and what I speak doth flow | in verse, and that my verse best wits doth please?' (74.9–11). As 'Propertius' before him claimed Cynthia as his inspiration, Astrophil asserts 'Sure, thus it is: | my lips are sweet, inspired with Stella's kiss' (74.13–14). As is the case with Propertius' Cynthia, Stella, as this chapter goes on to demonstrate, is a shifting literary figure: part muse, part text, part intended reader, part collaborative voice in the weaving of *Astrophil and Stella*.[35]

This chapter juxtaposes Propertius and Sidney's *Astrophil and Stella*, framed by the provocative entrance of the muse in *Astrophil and Stella* 1. Sidney's suggested reading and appropriation of Propertian elegy enables a metaliterary discourse but one different from that to be found in the Augustan poems we have looked at. Sidney's text, we will see, is concerned not so much with the negotiation of poetic authority but with questions about the moral status of poetry in sixteenth-century England.

'"Fool", said my muse to me; "look in thy heart and write"': but what is in Astrophil's heart, and what is the central subject matter of his verse to be? Sonnet 8 tells us that 'Love, born in Greece, of late fled from his native place' (8.1) and goes on to show us Cupid taking refuge 'in Stella's joyful face' (8.8). Finding her 'most fair, most cold' (8.12), Cupid takes flight again 'to my close heart, where, while some firebrands he did lay | he burnt unawares his wings, and cannot fly away' (8.13–14). So erotic love is what resides in Astrophil's heart and is the ostensible subject of the sequence to come. It is a self-consciously literary love taking its origins from Greek erotic verse ('Love, born in Greece', 8.1) and coming to Sidney's England via other incarnations including those of elegy and Petrarch, the latter particularly flagged through that 'most fair, most cold' (8.12), the archetypical description of the Petrarchan lady.

The opening sonnet of *Astrophil and Stella* might thus be read as a response to the programmatic statements of Propertius 1.1, Ovid's *Amores* 1.1 and Sulpicia's first poem ([*Tibullus*] 3.13) all of which merge love with writing, so that erotic desire is the instigator of the elegiac poetic project. In Astrophil's case, while 'loving in truth', he would 'fain in verse', playing on the slippage between 'fain' (willingly, gladly), and 'feign', to fashion or form. Taking its etymology from the Latin *fingere*, to form or mould, feign in Sidney's time has both the positive meaning to fashion or shape, but also a negative one which is to fashion fictively or deceptively, to invent or contrive, to dissemble or pretend. From the outset, Astrophil's love project, and the poetry which conveys it, is caught in this tension between 'truth' and 'fain', between his poetry being a representation of true love ('loving in truth') or of it being a true representation of his love, and of that love being, possibly, a deceptive contrivance which is itself embodied through poetry.

'Fain in verse my love to show' (1.1) contains a further syntactical complexity since 'my love' can refer either to Astrophil's emotions, or to the beloved reader to whom he wants to convey his feelings, the Stella of the sequence. The feigning can thus either mean that the deception is applied to his emotions, that the verse is a pretence of love, or that it is aimed at deceiving the object of his love, Stella – or, indeed, both. From the first line of this opening sonnet we are caught in a hermeneutic impasse which centres on the problematics of poetry: that it may not be a true representation of an authentic and sincere love but an invented contrivance with the intent to deceive.

The sonnet continues to outline what is at stake for Astrophil in his writing of poetry:

> That she (dear she) might take some pleasure of my pain;
> Pleasure might cause her read, reading might make her know;
> Knowledge might pity win, and pity grace obtain.
>
> (1.2–4)

By reading his verse, Astrophil anticipates, the married Stella may be induced to empathise with his plight, to pity him and bestow her 'grace' on the lovelorn poet. Grace here means Stella's favour, a privilege which Astrophil seeks for himself, and one which, as later sonnets elucidate, unequivocally means sexual submission. That Astrophil's desires and intentions are physical is made transparent in sonnets 52 ('Let Virtue have that Stella's self; yet thus, | that virtue but that body grant us'), 61, 62 on the tension between Stella's virtuous and Astrophil's physical love ('Dear, love me not, that you might love me more'), 63 ('I craved the thing which ever she denies') and, especially, the Second Song where Astrophil's frustration almost spills over into rape ('Her tongue waking still refuseth | giving frankly niggard "no"; | now will I attempt to know | what "no" her tongue sleeping useth'). 57 adds to this when it talks about Stella being 'pierced' by the sharpness of Astrophil's erotic laments. The sequence also makes clear that while Stella, though married, does fall in love with Astrophil (e.g. sonnets 66 where Stella's eyes 'guilty seemed of love', and 69 'For Stella hath, with words where faith doth shine, | of her high heart giv'n me the monarchy'), he equates the fact that she will not consummate this love with ultimate failure.

So Astrophil's writing of poetry has a specific outcome in sight: the seduction and sexual possession of Stella. The overtly physical nature of his aspirations, and the problematic use of that term 'grace' in an explicitly sexual way gives this poem a discordant position in relation to sixteenth-century neo-Platonism and the orthodox Petrarchan poetics built on it. Petrarch's own sonnets to Laura are founded on what became commonly known as the 'ladder of love' where a desire for the physical beauty of the earthly sonnet lady leads to an ascent towards an appreciation of divine beauty, heavenly grace and ultimate spiritual goodness.[36] The tension of the *canzoniere* springs, in part, from the conflict between the narrator's physical and spiritual desires, wryly recognised in 'Una candida cerva' when the narrator falls into the stream, but the neo-Platonic underpinning remains stable. Castiglione's *The Book of the Courtier* (1528) also draws on Plato ('as it is defined of the wise men of olde time, Love is nothing else but a certain coveting to enjoy beautie', 303) and, in the speech of Pietro Bembo in book 4, offers an exposition of sixteenth-century neo-Platonism which is a suggestive context for the reading of *Astrophil and Stella*:

> And therefore who so thinketh in possessing the body to enjoy Beauty, he is far deceived, and is moved to it, not with true knowledge by the choice of reason, but with false opinion by the longing of sense ... These kind of lovers therefore love most unluckily for ... they never come by their covetings ... Young men be wrapped in this sensual love which is very rebel against reason ... and when these youthfull years be gone and past, leave it off clean, keeping aloof from this sensual coveting as from the lowest step of the stairs, by the which a man may ascend to true love.
>
> (*The Book of the Courtier* 304–7)[37]

Castiglione's description of ardent male youth maps neatly onto the representation of Astrophil: ideas of deceit, the replacement of 'true knowledge' by 'false opinion', the privileging of sensual desire over reason, even the connection between youth and melancholy provide a productive frame for reading Astrophil's first sonnet. The notions of Astrophil's love as 'vain, oppressive and at odds with virtue', of Astrophil himself being a negative rather than a positive model of the lover are certainly not new.[38] This chapter extends these previous readings by concentrating on Astrophil not so much as a lover but as a problematic poet of love, and considers how this re-focus allows the text to intervene in debates about the moral status of poetry itself.

Astrophil, according to Castiglione's exposition, remains on the 'lowest step' of the 'stairs' or ladder of love, caught up solely in physical desire for Stella. As a poet Astrophil takes this ladder conceit and turns it into a travesty of neo-Platonism: 'pleasure might cause her read, reading might make her know; | knowledge might pity win, and pity grace obtain' (1.3– 4). Rather than guiding him to the 'true love' and 'true knowledge' of Castiglione, Astrophil's poetry leads Stella, he hopes, to the fallen 'grace' of adulterous consummation. The idiom and tropes of neo-Platonism are appropriated by Astrophil but only in a debased sense – and the writing and pleasurable reading of love poetry are shown to be central to this moral falling away from the spiritual elevation articulated in Castiglione. From his opening sonnet, the aim of Astrophil's poetry is shown to be corrupt.

We have already noticed the way Astrophil rejects *imitatio* as a mode of poetic production and can now posit a connection between the way in which the text is created and its deceitful aims. Astrophil scours pre- vious poetry ('oft turning other's leaves', 1.7) for inspiration but what he is seeking are 'fit words to paint the blackest face of woe' (1.5). 'Paint', like feign, has positive meanings at this period and can mean 'to express', but it can also have the negative connotation to represent or portray in a false way. So one way of reading this text is that Astrophil is searching for prior poetry to assist, reinforce, defend and authorise his own corrupt and sensual aims. Poetic production and morality become mapped onto each other, so that Astrophil's rejection of imitative orthodoxy both symbolises and reflects his ethical failures in striving to put poetry to debased use as a tool of temptation and seduction.

Past poetry defies Astrophil's quest, even attempts to block his pursuit of immorality: 'other's feet still seemed but strangers in my way' (1.11). But swollen with desire, 'thus great with child to speak' (1.12), Astrophil refuses to be diverted from his course. And so it is his wayward muse who acts as midwife, bringing his corrupt poetics to birth: 'look in thy heart and write'.

Astrophil's muse and his rejection of *imitatio* as a productive route to poetry have been read positively as indicators of 'an aesthetics for ori- ginality'.[39] But while the poem strikes a pose of – or feigns – innovation and inventiveness, it remains shaped by, and embedded within, literary conventions. As we have seen, in thematising its own status as poetry, it follows programmatic classical poems including those of elegy. The sonnet form is itself a gesture towards its Petrarchan inheritance, and the struc- ture of a sonnet sequence, the first in English, further asserts its relation to Petrarch. The ladder conceit of lines 3–4 owes a debt to neo-Platonism generally but also to Castiglione, and is itself based on *gradatio*, a standard trope of rhetoric. For all Astrophil's striving, and however much his muse might seem to endorse the idea of emotional authenticity, spontaneity, originality and artlessness, this is a complex and sophisticated text in which more seems to be happening than Astrophil is perhaps aware. It is in the space between Astrophil's understanding and the reader's that the virtuosity of the poem lies.

To contextualise the moral concerns which surrounded poetry at this time and which inform *Astrophil and Stella*, it is helpful to turn to Sidney's *Defence of Poesie*. Dating Sidney's texts is problematic but the *Defence* can be dated to after December 1579, and may have overlapped with the writing of *Astrophil and Stella*.[40] Probably written in response to Stephen Gosson's *Schoole of Abuse*, an anti-poetic treatise dedicated to Sidney, the very existence of the *Defence*, which takes the form of a forensic speech with Poetry being on trial, is a testament to the 'uncertain value of poetry' in this period.[41] William Tyndale, for example, in *An Answer to Sir Thomas More's Dialogue* (1530) calls the poet (in a generalising sense) 'the natural son of the father of all lies', so that the very term 'poet' might be used as a term of abuse.

In the *Defence*, the narrator rehearses 'the most important imputations laid to the poor poets' (905–6). These are that poetry is a waste of time, that it is 'the mother of lies' (908), and that it is 'the nurse of abuse, infecting us with many pestilent desires; with a siren's sweetness drawing the mind to the serpent's tail of sinful fancies' (909–10). Already we can see points of congruence emerging between Astrophil's poetics and cultural attacks on poetry by 'poet-haters' (845). Astrophil's deception and feigning, his 'pestilent desires' and his attempt to use poetry to tempt Stella from chastity are shown to imbue the sequence with precisely the facets of poetry that detractors used to attack it: Astrophil's verse corroborates rather than contests the criticisms laid against poetry.

The *Defence* goes on to argue that poetry can, and should, be a means to virtue: 'the final end is to lead and draw us to as high a perfection as our degenerate souls, made worse by their clayey longing, can be capable of' (296–8). All poets, the narrator claims, seek 'to know, and by knowledge to lift up the mind from the dungeon of the body to the enjoying of his own divine essence' (306–8). Astrophil, however, remains to the end of the sequence mired in his 'clayey longing', never escaping or transcending the desires of his body. The 'knowledge' that the virtuous poet attains and uses to raise himself towards the spiritual, becomes, in Astrophil's hand, Stella's knowledge of his own sexual desires and frustrations which, he hopes, will lead to the granting of the sexual favours he is pursuing. The *Defence* acknowledges the difficulty of achieving the status of a true and, implicitly, virtuous poet: 'by few men that art can be accomplished' (451–2). In Astrophil the opposite has been created, the corrupt poet, seeking not spiritual virtue but sexual gratification.

Before returning to *Astrophil and Stella*, it is worth looking at Gosson's text for the light that it, too, sheds on the dynamics at work in the sonnet sequence. *The Schoole of Abuse* is described by Gosson as 'a pleasant invective against poets'.[42] In it Gosson argues that 'amorous Poets ... discover their shame, discredit them selves, and disperse their poison through all the world' (1). That this 'poison' is specifically sexual in nature is made clear in his readings of Virgil and Ovid that immediately follow this opening statement: 'the one shows his art in the lust of Dido, the other his cunning in the incest of Myrrha, and that trumpet of Bawdry, the Craft of Love' (2). Beneath the surface wit of the poets lie, he contends, 'vanity ... wantoness ... folly' (2), where wit is like 'chaste Matrons apparel on common Courtesans' (2). The unwary reader risks being seduced by poetry which is not just likened to a prostitute but also to the cups of Circe which 'turn reasonable Creatures into brute Beasts' (2), and the golden apples which diverted Atalanta from chastity and the path of virtue to sinful lust (2). Gosson, it should be said, shows no apparent sense of irony in using classical myth and literature to castigate poetry.

To ensure that no one can misunderstand a message couched in such literary terms, Gosson clarifies that poetry is 'the blocks of the Devil that are cast in our ways' (2). In order to authorise his argument against poetry, Gosson calls on Plato: 'no marvel though Plato shut them out of his School, and banished them quite from his common wealth, as effeminate writers, unprofitable members, and utter enemies to virtue' (2–3). Plato is supplemented by 'Tullie' (Cicero) who 'accounted them the fathers of lies, Pipes of vanity, and Schools of Abuse' (3). It is worth noting here the association between poetry, effeminacy, lack of virtue and civic failure since these exact faults are demonstrated by Astrophil in the sonnet sequence. Poems 18 and 21 show the moral lassitude brought on by Astrophil's desire; 30 centres on his abandonment of political and civic interests, and 53 on his social shame; 47 foregrounds his fall into erotic slavery, an effeminising position, and 49 emphasises this with its image of Astrophil as a horse being ridden by Love.

Gosson employs an inverted 'ladder' conceit which itself speaks back to Castiglione and neo-Platonists when he traces the movement from poetry to an ultimate state of sin: 'from Piping to playing, from play to pleasure, from pleasure to sloth, from sloth to sleep, from sleep to sin, from sin to death, from death to the devil' (6–7). Astrophil, possibly following Gosson, does not challenge his representation but fulfils it: he is a figure for the 'amorous' and 'wanton' poets that Gosson denounces, who use the allurements of poetry in order to seduce their readers.

So *Astrophil and Stella* I stages a complex intervention in debates about the moral status of poetry. Astrophil, the poet within the narrative, is not represented as the ideal poetry-maker of the *Defence*, one who writes to 'teach and delight' (222), at least, not in any simple way. Instead, he is constructed to embody the faults culturally attributed, at least partially, to poetry: his verse is deceptive, designed only to seduce its readers, the foremost of whom is Stella, and to tempt her from chastity to sexual sin. Astrophil's rejection of *imitatio* and move away from an orthodox poetics is also a step towards moral bankruptcy so that the mode of poetic production is itself calibrated on an ethical scale. Astrophil's pursuit of originality and his move towards apparent emotional authenticity, sanctioned by his muse, is shown to be a paradoxical fall back into the common faults attributable, by its detractors, to poetry. His failure to live up to the ideal role of the poet offered by the *Defence* – to teach and delight – is instead turned into a negative exemplar – Astrophil is the illustration of a poet whose example we are not to follow.

But what of Stella? She is quite separate from the muse of the opening sonnet, and is instead positioned as the intended reader of the poetry. But at other points in the sequence she is shown to shift between reader, source of inspiration and, eventually, as a speaking voice, even a poet, in her own right. Like Cynthia, she is an unstable figure, alternatively complicit with, and oppositional to, the main poetic voice of Astrophil. In exploring the various roles allocated to Stella, we can investigate how she is made to work within the sequence, and assess the implications of her emerging voice for the metapoetic discourse we are tracing.

In many of the early poems, Stella is the archetypically objectified mistress. Especially characteristic is the extravagant blazon of sonnet 9 where she is described through an extended – and poetically stretched – architectural metaphor. Astrophil who claims in sonnet 3 that he will not follow those who 'cry on the muses nine' (3.1), or 'Pindar's apes' (3.3), or even those who 'with strange similes enrich each line' (3.7), falls definitively into the latter category as he describes Stella's face as 'Queen Virtue's court' (9.1), her mouth as a 'door' of 'red porphyry' (9.5–6), and her cheeks as 'porches rich' (9.7). This sonnet, like the other blazon poems, refuses all

subjectivity to Stella, turning her into no more than an ornamental artefact, an opportunity for Astrophil to display his own poetic wit.

In other poems Stella is a muse figure and a source of poetic inspiration.[43] The First Song blends these versions of Stella so that she is part
muse, part reader or listener, and part poetic material as she is blazoned
at length. Sonnet 67 makes her into a text which Astrophil strives to first
read, 'look on again, the fair text better try; | what blushing notes dost
thou in margin see?' (67.7–8), and then, in hope, to deliberately mis-
read: 'I am resolved thy error to maintain, | rather than by more truth to
get more pain' (67.13–14). Sonnet 45 shows us Stella as a potential reader of
Astrophil as text: 'then think, my dear, that you in me do read | of lover's
ruin some sad tragedy: | I am not I, pity the tale of me' (45.12–14). This
mini sequence culminates in sonnets 57 and 58 where Stella is shown not
just reading Astrophil's poems but reading them aloud to him in 58 ('the
anatomy of all my woes I wrote | Stella's sweet breath the same to me did
read', 58.11–12), and putting them to song in 57: 'she heard my plaints and
did not only hear, | but them (so sweet she is) most sweetly sing' (57.9–
10). In the Third Song she sings again and is likened to Orpheus. In all
these poems we learn that Stella reads and sings but we do not hear her
voice for ourselves. The first instance of direct speech from Stella is in the
Fourth Song.

The Fourth Song is set during an assignation at night between Astrophil
and Stella. The previous two sonnets, 84 and 85, sketch in a narrative which
brings Astrophil to the house of Stella's mother where she is staying. The
scene is set, tantalisingly, in Stella's bedchamber ('Your fair mother is abed,
| candles out and curtains spread; | she thinks you do letters write', 37–9),
and Astrophil makes pointed reference to the bed and its covering: 'these
sweet flowers on fine bed too' (15). We cannot tell whether Stella is complicit in this secret meeting or whether Astrophil has crept unasked to her
room, 'only joy, now here you are' (1), but his intent is unmistakeable: 'let
my whispering voice obtain | sweet reward for sharpest pain' (3–4). Of the
nine stanzas of the poem, the first eight end in the same refrain: 'take me
to thee and thee to me', and Stella's constant answer is 'no, no, no, no, my
dear, let be'.

On the narrative level, this song enacts the conflict between physical
desire and virtuous love which informs the sequence. Stella, by this stage,
has made her love for Astrophil clear and yet she will not succumb to
his seductive appeals and surrender her chastity. As Astrophil touches her,
she pushes him away ('Sweet, alas, why strive you thus? | Concord better

fitteth us. | Leave to Mars the force of hands', 43–6), until even Astrophil realises that she cannot be overcome: 'cursed be my destinies all, | that brought me so high, to fall' (51–2).

Re-writing the biblical Fall, Astrophil's 'fall' is into unwanted virtue rather than sin, and his expulsion is from Stella's bedroom, the site of his fantasies of a sexual Eden. His 'Eve' is not a tempter but the protector of the moralities which underpin this sequence. The Fifth Song, too, shows us an Astrophil who strives to undermine Stella's moral standing within the text by likening her to 'a devil, though clothed in angel's shining; | for thy face tempts my soul to leave heaven for thee' (81–2). Astrophil's inversion of the Genesis story may be read as being sanctioned by the subversive muse of the opening sonnet who privileges the debased desires of his heart.

Astrophil's tainted re-writing of the Eden story leads us back to a comparison between his poetry and the power of the poet as depicted in the *Defence*: 'freely ranging only within the zodiac of his own wit' (181–2) he can create a better world than Nature: 'her [Nature's] world is brazen, the poets only deliver a golden' (188). Readers and writers in Sidney's time had inherited a medieval equation between a classical golden world and the biblical Eden, so that it is partly an ideal of lost perfection. At the same time, accounts of the New World figured America, in particular, as a golden world both literally in terms of material wealth as well as sexually, 'in which no laws governed male sexual appetite, and nudity and sexual license prevailed'.[44] Astrophil's fantasies of an Eden in Stella's bedchamber with its 'sweet flowers on fine bed' (15) is clearly inflected by the latter accounts. Through his poetry he strives to recreate another Edenic golden world, but one filled only with sexual pleasure and erotic delight.

Within the context of the *Defence*, the poet's power is positioned as an overwhelmingly positive one, one which has the ability to draw human nature up from its 'clayey longings' (297) to 'as high a perfection as our degenerate souls … can be capable of' (296–8). But the *Defence* also foregrounds through this creation of a poetic golden world what is so disquieting about poetry to Renaissance thinkers: its capacity to be hubristic, to invert the natural order, to transform man into a god, and create a duplicate, counterfeit and false world. The danger is that poetry in the hands of a debased poet like Astrophil, whose only purpose is seduction and the sating of his sexual desires, has the power to corrupt rather than to uplift. Astrophil's re-writing of Stella as Eve, her bedchamber as Eden, and his own fall from the nearness of erotic satisfaction, illuminates exactly the threat of poetry, and the source of the anxiety it engenders about its right use which can be seen in Gosson's anti-poetic treatise as well as the *Defence*.

So in terms of the literary discourse which permeates the sequence, the Fourth Song is an important poem since it embodies sixteenth-century anxieties about the mis-use of poetry. It also performs the conflict between Petrarchan and neo-Platonic conventions and Astrophil's attempt to surmount them. His incursion into Stella's bedroom at night, his sexual insistence, his physical pressure on her, all speak to the overturning of conventional sixteenth-century literary erotics, an attempt, perhaps, to return to the underlying sexual mores of elegy which had been sanitised by Petrarch, but which re-emerge in Wyatt's poetry and, as we will see in the next chapter, that of Donne. In this struggle, it is Stella who safeguards Petrarchan and neo-Platonic virtue and morality, who keeps the sequence in order with her 'no, no, no, no' which closes each stanza. If Astrophil is the 'wanton', 'degenerate' poet of both Gosson and the *Defence*, then Stella is the moral exemplar and, perhaps, even the true poet conjured up by the *Defence*. Her role is that of both moral guardian and also defender of a mode of poetics which Astrophil strives to over-reach.

Importantly, too, Stella becomes a collaborative poetic voice which sustains this poem. The six-line stanzas which make up the song are built on four lines of Astrophil's persuasion, followed by his reiterated plea: 'take me to thee and thee to me'. Each stanza is then capped and closed by Stella's refusal, 'no, no, no, no, my dear, let be'. That final rhyming couplet repeated nine times is thus dependant on the combined voices of Astrophil and Stella, and the stanza would itself be incomplete without Stella's voice. Her following of his simple monosyllabic diction and metre mark Stella's complicity in this song, even while her refusal to accede to Astrophil's erotic demands demonstrates her rejection of the matter of his poetry. In contesting the contents while completing the form of the poem, Stella serves to displace, albeit in a minor way, the subversive muse of the opening sonnet, and presides over a poetic dialogue which merges narrative with metapoetic discourse.

The Fourth Song is an indicator of the emergence of Stella from source of inspiration, text and reader, to collaborative poetic voice. The Eleventh Song, the last song of the sequence and situated four sonnets from the end, shows an expansion of her role. In this poem Stella is no longer merely the respondent and her words are not confined to a single refrain. Also built on nine stanzas, this last song starts each stanza with Stella speaking in two lines, and then allows Astrophil to reply in three. The dynamic between the speakers is reversed as Stella interrogates or poses a question, and Astrophil responds. The rhyme scheme links their words, but now it is Stella who sets the precedent and Astrophil who follows after.

This is, in effect, Stella's farewell poem ('Come no more, lest I get anger', 37; 'well, be gone, be gone, I say', 41) and while in the narrative an emotional stalemate has been reached, the literary implication is that once Stella has achieved the status of poet in her own right, her function can be extended no further and she disappears from the text. The two sonnets which follow re-confirm her physical absence though she still, of course, haunts Astrophil's sonnets: 'unhappy sight, and hath she vanished by' (105.1), 'o absent presence, Stella is not here' (106.1). Within the story of the sequence, by the Eleventh Song Stella has admitted her love for Astrophil but will not compromise her chastity: her farewell is a sad one for both of them, though the song ends on a note of bathos as Astrophil has 'from louts to run away' (45).

Nevertheless, there is a moment within this song which indicates some moral development on the part of Astrophil. In stanza five, Stella tries to console Astrophil by telling him he will get over her loss and attach himself to other women, an idea which he rejects: 'I will think they pictures be, | image-like of saint's perfection, | poorly counterfeiting thee' (23–5). When she tells him that his reason should lead him away from such thinking, he counters: 'Dear, do reason no such spite; | never doth thy beauty flourish | more than in my reason's sight' (28–30). Recalling Castiglione, we remember that sensual love, epitomised throughout this sequence by Astrophil, is opposed to reason ('young men be wrapped in this sensual love, which is very rebel against reason', 305). Now Astrophil is perceiving and appreciating Stella through his reason, not just as a physical beauty but as a moral one. Her emergence as a poet and a presiding deity over this song allows Astrophil to gain some ethical and philosophical insight which supersedes his sexually acquisitive nature most usually foregrounded throughout the sequence.

This moment is, however, ephemeral. Stella retreats into silence and is heard no more in the final four sonnets, and Astrophil in 105 deems himself 'not in fault' (6) and 'guiltless' (10) in his love. And yet, there is a darker, more despairing note as the sequence ends with at least some intimations of Astrophil's possible maturing: 'that in my woes for thee thou art my joy, | and in my joys for thee my only annoy' (108.13–14).

Stella's emergence takes place not in the sonnets but in the songs, those points in the sequence which are interspersed between the overriding Petrarchan structure, thus liberating Stella's voice from the confining fourteen-line sonnet form and the muted nature of Laura. Laura, we should note, takes over from the voice of 'Petrarch' not in his sonnet sequence but in the *Triumph of Death*, a poem translated by Mary Sidney which we will look at in Chapter 5. When she speaks, Stella contests the anti-poetic arguments made by Gosson and personified by Astrophil. In her chastity, she represents a virtuous, constant morality which, towards the end of the sequence, is given equality with, perhaps even dominance over, the more questionable ethics – and poetics – of Astrophil. Stella's voice recuperates and compensates for that of Astrophil and becomes the moral guardian not just of this sequence but of poetry more generally. The female gendering of the muses and sibyl predetermine the metapoetic valence of female characters and voices, and protect a space within poetry which allows them to speak – even if only as ventriloquised personas of male poets. Chapter 5 returns to this issue and considers how these prior incarnations of female poetic voices might open up certain modes of writing to female author-ship, specifically by Sulpicia, Mary Sidney and Mary Wroth.

So *Astrophil and Stella* is a complex, sophisticated sequence that merges a compelling narrative and poetic virtuosity with a deeper engagement with the moral status of poetry itself. By reading it in conjunction with Propertius we can identify a preoccupation with writing and poetry, a discourse marked through the wayward muse of the opening sonnet and continued via Stella who, like Cynthia, shifts between muse, text, reader and poet. The struggle between Astrophil and Stella partly draws on that between 'Propertius' and Cynthia with both female figures emerging as creators of their own texts towards the end of the work, but the deeper substance of that dialogue differs, shaped by the varying literary concerns and anxieties of Augustan Rome and late sixteenth-century England. The Propertian text, in dialogue with the *Aeneid* and *Metamorphoses*, is interested in questions about the authoritative status of poetry, the *Astrophil and Stella* with its moral condition. Both sets of texts are, though, alive to questions of self-identity, with what it means to be a poet in Augustan Rome, and in Elizabethan England.

Sidney's Propertius can thus be read as certainly an erotic poet, but not one easily categorised or simply understood. The metapoetic subtext in Propertius serves as productive stimulus to the creation of *Astrophil and Stella* and animates it with a literary resonance and moral seriousness beyond that of simple poetic virtuosity. Astrophil and his wayward muse may certainly turn their backs on *imitatio* as a route to poetic excellence, but Sidney does not.

CHAPTER 4

'In Six Numbers Let My Work Rise,
and Subside in Five'

Authority and Impotence in Amores *1.5* and *3.7*,
Donne's 'To His Mistress Going To Bed' and Nashe's
Choice of Valentines

In this chapter we will explicitly practice the 'backwards reading' methodology discussed in the introduction. The reciprocal readings offered here
are thus separated into two stages: the next section starts with *Amores* 1.5
and 3.7, and considers what an association with Ovid enables in Donne's
and Nashe's texts. The following section then reverses the direction of interpretation and explores how readings of these Ovidian receptions might
inflect and reflect back on *Amores* 1.5. In line with Martindale's propos-
ition, re-reading Ovid via Donne and Nashe offers new perspectives on
a familiar text, and serves as a model for bringing previously unexplored
aspects of this elegy into focus via its later receptions.

Amores 1.5, the story of a successful sexual encounter, and 3.7, the impotence poem, have been read together before.[1] As both Alison Keith and
Alison Sharrock point out, Ovidian elegy might be read as 'programmatically impotent' so that 3.7 stands in for the general character of the genre
which frequently defines itself as 'soft' (*mollis*).[2] And yet, at the same time,
poems such as *Amores* 1.5 present a contrasting view of elegy as being built
on an aggressive and potent masculinity which positions seduction as
close to assault.[3] These two postures are reflected in the dynamic between
servitium amoris, 'the slavery of love', and *militia amoris*, 'the soldiering
or military campaign of love', the systems of tropes routinely utilised by
elegy.[4] *Amores* 1.1 also embeds this binary at the heart of elegy as 'Ovid'
describes the elegiac couplet: 'in six numbers let my work rise, and sink
again in five' (*sex mihi surgat opus numeris, in quinque residat*, 1.1.27).[5]
The phallic imagery is unmistakeable as the rise of the 'hard' hexameter
associated with epic is followed by the deflation of the 'soft' pentameter so
that the elegiac couplet is given the 'sexual rhythm of male performance'.[6]
What we have here are two systematic arrangements where hexameter,
epic, *militia amoris* and sexual conquest, are set against the pentameter,
elegy, *servitium amoris* and sexual failure, and the two alternate to create

both the elegiac couplet and elegy itself. In this model, *Amores* 1.5 and 3.7 may be read as the quintessential elements of the genre which constitute and embody what elegy is.

Turning to Donne and Nashe, what we will see in the texts studied here is that these two states of phallic power and disappointment are contained within single poems: the *Choice of Valentines* which alternates between sexual triumph and collapse, and 'To His Mistress Going To Bed' which, as read here, appears to be a poem of erotic achievement but conceals a subtext of fretful anxiety and unease.⁷ All four texts are built around a detailed sexual engagement between a man and his mistress, and the encounter is described with varying degrees of explicitness. Both the male and female bodies in these texts are thus symbolic constructs, and one of the aims of this chapter is to assess what cultural work they are made to perform in the texts under investigation, how the sexual acts they depict are made to signify.

As we shall see, Nashe positions his *Choice of Valentines* unequivocally as a response to Ovid.⁸ That Donne imitated Ovid and, particularly, the *Amores* is also widely recognised: M.L. Stapleton cites the general influence of the *Amores* on Donne's love poetry, principally through the characterisation of the narrative voice; Laurence Lerner sees Donne's *Elegies* as prime imitations of Ovid; Alan Armstrong goes so far as to call the *Amores* 'a valuable textbook for the poet [Donne]' and Jonathan Bate remarks on the influence of Ovid's Corinna on Donne's women.⁹ Prior to these critics, A. LaBranche discussed Donne's debt to Latin love elegy more generally, and described Donne's *Elegies* as 'the most original and carefully fashioned imitation of the classical genre'.¹⁰ Despite acknowledging the influence of Catullus and Propertius, LaBranche sees Ovid as 'the most certain source of elegy for Donne'.¹¹ John Carey agrees with LaBranche on the dominant influence of Ovid on Donne but contends 'there was more going on in their creator's brain than Ovid dreamed of'.¹² More particularly, Arthur Marotti, Carey and J.B. Leishman all agree that *Amores* 1.5 serves as a direct model for 'To His Mistress Going To Bed', and Marotti supports Carey's reading of Donne's text as a 'striptease' poem which takes delight in humiliating the woman at its centre through the act of commanding her to undress.¹³ The readings here offer a more complicated view of both Donne and Ovid, and the intertextual relationship between them.

Neither Donne's Elegy 2 nor Nashe's *Choice of Valentines* can be dated with accuracy but both have generally been attributed to c.1593. Donne was in his twenties at that time and finishing his education at Lincoln's Inn after studying at Oxford and Cambridge.¹⁴ His poem circulated in manuscript and its initial audience was most likely to have been his fellow

Inns of Court students: male, young, well-educated, both aspiring towards high social position and yet also asserting a rebellious and cynical attitude towards the Elizabethan court and its courtiers. When Donne's poems were first published posthumously in 1633, 'To His Mistress Going To Bed' was excluded from the collection, and the poem was not put into print until 1669 after the Restoration of Charles II.

Nashe's poem also circulated in manuscript and was not printed until 1899.[15] The poem is dedicated to Ferdinand Stanley, Lord Strange, who died in 1594 so it was certainly written before then. If it were one of the 'filthy rhymes' Gabriel Harvey accused Nashe of writing in his *Pierces Supererogation* (1593) then a composition date of 1592–3 seems indicated. There is, therefore, a strong possibility that the *Choice of Valentines* was actually circulating in manuscript in 1593, the same year as Donne's poem. Both poets were associated with the universities and Inns of Court, and both draw attention to Ovidian precedents.

Despite Nashe's explicit declaration of Ovidian *imitatio* in its epilogue, the *Choice of Valentines* still receives little critical attention other than by scholars concerned with trying to re-construct the boundaries of Renaissance 'pornography'.[16] Almost all Nashe scholars have dismissed the *Choice of Valentines* as being from the 'disreputable' part of his career, as a 'notorious pornographic verse narrative', as 'unadulterated' pornography or have ignored it all together.[17] By placing it alongside Donne's elegy and Ovid's *Amores*, the readings here challenge these superficial, even coy, judgements and attend to Nashe's text as certainly a bawdy poem but one with important things to tell us about Ovidian reception in the early 1590s.

'Her Arms Are Spread, and I Am All Unarmed Like One with Ovid's Cursed Hemlock Charmed': Reading Donne and Nashe through Ovid

Amores 1.5 stages the belated entrance of Corinna five poems into the first book.[18] In his opening poem, 'Ovid' has already been converted by Cupid from a potential writer of epic (*arma … violentaque bella*, 'arms and the violent deeds of war', 1.1.1) into a reluctant writer of elegy but, as he admits himself, has no object for his amatory verse, 'neither a boy, nor a maiden with long and well-kept locks'.[19] Drawing attention to the fact that an absence of a suitable love object does not necessarily preclude the writing of elegy, this first poem poses a question about the authenticity of the mistress (*puella*) which is carried through the rest of the book.[20] The *Ars Amatoria*, tentatively dated to c.2 BCE even comments on this ambiguity: 'and many ask, who is my Corinna'.[21] The arrival of Corinna in 1.5 might thus be seen as the 'true' beginning of the narrator's erotic enterprise and it is worth examining how this central poetic material is introduced.

> look! Corinna comes, draped in unfastened tunic, with divided hair falling over fair, white neck – such as 'tis said was beautiful Semiramis when passing to her bridal chamber, and Laïs loved of many men.

> Ecce, Corinna venit, tunica velata recincta,
>   candida dividua colla tegente coma –
> qualiter in thalamos formosa Semiramis isse
>   dicitur et multis Laïs amata viris.
>
> (1.5.9–12)

The injunction (*ecce*) draws immediate attention to Corinna's status in this poem as an object to be viewed, and the present tense of her arrival (*venit*) places her before us, as much for the readers' visual pleasure as for the narrator's. Her body is veiled (*velata*) by her tunic, both concealing and provocatively revealing itself at the same time, and the tunic is itself seductively 'unfastened' (*recincta*). Her hair, too, is loose on her neck rather than being formally dressed, and she is likened (*qualiter*) to Semiramis, the mythical Eastern queen of Babylon, a ruler in her own right and a woman known for her sexual prowess; and Laïs, a name associated with a number of expensive Greek courtesans. Images of the East, luxury, decadence, and an acutely sexualised beauty are all present in this crucial first description of Corinna. Possible allusions to Cleopatra and Virgil's Dido may be traced here, both Eastern queens like Semiramis, and associated with a disruptive female sexuality. There are also traces of Venus to be found, a goddess associated with the East via her birth near Cyprus, who is connected to prostitutes and prostitution generally and, especially, Laïs, whose ephemeral loveliness was traditionally contrasted to the immortal beauty of the goddess.[22]

Ovid's Corinna is thus a sexual spectacle created by the voyeuristic gaze of the narrator as an erotic object, and is placed within a tradition of images of women who exist, at least partially, for the sexual pleasure of men.[23] Despite the fact that she moves into the room while he is lying down, she is made a passive image of visual pleasure controlled by the watcher's eye and is without a reciprocal gaze of her own. The vision of the poet-narrator creates the matter of his poetry and then renders that controlling and productive gaze in words so that our pleasure in 'seeing' Corinna is a reflection of his: our eyes re-perform, through reading, the voyeuristic creative act of the poet.

To be looked at in Roman culture is not necessarily to be disempowered and to be the viewer does not always equate with being the winner in the visual hierarchy but certainly positions of authority and dominance are negotiated through the visual.[24] Since literary *eros* as articulated in erotic elegy is almost always non-reciprocal, it is not surprising that visuality is one of the spheres in which the asymmetry of this particular type of eroticism is played out.

So to return to *Amores* 1.5, it is worth examining the scene before Corinna's arrival. It is a hot day (*aestus erat*), just past noon, and the narrator is lying in the middle of his bed (*medio … toro*). The shutters to his window are half-opened (*pars adaperta fuit, pars altera clausa fenestrae*), and the resultant dimness in his room is likened to that of a shaded woodland, or twilight or the break of day.[25] The reiteration of words conveying intermediate or liminal points is striking: 'the middle hour' (*mediamque … horam*), 'the middle of the couch' (*medio … toro*), 'one part … the other part' (*pars … pars altera*), 'twilight' (*crepuscula*), 'when night has gone but the day has not yet sprung' (*ubi nox abiit, nec tamen orta dies*). The scene set is both a prosaic time for rest in the hottest part of the Mediterranean day but also a time between time heralding the possibility of dreams, visions, epiphanies. Noon, for the ancient Greeks and Romans, is as replete with 'paranormal possibilities' as midnight.[26]

As well as this eerie sense of being on a threshold which seems to presage something supernatural, the text simultaneously points to an atmosphere of sensuality, albeit one with hints of fear and violence. *Aestus* might mean 'hot' or 'sultry' but it also means 'passion' which, together with the image of the narrator lying on the sleeping couch, creates an aura of sexual anticipation. The imagery of woodland (*silvae*) invokes the potentiality of the *locus amoenus*, recalling the site of many of the rapes of nymphs in Greek myth and in Ovid's own (not yet written) *Metamorphoses*. *Fugiente … Phoebo* is a metaphor for the departure of the sun, but *fugiente*, 'fleeing', also reminds us of the number of mythic female characters who flee from the pursuing Apollo, not least, of course, Daphne who would become the archetype of the elegiac – and Petrarchan – beloved. And the narrator himself describes the shadowy light as that which 'shrinking maids should have whose timid modesty hopes to hide away'. The image of 'modest girls' (*verecundis … puellis*) whose chastity (*pudor*) leads them to seek hiding places (*latebras*) supports the subtext of mythic sexual pursuit and the girls who try to escape sexual violation. It thus serves as an ironic prefiguration of Corinna's arrival whose own appearance and behaviour have a complex relationship to ideas of modesty, chastity, hiding and sexual aggression.

So how does the text enable our understanding of Corinna who arrives so enigmatically after this build up of atmosphere and mystery? One way in which Corinna has been read is as a figment of the narrator's sexual imagination.[27] In this account, she is created by the poet as a sexual fantasy and offered to us as readers to share, implying an ideal audience of male readers. This notion fits with the problem already aired in 1.1 that 'Ovid' has been turned from epic poet into elegist by Cupid but has no 'real' material with which to work. Propertius, as we have seen, constructs Cynthia as textual *materia* for his elegies and as the embodiment of the poetry produced so it is unsurprising that Ovid's texts adopt a similar trope following his elegiac predecessor. Propertius 1.3, especially, where the narrator gazes on a sleeping Cynthia and re-constructs her in his imagination as always 'like' (*qualis*) something else (Ariadne helpless and abandoned by Theseus; Andromeda lying in bed after having been rescued by Perseus; a sleeping bacchante exhausted by her frenzy, 1.3.1–6) is recalled by Ovid's use of *qualiter* in describing Corinna.[28] Both Cynthia and Corinna are likened to mythic (or semi-mythic in Ovid's case) women who are associated with an overt sexuality (Semiramis, Laïs, Ariadne, a bacchante) which prefigures their own appearances and suggests their sexual availability in the eyes of each narrator. Each female figure is composed from a pre-existing repository of erotic images which shade and narrow the possibilities through which we might view these women, making them appear inevitably and almost teleologically sexual.

Specific aspects of Augustan visual culture might inflect the creation and representation of Corinna in this poem. Scholars have commented on the overwhelming number of sexually explicit images commonly available in Rome at this time.[29] Erotic frescoes, paintings, engravings, sculptures abound in both a public and private context: on the walls of public buildings such as bath-houses and of private homes; on cups, gemstones, mirrors and lamps. The paintings found in the luxurious Villa Farnesina on the Tiber, for example, have been dated to c.20 BCE, close to the time the *Amores* were being written, and are examples of the Roman taste for sophisticated erotic paintings showing beautiful Hellenised bodies and a penchant for mythic scenes.

Ovid himself gives us further examples of the contemporary prevalence of erotic art: in the *Tristia* he writes 'surely in our houses, even as figures of old heroes shine, painted by an artist's hand, so in some place a small tablet depicts the varying unions and forms of love'.[30] In the *Ars Amatoria*, too, he mentions books detailing sexual postures, and describes various sexual positions which, according to John Clarke, might be based on erotic

images in sexual handbooks.[31] In his description of the bedroom in which
he is lying in 1.5 'Ovid' does not describe the walls as being painted but the
possibility does exist that his Corinna is not just a sexual fantasy conjured
up from within his mind but an embodiment of a scene he might be
looking at, an actual incarnation of a wall-painting or statue, art brought
to life. This reading invokes the myth of Pygmalion, foreshadowing Ovid's
own version in the *Metamorphoses*, of the male artist and his female creation.[32] Prior to the *Metamorphoses*, *Amores* 1.5 operates in the same aesthetic space: the transformative nature of the imagination is shown to be
determinedly gendered as both 'Ovid' and Pygmalion obscure the distinction between art and female flesh.[33]

The idea of Corinna as a perfect piece of art is borne out in the detailed
description of her naked body:

> As she stood before my eyes with drapery laid aside, nowhere on all her
> body was sign of fault. What shoulders, what arms did I see – and touch!
> How suited for gripping is the form of her breasts! How smooth her body
> beneath the faultless bosom! What a long and beautiful side! How youth-
> fully fair a thigh!

> ut stetit ante oculos posito velamine nostros,
>   in toto nusquam corpora menda fuit.
> quos umeros, quales vidi tetigique lacertos!
>   forma papillarum quam fuit apta premi!
> quam castigato planus sub pectore venter!
>   quantum et quale latus! quam iuvenale femur!
>
> (1.5.17–22)

Corinna's body is produced through the visual description of what the
narrator sees and feels, recreating the artist's vision and touch in words.
Menda, translated here as 'fault', also means a textual correction, the
ancient equivalent of a printer's or typesetter's error, thus revealing Corinna
in terms of a perfect textual artefact. At the same time, her physical perfection is that of a work of visual art: not just a poem or a book of poetry
but also a statue or carving of marble or ivory. Especially telling is the sense
that this Corinna is more beautiful than a real woman could be.

So one way of reading Corinna which is sanctioned by the text is as a
piece of hyper-real erotic art brought to life through the force of the viewer's
imagination. Another is to see her in the context of divine epiphany, and
the Latin precedent suggested by several scholars as an intertext for this
reading is Catullus 68 where Lesbia comes to meet the narrator at the
borrowed house of Allius:[34]

Thither my fair goddess delicately stepped, and set the sole of her shining
foot on the smooth threshold, as she pressed on her slender sandal.

> quo mea se molli candida diva pede
> intulit et trito fulgentem in limine plantam
> innixa arguta constituit solea.
>
> (68.70–2)

The textual joke of Catullus' *candida diva* being turned into Ovid's *candida dividua* is cited as support for this reading, and the idea of epiphany is certainly upheld by the mysterious atmosphere evoked at the start of the poem. Chapter 4 will return to these notions of Corinna as art-work and as divinity after reading Donne and Nashe, and will examine how these later receptions of 1.5 allow us to combine both ideas and recalibrate what they might be made to mean. For the moment, though, it is instructive to consider the nature of the physical encounter between the narrator and Corinna, and the way that it is inverted in *Amores* 3.7.

'I tore away the tunic … but still she struggled to have the tunic shelter her' (*deripui tunicam … pugnabat tunica sed tamen illa tegi*, 1.5.13–14): in keeping with the tropes of *militia amoris*, physical love is represented as a battle (*pugnabat*) where instead of seduction we witness the violent ripping away (*deripui*) of Corinna's clothes. Once naked, the aggression is transferred from the woman's coverings to her body itself: 'how suited for gripping is the form of her breasts!' (*forma papillarum quam fuit apta premi*, 1.5.20). 'Suited for' (*apta*) suggests this suppressed violence is provoked by Corinna's own body. In terms of the binary being traced between hard (*durus*) and soft (*mollis*) this poem aligns itself with the conditions of epic struggle, with the 'rise' of the hexameter, and the successful completion of the act of love.

There are two further points worth noting in this poem in preparation for the way in which they are treated in 3.7 as well as the sixteenth-century receptions: the aftermath of this encounter is depicted in terms of mutual pleasure ('outwearied, we both lay quiet in repose', *lassi requievemus ambo*, 1.5.25); and the sexual act itself is glossed decorously ('who does not know the rest?', *cetera quis nescit?*, 1.5.25). The presence or absence of reciprocity, and the articulation or silencing of the actual mechanics of intercourse become key indicators to the way the other texts under consideration locate themselves in relation to *Amores* 1.5.

Amores 3.7 may be read as an instructive companion piece to 1.5.[35] In this text 'Ovid' recounts a story of sexual failure, an encounter marred by his body's refusal to perform. The mistress in this poem appears not to be Corinna, but is beautiful (*formosa*, 3.7.1), longed for (*votis saepe petita*, 3.7.1), and willing (*osculaque inservit cupida luctantia lingua*, 'and with eager tongue implanted wanton kisses', 3.7.9). Despite this, however, the narrator's body remains 'limp, powerless' (*languidus*) and he lies uselessly on the bed, in contrast to his earlier triumph. The girl tries to arouse him through enticing words and flattery (*et mihi blanditias dixit dominumque vocavit*, 3.7.11), but her calling him 'master', a hierarchical term of status and dominance, only serves to underscore his lack of potency at this moment. His own laments centre on his lack of masculinity: 'what is the point of being young and male? My girlfriend found me neither young nor male' (*quo me iuvenemque virumque?* | *Nec iuvenem nec me sensit amica virum!*, 3.7.19–20), 'though she had no man in her grasp' (*sed vir non contigit illi*, 3.7.43). The girl tries more direct means of stimulation: 'applying her hand and gently coaxing it' (*molliter admota sollicitare manu*, 3.7.74), but to no avail: 'no rising was possible through skill or tricks' (*nullas consurgere posse per artes*) and 'it' continues to 'lie down' (*procubuisse*, 3.7.76). Eventually the girl flounces from the bed still wrapped in her unbound tunic (*tunica velata soluta*, 3.7.81), so like the one worn by Corinna in 1.5 (*tunica velata recincta*, 1.5.9), and is forced to cover up the 'shameful' fact that her lover is unable to perform.

Amores 3.7 thus serves as a counter to 1.5, and is an embodiment of 'softness' (*mollitia*) as the vigorous masculinity of the earlier elegy falls away and is replaced by a wry poem of lethargy and limpness. The (eventual) reciprocal sexual pleasure of 1.5 is turned into a mutual frustration, and the visualisation of Corinna's body is exchanged for a greater focus on the under-performing male body which calls the narrator's masculinity into question. If 1.5 incorporates the 'hard' rise of the hexameter of elegy and the values encoded alongside it, then 3.7 embodies the 'soft' pentameter. Importantly, though, the impotence represented by 3.7 is a temporary one, and the poem itself foregrounds this point when the narrator addresses himself to his errant member: 'Now, too late, just look at it, it is well and strong, now clamouring for business and the fray.'[36] The movement is a cyclical one, alternating as do the metrical elements of the elegiac couplet. Other metaliterary readings of 3.7 suggest that it operates as a disengagement with the elegiac project, and as a farewell to the genre, suggestive ideas for our reading of Nashe to come.[37] Also worth noting here in advance of turning to Donne and Nashe is that this poem, in line with 1.5, while dealing explicitly with a sexual encounter – even a failed one – remains 'lexically inoffensive'.[38] The ways in which our sixteenth-century receptions either conform (Donne) or abandon (Nashe) this practice will be assessed for what they might tell us about those poems, their relationships to each other, and their use of Ovid.

Situated like *Amores* 1.5 in the intimacy of a bedroom, Donne's 'To His Mistress Going To Bed' (Elegy 2) is another voyeuristic text which implicates the reader in watching and overhearing an erotic engagement between the narrator and his mistress. It takes the form of a monologue given only through the male lover's voice, and has an undecided narrative status: it might be a textual representation of an encounter where the words of the poem are spoken aloud by the lover; it might represent the private thoughts of the lover that exist only in his mind as he watches his mistress prepare for the night; or it might be the sexual fantasy of a lone would-be lover creating a mistress out of his imagination – perhaps with the literary help of erotic texts such as Ovid's 1.5. If the latter, Donne's narrator can be read as becoming 'Ovid' in this poem, re-enacting the prior text for his – and our? – sexual, but also literary, pleasure.

The elegy is articulated via a series of imperatives: 'off with that girdle' (5), 'unpin that spangled breastplate' (7), 'unlace yourself' (9), 'off with that happy busk' (11), thus encoding a familiar gender dynamic and hierarchy of command: the dominant and dominating male unclothing, even if only through words and not deeds, a silent and sexually accommodating mistress. Where 'Ovid' tears off Corinna's tunic, Donne's lover orders his mistress to undress herself. Masculine power and prerogative are eroticised as a sexualisation of authority, an equation between the entitlement to demand and a state of sexual licence which turns the love object into an eroticised and objectivised spectacle to be enjoyed.

Undermining this position, however, is a strange visual absence at the heart of Donne's text. While the mistress' costume is elaborately described even as it is discarded (her girdle 'like heaven's zone glistering', 5; her bodice as a 'spangled breastplate', 7), her underlying body remains invisible. Contrary to the expectations set up by *Amores* 1.5, we are refused, even cheated of, the sexual description of the female body which the text implicitly promises. Instead, the mistress' clothes become a substitute and proxy for her self and are themselves fetishised in place of the body beneath.

When the mistress is ordered to 'unlace yourself' (9), the sound of her clothes coming off replaces her voice: 'for that harmonious chime | tells me from you, that now 'tis your bed time' (9–10). It is not the mistress who speaks but her coverings, so that communication is between the lover and her clothing. His 'envy' (11) a line later is for her 'happy busk' (11), again foregrounding the emotional relationship that seems to exist between the male lover and his mistress' elaborate costume. (Busks, to which we will

return presently, were placed within a bodice as stiffeners.³⁹) Where we
might expect to find a detailed and itemised description of the mistress'
body (the equivalent of Ovid's 'What shoulders, what arms did I see – and
touch! How suited for pressing the form of her breasts! How smooth her
body beneath the faultless bosom! What a long and beautiful side! How
youthfully fair a thigh!', 19–22) instead we find something depersonalised,
depicted in unspecific topographical terms: 'a far fairer world' (6), 'your
gown going off, such beauteous state reveals | as when from flowery meads
th'hill's shadow steals' (13–14), and the famous cartographical evocation
of the woman's body as 'O my America, my new found land' (27). This
unexpected resistance to *Amores* 1.5, this refusal to display the female body
purportedly at the centre of this poem, forces us to re-consider what this
text is actually 'about': how can we read this textual rejection of the blazon,
the visual representation of a naked female body, and what is at stake in
this repudiation?

   While the mistress' body is concealed beneath elaborate territorial
metaphors, it is the male lover's body which, in contrast to the case of the
specific Ovidian and generic elegiac precedents, is displayed in unequivo-
cally sexual terms: 'the foe oft-times having the foe in sight | Is tired of
standing though they never fight' (3–4). This exploits the trope of *militia
amoris* but here it is not just the idea of courtship which is imagined as a
struggle between two lovers (as is the case, for example, in *Astrophil and
Stella*) but the act of love itself is imaged as an act of warfare, an idea we
have already seen in *Amores* 1.5. The text merges the witty and sexual language so associated with Donne with a vocabulary of dominance as well
as the terms of politics ('foe'). Critically, though, while the text certainly
gestures towards the kind of masculine dominance we might expect, it is
the sexualised male body which is put on display in line 4, and it is the
naked male body which covers and continues to conceal the female at the
end of the poem: 'to teach thee, I am naked first, why then | what needst
thou have more covering than a man?' (47–8).

   So what is happening in this text? The brisk and dominating masculinity of the opening line ('all rest my powers defy', the implied impatience
of that repetition of 'come') surrenders to an appropriation of the female
imagery of pregnancy ('until I labour, I in labour lie') thus creating a fissure
in the textual gendering of the narrator. The image of being swollen with
rampant desire is an explicit reference to the male narrator's sexual arousal,
a visible signifier of masculinity, as is made clear in lines 3–4 ('the foe
oft-times having the foe in sight | Is tired of standing though they never
fight'). But that 'tired' (4), implying both eager sexual impatience and the

possibility of an exhausted detumescence, points to an unsettling gender ambiguity. Masculinity is set against varying opposites: femininity in the pregnancy imagery, emasculation in the potential loss of virility, rendering the narrator disturbingly hermaphroditic in the visual imagery which represents him.

Discussing Ovid's figure of the hermaphrodite in the Renaissance, Jonathan Bate describes it as the representation of 'complete union', perfect in itself, derived from the myth of unified beings in Plato's *Symposium*.[40] Golding's translation of Ovid's Hermaphroditus tale, though, tells quite a different story, and one more sensitive to Ovid's text. For both Ovid and Golding, this story is a troubling account of unsettled gender allocation resulting in the closest thing in the *Metamorphoses* to a female rapist.[41] Significantly for a story which is so centrally about gender, it is the nymph Salmacis who takes on the hunter-voyeur role most usually gendered masculine, and Hermaphroditus, with his 'tender skin' (4.426) and 'naked beauty' (4.427) who becomes the object of her masculinised gaze. The two do become one but the result, not surprisingly, is not the perfect one which Bate suggests: 'they were not any longer two but, as it were a toy | of double shape. Ye could not say it was a perfect boy | nor perfect wench' (4.468–70), and Hermaphroditus' own lament is for his lost manhood. The text describes him as 'weakened' (4.472), as 'but half a man' (4.473), and when he prays that other men using the spring might also be rendered as tainted as he is, he terms it 'infected' (4.481). Golding's own comment on this story in the 1567 dedicatory epistle describes Hermaphroditus as 'effeminate … weak' (116).

The Hermaphroditus story is one of a struggle for gender dominance rather than a merging of qualities, a dilution of masculinity rather than a unifying and strengthening, and so it is worth considering how these ideas might be present in the hermaphroditic imagery used at the start of 'To His Mistress Going To Bed': to what extent might the myth of Hermaphroditus be a shadow text hidden beneath the surface of Donne's elegy, another version of the loss of masculinity depicted in *Amores* 3.7? Certainly the refusal of the text to display visually the mistress in the way that Corinna is flaunted in *Amores* 1.5 confounds our expectations. The text complicates matters still further by at least partially presenting an overtly sexual view of the male narrator's body which is itself centred on a single body part, and that one which is most closely associated both with masculine potency but also potentially with its opposite, the impotency which haunts *Amores* 3.7. The fact that it is the narrator's sexually aroused body which is made the object of the gaze in Donne's text serves to render the narrator simultaneously hyper-masculine, a kind of concentrated phallic object, yet also effeminised through his positioning as a fragmented, visualised sexual object, of being looked at in the way women are cultur- ally, and textually, looked at.

Gender disruption also appears later in Donne's elegy in an allusion to the Atalanta and Hippomenes tale which Venus tells Adonis in the *Metamorphoses*. Donne's narrator muses:

> Gems which you women use
> Are like Atalanta's balls, cast in men's views,
> That when a fool's eye lighteth on a gem,
> His earthly soul may covet theirs, not them.
>
> (35–8)

In Ovid's text (*Metamorphoses* 10.560–707) Atalanta is a huntress who refuses marriage while Hippomenes is, like Hermaphroditus, a beau- tiful man-boy. Donne's text adds another twist as he reverses the gender roles: in the myth it is Hippomenes who throws down the golden apples given to him by Venus to distract Atalanta from the race and, thus, to win her as his wife. Donne's text inverts this story so that it is women who distract masculine eyes with their gems. It is men, in Donne's poem, who take on the female role of Atalanta, diverted from their (sexual) course, while women become the Hippomenes figure. The fact that both Atalanta and Hippomenes are themselves already confused in terms of gender markers only adds to the disorder. We should also note the opposition in Donne's text between the gems, the things that are 'theirs', women's, to be coveted, and 'them', women themselves – foregrounding the tension noted earlier between a woman's costume and the woman's body concealed by it.

Donne's text takes issue here with the problematics of vision, so intri- cately interwoven with the subject of gender: women's gems are displayed by them in a self-protective gesture to ward off the sexually possessive and penetrative male gaze just as, earlier in the poem, the 'spangled breastplate' serves as armour to deflect 'th' eyes of busy fools' (8). The mistress' clothing and ornaments become contested objects which serve to conceal her body from the multitude of male eyes while simultaneously revealing it to her male lover, so that the act of sexual seeing is itself a triumph of masculinity articulated in terms of competition against other men. To confirm this, the text proceeds to liken clothed women to 'books' gay coverings made | for laymen' (39–40) while their unclothed bodies are 'mystic books, which only we … must see revealed' (41–3). That 'must' (43), however, disrupts the confidence of the claim and opens up a space between what ought to be the case – that the lover alone should see his mistress unclothed – and a potential other reality which might have her revealing her body to his male rivals. The insistence on her clothing as a form of protective armour serves to separate the privileged lover from other men thus confirming his possessive masculinity which is itself dependent on refusing other men a sight of his mistress. This authoritative position, however, is intensely vulnerable since any display of the mistress' body to competitor male eyes will serve to damage the lover's own masculinity, undermining the exclusive visual power upon which it is partially reliant.

The correlation between absolute possession of the female body and secure masculine status is foregrounded in the imperial metaphor of mistress as new world territory: 'O my America, my new found land | my kingdom safeliest when with one man manned' (27–8). The male lover is figured as a colonist not just appropriating her body to himself but enhancing his rank and position, turning himself into a king through his possession of a 'kingdom' (28). But the sense of conquest is irrevocably linked with an awareness of the fragility of this state: the security of his 'kingdom' can only be protected by the exclusion of other men, and the repetition of 'man manned' (28) reiterates the association between possession and masculinity. Turning the female body into metaphorical geographical territory is an attempt to make her akin to property, a commodity which can be legally owned ('where my hand is set, my seal shall be', 32), in a way in which a mistress, perhaps, cannot be, being instead a possession with the inherent power to undermine the status of its purported owner. The awed and confident voice of ownership within the text ('my mine of precious stones, my empery | how blessed am I in this discovering thee!', 29–30) co-exists with a consciousness of its own vulnerability based on the slippery and inconstant nature of women, not least within Donne's other elegies as well as their Latin precedents.

The anxiety of masculinity articulated in sublimated form in this poem leads us back to the busk of line 11 which the narrator says 'I envy | that still can be, and still can stand so nigh'.[42] The busk is a phallic object ('straight, erect and hard') made of a rigid material such as whalebone, ivory or wood, used to stiffen a woman's bodice or corset. The fear, however wittily expressed by the narrator, is that unlike the 'happy busk', which remains consistently erect despite its nearness to the mistress, his own body might let him down in proximity to what he most desires. The text returns a number of times to this image of male arousal: the 'standing ... foe' of line 4, the busk of line 11, and lines 21–4 when the difference between 'ill spirits' and 'angels' can be seen in the response of the male body as 'those set our hairs, but these our flesh upright' (24). The almost obsessive repetition of this image of masculine potency simultaneously contains within it the insidious reminder of impotency: both the failure of masculine bodily virility which does not have the permanent capacity of the 'happy busk', and the helpless absence of arousal such as might be caused by the 'evil sprite' of line 23 which only sets a man's hairs upright.

To press this idea further, Sandy Feinstein points out that the busk and corset were, in the late sixteenth century, thought to have the potential to make women look more like men as they served to flatten their breasts and stomach.[43] It was also feared that they might act as a form of contraception, preventing women from getting pregnant because of the pressure on, and restriction of, their bodies, or even bring on abortions thereby promoting female sexual promiscuity free from the threat of pregnancy. The busk, then, functions not just as a visual signifier of physical masculinity but also as a cultural symbol for the threat of women appropriating masculine looks as well as masculine sexual morals. It is a subtle form of cross-dressing that confuses the physical differentiation of male and female. Within the context of Donne's poem, it hints that the hermaphroditic imagery noted in relation to the narrator might also encompass the mistress, turning her into a disturbingly androgynous figure. Importantly, however, the text strips the woman, or at least wishes to, of precisely this masculine attribute ('off with that happy busk', 11) which might itself be seen as a gesture towards 'correcting' and reasserting a more conventional gender differentiation.

Nevertheless, the implicit comparison with the eternally erect busk brings to our attention the potential for failure and impotence on the part of the male body, and is, therefore, the source of the narrator's explicit 'envy' (11). The mistress' busk functions as a form of portable masculinity which might be assumed or discarded at will. Within the poem, it is the narrator's command that the busk be removed thus eliminating any potential for competition even while acknowledging the busk as a possible substitute for the male lover himself.

Nashe's *Choice of Valentines* offers a suggestive context within which to situate Donne's elegy since Nashe's text also takes these themes of masculine anxiety and potential phallic substitutes and builds an entire semi-obscene, comic narrative around them. Indeed, its alternative manuscript title, *Nashes Dildo*, locates these issues right at the centre of the text.[44] Set in a city brothel ('an house of venerie', 24), the *Choice of Valentines* recounts the stages of an extended and explicit amorous encounter between the male narrator, Tomalin, and his prostitute lover 'Mistris Francis' (56). Written in a bawdier erotic register than the Donne text, Nashe's poem indulges the reader with a detailed description of the heroine's sexual parts:

> A pretty rising womb without a weam,
>   That shone as bright as any silver stream;
> And bore out like the bending of an hill,
>   At whose decline a fountain dwelleth still;
> That hath his mouth beset with ugly briars,
>   Resembling much a dusky net of wires.
>
> (109–14)[45]

Topographical imagery for the female body ('silver stream', 'hill') links this to Donne's description of the mistress but Nashe's text has no qualms about the explicitness of what he is describing. Nashe's use of *Amores* 1.5 can also be traced from line 109 where 'weam' meaning 'wen' or a spot or blemish recalls Corinna's description at *Amores* 1.5.18: 'nowhere on all her body was sign of fault'. 'Wen' is the word used for *menda* in Christopher Marlowe's translation of *Amores* 1.5: 'not one wen in her body could I spy', though Nashe certainly read Ovid in the original Latin as well.

As the poem progresses, it seems that it is the details and specificities of Francis' erotic charms which crucially overwhelm her male lover, paralysing him rather than inciting him to perform:

> It makes the fruits of love eftsoon be ripe,
> And pleasure plucked too timely from the stem
>   To die ere it hath seen Jerusalem.
> O Gods, that ever any thing so sweet,
>   So suddenly should fade away and fleet.
> Her arms are spread, and I am all unarm'd
>   Like one with Ovids cursed hemlock charm'd.
>
> (119–24)

The connection between female attractions explicitly described and the male lover's phallic inadequacies is made graphically clear so that it is precisely the blatant and quasi-pornographic nature of the textual description which serves to emasculate the lover ('I am all unarm'd', 121). 'Unarm'd' recalls both the 'foe' of Donne's elegy as well as the more pervasive imagery of elegiac *militia amoris*. *Amores* 3.7 is explicitly recalled both where 'Ovid' describes his failed and paralysed body: 'my body, as if drugged with chill hemlock' (*tacta tamen veluti gelida mea membra cicuta*, 13), and in the imagery of the drooping rose (*languidiora rosa*, 3.7.66) in Nashe's 'plucked too timely from the stem' (120).

By placing Nashe's text beside Donne's, we can clarify one of the reasons why Donne's narrator refuses to articulate a frank and uninhibited description of his mistress' naked body, and instead veils it in metaphor ('O my America, my new found land'), in 'white linen' (45) and, finally, masks it with his own body (48). The fear of sexual failure, as represented by Nashe's Tomalin, appears to be staved off by the narrator's poetic distraction, and masculinity is maintained by obscuring overwhelming female charms beneath textual extravagance and ornament. The linguistic lavishness and expansiveness of Donne's text serve not just a literary purpose but also a narrative one, that of displacing the narrator's sexual fervour ('until I labour, I in labour lie') and allowing him a sense of sexual control, a quality which is itself gendered masculine.

In the face of Tomalin's sexual failure, Francis, in Nashe's text, does not hide her disappointment and, like the mistress of 3.7, resorts to manual stimulation: 'Unhappy me, quoth she, and will it not stand? | Come, let me rub and chafe it with my hand' (131–2). In an unexpected departure from the Ovidian precedent, she succeeds in rousing her lover. The act of intercourse proceeds with great gusto ('now high, now low, now striking short and thick; | now diving deep, he touched her to the quick', 147–8), but the narrator's pride in his prowess is short-lived and, with the plea 'but what so firm, that may continue ever?' (178), he is forced to bring the encounter to an unexpectedly rushed end, despite his lover's entreaties that he continue. Francis is not, however, completely dependent on the untrustworthy male body, that 'faint-hearted instrument of lust' (235). She has a substitute ready, 'my little dildo' (239) which 'stands as stiff as he were made of steel' (242). Taking her own pleasure, she gloats at the way the penis substitute 'usurps' (249) 'poor Priapus' (247) 'in bed and bower | and undermines thy kingdom every hour' (249–50).

Despite the narrative arc, this is not a poem which celebrates or is even interested in female sexual autonomy or pleasure: instead it offers graphic images of the female body in positions designed to give voyeuristic sexual gratification to its primarily male readers.[46] At the same time, beneath the surface bawdy, it tells a potent 'warning story' of what happens to masculinity when women are allowed to possess a phallic surrogate of their own. The notion of the emasculated male becomes intimately entangled with the masculinised female so that the hermaphroditic imagery encompasses both, and one transgressively gendered position is caused by, and matched with, the other. Nashe's Francis is masculinised not just by her ownership of the dildo which makes her male lover obsolete but by her ambiguously gendered name, the description of her 'manly thigh' (103), and a strange use of 'his' in the description of her 'womb': 'that hath his mouth beset with ugly briars' (113).

The textual interactions between Ovid's *Amores*, Nashe's *Choice of Valentines* and Donne's elegy offer reasons for both Donne's narrator's sexual 'envy' of his lover's busk as well as his command that she discard it. The 'kingdom' (28) which the narrator of Elegy 2 wants to possess exclusively, the rulership which 'Ovid' achieves but is unable to exploit (*quo regna sine usu*, 3.7.49), is endangered by Nashe's Francis and her sexual toy which 'undermines thy kingdom' (250). The shadow of *Amores* 3.7 threatens the outcome of Donne's text just as *Amores* 1.5 protects and endorses it.

So the Donne and Nashe texts read here each encompass both *Amores* 1.5 and 3.7, and merge them into a single poem; and each of these poems incorporates the two postures of elegy, encoded via extended ideas of 'hard' and 'soft'. Donne's poem maintains the unobjectionable diction of Ovid, keeping it within the bounds of what modern scholars have called the 'erotic' without crossing over into the so-called 'pornographic' of Nashe's poem, but these are clearly problematic categories to apply retrospectively whether to Roman or to early modern texts.

What we can say, though, is that these texts themselves appear to be testing the boundaries of how far they are able to go, what is culturally authorised in poetry, or a certain type of poetry, and where the limits might be reached. *Amores* 1.5 dwells on the eroticised description of Corinna's body, but then coyly looks away when it comes to the actual sexual engagement: 'who does not know the rest?' (1.5.25). 'To His Mistress Going To Bed' teases the reader and flirts with his or her expectations but settles on an absence where the eroticised description of the female body 'ought' to be. The *Choice of Valentines* takes the opposite stance and outdoes Ovid making its sexual description explicit. From the dedicatory proem the text states that it is a 'verse of loose unchastity' (Proem, 5) and that it will be 'painting forth the things that hidden are | since all men act what I in speech declare' (Proem, 6–7). The epilogue, too, returns to this question of how far poetry might go: 'yet Ovid's wanton Muse did not offend. | He is the fountain whence my streams do flow' (Epilogue, 4–5). Nashe, of course, knew quite well that Ovid's poetry did apparently transgress unstated rules and that he was exiled from Rome: the fictional 'evidence' of Ovid's own poetry claims the cause to be a poem (*carmen*) as well as a mistake (*error*).[47] Since Ovid's exile was a central component of his persona in the sixteenth century, this statement by Nashe has to be read as a disingenuous and deliberately provocative one.[48] Nashe appears to be defending himself with the dubious authority of Ovid, but he is also speaking against the cultural idea that poetry should be moral, that it should 'teach and delight', an idea we have already seen being debated by Philip Sidney's texts in the previous chapter.

The *Choice of Valentines* exceeds the boundaries of, and extends, *Amores* 3.7: where Ovid's poem leaves the mistress frustrated, Nashe's text allows her to achieve her own sexual satisfaction without the use of a male body at all, rendering Tomalin not just impotent but unnecessary. The dildo thus operates both as a move away from 3.7, taking it into new territory, and as an extension of its reasons for anxiety. The covert disquiet about the ever-erect busk evinced in 'To His Mistress Going To Bed' is made overt, and is proved to be scarily (if comically) accurate: Tomalin is too easily displaced by a woman with her own phallic substitute.

So these texts by Donne and Nashe rework issues of sexual power and impotence already present in Ovid. At the same time, they demonstrate a more specific disquiet, even dissent, concerning gender which may register as a contemporary 1590s resonance centred on problematic issues concerning female autonomy and empowerment. Written and in circulation in c.1593, during the final troubled phase of Elizabeth I's forty-five-year reign, it is possible to read these texts as having political overtones concerned with ideas of masculine hegemony, female power and the contestation of authority.[49] The next section looks at how these ideas are put to work in the Donne and Nashe texts and then returns to *Amores* 1.5 to read the politicised back into that poem.

'O My America, My New Found Land': Re-Reading Ovid's Corinna through Donne and Nashe

On 1 June 1599 John Whitgift, Archbishop of Canterbury, and Richard Bancroft, Bishop of London, issued an order to the Stationers' Company that 'no Satires or Epigrams be printed hereafter'.[50] Known as the Bishops' Ban, this edict led to the confiscation and burning of books which included Marlowe's translation of the *Amores*, verse satires by John Marston and John Davies, the published pamphlets in the public quarrel between Gabriel Harvey and Thomas Nashe, and all of Nashe's other works. The *Choice of Valentines*, having never been printed, escaped the ban.

This was not the first time that Nashe had found himself in trouble with the authorities. In 1597 he had written the first act of a play called the *Isle of Dogs* and left it with the theatrical company, Pembroke's Men, with whom he was working. Ben Jonson completed the play, and it was performed for the first and only time in July 1597 before being suppressed by the Privy Council at the request of the Lord Mayor and Aldermen of the City of London.[51] Ben Jonson was arrested and thrown into the Marshalsea. Nashe's rooms were searched and he only evaded prison by fleeing London for Norfolk. Sadly, the play was destroyed, but it seems to have been a political satire attacking the Elizabethan court and its institutions such as the Privy Council. The instructions given by the Privy Council to Richard Topcliffe were to trace those responsible for this 'lewd play ... containing very seditious and scandalous matter', and ensure that the 'lewd and mutinous behaviour' of the players be punished. When the case against Ben Jonson was heard on 15 August 1597, the play was again described as 'containing very seditious and scandalous matter'.

The *Isle of Dogs*, written in part by Nashe, provides a suggestive context through which to read the earlier *Choice of Valentines*. Both texts could be read as showing a rebellious stance towards forms of authority: explicitly political power and influence in the case of the play; a more generalised engagement with the way in which literature and gender may be put to contested and subversive use in the poem. The *Choice of Valentines* has been described as an 'anti-Petrarchan' poem which disrupts the neo-Platonic underpinning of that mode of writing, and re-locates itself in a city brothel, the site of '(relatively) autonomous women'.[52] As many scholars have noted, Petrarchan tropes were widely appropriated to structure the Elizabethan court, facilitating female rule while allowing both the servitude of male courtiers and an insistence on the chastity of the monarch.[53] Contesting the Petrarchan, then, as Nashe does, has decisive and, possibly, scandalous politicised overtones.

The *Choice of Valentines* also, as we have seen, upsets the authority of Ovid's poem, turning 3.7 from a poem of frustration into one of female usurpation of masculine prerogatives and resultant sexual satisfaction. The poem sanctions female empowerment but only at the cost of masculine hegemony. It thus seems to give local expression to a wider cultural anxiety about the rightful hierarchy of gender which is especially potent given the presence of a female monarch on the English throne. The 'kingdom' which is at stake in Donne's poem is destabilised by Francis and her portable 'penis' which 'undermines thy kingdom every hour' (250).

A brief return to Donne's elegy may be instructive here. A number of scholars have particularly drawn attention to correlations between Elizabeth's natural or physical body, her body as political entity and Donne's metaphor of his mistress' body as America: an implicit, though unverbalised, association with Virginia, both geographical territory and itself a kind of hallucinatory vision of the queen's virgin body.[54] The language of sovereignty and exploration is part of a discourse of power articulated in the poem but control, authority and supremacy shift within Donne's text in suggestive ways. Only the queen and her government had the power to authorise ('licence', 25) 'rovers', government-sponsored privateers like Raleigh and Drake, and the movement of the text takes the male lover from the position of a man seeking patronage and permission ('licence my roving hands', 25) to the possessor of the authorising female body. 'My mine of precious stones, my empery' (29) with its insistent double possession ('my mine') at the start of the line makes it clear that the power dynamic has altered and that the sovereign has become the colonised. The shift from female to male authority is completed as 'where my hand is set, my seal shall be' (32) where the act of sealing up the female body through sexual consummation is also figured as taking control of the Great Seal of England, and putting it back under male control. The female body of Donne's text thus becomes an index of politicised power as well as masculinity, as the lover moves from suppliant to imperial conqueror. The fantasy enacted by the text is not simply an erotic one, but also one which enables the almost treasonous political usurpation of female rule and the restoration of male authority.

So both Donne's and Nashe's texts can be read as having a politicised overlay. They use Ovid's representations of sexual encounters in *Amores* 1.5 and 3.7 to articulate transgressive ideas about gender hierarchies, imperial politics and the political appropriation of Petrarchism at the Elizabethan court. They employ Ovid, in other words, to enable an engagement with the pressing concerns and anxieties of elite, educated, sophisticated and relatively young men (and, possibly, some women) in 1590s England. But can we, following Martindale, read these concerns back into Ovid's texts, 'unlocking' fresh interpretations? If the male and female bodies in Nashe and Donne are inscribed with issues of contested authorities and political mythologising, then how might we re-read Ovid? It is certainly not new to detect the 'political commitments' of Ovid's poetry.[55] As Alison Sharrock says, 'the entire Ovidian corpus is in dialogue with the most powerful contemporary signifiers of the masculine order: Augustus, *arma* ... and political life'.[56] Picking up on the earlier discussion of how Corinna in *Amores* 1.5 is associated with the idea of epiphany, and is depicted as being like a perfect work of visual art, the next section argues than the natural correlation would be with Venus, specifically statues of Venus, thus allowing a covert dialogue with the political myths which support, and are proliferated by, the Augustan regime.

The literary tradition of men who desire statues, and for whom statues come to life, particularly statues of Aphrodite or Venus, is a long one.[57] The classic case in antiquity is the famous story of the man who fell in love with Praxiteles' Aphrodite of Cnidos.[58] So enamoured was he that he contrived to be locked in the temple overnight with the statue. By morning, when the temple was unlocked, the physical evidence of his passion was clear to see from the stains on the marble: and Aphrodite herself was so offended that she punished the man by sending him mad.[59] Roman copies of the Cnidia from around the first century BCE show her standing in a classic *pudica* (modest) pose with one hand covering her pubic area and the other (sometimes) over her breasts.[60] While this gesture shows the goddess screening her body against the invasive gaze of the viewer of whom she seems acutely aware, it also draws attention precisely to what is supposedly concealed, not surprising given that this is a representation of the goddess of sexual love. The function of Corinna's half-open tunic in 1.5.9 may be read as parallel to that of Venus' hands, drawing attention to a comparison between the goddess and 'Ovid's' view of Corinna. Roman statues of Venus from around the first century BCE frequently showed her veiled by sheer drapery making the likeness even closer.

Praxiteles was said to have modelled his Aphrodite on his mistress, the courtesan Phryne (who is mentioned in Propertius 2.6), so that the story, at least from Pliny's time, and almost certainly earlier too, blurred the two categories of women – courtesan/mistress and goddess – into a single figure. Corinna too, along with Cynthia and Tibullus' Delia, has sometimes been seen by modern scholars as a Hellenised courtesan, and comparisons have been drawn between the mistresses of elegy and nude statues of Venus.[61] In a Hellenistic source for the Pygmalion story, the statue was not just brought to life with the support of Venus, as is the case in Ovid's version, but was actually a cult image of the goddess.[62] Ovid's ecstatic catalogue of Corinna's physical flawlessness (*in toto nusquam corpore menda fuit*, 'nowhere on all her body was sign of fault', 1.5.18) thus enables a textual slippage between elegiac mistress, perfect artistic artefact, and Venus, the archetype of the transcendent eroticised female body.

Later poems in the *Amores* make Corinna an explicit analogue to Venus: in 1.7 when 'Ovid' hits her, the violence is likened to Diomedes' attack on Aphrodite as she carries Aeneas from the battle (*Iliad* 5.330–52): 'he was the first to smite a goddess – I am the second!' (*ille deam primus perculit – alter ego!* 1.7.32). And in 2.14, the abortion poem, the narrator contrasts Corinna to Venus: 'If Venus had violated Aeneas in her pregnant belly the future world would have been bereft of Caesars' (*si Venus*

Aenean gravida temerasset in alvo | Caesaribus tellus orba futura fuit, 2.14.17–
18). These mentions of Aeneas, Venus and 'Caesars' are crucial markers of
how these texts engage obliquely with Augustan mythologising about the
foundation of Rome. Of particular importance to our reading of 1.5 is the
Augustan regime's use of the myth of the Julian family springing from
Venus to support its legitimacy.[63] Reading back from Donne and Nashe to
Ovid with a careful eye for the political mythologising of female bodies,
and an active engagement with the sexual politics of a ruling administra-
tion proves a productive way to re-orient *Amores* 1.5.

The *Amores* would not be the only Augustan text to interrogate the political appropriation of Venus. The *Aeneid*, a central Augustan text to which
we will presently return, embeds Venus at its heart as the mother of Aeneas
and, hence, the future Julian family through his son Ascanius/Iulus. Julius
Caesar claimed descent from the goddess and dedicated a temple to Venus
Genetrix in 46 BCE.[64] Visual representations of the goddess and her cult
worship were an important part of Augustus' 'revival' of Rome after the
bitter years of civil war.[65] The Forum Augustum, especially, with its statuary
of Venus and Aeneas was a crucial monument of political myth-making.[66]
Reliefs in the temple of Mars Ultor (Mars the Avenger) in the forum seem
to have featured cult groups including Mars and Venus, often with Cupid.
Along the sides of the forum, too, were stone processions of Romans, the
'best or greatest men' (*summi viri*), including Aeneas, his father Anchises,
and the Julii family. At the centre was a statue of Augustus in a war chariot labelled *pater patriae*, 'father of the country'. The whole construction
was a magnificent visual narrative, unrelentingly didactic, that positioned
Augustus as the inevitable, legitimate and rightful leader of Rome, in a
line which starts from Venus and Anchises. By offering a representation of
Venus, however indirectly, *Amores* 1.5 sets up not just literary resonances
with Virgil's text but also constructs a dialogue with the politics and
ideology of Augustus' reign made visible throughout the city.[67]

As previous scholars have noted, it is reductive to see the Augustan
exploitation of visual imagery as merely propaganda, especially as its specific forms did not necessarily originate with Augustus himself.[68] What we
might call Augustanism is 'a product of contestation and dialogue' so that
so-called 'anti-Augustan' texts are as 'Augustan' in nature as the political
ideology they might superficially appear to reject.[69] But certainly the use of
art, buildings, religious ritual, public ceremony, even the proliferation of
visual imagery in Augustan texts such as the *Aeneid* with its extended and
numerous ecphrases and visions, are a testament to the primacy of looking
and the importance of visual communication under Augustus.[70] It is

against this background that we can read the images of Corinna mobilised in *Amores* 1.5 as an embodiment of Venus.

It has become commonplace to recognise the problematic nature of Venus as founding ancestor of the Romans. While Augustan ideology worked hard to foreground her maternal role as Venus Genetrix, it proved impossible to completely repress her association with unbounded sexuality and disruptive erotic passion, and she remained a metonymy for sexual pleasure. The adulterous 'family' group of Venus, Mars and Cupid made prominent in the Augustan Forum is especially problematic in relation to Augustus' moral legislation and the attempts to regulate marriage and criminalise adultery.[71] The laws attempted to re-establish the polarity between '*matrona* and *meretrix*' which had allegedly become somewhat blurred in Roman society, but this is precisely a dichotomy which Venus herself refuses to endorse. Famed for her liaison with Mars, Venus turns her betrayed consort, Vulcan, into a source of both laughter and scorn. *Amores* 2.5 draws attention to this aspect of Venus when the goddess is figured as a precedent for the unfaithful mistress giving passionate kisses 'such as Venus bestowed on Mars' (*sed Venerem Marti saepe tulisse suo*, 2.5.28). *Amores* 1.8 claims that 'Venus reigns in the city of her Aeneas' (*at Venus Aeneae regnat in urbe sui*, 1.8.42), a statement which might be read as having positive connotations in terms of Augustan ideology – until we remember that the words are in the mouth of a nurse or, in elegy, more probably a brothel owner (*lena*) who is advising a young girl new to the profession. *Amores* 1.11, too, specifically mentions the temple of Venus (*Veneris ... aede*, 1.11.26) when the narrator promises to dedicate his tablets to the goddess if they prove to be successful aids in his acts of seduction.

So the reign of Venus can be used to either promote or undermine official morality, playing on the complexity of image already invested in Venus, despite attempts to stabilise her as a grave and protecting maternal figure. Returning to *Amores* 1.5, it seems that the multiple interpretations of Corinna that it enables – as human mistress, erotic artwork, statue or even Venus herself – serve as a critique of any attempt to unify the inherently multifaceted nature of Venus and narrow it down to a single interpretation. The Ovidian text insists on remaining open, refusing the closure of a defined and uncontested interpretation, and so opposes not just a single meaning for Corinna but combats the process of interpretative closure itself.

Ovid is not alone, however, in problematising Venus: the *Aeneid*, too, allows a disconcertingly disruptive and unruly side of Venus to intrude into a text which appears to be concerned with, amongst other things, the containment of passion and the establishment of order. Venus in her maternal, nurturing and protective role is prominent at the start and end of the poem. When she goes to Jupiter in book 1 she is depicted as saddened (*tristior*, 1.229) and with her eyes brimming with tears (*lacrimis oculos suffusa nitentis*, 1.229), a sober picture of anxious and vulnerable motherhood. Her concern is not just for her son but for the whole race of Romans who are to spring from his line as rulers (1.230–55) and it is her loving concern which prompts Jupiter's great prophetic speech (1.257–96) of Roman 'dominion without end' (*imperium sine fine*, 1.279). In book 12, too, after Aeneas is wounded in battle, Venus herself fetches herbs from Mount Ida to staunch the wound and take away all his pain (12.411–22). However, after the book 1 prophecy, in a much discussed episode, Venus' interaction with her son takes on an unsettling flavour which provides a suggestive frame for our reading of *Amores* 1.5.[72]

After the storm Aeneas, with a few of his ships, is washed up on the shore of Carthage. He ventures inland with Achates for companion and is met by his mother 'amid the forest' (*media ... silva*, 1.314). Faint cross-echoes can be heard between this and the forests of *Amores* 1.5.4 (*quale fere silvae lumen habere solent*), and the reiteration of forms of *medius* already noted. The intertext with the Odysseus–Nausicaa episode in *Odyssey* 6 is well established.[73] That encounter, too, takes place in a wood, and the naked Odysseus is dependent on a strategically held branch to cover his exposed body.[74] Woods are notorious sites in Greek myth for erotic encounters with gods, goddesses, nymphs and satyrs. Aeneas' mother is dressed as a virgin huntress (*virginis os habitumque gerens et virginis arma*, 1.315) foregrounding her ironic appropriation of the guise of the chaste followers of Diana as well as prefiguring the first sight of Dido later in the book who is herself likened to Diana (1.498–504). The Virgilian text dwells for eight lines on Venus' appearance and makes her a sensuously enticing figure: 'she had ... given her hair to the winds to scatter; her knee bare, and her flowing robes gathered in a knot'.[75] The picture of her undressed hair and semi-covered body recalls and anticipates Corinna's first appearance in *Amores* 1.5.

The Odysseus–Nausicaa encounter is modified in a number of ways in the Virgilian text: the nakedness is transferred from the man to the semi-clothed goddess; Odysseus' likeness to a hungry lion hunting cattle or sheep (*Odyssey* 6.130–4) is re-written as Venus the huntress (*venetrix*); Odysseus speaks first in Homer, but in Virgil Venus does (1.321), before Aeneas has the chance to fulfil his Homeric role, and her speech is ambiguously teasing: 'tell me, youths, if perhaps you have seen a sister of mine straying here' (*Iuvenes, monstrate, mearum | vidistis si quam hic errantem forte sororum*, 1.321–2). *Errantem* means to go astray figuratively as well as literally, so 'to stray from the path of virtue'. Given the woodland setting, the idea of a nymph going sexually astray is implicit so Venus' words are both uncomfortably flirtatious in speaking to her son, and also foreshadow the consummation of Dido's doomed love for Aeneas which takes place during a hunt.[76]

Pre-empted in this way, Aeneas' reply returns to the Homeric model: 'but by what name should I call you, o maiden? For your face is not mortal nor has your voice a human ring; o goddess surely!' (*o – quam te memorem, virgo? Namque haud tibi vultus | mortalis, nec vox hominem sonat; o dea certe!*, 1.327–8).[77] The self-conscious and gently erotic flattery of Odysseus, known for his cunning and eloquence, sits uneasily with Aeneas, and is made doubly disturbing by the fact that he really is speaking to a goddess, and that she is his mother.

To compound the disquiet generated by this version of Venus, the Virgilian text is here replaying not just an Odyssean model but also the scene in the 'Hymn to Aphrodite' which recounts the original sexual encounter between Venus and Anchises, Aeneas' father, which resulted in Aeneas' own birth. In that text, too, Venus appears as 'an unmarried girl' (82), and Anchises' first words on seeing her are 'hail, lady, whichever of the blessed ones you are that arrive at this dwelling, Artemis or Leto or golden Aphrodite' (92–3).[78] There are further parallels, too, as Anchises promises 'I will build you an altar on a hill top, in a conspicuous place, and make goodly sacrifices to you' (100–1); echoed by Aeneas' 'many a victim shall fall for you at our hand before your altars' (1.334).[79]

In the Hymn, Aphrodite wakes Anchises after their sexual encounter and reveals herself to him as a goddess: 'but when he saw the neck and lovely eyes of Aphrodite he was afraid and averted his gaze' (181–2). He accuses her of deception, 'but you did not tell the truth', and fears his punishment for sleeping with a goddess. The revelation of Venus in the *Aeneid* re-writes this prior text. Venus, having prepared Aeneas for his meeting with Dido, drops her disguise and one of the indicators of her divinity is her bright rosy neck (*rosea cervice refulsit*, 1.402). Then comes an ambiguous line: 'down to her feet fell her raiment, and in her step she was revealed, a very goddess' (*pedes vestis defluxit ad imos, | et vera incessu patuit dea*, 1.404–5). We have already seen Venus described with her tunic knotted up above her knees and so it is often assumed that her tunic is untied so that it flows down to her feet thus covering her from the knee down in a dignified matron's pose.

Kenneth Reckford, however, offers a different and intriguing reading: he proposes an understanding of *defluxit* not just as 'flowed down, descended' but also as 'slipped away' so that the tunic does not flow down from the knee but slides off completely leaving Venus naked to her son's eyes. The step that then reveals Venus as a goddess is a step out of her clothes, and the revelation is partly a recognition (*adgnovit*, 1.406) since Venus, as we have seen, is frequently represented as naked. Aeneas, who fails to recognise the goddess clothed, identifies her immediately once her clothes slip off.

The 'Hymn to Aphrodite' is again recalled here, since Anchises does not just see Venus naked but actually unclothes her himself: 'he undid her girdle and divested her of her gleaming garments' (164–5). Aeneas, too, like his father before him, reproaches Venus for her deception, accusing her of mocking him with false words and images: 'You are cruel! Why do you mock your son so often with vain phantoms? Why am I not allowed to clasp you hand in hand and hear and utter words unfeigned?' (*quid natum totiens, crudelis tu quoque, falsis | ludis imaginibus? Cur dextrae iungere dextram | not datur ac veras audire et reddire voces?*, 1.407–9).

This reading of the Virgilian Venus undermines the decorous representation of the goddess of Augustan political orthodoxy as the disturbingly eroticised encounter with her son replays a previous sexual engagement with his father, thus subtly associating the goddess with a form of incest. Rather than appearing as the grave and serious mother of the Roman race, Venus is an acutely problematic maternal figure for Aeneas, and it is significant that this disquieting fissure in the image of the goddess is indicated through an uncertainty over what Aeneas sees. The extended description of Venus' appearance functions like an ecphrasis, and serves as a site of intertextuality, complicating the text.

The figure of Venus even in the *Aeneid* is thus seen in a plurality of ways shifting between protective and seductive, grave and frivolous, clothed and naked, mother and virgin, a force for order or for chaos. As is the case in *Amores* 1.5, the single view of Venus Genetrix central to Augustan legitimisation is resisted and contested, and that uncertainty is negotiated through the visual representation of a sexualised female body.

Amores 1.5, then, rather than being a purely private, erotic poem, interacts imaginatively with the visual culture of Ovid's Rome, specifically with erotic visual art, with ecphrastic moments in the *Aeneid*, and with the ideological use of imagery to support Augustan power. This is not, of course, to deny its status as an erotic poem, but the voyeuristic gaze which makes a sexual spectacle of Corinna itself serves to position the text as one which is engaging sceptically with the politicised use of visuality in the Augustan city. Enabling Corinna to be viewed as mistress, courtesan, goddess, perfect art object and even an analogue to Venus herself, the text refuses any form of interpretative closure and remains defiantly open. At the same time, the text draws attention to some ambivalent and deeply problematic moments in the *Aeneid*, just as the *Metamorphoses* will do. By foregrounding the blatant sexuality of Venus-Corinna, *Amores* 1.5 surreptitiously equates 'Ovid' with both Mars and Anchises, and responds in a sly, mischievous way to the Virgilian text and its Homeric predecessors, as well as the attempts of Augustan ideology to delimit the meanings of Venus.

Politicised readings of Donne's elegy and Nashe's *Choice of Valentines* thus re-calibrate interpretations of *Amores* 1.5, and offer valuable insights into what appears, on the surface, to be a simple, though slippery, text of an afternoon sexual encounter. All these poems make use of the textual production of a female body to serve as a form of vocabulary which bridges erotic and politicised discourse, thus breaking down any easy distinctions between them. Officially sanctioned stories of female virginity, chastity and moral probity are countered by poetry which refuses to accept or uphold the politicised narratives which legitimate and support specific cultural and political regimes. In Ovid's elegy, the placing of a Venus figure in this openly sexual poem problematises Augustan mythology which strives to harness and curtail Venus, to re-appropriate the qualities associated with her, and to re-write her story. By recalling and presenting us with the 'other' Venus, Ovid's text places itself in dialogue with the politicised monuments of Augustan Rome, and participates in a discourse where the political and the erotic become intertwined.

The 'anti-Petrarchan' nature of Donne's and Nashe's texts perform a similar cultural work in undercutting, and exposing, the Petrarchan appropriations of the Elizabethan court, built around the uneasy concurrence of female virginity and potentially emasculating female monarchical authority. Notably, these poems are acutely dependent on phallic models of power, and representations of penetration, or the failure to penetrate, are used to confirm or destabilise conventional hierarchies of gender, status and authority. Fantasies of sex and power are enacted on, with and through both male and female bodies but not in a straightforward way. They do not make an uncomplicated textual exchange where the poetics of love are merely a coded way of talking about politics.

The dialogue between these texts is a complex one. Donne and Nashe in their receptions of *Amores* 1.5 and 3.7 show themselves to be astute, sensitive and creative readers of Ovid, and demonstrate the ability to re-make his texts to have specific resonance in 1590s England. Importantly, their

Ovid is not merely a poet of frivolous, erotic verse but also a politicised poet in the broadest sense, one who provides a model for constructing and articulating transactions with imperial or political power through images of sex and desire. The language of sex as power is already present in the Augustan appropriation of Venus, and the Elizabethan requisition of Petrarchan dynamics, and so these texts site themselves within, as well as against, these pre-existing discourses, contesting their authority from the inside.

The playful and pointed Ovidian wit seems to have been particularly attractive to communities of readers and writers associated with the universities and Inns of Court, and his transgressive response to Augustan ideology perhaps finds a natural home amongst the young, well-educated, worldly, cynical and sceptical communities to which Donne (at this stage of his life) and Nashe belong. It should be remembered that reading potentially subversive texts could be as transgressive an act as writing them – as the Bishops' Ban of 1599 recognises.

The 'backwards-reading' which Martindale advocates proves to be a productive approach to unpacking the complex dialogues between these texts. In reality, however, it is difficult to isolate readings in strict chronological fashion, in whichever direction, and we always, to some extent, read poetry against other poems privileging a relational intertextual reading practice over one centred on a temporally based 'influence'. Nevertheless, approaching Ovid through Donne and Nashe can open up even such a familiar text as *Amores* 1.5, re-calibrating the way it can be made to mean, and bringing unexpected readings into focus.

The texts considered in this chapter take images of eroticised female bodies and manipulate them to participate in varying discourses sometimes quite separate from that of female sexuality. The female body itself seems to be a common cultural currency which places it at the disposal of male authors, and the question of who ultimately 'owns' women's bodies remains unresolved. The next chapter pursues this issue and looks at what happens when female authors intervene in elegiac and Petrarchan discourse. The complicated and problematic relationships between female authorship, women's narrative voices and representations of the eroticised female body will be the subjects of our investigations into the elegiac texts of Sulpicia, the 'Petrarchan' translations of Mary Sidney and a sonnet of Mary Wroth.

CHAPTER 5

'My Heart ... with Love Did Inly Burn'

Female Authorship and Desire in Sulpicia, Mary Sidney's Antonie *and Mary Wroth's* Pamphilia to Amphilanthus *1*

Petrarch's sonnets are organised around the narrator's hopeless, unrequited love for the chaste, virtuous Laura. As is well known, she is cold, disdainful, sometimes unkind, and it is her very elusiveness which sustains and perpetuates the Petrarchan narrative, giving it its unfinished, always-still-happening character. The *Triumph of Death*, however, shatters this narrative in a provocative, and hitherto under-explored, fashion, and does so through the ghostly voice of Laura whose shade returns from the dead. Drawing explicitly on the narrative situation of Propertius 4.7 where Cynthia comes back from the underworld, this poem has 'Petrarch' asking Laura whether she has ever regretted her refusal of his love. Her response, taken from Mary Sidney's c.1599 translation, is this:[1]

> Never were
> Our hearts but one, nor never two shall be:
> Only thy flame I tempered with my cheer;
> This only way could save both thee and me;
> [...]
> A thousand times wrath in my face did flame,
> My heart meanwhile with love did inly burn,
> But never will my reason overcame.
>
> (2.88–102)

Laura's revelation is that she was never the chill and aloof beloved of the 365 sonnets, and that 'Petrarch's' love has not been unrequited: like the Petrarchan lover himself, her 'heart ... with love did inly burn' (101).

This statement couched in Laura's voice annihilates the emotional basis which has sustained the *canzoniere* and collapses the structure upon which Petrarchan erotics have been built. If Laura has always reciprocated 'Petrarch's' love, then this poem does not just challenge and complicate the Petrarchan narrative but destroys it completely. The sonnets turn out to be purposeless, almost comically mistaken, and Laura's revelation throws the Petrarchan mode into an existential crisis. Significantly, this disruption is encoded through a female voice which thus characterises itself as an ideological force for poetic chaos and a form of literary anarchy.[2] Might this, then, be a reason why Sidney was drawn to translate this poem, offering, as it does, the opportunity for a female voice to speak out against the genre from within its very heart?[3]

The Petrarchan genre is a capacious and accommodating one that does not irretrievably shut out a female voice, and the evidence comes from Petrarch's own text, where Laura herself subverts the dominant narrative, breaking down the hierarchies of lover and beloved, male and female, subject and object. While Laura speaks and declares her love, separating herself from her previous representations through the view of 'Petrarch', she also blends her characterisation back into his. The reason for her silence, she explains, was always the support of his own troubled virtue: 'only thy flame I tempered with my cheer; | this only way could save both thee and me' (2.90–1). The moral high ground remains with Laura who 'never will my reason overcame' (2.102) even when she turns from beloved into lover.

It remains, of course, disturbing that Laura is only allowed to speak and articulate her love when she is dead: she never quite relinquishes the chaste and now almost angelic nature with which the earlier texts had imbued her. Nevertheless, this poem is an important example of the way in which the female voice, even when ventriloquised in male-authored Petrarchan texts, may be manipulated to open up the dominant narrative and contest it from within. It may be precisely this space within the genre to which Mary Sidney's translation chooses to draw attention,

Chapters 2 and 3 have already demonstrated that ventriloquised speech attached to female characters can be used by male authors to weave alternative voices into their texts, rendering them complex and multivocal.[4] This chapter concentrates on the ideological space mapped out by these frequently disruptive voices and considers how these prior male appropriations of the female voice in elegy and Petrarchan poetry might serve to invite, even provoke, the intervention of female authors – in this case Sulpicia, Mary Sidney and her niece, Mary Wroth.[5] What happens when these fictional voices are inhabited not by male authors but by female writers, and how do they enable women to insert themselves into literary genres whose categories and concerns have been described as overwhelmingly gendered masculine? This chapter investigates how male authors, by creating disruptive female voices within their own texts, prime elegy and its Renaissance cognate of Petrarchan poetry as a mode of writing accessible to female authorship actively, if unintentionally, enabling women writers to insert themselves into these poetic genres without irretrievably distorting or destroying the contours and conventions which serve to characterise the forms.[6]

Recognising that instances of female speech may already be manipulated to provide an alternative and, frequently, transgressive voice within male-authored erotic texts, this chapter investigates how this opening is productively exploited by the authentic female voices of Sulpicia, Mary Sidney and Wroth who thus collude with the pre-existing conventions even while they disrupt them. Genre, however unstable, certainly plays a role in shaping the production of gender in elegiac and Petrarchan texts – but where does the agency lie when a woman chooses to write in one of these modes? To what extent can she negotiate a gender position that is contained within the poetic practices already laid down by previous male poets and yet, somehow, not be constrained, or have her voice muted, by those same conventions?

The main concerns of this chapter are thus not Mary Sidney's or Wroth's imitation and direct reception of Sulpicia, something which cannot be proven, but the ways in which both women actively engage with, and exploit, elegy's already existing space for notions of female desire and authorship. Cynthia's re-writing of the Propertian master-narrative in 4.7, the disorderly voices of Laura and Stella who refuse to remain as silent, worshipped women and assert themselves as lovers in their own right, the voice of Francis in Nashe's poem who contests the dominant cultural narratives of patriarchy and masculine sexual hegemony, all offer transgressive precedents which permit authentic female voices access to this mode of poetics, even if always in a problematic fashion.

The next section offers readings of Sulpicia's elegies, transmitted in the corpus of Tibullus, and is especially concerned with the way in which she draws attention to her disruptive presence as a female lover within the elegiac world.[7] Always knowing and acutely self-conscious, Sulpicia's texts exploit and re-shape the gender models upon which elegy is constructed. Turning to Mary Sidney, the subsequent section focuses on her *Antonie*, a closet drama which she translated from Garnier's French play *Marc Antoine*.[8] The play is not conventionally labelled 'Petrarchan' in nature but is read here as reworking the gender dynamics of the elegiac and Petrarchan modes, especially in the love dialogue constructed through the voices of Antony and his queen, and the articulation of female desire by Cleopatra. The final section moves forward to the beginning of the seventeenth century, exploring how Wroth's opening sonnet in her *Pamphilia to Amphilanthus* sequence responds to Roman elegy, especially, perhaps Ovid, as well as the texts of her aunt, Mary Sidney, and uncle, Philip Sidney.

Sulpicia, Sidney and Wroth, we will see, re-write some of the fundamental tenets which shape the literary representation of female desire in
each of the periods under investigation, though certainly not without
some necessarily complex manoeuvring to accommodate the radical re-
positioning of their personas and characters. By drawing attention to their
participation in contemporary literary modes, all three women make bold
and forthright statements about their status as accomplished and authoritative readers, as well as their confidence, even audaciousness, as writers.

The intertextual dialogues being traced in this chapter are multiple: those
between Sulpicia's texts and prior elegy; between Sidney, Wroth, Roman
elegy and the Petrarchan mode; and also the perhaps unintentional
though, nevertheless, revealing congruencies between these three women
poets. All of them, as we will see, exploit pre-existing literary conventions
to find their own ways into what have appeared to be overwhelmingly
masculinised poetic discourses. Male-authored imitations of Latin elegy
continue to encode erotic transgression as a partially feminine quality
figured through appropriations of a female voice and thus, this chapter
demonstrates, render this mode of poetics open to, even welcoming of,
female authorship.

While there has been much interest in female authorship and female
'Petrarchan' poetry in the early modern period, scholars have not asked
why this specific mode of poetics is so accessible to women. Ann Rosalind
Jones briefly recognises Roman love elegy as an 'amorous discourse' potentially available to European Renaissance women writers but does not follow
up this statement or interrogate why this might be the case.[9] The work here
thus builds on the existing literature on female-authored Petrarchan poetry
and suggests a reason why this poetic mode might prove so accommodating and productive, albeit in a problematic fashion, to women poets.
The classical model of Sulpicia whose own texts stage such a provocative
intervention in relation to elegy serves as an example of elegiac reception in its own right, as well as an authoritative paradigm of female erotic
authorship.

'At Last Love Has Come': Sulpicia's Elegies and
the Lexicon of Love

Tandem venit amor, 'at last love has come' (3.13.1):[10] like her elegiac
predecessors, Catullus and Propertius, Sulpicia's opening poem is self-
consciously programmatic, setting out both her narrative fiction – that
she is a woman in love for the first time – as well as her literary agenda.[11]

Elegy predefines the narrator-lover as male and so, from her opening words, Sulpicia's text unsettles the dominant narrative of the enslaved male lover and the hard or cruel (*dura*) female beloved. *Tandem*, 'at last, finally' contrasts with the *prima*, 'first' of Propertius' opening line where 'Cynthia first ensnared me, poor wretch, with her eyes'.[12] While 'Propertius' is wrestled down and 'Ovid' ambushed by Cupid, 'Sulpicia', it seems, has been waiting for love.[13] Love, as readers of elegy know, is the initiator and inspiration for the poetic project we are reading, and the two roles of lover and author are inexorably and inextricably linked. 'Sulpicia' has to be in love in order to be an elegist and so already from her opening words we can see that her poetic persona is shaped by the codes, conventions and needs of the genre as established by Catullus and Propertius.[14]

Claiming the status, however, of lover and poet is intrinsically problematic when the narrator is female. We have seen already that the social position of the mistress is ambiguous at best, and associated with adultery and prostitution.[15] By openly declaring her love, however fictional it might be, 'Sulpicia' exposes herself deliberately to social and sexual censure, but manipulates the prevailing discourse to liberate and complicate the idea of female sexuality rather than allowing it to be forestalled and contained. The rumour (*fama*) that she had concealed (*texisse*) her love, she says, would be a greater cause of shame (*magis … pudori*) than to have laid it bare (*nudasse*).[16] Especially notable is the diction and choice of vocabulary here: 'concealed' and 'made naked' both recall the way in which the eroticised covering and stripping of female bodies is a prime concern of Catullan and Propertian poetics: in 2.15, for example, Propertius writes 'but if you persist in going to bed clothed, you will, with your gown ripped, experience the violence of my hands'.[17] Ideas of rumour or renown (*fama*) and shame or decency (*pudor*), too, to which we will return shortly, carry a particularly significant weight in other texts from this period, and Roman moral thought more generally.[18]

Sulpicia's verse takes the imagery of physical exposure and translates it into an emotional and literary quality. To conceal or cover her love is to keep silent, to mute her female voice and inhibit her poetic undertaking just as it has begun. Unlike the silenced women of Propertius 2.15 and *Amores* 1.5 whose very wordlessness is critical to the progress of those particular poems, Sulpicia's texts only exist through her refusal to be voiceless, itself imaged as a physical laying bare of her self. The association between women's speech and their dress permeates Roman texts and provides one of the common metaphors for the propriety – or its opposite – of female conduct.[19] To be decently attired is frequently a synonym for moral integrity, one aspect of which, for women especially, is vocal reticence. In the *Ars Amatoria*, for example, the narrator describes the women who should avoid his disreputable poetry by depicting them in terms of their dress: 'keep far away, slender fillets, symbols of modesty, and the long skirt that hides half the feet in its folds'.[20] While this is comically disingenuous on Ovid's part, it still participates self-consciously in the moralising discourse which Sulpicia's text foregrounds, only to reject, in her opening poem. If to read, and write, erotic texts is to compromise both the dress and moral code that differentiates respectable from other Roman women, then 'Sulpicia' is prepared to accept and embrace the conventions of her poetic predecessors and strip herself, metaphorically but scandalously, bare.

In male-authored elegy it is, of course, the mistress' body which is revealed, not the narrator-lover's. Sulpicia's opening two lines therefore stress the tension created when a female voice inverts the established narrative hierarchy and appropriates the role of the controlling poet-lover rather than being the constructed object of poetic desire. Propertius' Cynthia in 4.7 has already put pressure on the contours of 'Propertius'' story when she contests the narrator's master-narrative, and Sulpicia has the same disorienting effect. Her texts test the limits of elegy, prefiguring Ovid's later experiments in the exile poems, by overturning the gender distribution while still maintaining other recognisable qualities. Her adoption, for example, of a cultural position of sexual infamy, reclaimed as one of erotic and poetic renown, mirrors the worthlessness (*nequitia*) of 'Catullus' and 'Propertius' as they reconfigure, however temporarily, what it means to be a slave, a soldier, and a Roman man. Sulpicia's defiant sexual stance is thus actually a subservience to the qualities already embedded in this mode of writing by her male predecessors. Even while she disturbs some of the elements that contribute to the establishment of elegy as a genre – the gendering of the poet-lover as male, for example – she equally conforms to others so that it is her female body which is metaphorically put on display within the text, not that of her male beloved. Unable to completely abandon the 'dominant cultural repertoire', Sulpicia is forced to represent herself as an eroticised, unclothed body if she is to find a place within elegiac discourse at all.[21]

Sulpicia, by adopting the posture of lover-narrator embraces the sexual marginalisation and gender dissonance already established by Catullus and Propertius, and blends textual qualities of masculinity and femininity in her self-representation. However, she also prioritises a discourse of clothing, a kind of metaphorical cross-dressing, which, while it exists in Propertius' Vertumnus poem (4.2), is not applied directly to

'Propertius' as lover. Certainly we might read Propertius' Vertumnus as a figure for the poet switching textual gender and personae as he does so frequently in book 4, ventriloquising the voices of Arethusa (4.3), Tarpeia (4.4), Acanthis (4.5), Cynthia (4.7) and Cornelia (4.11). Vertumnus's opening line foregrounds the multiplicity of physical forms which exist within his single body: 'you who marvel that my one body has so many shapes' (*qui mirare meas tot in uno corpore formas*, 4.2.1), just as so many ventriloquised female voices spring from the male poet's body. Vertumnus goes on to emphasise the way in which clothing produces gender: 'clothe me in Coan silks, and I will become a not prudish girl: and who would deny that, wearing the toga, I am a man?' (4.2.23–4).[22] The specificity of Coan silks seems to be a deliberate recollection of Cynthia's dress in 1.2 and 2.1, thus drawing attention to the constructed nature of Cynthia in particular, and the textual performance of gender more generally. Sulpicia's 3.13 with its images of clothing and unclothing situates itself within this discourse where the fact of being undressed, even figuratively, authenticates her gender. At the same time, the text puts her feminine status in jeopardy by allowing her to take control of the act of dressing and undressing herself, a stark contrast to the Propertian and Ovidian mistress who so frequently has her clothing removed with various degrees of force and violence.

Sulpicia's 3.16 returns to the volatile relationship between dress and gender and might even be read as a reply to the question posed by Propertius' Vertumnus: 'who would deny that, wearing the toga, I am a man?' (4.2.24). In Sulpicia's poem, she accuses Cerinthus of being unfaithful, following the previous accusations of sexual incontinence against Lesbia and Cynthia. The object of her competitive disdain is a prostitute (*scortum*, 4) significantly wearing a toga (*togae*, 3). This masculine garment was the mark of the street prostitute, possibly identifying her as a 'public' woman as opposed to the dress of the respectable woman.[23] Importantly, however, it also destabilises the way Propertius' Vertumnus constructs gender through dress and presents a different answer to his question: Sulpicia does deny that a person wearing a toga is always a man, since it might, as in her text, be a woman. To dress a woman in male attire is, in this case, a cultural code for her social and sexual marginalisation, a way of visibly distinguishing her from the category, however problematic, of 'respectable' women. Within the context of Sulpicia's texts the cross-dressed woman is also a figure for the poet herself as she adopts the literary clothing of the male poet-lover, and builds her poetic reputation on her outspoken declarations of erotic love.

3.16 has been read as a form of invective, and therefore might be seen as a site of deliberate intertextuality with Catullan abuse poems written about the supposed sexual exploits of Lesbia such as c.11 where she is depicted with three hundred lovers at once, c.37 where she takes her seat at the 'lascivious tavern' (*salax taberna*) and c.58 where she serves men in the alleys and crossroads of Rome. But the alignment of 'Sulpicia' with 'Catullus' as the injured party is not completely secure. However much Sulpicia's text persuades us into an empathetic response to the narrator's predicament, her polarisation of her rival as a prostitute, ignoble (*ignoto*, 6), public, male-dressed, and excluded from good society, versus her own status as noble (*Servi filia Sulpicia*, 4), secure within the safety and affection of her family and metaphorically dressed as a woman, does not quite stand up to scrutiny.

The direct eroticism of her declarations in 3.13, her overt revealing of her self, the inversion of Roman social and sexual conventions, all blur the lines which supposedly separate 'Sulpicia' from the street girl so that the text interrogates both the elegiac master narrative which primarily seeks to attribute infidelity to the woman, as well as larger cultural categories which seek to essentialise classifications of women. By drawing attention to the similarities between 'Sulpicia' and the prostitute – their male 'clothing', their overt expressions of sexuality, even their sharing of Cerinthus – Sulpicia's texts reveal the problematic position of the female writer who inserts herself into this mode of love poetry. Her self-representation is partially controlled by a previous textual gender ideology which associates a woman with a form of sexual expression which is always slightly out of control, whether she is the Hellenised courtesan of Propertius or Ovid, or the adulterous married woman of Catullus. Sulpicia certainly extends the type, since 'Sulpicia' is a young, unmarried woman, under the guardianship of her male relation, Messalla, but cannot escape the moral hangover from her literary predecessors even when she claims the position of lover rather than beloved. Nevertheless, however much Sulpicia's voice might be controlled, conditioned and constrained by the master narrative established by prior male authors, it seems that she still has the power to unsettle elegy.

One of the tropes which Sulpicia exploits to stage her intervention is the association of the mistress with the reading and, possibly, writing of love poetry. Catullus' pseudonym for his lover, Lesbia, itself raises the idea of female erotic authorship through its allusion to Sappho, although ironically, of course, Catullus' c.51 serves to at least partially silence Sappho as he writes over and reconfigures her words.[24] The presence, however, of even this muted female voice inextricably blended with a masculine one, still permits and facilitates the insertion of an authentic female vocal presence attached to a female author.[25] Lesbia's voice, too is 'heard' within Catullan texts, though usually indirectly such as in c.70 and c.72. C.35 demonstrates, comically, the connection between writing and love as Caecilius' mistress, 'a maiden more scholarly than the Sapphic muse' (35.16–17) burns for him after reading the draft of his poem.[26] C.36 continues the theme as 'my beloved' exercises her poetic judgement and confers to the fire (an alternative form of burning) the writings of the 'worst of poets' (*pessimi poetae*, 36.6) – though we are not quite sure whether she means Volusius' 'excremental sheets' (*cacata charta*, 36.1) or Catullus' own 'wild iambics' (*truces ... iambos*, 36.5). Propertius in 2.3 explicitly positions Cynthia as an erotic poet: 'and when she pits her writings against those of ancient Corinna and deems Erinna's poems no match for her own' (*et sua cum antiquae committit scripta Corinnae | carminaque Erinnae non putat aequa suis*, 2.3.21–2), although he cunningly withholds his own artistic judgement on her poetic skills; and Cynthia, as we have seen, composes her own epitaph in 4.7. Ovid's *Amores*, too, though possibly written after Sulpicia's poems, gesture towards the female reader in 2.1, and comment wittily on how reading elegy has taught Corinna all the skills of the mistress: to elude her guardian and slip out of bed at night to meet her lover.[27]

We should be wary, of course, of accepting the references to women reading and writing in these texts as indicative of some kind of historical reality, but it can be said that in the elegiac world women, at least mistresses and potential mistresses, commonly participate in the production, circulation and even destruction of the texts which contain them: in 4.7, as we have seen, Cynthia begs 'Propertius' to burn the poems about her, just as Lesbia burns the poems above. That 'Sulpicia' should therefore be an acute reader of prior texts, as well as a writer of her own, is not surprising: indeed, in order to secure her reputation as an inhabitant of this fictional world she could be nothing else. The relation, however, between the literary skills and ambitions of the mistress and the status of actual writing women in Rome is a problematic one which complicates the way Sulpicia negotiates her own writerly presence within her texts.

We know of female writers from classical Rome but, apart from Sulpicia's texts, only fragments of their writings have survived.[28] The moral reputation of women writers is strikingly polarised depending, it seems, on the genre, content and moral purpose of what they wrote. The letters of Cornelia, the mother of the Gracchi (b.195–190 BCE), were published, according to Cicero, but seem to have been deemed morally unthreatening since they were written to support the masculine virtues and prerogatives of her sons, and encode her own status as wife and mother, the ideal and idealised position for a Roman matron.[29] From Plutarch's life of Pompey we know that Pompey's third wife, also Cornelia, 'was well versed in literature', a fairly neutral statement.[30] The other two known women writers, however, from the period before Sulpicia, Clodia Metelli and Sempronia, are far more problematic according to the sources and, arguably, exhibit pronounced similarities, in their purported behaviour and their writing, to Lesbia, Cynthia and Sulpicia. A prime source for Clodia, as we saw in Chapter 2, is Cicero's *Pro Caelio*. The importance of this to Sulpicia comes from Cicero's positioning of Clodia as an 'experienced ... poetess' (*veteris ... poetriae*) of 'many comedies' (*plurimarum fabularum*). Although Clodia is not represented as writing love poetry, the ideas here of experience, implying illicit sexual as well as literary expertise, and the creation of *fabulae*, 'stories, plays, dramas, fiction' combine to discredit her both as a legal witness and as a respectable woman. Her very fluency is itself articulated as a flagrant repudiation of moral probity and integrity, thus serving to reinstate the association between female silence, both spoken and written, and virtue. Cicero continues to exploit this image of Clodia as poet and positions her as a not very good one despite her experience: 'how devoid it is of plot, how utterly it fails to find an ending!' (*quam est sine argumento, quam nullum invenire exitum potest! Cael.* 64). The comment about the ending, despite the genre difference, is especially suggestive in relation to Sulpicia (as well as Catullus and Propertius) since the abrupt discontinuation of her narrative after 3.18 has itself given rise to speculation about the order of the poems, with some scholars, as noted above, arguing for 3.13 with its 'at last love has come' as following 3.18 since they, like Cicero, desire a more obvious and neat ending.

Sallust's Sempronia, described in his *Catiline*, is another model of the dissipated female writer which seems to inform the creation of the elegiac mistress. Recounting the 'conspiracy' of Catiline which took place in 63 BCE, Sallust's history was written sometime after 53 BCE (possibly at around the same time that Catullus was active) and was put into circulation between about 44 and 40 BCE.[31] There is no evidence for Sempronia other than Sallust which does force the question of her historical authenticity, but whether she is a 'true' portrait or an ideologically driven construct, she provides a useful template against which we can read Sulpicia. Sallust describes Sempronia as follows:

> she was well read in Greek and Latin literature, able to play the lyre and dance more skilfully than a respectable woman should and had many other

accomplishments which minister to voluptuousness. But there was nothing she held so cheap as modesty and chastity; you could not easily say whether she was less sparing of her money or of her reputation; her desires were so ardent that she sought men more often than she was sought by them … nevertheless, she was a woman of no mean endowments; she could write verses, tell jokes, and use language which was modest or tender or wanton; in effect, she possessed a high degree of wit and charm.[32]

The correlation between artistic skills – reading and writing verse, playing the lyre, dancing – and decadence, sexual impropriety and promiscuity is transparent. As well as the literary skills we have already identified in the elegiac mistress, we should remember that Cynthia, in particular, is shown to be accomplished at playing the lyre (e.g. Propertius 1.3.42, 2.1.9). The sexual forwardness of Sempronia ('her desires were so ardent that she sought men more often than she was sought by them') has a striking echo in Sulpicia's 3.13 where Cerinthus (unnamed) is brought and dropped into the narrator's arms (*sinus*, also 'lap, breast') following her prayers to Venus.[33] 'Sulpicia' is thus positioned as the sexual initiator and pursuer in the relationship, an overtly aberrant position for an unmarried Roman woman. Sallust's emphasis, too, on linguistic fluency, on Sempronia's accomplished and nuanced use of language, on her wit and her charm (qualities commented on by Scaliger, as we saw, when discussing Sulpicia's poems) are all re-used by Sulpicia's texts but presented within a very different moral framework. We should also note Sallust's references to 'reputation' (*fama*) and 'modest chastity' (*pudicitia*), terms important to the containment of women, with which Sulpicia, as we shall see shortly, takes issue.

Sulpicia is probably writing at least thirty-five, possibly more, years after Cicero's speech and Sallust's history but the negative discourse which partially associates female speech and writing with sexual profligacy is still current and actively informs the construction of female gender. By embracing it, Sulpicia confronts this cultural notion and actively re-configures it, so that it is incorporated within her narrative even while the idea of the outspoken woman who refuses to be silenced about her erotic and poetic ambitions is itself placed at the centre of her texts and heroised: 'the rumour that I have concealed it would shame me more than disclosure'. Both Catullus and Propertius also, of course, partially invert conventional social and sexual morality, and disturb cultural constructions of gender, particularly masculinity. Their representations of wayward women in Lesbia and Cynthia are themselves the counterparts of the temporarily effeminised male lovers but the central concern of their poetry is not so much 'female mastery' as the interrogation of ideas of masculinity, subservience, dependency and powerlessness.[34]

Sulpicia's texts negotiate an unstable relationship to those of her literary predecessors, as she selectively expands and contracts the elements which they have established. So while she maintains the dynamic of the narrator as lover and poet, she switches the gender from male to female; she retains the moral inversion already established by Catullus and Propertius as they reject the public roles of the Roman man for a life of idleness (*otium*) but transfers it into a female sphere where to be a 'public' woman is itself a signifier of immorality. She even qualifies the definitions of 'public' women, drawing both contrasts and comparisons between the toga-wearing street prostitute of 3.16 and the female poet-lover. Notably, Sulpicia does not, or cannot, confine herself to the position of either the male lover or the female beloved. Despite the way previous male-authored texts allow instances of the female voice to emerge, these voices are still always restricted and curtailed by the needs of the male poet. In order to liberate her own voice, Sulpicia is forced to disrupt the limited freedom allowed to Lesbia and Cynthia, or even Clodia Metelli and Sempronia whose own voices we never hear, who never escape the discursive confines of their creators, and invent a novel way of intervening in the discourse that associates female speech and writing with sexual immorality.

'Never would I choose to entrust my messages to tablets under seal, that none might read them before my lover' (3.13.7–8):[35] Sulpicia's writing tablets consolidate these issues of gendered authorship, poetic predecessors, intertextuality, female sexuality, immorality and the revelation of the female body, and serve as a fine example of her dense, compressed style of writing that rewards close attention. Poems about writing tablets already exist in the texts of Catullus and Propertius, but are put to work in a different way.[36] Catullus 42 tells the story of the 'impudent adulteress' (*moecha turpis*, 3), who refuses to return his tablets to the narrator. The text does not tell us how she obtained them in the first place so we might deduce that they were given to her, that she was possibly another lover to whom he had written poems. What is worth noting is the pattern of abuse and its relation to the tablets: while she has them, she is the object of typical, if relatively mild, Catullan sexual invective: *moecha*, 'adulteress, slut' (3), *turpis*, 'shameful' (3), *putida*, 'foul, offensive' (11), *lupanar*, 'brothel' (13). Realising that she is unmoved, the narrator re-thinks his strategy and plans to flatter and shame her simultaneously into returning the tablets: 'give back the tablets, chaste and honourable maiden!' (*pudica et proba, redde codicillos!*, 24). In order to be named 'chaste, modest, virtuous' (*pudica*) and 'honest' (*proba*), the woman has to give up the tablets that she has been reading, thus re-forging the association between reading and immorality when the reader is female.

In contrast, we have c.50 which depicts a day when 'Catullus' and Licinius 'played many games with my tablets' (*multum lusimus in meis tabellis*), passing them back and forth as they exchange poems, and laughter and drink wine.[37] In this poem, too, the exchange is eroticised and the recipient of 'Catullus'' verses depicted in sexualised terms but, far from the denigrating abuse suffered by the woman, the male friend is associated with more gratifying terms: *lepor*, 'charm', *iucundus*, 'delightful', *facetiae*, 'wit', and the narrator himself cannot wait to speak with him again (*ut tecum loquerer simulque ut essem*, 13). The situation, of course, is not the same in the two poems, but the way in which the exchange of tablets is both gendered and sexualised, in negative terms with the woman, positive with the man, provokes a suggestive intertextual response from Sulpicia about the reading of her tablets.

Sulpicia refuses to seal her tablets or restrict their readership; indeed, she is not even concerned that her lover (*meus*) should read them in advance of a more general audience. By publicising both her love and her writing, she flouts the rules of silence which more usually bind women, and foregrounds the extent to which she might be positioning herself as more a poet or public writer than a lover. While both Catullus' and Propertius' texts at least partly invoke a sense of the writing of poetry as a private act, to be shared with intimates but which is or, ideally, should be, controlled by the poet himself, Sulpicia's text sets no limits to the circulation of her tablets, wishing them to be open to everyone. The slippage between physical elegies, either in tablet or book form, and the body of the elegiac mistress is well established, and we have seen in Chapter 3 how Propertius, especially, uses Cynthia as the embodiment of his Hellenistic poetics. If the female beloved's body is, partially, a textual one, then Sulpicia's tablets can be construed, figuratively, as a representation of her body. Yet again, she places herself in the position of a mistress despite also being both poet and lover, and the sexual discourse which equates erotic poetry with a female body is played out not in the figure of Cerinthus, but in Sulpicia herself. The public-private dichotomy reappears, so that the circulation and interception of Sulpicia's poetry is imaged as a public circulation of her body, prefiguring the prostitute, another public woman, in 3.16.

Replacing Cerinthus' body with her own is especially remarkable given the provenance of his name, which associates him with bees, honey and wax.[38] The poetic associations of bees and honey, and the idea of the hon-eyed mouth had been well established in Greek literature and Hellenistic

epigram; Roman writing tablets were covered in wax, confirming the literary connections. Because of these connotations Cerinthus is little more
than a name within Sulpicia's texts as she performs the roles of both male
lover and female beloved through the textual depictions of her own body.

This dynamic, so typical of Sulpicia's poetics, responds to Propertius'
2.23(24): 'Do you talk thus, now that your famous book has made you
a legend, and your Cynthia is read all over the forum?' (2.23(24).24–5),[39]
where the idea of Cynthia being 'read' (*lecta*) in the forum also evokes a
subtext where both the woman and the book are passed around between
men.[40] 'Propertius' continues by foregrounding the *nequitia*, 'vice,
debauchery' (29) of his position: 'a gentleman must either not pretend to
respectability or else keep quiet about his love life' (*aut pudor ingenuis aut
reticendus amor*, 27). 'The modesty of the free-born' is set in opposition to
the public articulation of love. But as the poem continues, we realise that
the shame is not that of an excessive expression of what should be kept
private, or even that of a man conducting a sexual relationship outside of
marriage with a woman who might be a courtesan, but stems from the fact
that Cynthia is making a fool of him through her infidelity:

> but if indeed Cynthia were smiling kindly upon me, I should not now be
> called the prince of debauchery; nor would my name be thus dragged in
> dishonour throughout Rome, and although she fired me with passion, at
> least she would not be hoodwinking me.
>
> quod si iam facilis spiraret Cynthia nobis,
>   non ego nequitiae dicerer esse caput,
>   nec sic per totam, infamis traducerer urbem,
>   ureret et quamvis, non mihi verba daret.
>   (2.23(24).28–31)

The illicit sexual relationship, it seems, can quite acceptably be talked
about, it is the public knowledge of where the power of the relationship
lies – with Cynthia – which is deemed reprehensible. The concepts of
shame, honour and dishonour are here redefined by Propertius, and provide a model for Sulpicia's own negotiations within the moral framework
applied to Roman women.

So Sulpicia's unsealed tablets create a site of intertextuality which allows
her to prise open the prior texts of Catullus and Propertius and insert
a discourse centred not on masculinity – both its loss and its recuper-
ation – but on female desire, both sexual and poetic, and the ethics of femininity in Roman culture. Confronting the notion which equates female
speech, and especially writing, with sexual incontinence and immorality,

she manoeuvres to embrace this argument and reject it at the same time. 'No, I love my fault' (*sed peccasse iuvat*, 9), she asserts, implicitly equating Cerinthus, her love, with the idea of a misdeed and thus upholding the dominant cultural master-narrative which is itself countered in Catullus and Propertius. At the same time, she embraces the very idea of sexual transgression, precisely because it allows her to step beyond the social norms of the well-born young Roman woman. However, she is wary enough to try to delimit the extent of her social and sexual deviation, hence the prostitute of 3.16 who serves to demarcate the distinction between the two women even while querying that very classification.

'Sulpicia's' syntax reiterates the integrity of her love: 'let all hear that we have made love, each worthy of the other' (*cum digno digna fuisse ferar*, 10).[41] The centring, in Latin, of *digno digna*, 'a worthy man, a worthy woman', foregrounds the kind of reciprocity that 'Catullus' fantasises about achieving with Lesbia but which evades him, indeed, has to for the narrative of sexual subjection to continue. Although 'Sulpicia's' love story is certainly not without its problems, it is striking that her very first poem dismantles the gendered and sexual hierarchy which underpins elegiac erotics and replaces it with a mutuality which is quite distinctive.

The rejection of the idea of a worthless love, which exists in Catullus and Propertius as their narrators expose the moral and sexual failings of Lesbia and Cynthia, again unsettles the typical narrative arc of previous elegiac texts. Significantly, though, the seeds of this reciprocity might already lie dormant. Catullus' c.70, for example, where we hear Lesbia's words through the mouth of the narrator, position her as professing her own love for 'Catullus': 'the woman I love says that there is no-one whom she would rather marry than me, not if Jupiter himself were to woo her' (*nulli se dicit mulier mea nubere malle | quam mihi, non si se Iuppiter ipse petat*, 70.1–2), and, though 'Catullus' goes on to bitterly deny her sincerity, the text still allows an opening for readers to refuse his subjective reading of Lesbia's words. Similarly, as we have seen in Chapter 3, Propertius 4.7 gives Cynthia's version of their love story, and it serves to challenge much that we have been told by the Propertian narrator. Sulpicia's texts seize upon these sparse moments of narrative contestation that already exist in her predecessors' poetry and transform them into the central substance of her own work. Her challenge, it appears, is not just to social convention and sexual morality, but also to the literary tradition to which she allies herself.

That the fault which she declares herself to love is as much one of writing as of loving is implicit within the text: *vultus componere famae | taedet,*

'[I] loathe to wear a mask for rumour' (9–10). This rather abrupt translation does little to unpack the density of expression here: *componere*, given
here as 'to wear', also means 'to construct or compose'; *vultus*, means 'face,
expression'; and *fama*, certainly might mean 'rumour' but also 'reputation,
fame', and is associated with one's public character. *Fama* is also what poets
strive for, the lasting reputation that extends beyond their death.[42] An alternative translation might, then, be 'I'm sick of composing my expression[s]
for the sake of my [sexual] reputation', thus acknowledging that poetic
fama, for Sulpicia, can only be achieved through the sacrifice of her social
fama. 'Mask' for *vultus* might recall Propertius' Vertumnus and the many
shapes or masks which he adopts, and the gap that exists between the historical Catullus, or Propertius or Sulpicia, and the constructed narrators
of the same name within their texts. Ironically, Sulpicia's poetic reputation
depends precisely on what we might call her sexual reputation, since it is the
intricate, delicate evocation of her erotic narrative for which she is valued.

The discourse of *fama* is widespread in Latin literature of this period,
but one particularly suggestive example occurs in relation to Dido in the
Aeneid.[43] We have seen how Propertius and Ovid both embed intertextual
responses to Virgil's text in their own poetry, and it is possible to trace the
way in which Sulpicia's texts serve to re-write, in miniature, the narrative
movement of the Aeneas/Dido love story, giving it a happy end.[44] The
arrival of love, female speech and silence, the politics of reputation and
sexual crime: this nexus of ideas articulated in 3.13 is also put to work, on a
larger scale, in *Aeneid* 4. It is worth noting that the idea of *fama* is particularly prominent just after the cave episode when Dido consummates her
relationship with Aeneas:

> That day was the first day of death, that first the cause of woe. For no more
> is Dido swayed by fair show or fair fame, no more does she dream of a secret
> love: she calls it marriage and with that name veils her fault.

> > Ille dies primus leti primusque malorum
> > causa fuit. neque enim specie famave movetur
> > nec iam furtivum Dido meditatur amorem;
> > coniugium vocat; hoc praetexit nomine culpam.
> > > (4.169–72)

Sulpicia's text, like Virgil's, locks together the public expression of female
desire, the idea of fault or error, and fame or reputation, but where for
Dido this conjunction will lead remorselessly towards her suicide, thus
serving as a warning story, policing female sexual reputation, Sulpicia re-
configures the elements more positively.

It is especially remarkable that Sulpicia is audacious enough here to challenge both the sexual orthodoxy of Roman morality, and also the cultural hegemony of Virgil's epic. Her allusions might be subtle and easily overlooked, but are as significant to the reading of her texts as Virgilian allusions are to Propertius and Ovid. This engagement with the *Aeneid* might be seen as another instance of Sulpicia blending her voice with those of her literary predecessors, adopting qualities of voice or viewpoint which can only be named as 'masculine' or 'feminine' in the most problematic of ways. Far more interesting, perhaps, is what this site of intertextuality might reveal about Sulpicia's reading and her expectations of her readers. 3.13 is particularly self-conscious about its status as a literary artefact, and sensitive to its own reception. Issues of disclosure, the unsealed tablets open to a general readership, all position this text as one which will be publicly available – a fact confirmed by its inclusion within the Tibullan corpus. Lines 5–6 draw especial attention to its audience: 'let my joys be told by all of whom it is said that they have missed their own' (*mea gaudia narret,* | *dicetur si quis non habuisse sua*). *Quis* is ungendered, so all we know about the purported audience is that they will be of good reputation since it is said (*dicetur*) that they do not have loves of their own. The sly *dicetur* playfully recalls the gap that might exist between public reputation and private behaviour, evoking the line which is tragically crossed by Dido. Sulpicia has not only read the *Aeneid* herself, but assumes that her readers will have too, and will have the literary expertise and fluency to reconstruct and decipher her own intertextual allusions to that text. Sulpicia boldly inhabits the literary realms of her predecessors and re-shapes their poetic discourse from the inside to suit her own sometimes radical, disruptive poetics.

Sulpicia's texts can thus be seen to exploit the pre-existing female ventriloquism of Catullus and Propertius and expand their use of the female voice to contest the various master-narratives at work within their texts. By contesting the fiction of the unfaithful and unfeeling mistress (*dura puella*), so entrenched, even though contested, in Catullus and Propertius, Sulpicia's texts serve to decentre one of the prime considerations of prior male-authored poetry – that of masculinity under pressure – and re-orient what this mode of poetry might be made to be about. At the same time, while her texts adopt some elements of what we might describe as elegiac femininity, such as the disclosure of her metaphorical body, and the discourse of chastity (*pudicitia*), her voice equally assumes the more typical stance of the masculine lover thus blending masculine and feminine in a single utterance. Notably, by performing the roles of both genders, Sulpicia's texts leave almost no room for Cerinthus. He is excluded entirely from the 'masculine' role of abject lover, and is only tentatively associated with the 'female' role of the uncaring beloved, a position which is erased in any case in 3.18. The mutual dependence of these two roles is foregrounded, as is their relative fluidity in gendered terms.

The numerous instances of intertextuality, the concern with writing and reception, the engagement with issues of *fama* or reputation all point to an intended audience of sophisticated Roman readers familiar with Virgil as well as Catullus and Propertius. Sulpicia's texts boldly insert themselves into male literary, and public, discourse, an extraordinarily confident position for a female writer to take.

Before turning to the Renaissance, it is worth briefly considering the response of the so-called *amicus* poet to Sulpicia's audacious interventions. 3.8, it seems, works very hard to cancel out the transgressions of Sulpicia's own texts, and replace her narrator within the confines of male-authored love poetry. 'Sulpicia', we learn in the opening line, is *culta*, 'dressed', also 'ornamented, groomed, cultivated' for the pleasure of Mars and, we infer, the poet's readers. The itemised description of her beauty which follows reminds us particularly of Propertius' Cynthia and Ovid's Corinna:

> Has she loosed her hair? Then flowing locks become her. Has she dressed it? With dressed hair she is divine. She fires the heart if she chooses to appear in gown of Tyrian hue; she fires it if she comes in the sheen of snowy robes.

> seu solvit crines, fusis decet esse capillis;
> 　　seu compsit, comptis est veneranda comis.
> urit, seu Tyria voluit procedere palla;
> 　　urit, seu nivea candida veste venit.
> 　　　　　　　　　([Tibullus.] 3.8.9–12)

The urge to suppress the contraventions of Sulpicia, and re-contain her within the objectivising discourse which her texts disturb is itself a fine testament to the way in which she upsets and unsettles the established paradigms of her male elegiac predecessors.

'Outrage Your Face': Petrarchan Contestations and the Voice of Cleopatra in Mary Sidney's *Antonie*

In 1621, in a vituperative letter written to Mary Wroth, Sir Edward Denny gives us a contemporary judgement of both Wroth herself and her aunt, Mary Sidney:[45]

> [I] pray that you may repent you of so many ill spent years of so vain a book and that you may redeem the time with writing as large a volume of

heavenly lays and holy love as you have of lascivious tales and amorous toys
that at the last you may follow the rare, and pious example of your virtuous
and learned aunt, who translated so many godly books and especially the
holy psalms of David.[46]

Attacking Wroth for supposedly libelling him and his family in her *Urania*,
a long chivalric romance which draws on Philip Sidney's two versions of
the *Arcadia*, Denny makes a negative comparison between her and Mary
Sidney. Sidney is 'virtuous' and 'learned', a 'rare and pious example', while
Wroth is the author of 'so vain a book'. Strikingly, however, in this sometimes rabid letter, Denny does not castigate Wroth for writing in itself,
but for the type of writing she has produced: 'lascivious tales and amorous
toys'. Rather than drawing here on customary anti-female invective (which
does appear in a second poem-letter by Denny to Wroth: 'leave idle books
alone | for wise and worthier women have writ none'), he instead points
her towards further writing as a moral corrective. She can 'redeem' herself
not through authorial silence but through penning 'heavenly lays and holy
love … godly books' – that is, by re-writing herself into the image of Mary
Sidney.

We will return to Denny's attack on Wroth in the next section but,
firstly, will ask: are Mary Sidney's writings quite as innocuous, even
exemplary, as Denny asserts? Acknowledged as her brother Philip's literary executor after his untimely death in 1586 at the age of thirty-two,
Sidney published authorised editions of his works including their joint
translations of the psalms.[47] She also wrote secular translations under her
own name without recourse to apology, disclaimer or conventional use
of a modesty topos. Her *Antonie*, a translation of Robert Garnier's 1578
French play, *Marc Antoine*, was composed in 1590, published under her
own name in 1592 and reprinted in 1595, pre-dating Shakespeare's play
(written c.1603–7) by over a decade. Sidney's prefatory Argument notes
its classical source as Plutarch: 'the history to be read at large in Plutarch
in the life of Antonius'.[48] Although translating an existing text, Sidney
clearly chose *Antonie* over Garnier's other plays, and we have further evidence of her interest in Cleopatra from her sponsorship of Samuel Daniel's
Cleopatra, dedicated to Sidney in 1594.[49] Sidney's drama has previously
been read as an instance of the *ars moriendi*, particularly drawing on her
grief for the death of her brother; and as Protestant political commentary
focusing on the problem of the succession, and intervening in debates
about Elizabethan foreign policy.[50] Here, though, we will focus on the dialogue of love which is articulated between Antony and Cleopatra. Framing
Sidney's lovers through love elegy generally, and with a special focus on

Sulpicia's negotiations with the genre, serves to bring into focus Sidney's concerns with female desire and authorship.

Sidney's *Antonie*, is usually classified as a quasi-Senecan closet drama, written to be read out loud, possibly by a group, rather than to be acted on stage. Garnier's alexandrine rhyming couplets are rendered by Sidney in blank verse, primarily iambic pentameter; and the long monologues of the protagonists (Antony, Cleopatra, Octavius Caesar) are broken up at the end of each of the five acts by the chorus who take a moralising, somewhat detached view of the conflict. The play is set after Actium and is remarkably lacking in physical action: the main event, Antony's suicide, is described in a messenger speech to Octavius, and the play ends before Cleopatra's own death. Instead, the play functions like a dramatic narrative poem of multiple voices, with elements of the Ciceronian forensic speech, particularly in the first two acts where first Antony, then Cleopatra make their 'case'. What is at stake is not so much political point-scoring following the disaster of Actium, as a debate about sexual constancy, much in the manner of that indicated in Propertius 4.7.

From Antony's opening speech, his recourse to an elegiac/Petrarchan narrative and idiom is immediately apparent:

> ... my queen her self, in whom I liv'd
> The idol of my heart ...
> For love of her, in her allurements caught,
> Abandon'd life, I honour have despised ...
> Contemn'd that power that made me so much fear'd,
> A slave become unto her feeble face.
>
> (1.5–16)

This abject Antony, caught in the erotic seductiveness of Cleopatra's wiles ('in her allurements caught', 1.11), neglecting his Roman responsibilities ('I honour have despised ... of the stately Rome | despoiled the Empire of her best attire', 1.12–14) and compromising his masculinity ('contemn'd that power that made me so fear'd', 1.15) is certainly recognisable from Plutarch. The lexicon of love which he uses, though, explicitly reflects the elegiac and Petrarchan, especially in the usage of 'idol of my heart', and the imagery of the male lover as slave. 'My queen' might reflect the specifically Elizabethan context of this drama, and the separation of love from honour or political authority reminds us of the self-proclaimed moral worthlessness (*nequitia*) of Propertius as well as various sonnets in the *Astrophil and Stella*, such as 30 where Astrophil cannot attend to European politics 'for still I think of you' (30.14).

Antony's surrender to Octavius is figured in sexualised terms making the slippage between political and erotic submission clear:

> But these same arms which on my back I wear
> Thou should'st have them too, and me unarmed
> Yielded to Caesar naked of defence.
>
> (1.24–6)

This imagery is continued in that of the triumph, making allusion to Roman spectacle as well as the eroticised appropriation of the triumph in, for example, *Amores* 1.2, and Petrarch's *Triomphi*. Antony claims that he will never appear in Octavius' military triumph ('let Caesar never think | triumph of me shall his proud chariot grace', 1.27–8), since he already has his place in Cleopatra's 'triumph of love':

> Thou only Cleopatra triumph hast,
> Thou only hast my freedom servile made,
> Thou only hast me vanquished ...
> None else henceforth, but thou my dearest queen,
> Shall glory in commanding Antonie.
>
> (1.31–3, 37–8)

Antony, who will never submit to Octavius, has already capitulated to Cleopatra, but makes it clear that it is an active erotic surrender, and one with which he is complicit: 'Thou only hast me vanquished: not by force | (for forced I cannot be)' (1.33–4).

Sidney's text blends the 'historical' Antony of Plutarch with the Petrarchan lover of so much erotic poetry from this period, not least that of her brothers, Robert and Philip. She subtly re-writes Garnier's original to underscore her interest in the moral significance of her lovers: where Garnier's original gives 'esclave devenu de son visage feint' ('a slave become of her dissembled face', 1.16), Sidney turns 'feint' into 'feeble', lacking moral strength – indicating Antony's prejudiced judgement of Cleopatra at this stage of the drama.[51] Garnier's 'feint' (feigned, dissembled, pretended, sham) refers back to his Argument where Cleopatra is negotiating with Octavius, preparing to abandon Antony for her own survival. We should also remember Philip Sidney's slippery usage of 'fain' in *Astrophil and Stella* 1, and Sulpicia's refusal to compose her face for the sake of her reputation (*vultus componere famae* | *taedet*, [*Tib.*] 3.13.9–10). Antony's words position Cleopatra as akin to Astrophil, and as opposed to 'Sulpicia', a complicated arrangement which we will unpack further below.

Sidney's translation shifts the emphasis away from Garnier's focus on political betrayal and instead foregrounds the problematic moral status of her protagonists. Antony sees Cleopatra's beauty as the opposite of the neo-Platonic beauty of, for example, Petrarch's Laura or Philip Sidney's Stella, which is the visible emblem of their moral virtue and sexual chastity. By allowing himself to become enslaved to, and by, such a worthless beauty ('that face whose guileful semblant', 1.111), Antony castigates his own ethical failure ('that face … infect[s] thy tainted heart', 1.111–12). His slippage from the moral masculinity of Roman honour and power is into an effeminised state of subservience ('low, dishonoured, despised | in wanton love a woman thee misleads', 1.119–20) which is itself morally defective ('scarce master of thy self | late master of so many nations', 1.129–30), and reminiscent of the Catullan and Propertian male lovers we have met.

So, from this first act, a long soliloquy by Antony capped by a chorus, we are introduced to a shadowed version of the elegiac/Petrarchan dynamic, a partial subversion of the Laura/'Petrarch' or Stella/Astrophil relationship where the female beloved still directs and controls the moral status of the relationship but rather than holding the lover to a virtuous love, she entices him into something corrupt, debauched and decadent. Sidney's Cleopatra, at this stage of the drama and based only on Antony's narrative, is positioned as akin to Lesbia, Cynthia and Corinna with their slippery morals and uncertain sexual status.

This version of Cleopatra is complicit with her representation in Augustan texts written when the wars between Antony and Augustus were still fresh, and include, importantly, images constructed by Virgil and Propertius which would themselves have helped inform Plutarch's Life. The conflation of Cleopatra with Virgil's Dido – also a female, eastern, queen who tries to divert Aeneas from his imperial Roman mission – is well recognised.[52] The battle of Actium is depicted on Aeneas' shield in book 8, and Virgil's Cleopatra is given real stature here as the dangerous embodiment of everything non-Roman: 'on the other side comes Antony with barbaric might and motley arms … and there follows him (oh, the impiety!) his Egyptian wife' (8.685–8).[53] Virgil's Antony is aligned with the barbarous, uncivilised, effeminised east, so that his 'marriage' with Cleopatra is articulated as something contravening divine law. This is foregrounded in the description of the Egyptian gods, 'monstrous gods of every form and barking Anubis' (*omnigenumque deum monstra et latrator Anubis*, 8.698) who do battle against Neptune and Venus, pitching the Egyptian pantheon against the Roman. The *Aeneid*, though, is not itself immune to the allure of erotic love, and while Cleopatra on the shield is a terrifying figure, her alter ego, Dido, is frequently read as one of the most

sympathetic characters of the epic, personifying the human cost of masculine imperial values, representing the humanity which Aeneas perhaps
loses even as he gains the territory that will become Rome.

Cleopatra is also represented in Propertian texts, while Antony is
explicitly conflated with 'Propertius', the narrator and elegiac lover. In
2.16 'Propertius' mourns his own shame that despite Cynthia's visible and
public sexual betrayal, he is unable to free himself from his excessive love
for her. He continues by making a transparent comparison between himself and Antony:

> Look at the leader who lately, amid vain alarms, filled Actium's bay with
> his doomed soldiers: a base love made him turn his ships in flight and seek
> refuge at the ends of the world.

> cerne ducem, modo qui fremitu complevit inani
>   Actia damnatis aequora militibus:
> hunc infamis amor versis dare terga carinis
>   iussit et extremo quaerere in orbe fugam.
>   (2.16.37–40)

By comparing himself to Antony, the Propertian narrator is elevating the
'heroic' nature of his love, even while condemning it. The notion of 'a base
love' (*infamis amor*) underpins Sidney's 'a slave become unto her feeble
face', and Antony's flight from battle is equated with 'Propertius' turning
away from Rome's urban entertainments, the elegiac equivalent of warfare,
where sensuous pleasure replaces something far more martial. The implication in 2.16 is that Antony's retreat from battle is towards an erotic and
decadent refuge in Egypt, both geographically and morally at a distance
from Rome. And yet, Propertius tells us, 'Antony' is still also present at
the heart of Rome, contesting ideologies of Roman, Augustan manhood
from within, through the existence of the elegiac lover. Virgil's Aeneas
may have freed himself from Dido's love, but 'Propertius' revels in his
own abasement, countering the dominant, though certainly not the only,
reading of the *Aeneid* and taking the part of Antony rather than Augustus.

Propertius 3.11 extends this conflation of 'Propertius' and Cynthia with
Antony and Cleopatra. In a poem which purportedly seeks to absolve the
narrator's own compromised masculinity, he compares himself to mythic
heroes who were also bound in sexual thrall to a woman: Jason to Medea,
Achilles to Penthesilea, Hercules to Omphale, before returning to Antony's
union with Cleopatra:

> What of her who of late has fastened disgrace upon our arms, and, a woman
> who fornicated even with her slaves, demanded as the price of her shameful

union the walls of Rome and the Senate made over to her dominion? ... to
be sure the harlot queen of licentious Canopus, the one disgrace branded on
Philip's line, dared to pit barking Anubis against our Jupiter.

> quid, modo quae nostris opprobria nexerit armis
>   et, famulos inter femina trita suos?
> coniugii obsceni pretium Romana poposcit
>   moenia et addictos in sua regna patres [···]
> scilicet, incesti meretrix regina Canopi
>   una Philippei sanguinis usta nota
> ausa Iovi nostres latrantem opponere Anubim.
>   (3.11.29–41)

Again, the Propertian narrator aligns himself with Antony and articulates
his relationship with Cynthia in relation to that of Antony with Cleopatra,
so that the Propertian texts celebrate the shameless love of elegy even
while acknowledging the abjectness it imposes on Roman masculinity.
Cynthia, already portrayed as a Hellenised courtesan, becomes associated
with Cleopatra's prostitute queen (*meretrix regina*), both a comment on
Cynthia's ambiguous social and sexual status (*meretrix*) and her erotic power
over 'Propertius' (*regina*). It is also worth noting the echo in *latrantem ...
Anubim* (barking Anubis) of Virgil's *latrator Anubis* quoted above, and we
will return presently to this in relation to Mary Sidney.

Co-locating these constructions of Antony and Cleopatra with Mary
Sidney's *Antonie* is productive: by engaging with these characters and the
literary and ideological values they have been made to represent, Sidney
is also, if indirectly, engaging with Roman love elegy. Her Antony also
gestures towards the Aeneas/Dido story, and Virgil's text. In his long
opening monologue, Antony recalls his attempt to leave Cleopatra and
return to war:

> The looks, the grace, the words,
> Sweetness, allurements, amorous delights
> Entered again thy soul, and day and night
> In watch, in sleep, her image follow'd thee:
> Not dreaming but of her, repenting still
> That thou for war hadst such a goddess left.
>   (1.101–6)

'In watch, in sleep, her image follow'd thee' recalls the substance of Dido's
anguished words to Aeneas when she vows to follow him in death as in
life, though Dido's agency and haunting sense of retribution is erased from
Antonie's vision and foregrounds the differing perspectives at work here.[54]
While Aeneas cannot assuage Dido's grief at being abandoned for war in

Italy, Sidney's Antonie expresses his repentance and returns to his 'Dido'. As we have already seen, Sulpicia's 3.18 is also a subtle re-writing of the parting of Dido and Aeneas, re-configuring the episode so that 'Sulpicia' takes on the male role and articulates her intention to return to her lover whom she left the night before. Sidney's text takes an elegiac stance in revisiting and radically revising the *Aeneid* and the central love relationship which it contains: her Antony, too, is, in some measure, a transgressive anti-Aeneas. This allusion to Virgil is confirmed in Antony's last words in his Act 1 speech. He ends with an aphorism on women's changeability: 'but ah! By nature women wav'ring are | each moment changing and rechanging minds' (1.145–6), which seems to deliberately recall Virgil's *varium et mutabile semper | femina*, 'a fickle and changeful thing is woman' (*Aeneid* 4.569–79). The words are spoken by Mercury in a dream to Aeneas and are proved profoundly wrong in relation to Dido – and Sidney's text, too, goes on to challenge Antony's estimation in Act 2 when Cleopatra takes on a voice of her own.

It is difficult know with certainty whether Sidney knew Latin: she certainly had excellent French and Italian, and it has been speculated that she knew Latin and Greek and, maybe, also Hebrew.[55] In support of her having Latin, it is worth noting what may be an echo of Propertius or Virgil, or both. In the second act, Cleopatra laments Antony's 'suspect' (2.433) about her constancy and swears her fidelity by 'barking Anubis, Apis bellowing' (2.422). We have seen that the Propertian and Virgilian texts quoted above both mention Anubis barking (*latrator Anubis, latrantem … Anubim*) and this is one of the instances where Sidney departs from Garnier's French text. Garnier gives 'I swear by bellowing Apis, and I swear also by you, venerable Anubis', 677–8 ('j'en atteste et le beuglant Apis | et t'en atteste aussi, venerable Anubis'), making no mention of Anubis barking, the key descriptor in the two Latin texts, which reappears in Sidney's drama.[56] She certainly inserts other subtle allusions which are not part of the French text: for example, Antony's 'whome she, false she' (3.29) seems to operate as a metrical and syntactical recall of Philip Sidney's 'that she (dear she)' in *Astrophil and Stella* 1.2. Garnier simply gives us *qu'elle*, 'whom she', and qualifies 'elle' later in the line with 'l'inhumaine' ('cruel', 892). This reminder of Philip Sidney's Stella works to undermine Antony's assertion of Cleopatra's unloving deception since Stella, as we know, might have appeared cold and unmoved on the surface but actually hides her love for Astrophil for the protection of his own virtue. Garnier later utilises Catullan allusions to the kiss poems, cc.5 and 7: 'of a thousand kisses, and a thousand, and a thousand more', 1996 ('de mille baisers, et mille et mille encore'). Sidney expands this motif in Cleopatra's last speech: 'a thousand sobbes' (5.185), 'with thousand plaints' (5.186), 'a thousand kisses, thousand thousand more' (5.205). Certainly Sidney's allusions are not conclusive evidence, but they do draw attention to the possibility that she had knowledge of Latin and elegy in the original, perhaps via her brothers.

As the accumulated evidence indicates, Mary Sidney's *Antonie* may be read as an important, though overlooked, intertext to Roman elegy and, in some ways, is closer to its 'source' than Petrarch's moralised, neo-Platonic poetry. This affinity is made especially clear in the Argument that prefaces the drama: Antony is 'entertained … with all the exquisite delights and sumptuous pleasures, which a great prince and voluptuous lover could to the uttermost desire' (9–10). His adoption of elegiac values is made overt in the language used, and through his rejection of Octavia 'his virtuous wife … by whom nevertheless he had excellent children' (12–13). The latter may be usefully compared to Propertius' first poem where his defeat by Cynthia and Cupid leads him, also, to reject respectable girls for the disreputable pleasures of the elegiac mistress: 'the villain [Cupid] taught me to shun decent girls and to lead the life of a ne'er-do-well' (1.1.5–6).[57] As in Sulpicia's texts, the sexual status of the competing women is made prominent as Antony rejects virtue for something far more sexually enticing. The 'sumptuous pleasures' of Cleopatra are contrasted with the moral integrity of Octavia who conforms to what a 'proper' wife should be, though Sidney certainly, as we shall soon see, goes on to contest this easy separation of 'good' and 'bad' women. The mention of Antony's children draws attention to his sexual promiscuity ('nevertheless') while it confirms Octavia in her traditional role of Roman matron.

One of the dominant emotions of the elegiac lover is his sexual jealousy and suspicion of his mistress, and this, too, is drawn into Sidney's Antony: 'Antony finding that all that he trusted to fail him, beginneth to grow jealous and to suspect Cleopatra' (Argument 21–2). Strikingly, Sidney reworks Garnier at this point, condensing his more detailed description of the battle of Actium, and minimising his political nuances: 'he had the thought that Cleopatra had reached an understanding with him [Octavian] to ruin him [Antony], and by his ruin to contrive her bargain' (Garnier's Argument).[58] By eliding this politicised Cleopatra, manoeuvring for the survival of her reign over Egypt, Sidney focuses more closely on what we might call the erotic Cleopatra, foregrounding Antony's suspicion over her sexual morals, where it is her fidelity and constancy, so important to Catullus' Lesbia and Propertius' Cynthia, which are at stake: 'justly complain I she disloyal is | nor constant is, even as I constant am' (1.141–2).

So by the end of this first act, we think we recognise the erotic contours of this play: Antony is enthralled by his decadent mistress who is prepared to abandon him for Octavius in order to promote her own self-interest. We are reminded not just of Lesbia and Cynthia, but also the fickle, changeable women of Wyatt's Petrarchan verse, and the deceptive beloved of Robert Sidney's bitter love poetry. The second act, however, overturns these expectations and achieves this reversal through the voice of Cleopatra. From her first appearance, she challenges Antony's representation of her, just as the female voices of Cynthia and Sulpicia contest the dominant elegiac narrative:

> That I have thee betrayed, dear Antonie,
> My life, my soul, my sun? I had such thought?
> That I have thee betrayed my Lord, my King?
> That I would break my vowed faith to thee?
> Leave thee? Deceive thee?
>
> (2.151–5)

Cleopatra's opening speech rejects her previous representations as deceiving and untrustworthy, and repositions herself as the faithful and constant lover, making herself the subject of the Petrarchan narrative. Antony is described in typical hyperbole: 'my life, my soul, my sun', where 'sun' may deliberately recall, and supersede, Philip Sidney's astronomical imagery of Stella and Astrophil – the star and star lover. Cleopatra's words recuperate Antony's compromised masculinity and political status ('my Lord, my King') even while her assumption of the lover's role reduces him, temporarily, to the beloved object. The complexities of erotic power dynamics are made manifest as both Antony and Cleopatra claim, separately, the position of faithful lovers, and both compete in terms of the sexual abasement required from this literary mode of love. Cleopatra goes on to articulate the kind of reciprocity we have already noted in Sulpicia's texts when she stresses her queenly status, 'my royal heart' (2.163), the counterpart to Antony as 'my King'. The trope of erotic death which is so prominent in Propertius is adopted by Cleopatra, and her wish 'to have one tomb with thee' (2.178), echoes Cynthia's promise (or threat) that her bones will be mixed with 'Propertius'' (*mixtis ossibus ossa teram*, 4.7.94).

It is not unusual for Petrarchan discourse to appear in drama from this period, but Sidney's *Antonie* is notable for the way in which it uses a female voice to confront and challenge, in an extended way, the gendered norms of the form, and expose the ease with which they might be reconfigured. Sidney does not discard the Petrarchan model but instead, like Sulpicia with elegy, exploits the way in which it already contains a space for the female voice, one previously employed by male authors to contest their own stories from within the text, rendering both elegy and Petrarchan discourse explicitly multivalent and multivocal. Cleopatra's voice, while nominally female within the text, at this point is more or less equivalent to Antony's as they both perform the role of the lover let down, they believe, by their beloved, reclaiming their own constancy in the face of the other's perfidy. This is reflected in the correspondence of their diction as they unknowingly echo each other: his 'my Queen', her 'my King'; his 'idol of my heart', her 'my life ... my sun'. We have seen that Sulpicia's texts could find no significant role for Cerinthus, that the female narrator was forced into performing the roles of both lover and mistress: in Sidney's drama the two opposing roles of lover and beloved do have a presence but it is a strikingly blended one which is adopted simultaneously by both protagonists, both loved and loving, both masculinised and feminised, extinguishing the hierarchies upon which standard male authored elegy and Petrarchan poetry is primarily constructed.

Antony's Act 1 speech presents a complex mix of guilt and responsibility as he manoeuvres to both blame Cleopatra for his state and accept accountability on his own behalf ('For her have I forgone | my country' (1.7–8), 'thou threw'st thy cuirasse off, and fearful healm | with coward courage' (1.74–5)). Cleopatra in Act 2 does not try to evade her own guilt: when Eras asks, 'are you therefore cause of his overthrow?' (2.211), Cleopatra confesses, 'I am sole cause: I did it, only I' (2.212). Her acceptance of blame in the Actium disaster gives her back moral stature in this play, perhaps exceeding that of Antony. As Stella proved to be the moral guardian of Philip Sidney's sonnet sequence, so Cleopatra takes on that mantle here: 'if we therein sometimes some faults commit | we may them not to their high majesties | but to our selves impute' (2.239–41). In acquiring a narrative voice of her own, Cleopatra undermines her representation as the immoral Egyptian queen and adopts a philosophical role.

She goes on to demonstrate her constancy to Antony through her rejection of political expediency with regard to Octavius. Charmion presses her to abandon Antony to protect herself and Egypt:

> Then, madam, help your self, leave off in time
> Antonie's wreck, lest it your wreck procure:
> Retire you from him, save from wrathful rage
> Of angry Caesar both your realm and you.
> (2.287–90)

Cleopatra, though, remains faithful: 'sooner shining light | shall leave the day, and darkness leave the night ... | then I thee, Antony, leave in deep distress' (2.297–302). In speaking her own constancy, Cleopatra is like Cynthia in 4.7 who had rejected the role of the cruel mistress (*dura puella*) and re-made herself into a female version of the elegiac lover. Like Stella and even Laura in the *Triumph of Death*, Cleopatra's is a female voice which takes issue with a prior male narrative which has tried to contain her, and liberates herself from it when she is allowed to speak on her own behalf.

Roman elegy gives us image after image of violence enacted against the female beloved's body: in Propertius 4.7, for example, Cynthia's body is charred from her funeral pyre and her lips withered from her crossing to the underworld. The physical spoiling, by death, of her previous beauty becomes almost a twisted emblem of her maligned reputation in Propertius' texts. Her return from the underworld is to write her own epitaph which both re-configures her role in the narrative, from faithless mistress to constant lover, and restores her beauty: 'here in Tibur's soil lies golden Cynthia' (*hic Tiburtina iacet aurea Cynthia terra*, 4.7.85). Sulpicia's texts, too, make use of this discourse centred on the female body: they write out the sadism so often inscribed on the bodies of elegiac women, but are still forced to put 'Sulpicia's' body into public, sexualised circulation for the pleasure of her readers. Sidney's text makes a striking intervention as her Cleopatra, notorious (in literary texts, at least) for her beauty, makes moves to destroy the very beauty which so often defines her.

Already in her Argument, Sidney plays down the focus on Cleopatra as a superb object to be looked at: Garnier's 'M.Antoine, ayant traversé és provinces d'Asie, fut tellement espris de la singulière beauté de Cleopatre Roine d'Egypte' is reworked as 'but coming in his journey into Syria the places renewed in his remembrance the long intermitted love of Cleopatra, Queen of Egypt' (Argument 6–8) markedly removing the reference to her 'singular, or notable beauty'. Sidney already seems to be foregrounding a distinctive response to the concept of the Petrarchan blazon, the Renaissance adaptation of the elegiac cataloguing of female beauty such as we see in *Amores* 1.5. The practice of blazoning the beloved is, of course, one way in which she is objectivised, textually dismembered as a collection of exquisite body-parts to be lingered over.[59] Sidney's refusal of this device, gestured towards in Garnier's Argument, is a first hint that her Cleopatra might not conform to the usual status assigned to women in love narratives, that she might, at least partially, contest her position as the object of male sexual desire.

In Act 2, Cleopatra advances what might be identified as an anti-beauty or anti-blazon discourse when she blames her face for her plight: 'my face too lovely caus'd my wretched case. | My face hath so entrapp'd, to cast us down' (2.194–5). This is another subtle reworking of Garnier who makes Cleopatra's beauty the cause of her and Antony's joint troubles ('ma beauté trop aimable est notre adversité', 430), and it is worth noting that Sidney does not use the word 'beauty' here, instead reiterating 'face' twice. This might serve as an allusion to Ovid's Apollo and Daphne episode, which itself acts as a bridge between elegiac and Petrarchan narratives, where Daphne prays to have her beauty destroyed in an attempt to stop her terrifying pursuit and rape by Apollo: 'change and destroy this beauty by which I pleased o'er well' (*qua nimium placui, mutando perde figuram*, *Metamorphoses* 1.547). This denunciation of physical beauty on the part of both Daphne and Cleopatra appears to be a muted struggle for agency, a compromised striving to escape the way they are positioned within the texts which contain them, where to be beautiful is conflated with being the victim or object of masculine texts. These acts of female speech seem to be correlated with the rejection of the blazon, so that rendering one of the prime signs of elegy and Petrarchism unviable is itself one of the aims of these female voices. Cynthia, too, in contesting the Propertian master-narrative, re-constructs her loveliness on her own terms when she describes herself simply as 'golden' (*aurea*).

Diomedes' speech in Act 2 focuses on this tension which exists in *Antonie* between the rhetoric of blazon and anti-blazon, between Cleopatra as object and as subject, as articulated through male discourse and the way in which she strives to re-make herself through her own speech and actions. He begins by describing the 'Petrarchan' Cleopatra of the past:

> The alabaster covering of her face,
> The coral colour of her two lips engrains,
> Her beamy eyes, two suns of this our world
> Of her fair hair the fine and flaming gold.
>
> (2.477–80)

The formulaic nature of this description of her face with her skin like marble, her coral lips, her eyes like suns, and her hair like gold might be particularly foregrounded by Shakespeare's sonnet 130, which makes satirical play precisely with these absurdly clichéd similes and metaphors.[60] As Diomedes' speech progresses, however, into Cleopatra's present state, the blazon is turned into an anti-blazon:

> Careless of all, her hair disordered hangs:
> Her charming eyes whence murdering looks did fly,
> Now rivers grown, whose wellspring anguish is,
> Do trickling wash the marble of her face.
>
> (2.493–6)

This anti-blazon disrupts the Petrarchan mode but is still in and of it, as it utilises the same terms of reference (her hair, her eyes, her 'marble' face) even as it warps them, manipulating them into a distorted image that upsets the picture of the sensuous, wanton Cleopatra. It is Cleopatra herself who actively destroys her previously fetishised beauty, and she focuses not just on her face but also on her body, particularly her breast. Diomedes continues, 'her fair discovered breast with sobbing swollen | self cruel she still martyreth with blows' (2.497–8).

On one level, this recalls scenes of female mourning from other classical texts, but it also serves as Sidney's engagement with scenes of eroticised violence practised against the beautiful female body.[61] Here it is not a violent lover who rips off the woman's clothes as we have seen in Ovid's and Propertius' texts, but the woman who takes control of her own body and uncovers her breast ('discovered') in a gesture which becomes a grotesque parody of erotic unclothing. Like Sulpicia, Cleopatra puts her own body on display: she writes her fidelity to Antony on her breast, and intends that her dead and wounded body will stand as a masochistic monument to her faithful and constant love: 'for certain seal | of her true loyalty my corpse hath left' (2.444–5).

Cleopatra is not alone in her display; in Act 5 she urges her women to injure their own bodies too, in imitation of her, as a tribute to Antony:

> Martyr your breasts with multipled blows,
> With violent hands tear off your hanging hair,
> Outrage your face.
>
> (5.195–7)

The emphasis on the women's breasts is another instance of Sidney inserting her own ideas into the text. Garnier uses 'stomach' instead of breast: 'plombez vostre estomach de coups multipliez' ('pound your stomach with multiple blows', 1986). Sidney's change gives her words an erotic charge missing from Garnier, so that even at the point at which she allows Cleopatra to tentatively escape the Petrarchan confines attached to her beauty, she constrains and delimits her, so that Cleopatra's anguish is eroticised and displays the very body she has tried to destroy. Indeed, the wounding or martyring becomes itself fetishised as the visible symbol of Cleopatra's unsatisfied, and now unsatisfiable, desire for the dead Antony.

Metaphors of 'love's wound' are ubiquitous, of course, in the love poetry under consideration here: the narrator in *Amores* 1.2, for example, foresees himself as 'with wound all freshly dealt' (*modo vulnus habebo*); and *Astrophil and Stella* is replete with images of Astrophil being pierced by Cupid's arrows.[62] But while male lovers might be figuratively injured by love, their texts do not linger over images of their hurt, even mutilated, bodies as is the case with Cleopatra. In the absence of a male body to blazon – and Antony's death is reported in a messenger's speech which only details how 'he his body pierc'd' (4.264) – Sidney's *Antonie* seems to have no recourse but to display a female body, just as Sulpicia puts her own textual body into public circulation. Cleopatra's disturbing violence against her breast replays, but also deepens and makes physical, the mostly psychological masochism of the male Petrarchan lover.

The female voice, then, certainly may find a space in, and from, which to speak but it is confined to certain modes of articulation. It might even tentatively be identified as a female voice precisely because it is forced to exhibit the body from which it comes. The female lover (Cynthia, 'Sulpicia', Cleopatra) may invert the tradition which primarily encodes the poet-lover as male but she cannot completely escape prior conventions. She colludes with them in blazoning her own body, even when it takes the form of a masochistic anti-blazon (Cleopatra), or an embracing of transgressive morality ('Sulpicia'). The form that this display takes is governed by the prior representation of women already produced by related male-authored texts: Sulpicia's texts put her body into an overtly sexualised form of public circulation, replicating the dubious social and moral status of Lesbia, Cynthia and Corinna. Cleopatra is perhaps the more ambiguous figure, partly because she has a place in a wider tradition and thus is already imbued with variant readings.[63] Sidney's drama seems to recuperate her moral status, turning her into a model of the constant lover, but her repudiation of her own sexualised image as she attempts to 'outrage' her face and body, recalls her erotic and eroticised past.

Sidney's *Antonie* does not end with Cleopatra's death. Despite the disturbing aesthetic of her self-tortured body, there remains the possibility of reconciliation between her and Antony, even if it is beyond the grave:

> To die with thee, and dying thee embrace:
> My body joined with thine, my mouth with thine,
> My mouth, whose moisture burning sighs have dried
> To be in one self tomb, and one self chest,
> And wrapt with thee in one self sheet to rest.
>
> (5.172–6)[64]

Cleopatra thus returns to the imagery of an eroticised death but, in contrast to the macabre nature of Cynthia's promise, Cleopatra's is an image of peace and final repose.

'But One Heart Flaming More than All the Rest':
Pamphilia to Amphilanthus 1

In a heated poem-letter, Lord Edward Denny, who we met in the previous section, attacks Mary Wroth as 'hermaphrodite in show, in deed a
monster'.[65] His fury had been ignited by what he read as an instance of
family libel in her *Urania*, something which Wroth denied, but the fer-
ocity of his textual assault seems to speak to something deeper. His terms
of abuse, 'hermaphrodite … monster', strike directly at Wroth's female
status and are bound up with her authorship as a woman who 'conceived
an idle book'. Despite her bold response to Denny in a poetic retort which
is the counterpart to his ('Hermaphrodite in sense, in art a monster …
your spiteful words against a harmless book | shows that an ass much like
the sire doth look'), Wroth went to some trouble to have her published
Urania recalled, even writing to the Duke of Buckingham to assure James
I that she meant no offence by it. The brief poetic correspondence thus
foregrounds a cultural discomfort with the idea of a writing woman, particularly, perhaps, a woman who writes of love.

Two of the many lovers in the *Urania* are Pamphilia and Amphilanthus,
and appended to the 1621 printed edition of the romance is a sequence
of sonnets written by Pamphilia, 'all loving', to her inconstant beloved,
Amphilanthus, 'lover of two' – the first full sonnet sequence written in
English by a woman.[66] The sonnets also appear to have circulated separately
in manuscript in advance of the romance: the Folger autograph manuscript has been provisionally dated to c.1610–13.[67] This sonnet sequence,
then, known as *Pamphilia to Amphilanthus*, is a complicated text which
locates itself both as part of, and yet independent from, the romance. Its
title refers back to *Astrophil and Stella* by Wroth's uncle, Philip Sidney, but
also recalls the letters of Ovid's *Heroides*, centring on a female lover writing
back to an absent male beloved. Indeed, Wroth pays tribute to Ovid in
her *Urania* when a poet-scholar is described as 'one who had been mad
in studying how to make a piece of poetry to excel Ovid, and to be more
admired than he is'.[68] Even more directly than her aunt, Mary Sidney,
Wroth wrestles with the question of what happens to elegiac-Petrarchan
erotics when the poet-lover is a woman.

Pamphilia to Amphilanthus 1 is set at the deepest point of night: 'when
night's black mantle could most darkness prove' (1.1), and conjures up a
psychological state where sleep has alienated, or perhaps liberated, the
narrator from her day-time self: 'when sleep, death's image, did my senses
hire | from knowledge of myself'.[69] This state gives rise to a dream-vision,

a staple form used by both elegy as well as the Petrarchan mode, in which Pamphilia sees Venus and Cupid on a chariot of love:[70]

> In sleep, a chariot drawn by winged desire
>   I saw: where sat bright Venus, queen of love,
>   And at her feet, her son, still adding fire
>   To burning hearts which she did hold above.
>   (1.5–8)

Recalling the triumphal form of Petrarch and evoking *Amores* 1.2 where 'Ovid' has a predictive vision of himself as a captive in Cupid's victorious display, Wroth shifts her emphasis to Venus who dominates over Cupid both in her primary position in the verse as well as in status: she is 'queen of love', he merely 'her son', crouched at her feet. The prominence of the female goddess taking precedence over the more usual Renaissance boy-god of love (e.g. *Astrophil and Stella* 8, 17, 20, 43) might itself be signalling a covert gender struggle at work within this text, and it is worth remembering that Sulpicia also makes use of Venus, 'Cytherea' (3.13.3), striking in texts which are otherwise free from mythological allusion. The benevolent ally to 'Sulpicia', however, dropping 'him' (*illum*) into her arms, is quite other in Wroth.

   Venus in her chariot drawn by doves is a common image in Renaissance love iconography: *Astrophil and Stella*, for example, has 'coupling doves, guide Venus' chariot' (79.4), drawing on Ovid, amongst other sources: 'then borne aloft through the yielding air by her [Venus'] harnessed doves' (*Metamorphoses* 14.597), and 'bind your locks with myrtle, yoke your mother's doves' (*Amores* 1.2.23).[71] It is also a prominent image in Sappho whose Ovidian 'biography' and 'Ode to Aphrodite' (fr.1 L-P) were well-known in the Renaissance.[72] Sappho's Aphrodite is summoned by the female narrator 'in your chariot yoked with swift, lovely | sparrows bringing you over the dark earth' (1.9–10) and is prayed to as a powerful erotic collaborator, perhaps the origin of Sulpicia's own positioning which is itself starkly at odds, as we have seen, with the more usual combative relationship between male elegists and Cupid.[73] That Wroth was familiar with Venus and Sappho can be seen from her *Urania*: the central Throne of Venus episode in book 1, which is also illustrated in the frontispiece, is used to distinguish the most constant lover (Pamphilia) from the unfaithful (for example, Amphilanthus); and at least two women throw, or attempt to throw, themselves off cliffs as Ovid's Sappho is preparing to do in *Heroides* 15.

   Nevertheless, Venus in Wroth's opening sonnet is no benevolent deity. In supervising Cupid, these gods of love are 'adding fire to burning hearts'

(7–8) – setting these organs violently alight with a blazing erotic love. Turning to the watching Pamphilia: 'but one heart flaming more than all the rest | the goddess held, and put it to my breast' (9–10). Playing on the image of the cold, aloof mistress of prior texts, Wroth's Pamphilia is given a fiery heart that makes her the most passionate of lovers ('flaming more than all the rest'), while also reminding us that those prior women, too, had long contested their attributed heartlessness.

At odds with the passivity of Pamphilia in this scene is the grotesque, though under articulated, vision of her breast ripped open, which it must be in order for the new heart to be placed, as Venus' own order makes clear: 'dear son, now shut said she: thus must we win' (11). Less overtly than Mary Sidney's Cleopatra, Wroth's Pamphilia, too, embodies a brutal version of the figurative 'love's wound' that is such a prominent motif in elegy and the Petrarchan. What is metaphor in male-authored verse becomes flesh for these women authors, placing the mutilated female body at the heart of erotic experience.

Wroth noticeably merges elements of prior gendered love poetry: unlike Sappho and Sulpicia, she is not waiting eagerly for love – she is ambushed in the way Propertius and Ovid are, and the combative 'thus we must win' spoken by Venus recalls the goddess' competitive erotics at the start of Ovid's tale of Proserpina when she entreats Cupid 'why do you not extend your mother's and your own empire'.[74] If Pamphilia's body is a battle-ground, then Venus and Cupid are the victors: 'he her obeyed and martyred my poor heart'. For Pamphilia, as for the Catullan or Propertian narrator, love is an oppression, bound up with questions of power and submission. And, like 'Ovid', she becomes a lover with no object for her desire: 'neither a boy nor a girl with long, polished hair' (*Amores* 1.1.20).[75] Despite this crucial absence, Pamphilia's dream-vision spills over into day: 'I, waking hop'd as dreams it would depart | yet since, o me: a lover I have been' (13–14).

This opening sonnet is remarkable for the way in which it blends prior influences: it operates programmatically such as is the case with Catullus and the elegists to equate the start of love with the beginning of a poetic project, yet it also evinces a marked departure from earlier texts in the matter of the dream-vision. Where male narrators of dream poems such as Propertius, Petrarch or Astrophil produce images of their beloved in sleep, the dynamic between lover and love object is disturbed in the case of Pamphilia who sees only herself. Her own body takes the place of Cynthia, Laura or Stella so that she is both the dreamer and the unsettling matter of the dream. Where Astrophil, for example, sees a vision of 'ivory, rubies, pearl and gold' representing Stella's 'skin, lips, teeth and head so well' (32.10–11), Pamphilia is faced with a dream in which is 'martyred my poor heart' (12). While Astrophil tries to court sleep in order to enjoy a sight of Stella ('I, seeing better sights in sight's decay | called it anew, and wooed sleep again', 38.12–13), Pamphilia only wants her dream to end: 'waking hop'd as dreams it would depart' (13).

Love, then, is, once more, the initiator of poetry and in this sense Pamphilia conforms to the conventions already laid down: her transformation into a 'lover' (14) is simultaneously a transition into becoming a poet, a status encoded within the sequence title, *Pamphilia to Amphilanthus*. The transplant of the flaming heart alters Pamphilia irretrievably as she absorbs and contains the vehicle of burning love within her own body. Bearing in mind the extent to which both elegy and the Petrarchan mode are immensely self-conscious, concerned as much with the understanding of their own metaliterary status and their relationships to prior texts as they are with a depiction of erotic love, we might additionally read this heart as itself a figurative stand-in for a tradition of love poetry which Pamphilia assimilates in advance of commencing her own sonnet sequence. That this is then 'shut' (11) into her body locks her into a nexus of intertextual relations and returns us to an equivalency between the representation of a female body and the text which we are reading.

Wroth might adopt Ovidian personas from both the *Amores* and the *Heroides* in her verse but this sonnet is quite different in tone and mood from either the jaunty, witty *Amores* or the often angry, vengeful or mournful letters of the heroines. Pamphilia's voice is inward looking, using the dream as a vehicle to probe and convey something about the psyche of a female lover in this mode of poetry. She is passive and mute in the poem's vision, unresisting of the torments imposed on her by Venus and Cupid. Unlike 'Propertius', for example, who, in his opening elegy, describes to Tullus how his head had been trampled by an aggressive Cupid, and later addresses a broader group of implicitly male friends, Pamphilia is solitary in her love and pain.[76] Her gender seems to isolate her from other female lovers as well as from Amphilanthus. The poem encapsulates a tension between her silence in the dream and her poetic voice in the sonnet, encoding a sense of social and psychic transgression from the start of this sequence. Disturbingly, too, there is a masochistic quality in that vision of a flaming heart being pressed and enclosed within Pamphilia's open breast: the image might recall the psychological masochism of Catullus and Wyatt, for example, in thrall to their unfaithful mistresses but Wroth's text makes the erotic wound vividly corporeal, even fetishised, as love cannot be separated from either poetry or pain.

We noted earlier that the *amicus* poems re-place Sulpicia into the subordinate position of the elegiac mistress as love object, and there is an interesting counterpart to this in the case of Wroth. Her cousin, William Herbert, with whom Wroth had an illicit affair, wrote a poem under the fictional authorship of Amphilanthus which Wroth inserts into the *Urania*.[77] What is so striking about this poem is the way in which it overturns and re-writes not just Pamphilia's articulations of constant love, but also the more usual Petrarchan dynamic. In Herbert's poem Amphilanthus acknowledges Pamphilia's love but judges it less powerful, less all-encompassing than his love for her which is itself articulated in conventional Petrarchan fashion: 'I do think no thought but thee | nor desire more light to see | than what doth rise | from thy fair eyes' (11–14). But he does not blame her for her inadequate love ('Dear I blame not they neglect' (15)) because it is due not to a personal fault within Pamphilia but the essential nature of women:

> Thou dost pretty love impart
> As can lodge in woman's heart
> None should be pressed
> Beyond their best.
> (18–21)

If Amphilanthus himself loved only as well as women do, there would be no cause for disappointment:

> Had I loved but at that rate
> Which hath been ordain'd by fate
> To all your kind;
> I had full requited been.
> (1–4)

This seems to be a marked revision of conventional Petrarchism which responds to Pamphilia's own texts of love and constancy, while still managing to manoeuvre a position of simultaneous masculine abjectness and superiority. Despite his name, Amphilanthus yet claims a moral high ground in relation to Pamphilia. Ironically, as the narrator of the *Urania* explains, this poem was written ostensibly to another woman, Antissia, but was really meant for Pamphilia. Wroth thus plays multiple games with her characters allowing Amphilanthus to expose his own dubious nature at precisely the moment in which he articulates the pre-eminent quality of his masculine love over that of Pamphilia specifically and women more generally.

The tone of disillusionment and resignation on the part of Amphilanthus recalls that of the Catullan and Propertian lover as well as the narrator of Wyatt's verse and that of Robert Sidney, Wroth's father, in his 'betrayal' poems, but what is especially notable is the extent to which this poem answers back to Pamphilia's texts. The debate about love and constancy that we have already traced in both elegy and the Petrarchan mode and which is especially foregrounded in the instances of female speech which break through the dominating male narrative is once more brought to the fore. But rather than decrying a lack of love on the part of Pamphilia, in line with 'Petrarch' or Astrophil, Amphilanthus is forced to accommodate her love and yet, somehow, still subordinate it to his own. This text, then, is fascinatingly responsive to Pamphilia's own verse and serves to revise her revision of poetic love narratives. Wroth's intervention can be seen as not just challenging and expanding the agenda, in however compromised a fashion, of previous male Petrarchan poetry, but as also provoking an innovation in at least one male author who follows her.

Reading Sulpicia, Mary Sidney and Wroth together raises questions about female authors' relationships to precedents and poetic 'traditions', and allows us to explore how they might use prior poetry to authorise their own interventions. All three women negotiate their presence within genres and erotic discourses that are more usually seen as masculinised but which, as shown here, can be opened up by, and to, women writers. The creative exchanges that take place are varied, and it pays to be attentive to the local and specific rather than generalising about 'women's writing' – crude gender binaries may obscure rather than illuminate. As we have seen, Wroth, for example, might appropriate Ovidian personas in some instances while overturning them in others. It is perhaps more helpful to apply models of difference and comparability, and participation and exclusion to investigate female writing. What is clear, though, is that the prior texts of Catullus, the elegists and Renaissance Petrarchism enable rather than prohibit female authorship in the early modern period.

Conclusion
'And Love Doth Hold My Hand and Makes Me Write'

Yet shall the better part of me assurèd be to climb
Aloft above the starry sky; and all the world shall never
Be able to quench my name. For look how far so ever
The Roman empire by the right of conquest shall extend
So far shall folk read this work. And time without all end
(If poets as by prophecy about the truth may aim)
My life shall everlastingly be lengthened still by fame.[1]

Ovid ends his *Metamorphoses* with a confident assertion, 'my name will be undying', and also a prophecy – *vivam*, 'I shall live'.[2] The *Metamorphoses* certainly had (and continues to have) a vital afterlife but, as this book shows, so did the *Amores* and the earlier texts of Catullus, Propertius and, possibly, Sulpicia. Roman erotic elegy, we have seen, is alive in, and helps to shape, the love poetry of sixteenth-century England, and its re-writing is complex and subtle. The forms of *imitatio*, intertextuality and reception with which we have been concerned here do not always advertise their sources; we have not been dealing with straightforward elegiac translations or overt re-writings. Early modern English poetry uses love elegy in ways which are nuanced, selective and, sometimes, revisionary. It can show us something new about the Latin texts, their latent potential, and the way they anticipate or speak forward to Tudor England. Roman love elegy, as read here, is capacious and fluid enough to lend itself very well to being 'Englished'.

The receptions and intertexts of elegy we have traced are rich, diverse and not easily categorised. There is, it seems, no single or unified way of reading, re-writing or responding to elegy in poetic terms, not surprising, perhaps, given elegy's own internal diversity, its capacity to be 'about' so many things. The English receptions explored here recognise, and take advantage of, the complexity inherent in elegy and so do different things with, and to, it. Notably, the critic Thomas Greene's influential reception narrative of loss and melancholy has not been borne out by the readings here. What we have traced in its place is an exuberant, un-anxious, creative and immensely productive set of practices that take elegy as their source or origin but re-shape it to articulate the varied preoccupations of the sixteenth-century poetry with which we are concerned.

Elegy, as we have seen, allows and enables ideas, tonalities and voices that Petrarch's sonnets do not: Wyatt, Donne and Nashe, for example, exploit the overt sexuality and sexualisation of the Latin mistress, something prohibited in Petrarch's own neo-Platonic idealisation of Laura. Sidney draws on elegy's model of gendered dialogues in his *Astrophil and Stella*, giving a voice to his Stella in counterpoint to Laura's silence. This move, added to the voices of elegy's mistresses, Sulpicia, and the woman in, say, Nashe's *Choice of Valentines* helps condition and enable the intervention of female authors into this mode of love-writing, something otherwise culturally counter-intuitive. Elegy, too, extends the tones available to 'love' poetry and erotic writing: playful, irreverent, sceptical, cynical, even sexually explicit in the case of Ovid's impotence poem, elegy challenges the qualities that might be deemed 'literary' and makes them legitimate and available, if not always respectable, to early modern poets and poetry.

We started this book with Philip Sidney's image of the re-writing of prior poetry as a metamorphic art ('turning others' leaves') and so it seems fitting to return here to his *Astrophil and Stella*, this time sonnet 90. With characteristic witty disingenuousness, Sidney has Astrophil repudiate the idea of poetry as a route to renown: 'Stella, think not that I by verse seek fame' (1), reminding us that he seeks nothing 'but thee' (2). Disowning both Ovid and Petrarch ('Nor so ambitious am I, as to frame | a nest for my young praise in laurel tree', 5–6), and even the title of poet ('In truth I swear, I wish not there should be | graved in mine epitaph a poet's name', 7–8), he yet ends this poem with the standard elegiac and Petrarchan trope of love being the instigator of the poetry we are reading: 'And love doth hold my hand, and makes me write' (14). Sidney's self-conscious, deft and simultaneous recognition, refutation and ratification of these tropes might serve as a summation of the various, even contradictory, ways in which elegy, sometimes mediated via the Petrarchan, is put to work.

Sidney's sonnets are important, too, for the way in which they showcase an assured blending of intertexts: Ovid and Petrarch above, Propertius as detailed in Chapter 3. This confident, even blasé, incorporation of elements from across the elegiac genre is not something particular to Sidney: Wyatt's use of a Catullan discourse of gendered speech is merged with Petrarch and the erotic hunt imagery so prevalent in Ovid, as we have seen; and Wroth's sonnet, too, authorises itself via vocal positions adopted from

Ovid's *Heroides* as well as Propertius' Cynthia and, possibly, Sulpicia. This untroubled 'pick-and-mix' approach of sixteenth-century poetics is perhaps one of the reasons why the intertextual relations between Catullus, elegy and this body of Renaissance poetry have been generally obscured to date: it is easy to focus on the undoubted and vital presence of Ovid and so overlook the other more varied elements that contribute to the nexus of intertexts. As the previous chapters have demonstrated, there is much to be gained hermeneutically by co-locating Renaissance verse with a broader range of Latin erotic poetry than Ovid alone.

Catullus, in particular, has emerged from the evidence as a significant presence in the early modern period. His previous incarnation as a racy epigrammatist mediated via Martial has been expanded here, and we have seen how Renaissance verse adopts both the sly sexuality of his sparrow poems, and the bitter keynote of a worthless love from the Lesbia texts. Both of these elements, together with the extensive number of sensual kiss poems composed in the period, indicate the presence of alternative erotic models from that of Petrarch which underpin early modern love lyric. We have seen, too, that Catullus has a presence in English verse from earlier than has been previously accounted, making his mark at the early Tudor and Henrician courts.

Nevertheless, it can be hard to isolate a single Latin 'source' for the texts read here: even Donne's debt to Ovid in 'To His Mistress Going To Bed', a relationship well-acknowledged in the literature, is seen here as being 'contaminated' positively by the influence of Virgil's Venus. Bearing in mind, though, firstly the joint transmission and printing of the elegists (excluding Ovid), and, secondly, the institutionalised practice of imitative intertextuality taught in schools via the commonplace book, we should not be surprised at the multiple intertexts that can be simultaneously uncovered in a single poem or poetic sequence. As we have seen Petrarch say, 'from many assorted elements a single thing is created, different and better'. Catullus, Propertius, Ovid and Sulpicia have been our focus here as some of the 'many assorted elements', but they are sometimes blended, and other intertexts have additionally been indicated throughout the preceding chapters. The early modern poetry studied here appears to be programmatically promiscuous in terms of its intertextual relationships.

The conventional methodology of reception which tends to posit, if only for practical analytical reasons, a one-to-one relationship between 'source' text and 'receiving' text thus needs to be enlarged to take account of Renaissance poetic practice. As we have seen repeatedly, the sixteenth-century poets read here think nothing of moving casually between Catullus, elegy, other Ovidian texts, even Virgil, and we need to be sensitive to the fact that our contemporary categorisations of genre may be too restrictive when it comes to unpacking Renaissance intertexts: Henry VIII's love letters and Nashe's 'pornographic' ballad prove surprisingly illuminating when co-located alongside our selected poetry.

Moving from a linear reception relationship to a network of intertexts proves productive but, at the same time, needs to be subject to some critical judgement; it allows us to take account of mediating texts, such as those of Petrarch, but also has the potential to make scholarly analysis unwieldy – where do we want to set our intertextual limits? The solution adopted here is to limit the number of Renaissance poems under investigation to allow narrow and deep readings that reach out to a nexus of various texts. While this might constrict the evidence and argument for the presence of elegy as a shaping component of sixteenth-century love poetry, the more panoramic 'reception' section in Chapter 1 offsets that, to some extent, and the added hermeneutic value of reading our texts via a relational network compensates for the deliberate focus. The approach taken here purposely aligns with the intertextual compositional practices of the early modern period, and suggests that reception methodology can be usefully conditioned by an attention to a culture's approach to reading and writing: that reception methodology can be historicised.

We have seen that intertexts or points of textual contact might consist of what we can loosely term plot or narrative content, character, images, phrases or words. They might shape a whole poetic text or be merely a subtle touch between texts. These intertexts may indicate connections with not just prior classical texts but contemporary sixteenth-century ones. They serve, then, not just as points of contact but as sites of complexity: to interpret them, meaning has to be understood in a comparative fashion. The chapters above indicate the value, even necessity, of expanding the relational complex through which we read sixteenth-century love poetry: for too long it has been more or less limited to Petrarch and a vague recourse to 'Ovidianism'. This delimited view of textual relations forecloses meanings that deserve to be opened up as this book has demonstrated.

As well as widening the interpretational grids through which we read both elegy and the Renaissance cognate verse, the previous chapters have also applied an interpretational anachronism. In most of the chapters this is a silent form of reading, but it is made explicit as a hermeneutic methodology in the Ovid–Donne chapter. While, obviously, acknowledging elegy as factually prior to sixteenth-century poetry, as readers striving to make sense of texts in the present moment that priority does not always hold. We do not necessarily read texts in chronological sequence – historical chronology becomes subordinate to a personal reading history, and elegy may be read as containing traces of Renaissance love poetry rather than vice versa. Casting this reading practice in a more theoretical light, we can say that later texts can illuminate our understanding of earlier ones: not through unlocking a stabilised, latent meaning, but by opening up new hermeneutic potentialities. This constitutes a shift away from a hierarchy of originary and 'receiving' text, towards a reciprocal dialogue as demonstrated in the Ovid–Donne chapter: two-directional, 'backwards reception' is, surely, the way forward.

It may be, then, that a fuzzy version of reception is appropriate when studying Renaissance lyric poetry and its elegiac (and other) intertexts. Asking questions about the extent to which both texts or groups of texts negotiate with and accommodate each other, what interventions they might make in the others' ideologies, and where or how one text or group might embrace or exclude the other prove to be profitable. Certainly, these approaches are especially useful when it comes to analysing how female authors insert themselves into forms dominated by male writers, but that does not preclude them being more generally applicable as texts from one cultural, social or historical period come into contact with texts from another. Sixteenth-century love poetry may assimilate elegy in the way that Pamphilia absorbs a blazing heart, but, as we have seen, sites of resistance and conflict are just as revealing as easy adoptions and adaptations.

The second concern of this book, closely bound up with the first, has been that of reading the erotic, where 'erotic' is a slippery, nuanced and – for those precise reasons – a valuable discursive category. The poetry of sex and desire as read here has not been interpreted as just a displaced way of discussing power relations between, for example, monarch and courtier, or as merely a way to shock and rebel against traditional, conservative values – though it may well do both those things. Instead, the chapters above have been interested in exploring how the vocabulary of sex and the 'lascivious' can be made to mean. What we have seen is that it is a polyphonic discourse: it is equally appropriated by official ideologies, religious and state powers, as well as the dialogues which query, challenge and oppose these.

There is, then, no single way of reading the erotic but it provides an idiom that deserves close and critical attention. The poets of love and sex with whom we have been concerned are not marginal to their cultures, are, in many cases, regarded as 'canonical' – and so their appropriation of erotic discourses warrants consideration. One of the ways to do this is by tracing the dialogues constructed through their verse: meanings may be dependent on what has previously been said, and read, by others. Uncovering these dialogic dependencies has been the substance of the preceding chapters, and we have seen how intricate yet meaningful are the connections between, for example, Ovid's impotence poem, Donne's busk and Nashe's dildo.

We cannot, though, easily transfer the insights gained from our reading of Ovid/Donne/Nashe, say, to the poetry of other chapters: what Catullus or Wyatt, for example, do with the erotic is not the same. Even more complicated are the negotiations of the women writers included here: Sulpicia, Mary Sidney and Mary Wroth all showcase their struggles to fit their female narrators to the contours of poetic discourses which both exploit and yet contest the voices of female characters. On one hand, the idea of female authors participating in literary culture via erotic poetry is counter-intuitive for both periods; on the other, there is a ready-made place for them conditioned by the prior voices of Lesbia, Cynthia, Laura and Stella.

The previous chapters, then, raise questions both about reception and intertextual methodologies, and about the hermeneutics of poetic erotics. There are no neat and easy answers – indeed, one of the conclusions reached here is that attention to the local and specific is more productive and illuminating than trying to find larger comparabilities. There is a danger that attempts to consolidate and unify may succeed, unintentionally, in flattening out differences and variations.

While classicists have been active in theorising the field of classical reception, more continuous interdisciplinary dialogue with early modernists would be valuable. The readings here have tried to be alert to the scholarship in both disciplines, but there is still much to be learnt about how to account for the relationships between texts which are mediated via other poets and intervening discourses such as is the case here with the Petrarchan. Methodologies and a critical vocabulary for managing the non-linear complexities of receptions, intertextual networks and literary 'traditions' still need to be honed.

So there is certainly more work to be done in this area. The close readings here are confined to English engagements with Catullus and the elegists but, as Chapter 1 indicates, early modern European love poetry, too, frequently locates itself in relation to elegiac erotics. Some scholarship exists on neo-Latin appropriations and re-writings of elegy, and will, no doubt, continue, but we can also usefully attend to vernacular receptions such as those of Pierre Ronsard and the Pléiade poets of sixteenth-century France.

The continued exploration of early modern female poets' engagement with classical texts generally, and elegy specifically, is also a fruitful area for further research. Christine de Pisan, Louise Labé, Pernette de Guillet in France; Mary Queen of Scots, Margaret Douglas, Isabella Whitney in Scotland and England; and a wide range of Italian women are all drawn to erotic poetic discourse that places them in the complicated and potentially subversive position of a desiring lover akin to Sulpicia. Veronica Franco, too, exploits the multiple and contradictory valencies of elegy as she negotiates her textual position as both famous Venetian courtesan and female poet. Investigating these women's poetics in detail will enable questions about issues of gendered receptions and intertextuality that deserve attention.

Above all, this book advocates the value of deep readings of a small number of poems: this approach may limit the broader conclusions which can be drawn about, in this case, the role and presence of Latin love elegy in shaping sixteenth-century poetics, but replaces the headline with particular, detailed and individualised examples of the multiple ways in which erotic elegy becomes 'Englished'.

Notes

Introduction

1 *Astrophil and Stella* 1.7–8: all quotations are from Duncan-Jones (1989, revised 2002).

2 'Genre' is used here as a form of shorthand, a quick way of referring to a set of codes and conventions which structure the relations between a group of texts.

3 To be precise, Catullus 1–60 are written in a variety of metres hence are often called polymetrics, including many in hendecasyllables; 69–116 are written in elegiac couplets but are epigrams not elegies in terms of genre. Among the longer poems 61, 65–8 are elegies.

4 Greene (1982) 51, 171.

5 On the reception of Ovid in the Renaissance see Barkan (1986), Martindale (1988), Bate (1994), Stapleton (1996), Enterline (2000), Taylor (2000), Lyne (2001), Pugh (2005), Kilgour (2012).

6 Gaisser (1993), Blevins (2004).

7 Martindale and Martindale (1990) 12; see also e.g. Bate (1994), Estrin (1994), Taylor (2000), Kilgour (2012).

8 Petrarch (2017) III.19.11: *curandum imitatori, ut quod scribit simile non idem sit,* the translation is lightly adapted from Fantham.

9 Petrarch (2017) III.19.13: *denique Senece consilio, quod ante Senecam Flacci erat, ut scribamus scilicet sicut apes mellificant, non servatis floribus, sed in favos versis, ut ex multis et variis unum fiat, idque aliud et melius.* Cf. Seneca's *Epistulae Morales* 84 (*Ad Lucilium*): *nos quoque has apes debemus imitari et quaecumque ex diversa lectione congessimus ... varia illa libamenta confundere, ut etiam si apparuerit, unde sumptum sit, aliud tamen esse quam unde sumptum est appareat,* 'we also should imitate these bees, and whatever we have gathered from various reading ... we should so blend these various libations so it may even appear, from wherever they may have originated, to be something different from that from which it came' (my translation); also Horace, *Odes* 4.2.27–32.

10 Quoted in Greene (1982) 150 from a letter from Angelo Poliziano to Paolo Cortesi.

11 *Satire* 2.25–30 dated to c.1590–3: all quotations from Donne are from Carey (1990, revised 2000).

12 Petrie (1983).

13 Revard (1986).
14 Gardner (1965).
15 Marotti (1986) 68, Miller (1991), Estrin (1994).
16 Dubrow (1995), Heyworth (2009) 179, Johnson (2009) 6. The elegies of Sulpicia were transmitted in the Tibullan corpus and so references in this introduction to Tibullus, who is not one of the poets studied here, can also be taken to include Sulpicia's texts.
17 Blevins (2004).
18 Blevins (2004) 5. On the ordering and authorial arrangement of Catullus' poems see Skinner (1981) and especially (2007b); also Hutchinson (2012).
19 On *militia amoris* see Cahoon (1988), McKeown (1995); on images of the military triumph in elegy, Murgatroyd (1975), Miller (1995), Beard (2007); on the trope of erotic sickness in Catullus, Booth (1997).
20 On Ovid in Petrarch, see e.g. Petrie (1983), Freccero (1986), Miller (1991), Estrin (1994), Dubrow (1995), Hardie (1999), Braden (2000), Heyworth (2009), Johnson (2009).
21 It is worth noting here that sexual morality is an ethical imperative to the Romans and that elegy delights in deliberately challenging, interrogating and subverting conventional expectations of sexual behaviour: see Langlands (2006); also Harper (2013) on the Christian transformation of sexual morality in late antiquity.
22 For example, Spiller (2001) 2–3, 'Petrarch … almost single-handedly supplied the whole of Renaissance Europe with the themes and motifs of love poetry'.
23 On 'anti-Petrarchan' as a term of analysis see especially Dubrow (1995), Blevins (2004).
24 Frow (1990) 46.
25 Braden (2000), quotations from 101.
26 Wyke (2002); also Miller (1994).
27 On the name Cerinthus see Boucher (1976), Roessel (1990).
28 Greene (1982) 1.
29 Greene's strategies are the 'reproductive' where a 'sacred original' is reproduced; the 'eclectic' where simple allusions or quotations are used in a sometimes random way; the 'heuristic' where the imitation announces its derivation from past texts but also distances itself from past culture; and the 'dialectical' which is the site of a 'struggle between texts and between eras', where texts 'criticise' each other: see Greene (1982) 38–48.
30 Greene (1982) 41.
31 Bull (2005).
32 Martindale and Martindale (1990) 14.
33 Greene (1982) 2. A single and universally agreed definition of intertextuality is impossible but Allen (2000) 5 offers a process which 'foregrounds notions of relationality, interconnectedness and interdependance'. For theoretical discussions on intertextuality see e.g. Frow (1990), Worton and Still (1990), Allen (2000), Orr (2003); for intertextuality in relation to the reception

of classical Latin texts Martindale (1988, 1993, 2006, 2013), Hinds (1998), Edmunds (2001); on the intertextuality of love elegy, O'Rourke (2012).

34 Greene (1982) 17–30.

35 On Donne's 'Ovidianism', see e.g. Armstrong (1977), Lerner (1988), Bate (1994), Stapleton (1996); also Easthope (1989), Low (1990), Belsey (1994), Singer (2009); also Chapter 4.

36 Wills (1996) 16.

37 Martindale (1993, 2013).

38 Frow (1990) 46; also O'Rourke (2012).

39 Aulus Gellius was a miscellanist writing in the second century CE: his twenty-book *Noctes Atticae*, 'Attic Nights', contains extracts from a great number of Greek and Latin works, and quotes extensively from Cicero and Virgil, contemporaneous, respectively, with Catullus and the Augustan elegists. The text was known in manuscript from the fifth century CE, and the *editio princeps* was printed in Rome in 1469. There was a second Roman edition and a Venetian edition both in 1472, with the Venetian edition being reprinted twelve times before 1500. The Aldine edition was published in 1515.

40 *Iucundum in modum Anakreonteia pleraque et Sapphica et poetarum quoque recentium elegeia quaedam erotica dulcia et venusta cecinerunt*: quotation and translation from Rolfe (1928): the Latin text gives 'Anakreontia' and 'elegeia' in Greek which has been transliterated here.

41 *Amavit hic puellam primariam Clodiam, quam Lesbiam suo appellat in carmine [...] Superiorem habuit neminem. In iocis apprime lepidus, in serio vero gravissimus extitit. Erotica scripsit*, written by Gerolamo Squarzafico for Aldus Manutius, quoted in Wray (2001) 3: Wray's translation is slightly adapted here.

42 'Eroticall' is first used by Richard Burton in his *Anatomy of Melancholy* (1621). Dates given are as first recorded in the *OED*.

43 E.g. Sidney's *Defence of Poesie* 222.

44 *The Boke Named the Governour* in Vickers (1999) 57.

45 All quotations from the *Faerie Queene* are from Roche (1987), quotation from 15.

46 *The Arte of English Poesy* in the Alexander edition (2004) 76.

47 Vickers (1999) viii.

48 Vickers (1999) 53.

49 Franz (1972), Talvacchia (1999), Moulton (2000), Brown (2004).

50 The 'Preface' whose full name is *A Preface or rather, a Brief Apologie of Poetrie and of the Author and Translator of this Poem*, is given in full in Vickers (1999): all quotations are from this edition.

51 Vickers (1999) 312.

52 *Aut prodesse volunt aut delectare poetae*, Ars Poetica 333.

53 Vickers (1999) 317.

54 *Et tamen ille tuae felix Aeneidos auctor | contulit in Tyrios arma virumque toros | nec legitur pars ulla magis de corpore toto,| quam non legitimo foedere iunctus*

amor, all quotations from the *Tristia* are from Owen (1963), translations from Wheeler, revised by Goold, 2nd edition (1988).

55 Vickers (1999) 317–18; the references to Venus and Vulcan are from *Aen.* 8.387–90, 404–6. Harington also uses Chaucer to defend the erotic: the Miller's and Wife of Bath's tales, he remarks, 'both in words and sense incurreth more the reprehension of flat scurrility' (318).

56 Martial 43.10.

1 'Ovid Was There and with Him Were Catullus, Propertius and Tibullus'

1 See Reynolds and Wilson (1968, revised 1991), Pfeiffer (1976), Reynolds (1983).

2 Heyworth (2007) vii. For details, Butrica (1984), summarised in Butrica (2006); see also Fedeli (2006).

3 *Propertius rediit ad nos*, quoted in Heyworth (2007) xxv.

4 Heyworth (2007) xxvi.

5 Heyworth (2007) xi, Gavinelli (2006).

6 Butrica (1984) 30, Heyworth (2007) xi, Gavinelli (2006).

7 Butrica (1984) 30, Heyworth (2007) xii, Fedeli (2012) 4.

8 Heyworth (2007) xv.

9 Heyworth (2007) xv.

10 U comes from Florence c.1465–70, C from Rome c.1470–1: Heyworth (2007) xv, xiv, xlviii.

11 Butrica (1984) 30.

12 *Catulli, Tibulli, Propertique libellos coepi ego Angelo Politianus iam inde a pueritia tractare et pro aetatis eius judicio vel corrigere vel interpretari*: Swann (1994) 106.

13 Stapleton (1996) 43–9.

14 See Stapleton (1996) ch.3 on the troubadours and ch.4 on Dante.

15 'I saw four great shades coming to us; their looks were neither sad nor joyful. The good Master [Virgil] began: "Mark him there with sword in hand who comes before the three as their lord; he is Homer, the sovereign poet. He that comes next is Horace the moralist, Ovid is the third, and the last Lucan".' *Inferno* 4.82–93.

16 Stapleton (1996) 4.

17 Stapleton (1996) 5. William Caxton had previously translated the whole of the *Metamorphoses* into English in 1480 but this had remained in manuscript: see Forey (2002) xiii.

18 Keach (1977) 29, Stapleton (1996) 134.

19 The text was printed by 'T.Creede for John Browne and to be sold at his shop in Fleetstreet, at the signe of the bible, 1600' (STC (2nd ed.)/ 18974.

20 Wilkinson (1955) 401.

21 *The Oxford Shakespeare: The Complete Works*, 2nd edition (2005).

22 Potter (2012) 18–31 on Shakespeare's education.

23 See Green (2009) on humanist education.

24 Green (2009) 222.

25 On florilegia and commonplace books on the medieval and Renaissance school curriculum, see Moss (1996).

26 *Summa petit livor; perflant altissima venti*: the translation is mine from *The Letters of Abelard and Heloise* (1974).

27 Fyler (2009). See also Wheeler (2000) on the *Heroides* in the medieval classroom and Heloise's use of them in her letters to Abelard.

28 Moss (1996) 53–4.

29 Moss (1996) 39–40.

30 Moss (1996) 67–70.

31 Moss (1996) 67–71.

32 Moss (1996) 87–90.

33 Moss (1996) 87–90.

34 Moss (1996) 190–9.

35 Gavinelli (2006) 404.

36 *Elegiam qui scribunt omnes puero negari debent. Nimium sunt enim molles, ut Tibullus, Propertius, Catullus et quae translatae est apud nos Sappho. Raro namque non amatoria scribunt desertosque conqueruntur amantes*: quoted in Kallendorf (2002) 223.

37 Quoted in Moss (1996) 84.

38 Green (2009) 218–19.

39 The allusion to Gallus is puzzling: Stockward might be referring to Virgil's *Eclogue* 10 where Gallus speaks as a character, or mentions in Ovid, or may simply not know that Gallus' poetry has been lost. Stockward's *A very fruiteful sermon preched at Paules Close the tenth of May last* was published in London in 1579, and is quoted in Kallendorf (2007) 373.

40 Scaliger in 1572 had questioned the attribution and created the *Appendix Vergiliana* into which the *Priapea* poems were placed: see Reeve in Reynolds (1983), Burrow (2008), Wallace (2011). As late as 1591, however, Spenser wrote *Vergils Gnat*, based on the contested *Culex* from the *Appendix*, so the question of Virgilian authorship seems to have remained open.

41 Green (2009) 147.

42 Green (2009) 219.

43 Gavinelli (2006) 411.

44 Green (2009) 127–90 on English school education.

45 Green (2009) 35.

46 Green (2009) 36–41.

47 Green (2009) 266–7.

48 *De Ratione Studii* 122.

49 Sig. F iiii + 1, quoted in Moss (1996) 90.

50 For example, LaBranche (1966), Armstrong (1977), Carey (1981), Freccero (1986), Barnard (1987), Lerner (1988), Miller (1991), Stapleton (1996), Hardie (1999), Braden (2000), Clarke (2000), Brown (2004). On the imprecision of the term 'Ovidian' as used by Renaissance scholars see Keach (1977).

51 'l'uno era Ovidio e l'altro era Catullo, | l'altro Properzio, che d'amor cantaro | fervidamente, e l'altro era Tibullo', translations from Petrarch's *Triumphs* are from Wilkins (1962).

52 Alexander (2006) 100.

53 See e.g. Lyne (1980), Keith (1994), Pincus (2004), Miller (2007), Myers (2012).

54 *successor fuit hic tibi, Galle, Propertius illi; | quartus ab his serie temporis ipse fui.*

55 On the Gallus fragments, Anderson *et al.* (1979), Putnam (1980), Fairweather (1984), Newman (1984), O'Hara (1989).

56 *Haec quoque lascivi cantarunt scripta Catulli, | Lesbia quis ipsa notior est Helena; | [...] et modo formosa quam multa Lycoride Gallus | mortuus inferna vulnera lavit aqua! | Cynthia quin vivet versu laudata Properti, | hos inter si me ponere Fama volet.* All quotations from Propertius are from Heyworth (2007), translations are lightly adapted from Goold (1990, revised 1999).

57 *carmina quis potuit tuto legisse Tibulli | vel tua, cuius opus Cynthia sola fuit?, Rem. Am.* 763–4: see also Boyd (1997) on the influence of Propertius on the *Amores*.

58 Gaius Valerius Catullus c.84–54 BCE was born in Verona to a propertied family but lived most of his life in Rome. He was at the centre of a group of young poets who rejected the traditional ideals of early Rome and turned towards Hellenistic Greek culture. His corpus of poetry is slim, comprising 114 poems which vary in length and form: sixty short poems in lyric metres, poems 61–68 which are longer and in a variety of metres, the remaining are epigrams written in elegiac metre. The 'Lesbia cycle' is loosely contructed and not in chronological order appearing across the short poems and epigrams.

59 *Ardeo, mi Galeaz, mollem reperire Catullum, | Ut possim dominae moriger esse meae. | Lectitat illa libens teneros lasciva poetas, | Et praefert numeros, docte Catulle, tuos,* 2.23–7 – quoted in Swann (1994) 97–8.

60 E.g. in his *Parthenopeus* and *Hendecasyllabi*: see Swann (1994). 'Catullus' refers to his poems as hendecasyllables, e.g. c.42.

61 *Amor Tibullo, Mars tibi, Maro, debet ... docto Catullo syllabae,* epigram 1.16.1–8, and *aeternumque, meae, frater, ave, lacrimae!,* 1.22 on the death of his brother, both quoted in Swann (1994) 104. Compare the latter with Catullus 101.10, *atque in perpetuum, frater, ave atque vale,* 'and forever, O my brother, hail and farewell'.

62 *Amavit hic puellam primariam Clodiam, quam Lesbiam suo appellat in carmine [...] Superiorem habuit neminem. In iocis apprime lepidus, in serio vero gravissimus extitit. Erotica scripsit:* quoted in Wray (2001) 3, the translation is lightly adapted here; this life was written by Gerolamo Squarzafico and is drawn from Jerome, Apuleius *Apology* 10, and possibly other now lost sources.

63 See especially Gaisser (1993) and (2009). On Martial as a mediator for the Renaissance Catullus, see Swann (1994).

64 On Poliziano, Reynolds and Wilson (1968, revised 1991) 140–3, also Pfeiffer (1976) 44–5 on Poliziano's lectures on classical poetry. Poliziano's Renaissance reading is available in Gaisser (2007), on the modern debate on the reading of *passer,* see Jocelyn (1980), Hooper (1985), Jones (1998), Pomeroy (2003).

65 On Catullan reception in England, see Duckett (1925), McPeek (1939), Gaisser (1993, 2001, 2009), Blevins (2004).

66 McPeek (1939) 44–5, Gaisser (2001) xxix, Blevins (2004) 19–22. Cheney (2011) 95–8 reads *Phyllyp Sparrow* as 'in the Roman elegiac tradition of Ovid'.

67 *Ite, Brittannorum lux o radiosa, Brittanum* | *carmina nostra pium vestrum celebrate Catullum!*, 'Go, o shining light of the Britons, and celebrate our songs, your worthy (*pium*) British Catullus!', *The Garlande or Chapelet of Laurell*, 1521–2. This quotation comes from Skelton's address to his book (*Skeltonis alloquitur librum suum*) which is itself an imitation of Catullan addresses to his poems, e.g. c.42, *adeste, hendecasyllabi, quot estis*, 'come hither, hendecasyllables, all of you there are' (42.1). All quotations from Skelton are from the Scattergood edition (1983) and silently modernised.

68 Carlson (1991) 102–6.

69 *qui nunc it per iter tenebricosum* | *illuc, unde negant redire quemquam*, 3.11–12.

70 Elegy 3.5 is Secundus' verse in honour of Erasmus.

71 All quotations from *Basia* are from Wright (1930), translations are mine.

72 *Non hic furta deum iocosa canto* | *monstrosasve libidinum figuras*, 12.3–4.

73 'Pastime with Good Company' in the *Henry VIII* manuscript, transcribed in Stevens (1979); Catullus: *otium, Catulle, tibi molestum est:* | *otio exultas nimiumque gestis.*

74 'But if I sit near her by | with loud voice my heart doth cry | and yet my mouth is dumb and dry | what means this?' (Wyatt, 103.21–4), and 'my tongue doth fail what I should crave' (103.26), cf. Cat. 51 especially 6–9: *nam simul te* | *Lesbia, aspexi, nihil est super mi* | *lingua sed torpet*, 'for whenever I see you, Lesbia, at once no sound of voice remains within my mouth, but my tongue falters'.

75 Herman (2010) 1–2, 50–1.

76 *Principum ac illustrium aliquot et eruditorum in Anglia virorum, encomia, trophaea, genethliaca et epithalamia. A Ioanne Lelando antiquario conscripta, nunc primarum in lucem edita*, 1589, London.

77 Carley (1986).

78 *Me tibi coniunxit comitem gratissima Granta: Naeniae in mortem Thomae Viati equitis incomparabilis*, 38: all quotations from Leland are from Sutton's online edition at www.philological.bham.ac.uk/lelandpoems which is based on the 1589 published edition edited by Thomas Newton, and a manuscript executed by John Stow now in the Bodleian Library (ms. 464 (4)).

79 *Mantua Virgilium genuit, Verona Catullum.*| *Patria Londinium est urbs generosa mihi.*

80 *Lesbia lascivo placuit formosa Catullo* | *[...]* | *Delitiae Galli docti clarique poetae* | *[...]*| *Lactea Peligni floret Nasonis amica,*| *Materiem numeris sueta Corynna dare: Cynthia laudatur detersi nympha Properti.*

81 See, especially, Wyke (2002), also Greene (1995b, 1998).

82 *Sunt qui admirantur, sunt qui venerantur, et usque* | *Carmina suspiciunt, docte Catulle, tua.*

83 *Quem si nunc dederis, novae studebunt* | *Formae, ac purpureum induent colorem* | *Ut sint persimiles Catullianis.*

84 *Tristi carmine passerem Catullus | Extinctum queritur parum pudicus,| Deflet Stella suae vices columbae | Vates molliculus, tener, cinaedus. | At nos qui colimus severiora,| Et Musas sequimur sacratiores | Lumen iudicii boni Viatum | Abreptum querimur dolore iusto.*

The reference to Stella is to Martial 1.7: *Stellae delicium mei columba | Verona licet audiente dicam | vicit, Maxime, passerem Catulli. | Tanto Stella meus tuo Catullo | quanto passere maior est columba*, 'The dove, the delight of my friend Stella – even with Verona listening I will say it – has surpassed, Maximus, the sparrow of Catullus. By so much is my Stella greater than your Catullus, as a dove is greater than a sparrow': this witty exposé of competitive manhood is testament to Martial's reading of Catullus' sparrow as more than just a pet bird; see also Martial 11.6.14–16 and discussion in Gaisser (2009) 170. Adams (1982) rather oddly accepts dove as sexual slang, but not sparrow.

85 Nash (1996) 115–17, Putnam (2009) editorial notes.

86 *Da mihi, mea lux, tot basia rapta petenti | quot dederat vati Lesbia blanda suo*: quotations from Sannazaro are from Putnam (2009); cf. *Da mi basia mille, deinde centum | dein mille altera, dein secunda centum*, 'give me a thousand kisses, then a hundred, then another thousand, then a second hundred', Cat. 5.7–8. All quotations from Catullus are from Mynors (1958), translations lightly adapted from Goold (1989) unless stated otherwise.

87 *Nulli se dicit mulier mea nubere malle | quam mihi, non si Iuppiter ipse petat.*

88 *Nulla meos poterit mulier praevertere sensus | ipsa licet caelum linquat, et astra Venus.*

89 *Dicit: sed mulier cupido quod dicit amanti | in vento et rapida scribere oportet aqua.*

90 *Iam sanxere semel nos inter foedera divi | foedera ad extremos non solvenda rogos.*

91 *Doctus ab Elysia redeat si valle Catullus | ingratosque trahat Lesbia sola choros | non tam mendosi maerebit damna libelli | gestiet officio quam, Ioviane, tuo.*

92 Croft's introduction to his edition of Robert Sidney's poems (1984) 54.

93 *nunc te cognovi: quare etsi impensius uror | multo mi tamen es vilior et levior.*

94 *huc est mens deducta tua mea, Lesbia, culpa | atque ita se officio perdidit ipsa suo.*

95 *eripite hanc pestem perniciemque mihi… ipse valere opto et taetrum hunc deponere morbum.*

96 *ambobus mihi quae carior est oculis.*

97 All quotations from Jonson are from Parfitt (1975, revised 1996).

98 *Soles occidere et redire possunt: | Nobis, cum semel occidit brevis lux, | Nox est perpetua una dormienda.*

99 See Roberts (1983) 16–17 on Jonson and the Sidney family. The 'Celia' poems appear in Jonson's *The Forest* just after his poem 'To Penshurst'.

100 *Da mi basia mille, deinde centum | Dein mille altera, dein secunda centum, | Deinde usque altera mille, deinde centum.*

101 *Quam magnus numerus Libyssae harenae | lasarpiciferis iacet Cyrenis | oraclum Iovis inter aestuosi | et Batti veteris sacrum sepulcrum | aut quam sidera multa, cum tacet nox | furtivos hominum vident amores, | … quae nec pernumerare curiosi | possint nec mala fascinare lingua.*

102 *Cynthia prima* 1.1. Sextus Propertius was born between 54 and 47 BCE in Assisi to a notable family and was dead by 2 BCE. His family's wealth was compromised by Augustus' property confiscations in c.41 BCE and we can note an irreverance, sometimes oblique, towards the Augustan regime in the poetry. Propertius' first book of poetry was published c.28 BCE and consists almost entirely of love poems, as does book 2. Books 3 and 4 are more diverse in subject matter but still include poems about Cynthia.

103 *Cinthia, si qua meo debetur fama labori | abs te suscipiam quicquid honoris erit. | Tu mihi das ipsas scribendi in carmina vives, tu facis ingenium, to facis eloguium*: quoted in Houghton (2013), translation lightly adapted.

104 *Ingenium nobis ipsa puella facit.*

105 Julia, Augustus' daughter, was banished in 2 BCE for adultery; Ovid was possibly implicated in the banishment of the younger Julia, Augustus' granddaughter, in 8 CE: see e.g. Thibault (1964), Boyle (2003) 4–6. The two Julias were, however, frequently confused or conflated in the Renaissance.

106 On Campion, see Manuwald (2012).

107 Manuwald (2012) 43.

108 Manuwald (2012) 43.

109 On the Accademia and their engagement with erotic elegy see Rosenthal (1992) ch.5, quotation from 210.

110 Puttenham (2004) 96.

111 It is possible to write in elegiac couplets without the resulting poem being elegy in genre terms.

112 Jonson also includes a translation of *Amores* 1.15 in the play, adapted from Marlowe: thanks to Charles Martindale for this reference; see also Stapleton (2014).

113 Poem 27 in Jonson's in *Underwoods*.

114 On the medieval Ovid, Hexter (2002), Fyler (2009), Clark *et al.* (2011). Publius Ovidius Naso, 43 BCE to 17 CE, was born at Sulmo and sent to Rome for his education. After holding some minor judicial posts, he concentrated on poetry and was a prominent and well-known poet in Rome before being banished by Augustus in 8 CE. All of his works were in elegiac couplets except the *Metamorphoses* which was written in hexameters, the metre of epic. *Amores* was originally a five-book collection but what we have is the three-book second edition published c.16 BCE. Ovid's other works are *Heroides, Ars Amatoria, Remedia Amoris, Fasti, Epistulae ex Ponto, Metamorphoses*.

115 Fyler (2009) 411.

116 E.g. Armstrong (1977), Barnard (1987), Martindale (1988), Bate (1994), Stapleton (1996), Hardie *et al.* (1999), Braden (2000), Taylor (2000), Lyne (2001), Wiseman (2008).

117 See e.g. Keach (1977), Burrow (1988), Brown (2004).

118 *Tristia* 2.207; earlier in the poem the narrator says 'verse caused Caesar to brand me and my ways by commanding that my "Art" be forthwith taken away', *carmina fecerunt, ut me moresque notaret | iam demi iussa Caesar ab*

Arte mea (*Tr.* 2.7–8), a reference to the removal of the *Ars Amatoria* from public libraries, but not necessarily the cause of his exile.

119 Hexter (2002) 432–4.

120 The quote is from Thomas Cooper's frequently reprinted *Thesaurus linguae romanae et brittanicae* (1565). See Bate (1993) 1 on Ovid's biography as an introduction to his works.

121 Gloss to ll.59–60. On Ovid's Renaissance biography see also Burrow in Hardie (2002).

122 Brown (2004) 36–52, quotes from 36.

123 Pugh (2005) 1.

124 Pugh (2005) 53. Also Hadfield (2003), in a passing comment, separates the 'Virgilian' and 'Ovidian' in the *Faerie Queene* which he characterises as order and chaos struggling for narrative control of the text.

125 On 'further voices' in the *Aeneid* see Lyne (1987).

126 Donatus' 'Life' is available in Camps (1969). On the *Priapea* poems as being understood to be by Virgil, see Kallendorf (2007) 191: he documents that they were, for example, printed in sixty-eight of the 131 editions of Virgil published in Renaissance Venice (191) and that, in some of the books that have come down to us, the *Priapea* poems have been manually cut out.

127 Introduction to *Aretino's Dialogues*, translated by Rosenthal (2005) 4.

128 *Ac coniugo spoliator ab Aenea, non esset parcitum: quod victis concede solet*: on Andrea Tordi's commentary on the *Aeneid*, see Kallendorf (2007) 356.

129 Cf. 'so saying, in burning rage he buries his sword full in Turnus' breast. His limbs grew slack and chill and with a moan his life fled resentfully to the Shades below', *hoc dicens ferrum adverso sub pectore condit | fervidus; ast illi solvuntur frigore membra | vitaque cum gemitu fugit indignata sub umbras*, *Aen.* 12.950–2; On Ariosto and Virgil, see Javitch (1984), Sitterson (1992).

130 This title-page is reproduced in Forey's edition of Golding's *Metamorphoses*, 2002, together with both the 1565 and 1567 prefatory epistles.

131 Gibson (1999) 19.

132 *Quia carmine ab omni | ad delinquendum doctior esse potest; quodcumque attigerit, siqua est studiosa sinistri / ad vitium mores instruet inde suos.*

133 *Nihil est hirsutius illis.*

134 *Ilias ipsa quid est aliud nisi adultera, de qua | inter amatorem pugna virumque fuit.*

135 *Aut quid Odyssea est nisi femina propter amorem | dum vir abest, multis una petita viris?*

136 *Posse nocere animis carminis omne genus.*

137 *Nil prodest, quod non laedere possit idem.*

138 *Omnia perversas possunt corrumpere mentes.* Augustus had endowed the Palatine library and in *Tristia* 1.1.69–72 'Ovid' advises his text not to hope to go there: see Gibson (1999) 31. In *Tr.* 2.237 'Ovid' asserts that Augustus has never actually read the *Ars* (*te numquam nostros evoluisse iocos*) but that that has not stopped him condemning it as immoral.

139 *Crede mihi, distant mores a carmine nostro – | vita verecunda est, Musa iocosa mea.* See also Catullus 16.5–6 for a similar separation between poet and text.

140 *Multa licet castae non facienda legant.*

141 Wilkinson (1955) 401.

142 Ovid would not, of course, have been the only source: Botticelli's Venus and Mars (c.1480) and his *Birth of Venus* (c.1485), both produced in Florence, would have been influenced by Ficino's neo-Platonism: see Wallace *et al.* (2007) 28.

143 See D'Ancona (1955) on the Villa Farnesina. Bacchus and Ariadne might have derived from Catullus 64 rather than Ovid: Ginzburg (1990) 84–5 proposes that Titian's *Bacchus and Ariadne* (c.1523) was also influenced by Catullus following a letter written to Titian by the friend who translated Cat. 64 for him as Titian did not have good Latin.

144 Hall's Chronicle.

145 On the history of *I Modi* see Lawner (1988) and Talvacchia (1999): both also contain copies of the engravings and translations of Aretino's sonnets, though Lawner, rather coyly, gives the obscene terms for the lovers' body parts in Italian.

146 Lawner (1988) 10–12. On the Laocoön, see Kallendorf (2007) 583.

147 Quoted in Talvacchia (1999) 6. Only sixteen illustrations and accompanying sonnets seem to have survived into the second edition.

148 Freedman (1995) 11.

149 E.g. Suetonius, *Tiberius* 43: 'a number of small rooms were furnished with the most indecent pictures and statuary obtainable, also certain erotic manuals from Elephantis in Egypt'; and Martial 12.43. Parker (1992) discusses the concept of ancient 'sex manuals'.

150 Quoted in Lawner (1988) 31–2.

151 From a letter from Aretino to Battista Zatti published in Venice in 1538 though the date of this actual letter is disputed to be between 1527 and 1537: quoted in Talvacchia (1999) 13, and Rosenthal (2005) 4.

152 Renaissance understandings of classical 'erotica' did encompass sexual encounters between non-divine participants since they were aware of lamps, mirrors and vases which depicted 'normal' people in sexual situations such as the Warren Cup: see Talvacchia (1999) 50, especially Clarke (2003).

153 *Ars Amatoria* 3.769–808.

154 E.g. *Orlando Furioso* 46.14, *ecco il flagello | de'Principi, il divin Pietro Aretino,* 'the divine Pietro Aretino, scourge of princes'. This seems to have been a reference to the fact that as a self-supporting writer and thus a man beholden to no patron, Aretino claimed a freedom of expression which was seen as radical and potentially dangerous: see Rosenthal's introduction to Aretino's *Dialogues* (2005) for his biography.

155 Rosenthal (2005) 5.

156 Talvacchia (1999) 19.

157 The Index of books forbidden in Catholic Europe was formally established in 1559 by Pope Paul IV: Machiavelli's political writings were on it as well as Aretino's works: see Findlen (1993).

158 See El-Gabalawy (1976) on Aretino's influence in England; also Moulton (2000) 31, 123ff.

159 See Bald (1970) 121.
160 Quotations from the *Ragionamenti* are from the Rosenthal translation (2005).
161 Little is known of Sulpicia other than information gleaned problematic- ally from her poetry. Sulpicia's six elegies have been transmitted in the third (sometimes fourth, depending on organisation) book of Albius Tibullus' poetry. They follow five poems, usually known as the Garland of Supicia or the *amicus* poems, which tell of the love of Sulpicia for Cerinthus.
162 On Sulpicia in the commentaries, Skoie (2002).
163 *Fingit alios amatores sibi esset, quibus dolet, quod uni Cerintho addicta sit. Fingit, inquam, ut iam tepentem pueri amorem accendat*, quoted in Skoie (2002) 90.
164 *Quod sane non potest dici, quam venuste ab erudito poeta commentum sit*, quoted in Skoie (2002) 90.
165 *Omnes Sulpiciam legant puellae* | *uni quae cupiunt viro placere;* | *omnes Sulpiciam legant mariti* | *uni qui cupiunt placere nuptae*: all quotations from Martial are from the Lindsay edition. Sulpicia, the wife of Calenus, is also praised in Martial 10.38.
166 My thanks to Charles Martindale for pointing out the Chaucer reference.

2 'For Truth and Faith in Her Is Laid Apart'

1 All quotations from Wyatt are from Rebholz (1978, revised 1997): the numbering of poems are from the 1997 edition. Sir Thomas Wyatt, 1503– 42, was a diplomat as well as poet at the court of Henry VIII. His father had been a Privy Councillor to Henry VII and remained as an advisor to Henry VIII. Wyatt was educated at Cambridge: see Brigden (2012) on his biography.
2 For example, Southall (1964), Estrin (1984), Dubrow (1995), Heale (1998), Cheney (2011). Some scholars have read Wyatt's fickle mistress as a coded way of talking about the capricious nature of fortune at court, or Henry VIII himself: Kamholtz (1978), Marotti (1982), Heale (1998).
3 All quotations from Catullus are from Mynors (1958), translations lightly adapted from Cornish, revised by Goold (1995).
4 Greene (1982) 255. Also Hannen (1974) 51–7 on the problematisation of elo- quence in Wyatt's poetry.
5 Skinner (2003) 82–95 tackles the teasing identification of Lesbia as one of the Clodias in c.79; Dyson (2008) 4–9 summarises the debate to date over the identification of Lesbia with Clodia Metelli; Gaisser (2009) 1 comments on the 'deceiving' accessibility of Catullan verse. Ives (2004) documents the historical relationship between Wyatt and Anne Boleyn but at least partially resists reading the poetry as purely autobiographical; as late as 2011, however, Cheney (2011) 102 discusses 'Whoso List to Hunt' as being about the histor- ical Anne Boleyn, and states unproblematically that Wyatt was in love with Anne and thus was in competition with Henry VIII for her regard (127).

6 Callimachus was a third-century BCE Hellenistic poet associated with the Alexandrian court: Catullus' c.66 is a translation of Callimachus, and he is mentioned in c. 116, Catullus' last poem. He is also invoked in Propertius 3.1.1, and his *Aetia*, now extant only in fragments, seems to have stood behind Ovid's *Metamorphoses* and *Fasti*: on Callimachus, Acosta-Hughes and Stephens (2012); on Callimachus, Catullus and elegy, Hunter (2006), Knox (2007), Gutzwiller (2012), Nelis (2012).

7 Translation by Nisetich, quoted in Gaisser (2009) 135; also in Knox (2007) where it is designated as epigram 25 Pf.

8 Gaisser (2009) 136.

9 Fitzgerald (1995), Wray (2001).

10 On *fides* in Roman cultural discourse see Galinsky (1996) 61, 272; also Corbeill (2005).

11 E.g. Fitzgerald (1995) 117–20, Galinsky (1996) 272, Skinner (2003), Corbeill (2005) 90.

12 Skinner (2003) 83.

13 Fitzgerald (1995) 117–20, Skinner (2003). See also Lyne (1980) and Krostenko (2001) on the 'language of social performance' in Catullus and Cicero.

14 See e.g. Skinner (1981), Fowler (1987), Greene (1995a), Dyson (2007). Certainly some of the texts support this reading: c.11, for example, uses the imagery of 'Catullus'' love as a flower cut down by a passing plough. This trope is used by Sappho to represent the loss of virginity on a bride's wedding night, but also appears in Homer associated with young warriors cut down in battle (e.g. *Il.* 8.303–5): the simile is reworked by Virgil in the *Aeneid* for the death of Euryalus (*Aen.* 9.434–7) which repeats Catullus' *veluti, flos* and *aratro*.

15 The gendered nature of speech acts is institutionalised in Roman law where women's ability to speak in legal contexts is severely limited: see Gardner (1986).

16 See Cicero, *De amicitia*; on the problematisation of *amicitia*, Oliensis (1997a); Williams (2012) 17–23, 174–85 on *amicitia* in Catullus.

17 *Dicebas quondam solum te nosse Catullum | Lesbia, nec prae me velle tenere Iovem*, 72.1–2.

18 Scholars have, on the whole, moved away from an easy and uncomplicated identification of Clodia Metelli with Lesbia but traces still exist, e.g. Wiseman (1985). On reading Catullus and Cicero together, see Fitzgerald (1995) especially ch.5, Krostenko (2001), Stroup (2010).

19 C.79 teasingly associates Lesbia with one of the three Clodia sisters when it describes Lesbius, a male relation, as *pulcher*, 'pretty' (79.1): Clodia Metelli's brother, Publius Clodius, has the cognomen *Pulcher*; the poem has Lesbia 'prefer' Lesbius to 'Catullus', and the *Pro Caelio* suggests unsubtly that the relationship between Clodia Metelli and P. Clodius Pulcher is an incestuous one e.g. 'that woman's husband – I meant to say brother; I always make that slip' (*istius mulieris viro – fratrem volui dicere; semper hic erro*, 13.32). On the other hand, Clodia's husband, Q. Metellus Celer, died in 59 BCE which does not 'match' c.83 where Lesbia is married. Apuleius' Apology 10 identifies

Lesbia as one of the Clodias, though not necessarily Clodia Metelli – even though it is based on information that is 'at least third hand', it reappears in fifteenth- and sixteenth-century editions of Catullus as noted below: see e.g. Booth (1999) xxxiv. Dyson (2008) 4–9 discusses the historical Clodia Metelli and the controversies over how to relate her to the fictional Lesbia, as does Skinner (1983) 273–87, (2003) 91–5, now (2011).

20 See Cicero's letters to Atticus on his relationship to Clodia and the 'incest' story: 9.1, 12.2, 14.1, 22.5, 23.3. These are discussed in e.g. Richlin (1992) 85, Booth (1999), Dyson (2008) which translates all the sources into English.

21 E.g. Leen (2000).

22 Skinner (2003).

23 The Loeb *Pro Caelio* gives a helpful context to this case, including background on M. Caelius Rufus.

24 '*posse versus facere ... iocum movere, sermone uti vel modesto vel molli procaci: prorsus multae facetiae multusque lepos inerat*', Cat. 25: all Latin quotations are from Reynolds (1991).

25 E.g. cc.12.9, 50.8 for *facetus*; while the term *urbanitas* does not appear in Catullan texts, the idea of a sophisticated, polished city lifestyle permeates the world which he depicts. All Latin quotations from the *Pro Caelio* are from Clark (1905), translations from Gardner (1958).

26 *quos simul complexa tenet trecentos,* | *nullum amans vere, sed identidem omnium ilia rumpens*, 'three hundred of whom she holds at once in her embrace, not loving one of them really, but again and again draining the strength of all' (11.18–20): *ilia rumpens* might more specifically be translated as breaking or destroying the groin or guts of her lovers, a deeply sexualised and grotesque image which conveys Lesbia's ability to crush the masculinity of her lovers; c.58.4–5: *nunc in quadriviis et angiportis* | *glubit magnanimi Remi nepotes*, where *glubit* has been read obscenely and explicitly as 'masturbates': see Lateiner (1977); Adams (1982) 74 more discreetly describes it as the act of 'retracting the foreskin'.

27 See e.g. Gildenhard (2007): 'the extent to which members of Rome's ruling elite could shower each other with abuse in the senate or lawcourts is striking' (174); the senate and law-courts are sites of almost exclusively male speech. On invective in Republican Rome, see Corbeill (1996) and the collections edited by Booth (2007), and Smith and Covina (2011).

28 See also *male dicendi* (3.7), *maledictis* (7.15) and 13.31 where Cicero asserts *omnia sunt alia non crimina, sed maledicta*, 'all the other matters complained of are not accusations, but slanders': this comes just after he has repeated Clodia's name twice in the sentence before, making an implicit connection between her and the calumny against Caelio.

29 Geffcken (1973), Leigh (2004), Harries (2007); also Gildenhard (2007), Tatum (2011).

30 See especially Skinner (2003) for the latter position: she reads Lesbia as a 'recognisable fictive analogue for the public figure of Clodia' (94) and as a symbol for illicit political relations in the troubled last years of the republic.

31 The date has been adjusted to a year beginning on 1 January: in Tudor England it was 1521 and some of the commentators on this event cite it in that way, e.g. Ives (2004) 37.

32 Edward Hall's *Chronicle* gives a near-contemporary record of this masque: educated at Cambridge, Hall was a contemporary of Henry VIII, whose reign he supported: see Hall, ed. H. Ellis (1809) 631, Howard (1994), Ives (2004) 27–8, Herman (2010) 16–27.

33 For complementary readings of the *château vert* see Howard (1994) and Herman (2010) 16–27.

34 The *château vert* is the first documented appearance of Anne Boleyn at a court performance. Having been educated at first the Hapsburg court of Burgundy, and then the French court in the service of Queen Claude, Anne had only very recently returned to England: Ives (2004) 18–29.

35 Ives (2004) 38.

36 Fragment B, 3871–2, here modernised. Usages documented in the *OED* show that Malebouche, during the fourteenth to sixteenth centuries, is also used as a personification of slander, something much closer to the concept of *maledictus* traced in Catullus and the *Pro Caelio*.

37 *Surripui tibi dum ludis, mellite Iuventi | saviolum dulci dulcius ambrosia. | verum id non impune tuli*, 'I stole a kiss from you, honey-sweet Juventius, while you were playing, a kiss sweeter than sweet ambrosia. But not unpunished', Cat. 99.1–3; 'Alas, madam, for stealing of a kiss | have I so much your mind there offended? | Have I then done so grievously amiss | that by no means it may be amended?', Wyatt 38.1–4.

38 *Non iam illud quaero, contra me ut diligat illa, | aut, quod non potis est, esse pudica velit*, 'No longer is this my prayer, that she should love me in return, or, for that is impossible, that she would consent to be chaste', Cat. 76.23–4; cf. 'Though I cannot your cruelty constrain | for my goodwill to favour me again, | Though my true and faithful love | have no power your heart to move' etc. Wyatt's 106.1–4.

39 E.g. Lever (1956), Greenblatt (1980), Ferry (1983), Mason (1986), Estrin (1994), Heale (1998), Falconer (2000), Cheney (2011).

40 E.g. Greenblatt (1980), Heale (1998).

41 E.g. Berthoff (1963), Friedman (1967), Estrin (1994), Heale (1998), Bates (2013).

42 E.g. Nelson (1963), notes to the Rebholz edition of Wyatt. All quotations from Ovid's *Amores* are from Kenney (1961, 1994).

43 For biographical discussions on Henry's letters to Anne, see Fraser (1992) 128–9; Ives (2004) 84–90; on letter-writing as a social practice, Barton and Hall (2000); on Renaissance letter-writing, Whigham (1981), Lerer (1997), Schneider (2005).

44 Lerer (1997), quotation from 3.

45 E.g. in letter 1, 'muy et mon ceur' ('me and my heart') changes to 'en nos faisant rementevoire' ('bringing to our mind') and 'o moins de nostre chosté' ('at least on our side'). Nine of the seventeen extant letters hand-written by

Henry VIII to Anne Boleyn were in French. All seventeen were published in English translation by Thomas Hearne in his *Robert of Avebury* (1720), and in the third volume of the Harleian Miscellany, but the French originals have never been published in England. The seventeen letters ended up in the Vatican library, possibly stolen from Anne Boleyn by the Imperial or Venetian ambassador. Napoleon removed the letters in 1797 and deposited them in the Bibliothèque du Roi in Paris where they were transcribed by M. Meon, the manuscript librarian. The letters were handed back to the pope in October 1815 and remain in the Vatican library today. The French transcriptions, together with French translations of the English letters, were published by George-Adrien Crapelet in Paris, 1826, and this is the edition from which French quotations are taken: the translations are mine. I have followed Crapelet's numbering but, where different, have noted other editors' ordering: the letters are not dated, but some can be provisionally ascribed according to external events. Letter 1 is numbered thus in all collections and has been dated to autumn 1526 by Ives (2004), 1527 by St. Clare Byrne (1936).

46 Fraser (1992) 128 dates Henry's pursuit from Shrovetide 1526; Ives (2004) 90 suggests Henry noticed Anne in 1522 from around the time of the *château vert* but also dates his courtship from 1526.

47 This letter is numbered 4 in all editions, and is dated by St. Clare Byrne to 1527: in it Henry makes reference to having been struck by the dart of love for more than one year ('ayant esté plus que ung anné dernyr attaynte du dart d'amours').

48 Ovid's Apollo and Daphne episode from the *Metamorphoses* (1.452–567) has long been recognised as the central myth of Petrarch's *canzoniere*, see e.g. Greene (1982) 127–46, Freccero (1986), Barnard (1987), Martindale (1988), Hardie (1999) and especially Estrin (1994), more recently Braden (2000), Heyworth (2009).

49 See Bates (2013) on the hunt.

50 Letter 10 is numbered 10 in the Harleian and in the Vatican collection but St. Clare Byrne dates it to 1527 and orders it as 5 in her edition (1936).

51 Letter 9 was written in English, is ordered 9 also in Harleian and the Vatican, but 12 in St. Clare Byrne who dates it to 22–30 June 1528: quotations from letters originally written in English are taken from St. Clare Byrne (1936) which have been modernised in terms of spelling.

52 See especially Lerer (1997) on the status of letters at the Henrician court.

53 See *Met.* 3.138–252 on Actaeon, the hunter who gets turned by Diana into a stag and is torn apart by his own hounds; Barkan (1980) on the way Diana and Actaeon structures other Renaissance literary texts; Vickers (1981) on this myth and the blazon, Bates (2013) on Actaeon and Tudor metaphors of hunting.

54 E.g. Boyd (1987) 200, Leen (2000).

55 All quotations from Petrarch's sonnets are from Mortimer (2002).

56 See Bath (1979) on the legend of Caesar's deer.

57 *Quin tu animo offirmas atque istinc teque reducis [...]; quae mihi subrepens imos ut torpor in artus | expulit.*

3 ' "Fool," Said My Muse to Me'

1 All quotations from *Astrophil and Stella* are from Duncan-Jones (1989, revised 2002). For other metapoetic readings of the sequence see Prendergast (1995, 1999).

2 The readings here assume a separation between the historical Philip Sidney and the fictional poet-narrator Astrophil, a distinction which is not always maintained in Sidney criticism: see e.g. Helgerson (1976) 131–41, Hager (1991). Sir Philip Sidney, 1554–86, was a prominent Elizabethan scholar, poet, courtier and soldier. His mother, Mary Dudley, was the sister of Robert Dudley, 1st Earl of Leicester, one of Elizabeth's favourites; his sister Mary Sidney and niece Mary Wroth are the subjects of Chapter 5. On Sidney's life see Duncan-Jones (1991) and Stewart (2000).

3 Quotations from *Africa* are from Bergin and Wilson (1977).

4 Quotations from *Gerusalemme Liberata* are from Wickert (2009).

5 Quotations from the *Faerie Queene* are from Roche (1978).

6 *Cingere litorea flaventia tempora myrto | Musa, per undenos emodulanda pedes*, 'Gird with the myrtle that loves the shore the golden locks on thy temple, O Muse to be sung to the lyre in elevens', *Am.* 1.1.29–30: Latin quotation from Kenney (1964, revised 1994), translation from Showerman revised by Goold (2002).

7 *Exorata meis illum Cytherea Camenis | attulit in nostrum deposuitque sinum*, 'won over by my Muse's prayers, Cythera's queen has brought and placed him in my arms', 3.13.3–4; all Latin quotations from Sulpicia are from Postgate (1924), translations from Cornish (1962).

8 All Latin quotations from Propertius are from Heyworth (2007), translations from Goold (1990).

9 On Cynthia as a muse and metaliterary figure, McNamee (1993) 224, Keith (1994, 2008: 98–9), Greene (1995a, 1995b), Wiggers (1997) 335, Wyke (2002), Pincus (2004), Johnson (2012) 40.

10 Spentzou (2002a) 8.

11 See Murray (1981, 2002), Spentzou (2002a).

12 See González (2000), Spentzou (2002b). On Callimachus, see Sullivan (1976) 107–58, Knox (1985), Arkins (2005) 19–34, Hunter (2006), Keith (2008) 45–85.

13 For an alternative reading of Sidney's response to Propertius, see Levy (1984).

14 Especially useful on the classical muse is Spentzou and Fowler (2002).

15 On 2.1, see Gaisser (1977), Wiggers (1997), Greene (2005a, 2005b), Heyworth (2007) 12–15, Keith (2008) 86–7, Johnson (2012).

16 *Ilias ipsa quid est aliud nisi adultera, de qua | inter amatorem pugna virumque fuit*, *Tr.* 2.371–2: quotation from Owen (1963), translation from Wheeler revised by Goold (1988).

17 Quotations from the *Aeneid* are from Mynors (1969), translations from Fairclough revised by Goold (2000).

18 Sharrock (2002a) 207.

19 Later invocations come at *Aen.* 7.37 where Erato is called upon, and 9.525–8 where the muse is Calliope: see Todd (1931), Toll (1989) on Erato, Lowrie (2009) on Virgil's muses more generally.

20 On the gendered and political implications of elegiac luxury, see Bowditch (2006, 2012); on the concept of luxury more broadly in the Roman world, Dalby (2000).

21 On 4.7 see Muecke (1974), Yardley (1977, 1983), Warden (1980, 1996), Allison (1980b, 1984), Papanghelis (1987) 145–98, Janan (2001), DeBrohun (2003), Richardson (2006) 454–61, Heyworth (2007) 463–73.

22 E.g. Fear (2000), Wyke (2002).

23 On voices, gender and writing in the *Heroides*, Verducci (1985), Desmond (1993), Gordon (1997), Kennedy (2002), Lindheim (2003), Spentzou (2003), Fulkerson (2005).

24 On voices in the *Aeneid*, see Parry (1963), Lyne (1987), Fowler (1990), Barchiesi (1997), Casali (1995), Perkell (1997), Behr (2005), Dinter (2005), Kallendorf (2007) explores early modern receptions of Virgilian voices.

25 On the underworld in 4.7, see Warden (1980) 38–50, Papanghelis (1987) 176–9, Richardson (2006) 454–61, Heyworth (2007) 463–73.

26 Dating can be only provisional, but the *Heroides* is usually dated to c.25–16 BCE, with Propertius' fourth book to c.16 BCE: Showerman revised by Goold (2002) on the *Heroides*, Goold (1990) on Propertius.

27 On the problem of the gates in the *Aeneid*, see Reed (1973), Austin (1977), Tarrant (1982), West (1990), Cockburn (1992), O'Hara (1996). On the gates of sleep in 4.7, Warden (1980) 58–9, Papanghelis (1987) 190.

28 Ovid's *Tristia* 1.7.15–25, 4.10.61–2 alludes to this story, further evidence that it was familiar in Augustan Rome; it was transmitted in Donatus' Life of Virgil available in Ziolkowski and Putnam (2008) 181–99.

29 *Met.* 5.251–678. All Latin quotations from the *Metamorphoses* are from Tarrant (2004), translations from Miller, revised by Goold (1977). On this muse episode, see Johnson and Malamud (1988), Cahoon (1996), Zissos (1999).

30 E.g. Richlin (1992), Johnson (1996), Zissos (1999).

31 E.g. *Met.* 1.173–6, 1.204–5; see Cahoon (1996), Zissos (1999); more generally, Barchiesi (1997).

32 On the sibyl as a figure associated with poetry, the poet and inspiration, see Fowler (2002).

33 Fowler (2002).

34 See Braden (1990) on Apollo/Daphne and Petrarch's sonnets.

35 On Stella as a text to be interpreted, see sonnet 67, 'the fair text better try; | what blushing notes does thou in margin see?' (67.7–8); if Stella as reader is implicated in the 'best wits' (67.11) then she might be read as a version of Cynthia as *docta puella*, 'learned girl'; on Stella's collaborative voice see Fienberg (1985), Prendergast (1995, 1999).

36 See Diotima's speech in *The Symposium* 210a–12a. On knowledge of Plato via Augustine in Petrarch's Italy, see Jayne (1995). On Marsilio Ficino's Plato see Allen *et al.* (2002), Allen (2008).

37 All quotations from Castiglione are from Thomas Hoby's 1561 English translation, spelling modernised here.

38 See Scanlon (1976), Sinfield (1980), Roche (1997).

39 Prendergast (1995). See also Quint (1983) on Renaissance concerns with how to reconcile 'counterfeit' or man-made fictions with the humanist valorisation of human creativity.

40 Duncan-Jones (1989, revised 2002) 371; all quotations from the *Defence* are from this edition. On the *Defence*, McIntyre (1962), Barnes (1971), Marotti (1999), on the relationship between the *Defence* and *Astrophil and Stella*, Weiner (1974), Sinfield (1980).

41 On Sidney and Gosson, Kinney (1972), Matz (2000) 60, Lehnhof (2008), Williams (2009); on anti-poetic treatises, see Matz (2000) quotation from 17, Herman (2009).

42 Quotations, with spellings modernised here, are by page number from the 1579 edition to which Sidney was most probably responding: STC 12097.5.

43 E.g. sonnets 15, 50, 55.

44 On the myth of the golden age in the Renaissance see Levin (1969); on the association between the New World and a golden world see Cunnar (1993), quotation from 186; also Hester (1987). Both Hakluyt and Ralegh who wrote of their voyages to the New World were at Oxford with Sidney: see Duncan-Jones (1991) 42. On the golden age in classical literature from Hesiod forwards, Wallace-Hadrill (1982), Barker (1996), Perkell (2002).

4 'In Six Numbers Let My Work Rise, and Subside in Five'

1 Keith (1994), Sharrock (1995).

2 Keith (1994), quotation from Sharrock (1995) 159. See Williams (2010) 140 on terms such as *delicatus, enervis, mollis or mollitia* being associated with effeminacy in Roman thought: 'softness is the antithesis of masculinity' (140). *Mollitia*, though, is a complicated term for the Romans which can be used in diverse ways to characterise 'an inability to act in a forceful "manly" way': see Edwards (1993) especially ch.2; quotation from 64.

3 E.g. Cahoon (1988), Keith (1994), Greene (1998), Sharrock (2002c).

4 Copley (1947), Lyne (1979), McCarthy (1998).

5 Latin quotations from the *Amores* are from Kenney (1961, 1994), translations from Showerman, revised by Goold (2002).

6 See Keith (1994) 34, Hallett (2012), also Morgan (2012). George Puttenham, in his *The Arte of English Poesy* (1589), describes the elegiac couplet as 'a piteous manner of metre, placing a limping pentameter after a lusty hexameter'.

7 John Donne, 1572–1631, had an adventurous life before becoming a cleric in the Church of England: Bald (1970) is the standard academic biography; for something more popular there is John Stubbs' readable *John Donne: The Reformed Soul* (2007). Thomas Nashe, 1567–c.1601, was a pamphleteer, playwright, poet and satirist: see Nicholl (1984) on his life.

8 On Nashe as an 'English quasi-Ovid' see Lyne (2002), also Crewe (1982), Franz (1989), Stapleton (1991, 1995), Moulton (2000).

9 Armstrong (1977), Lerner (1988), Bate (1994), Stapleton (1996); also Easthope (1989), Low (1990), Belsey (1994), Singer (2009) who all briefly comment on

Donne's 'Ovidianism'; Bald (1970) 47 on Donne's reading of Marlowe's translation of the *Amores* at Cambridge.

10 LaBranche (1966) 359.

11 LaBranche (1966) 360.

12 Carey (1981) 41.

13 Leishman (1951) 52–73, Carey (1981) 106, Marotti (1986) 53–4.

14 Carey (1990, 2000) xxiii, 422; on Donne's life, Bald (1970).

15 McKerrow (1958), Kuin and Prescott (2000), Moulton (2000). Both Donne's
   elegy and Nashe's poem are in the Rosenbach manuscript (Rosenbach MS
   1083/15 fols. 9v–11v) undiscovered when McKerrow edited the complete works
   of Nashe: see Marotti (1986) and Moulton (2000).

16 On pornography as a term in general see Hunt (1993); on 'pornography' in the
   Renaissance see Franz (1972, 1989), El-Gabalawy (1976), Merrix (1986), Young
   (1987), Findlen (1993), Talvacchia (1999), Moulton (2000).

17 Franz (1972), Hilliard (1986), Boehrer (1989), Hutson (1989); Hibbard (1962)
   57 dismisses it as 'valueless as poetry'. There are signs that Nashe is being
   rehabilitated however: Guy-Bray *et al.* (2013).

18 It is impossible to date the *Amores* with certainty but c.22–19 BCE after the
   death of Tibullus (19 BCE) is indicated: Boyd (1997), Davis (1999), Harrison
   (2002), Tarrant (2002).

19 *Aut puer aut longas compta puella comas*, *Am.* 1.1.20. For other readings of 1.5
   see e.g. Huntingford (1981), Papanghelis (1989), Gratwick (1991), Keith (1994),
   Sharrock (1995), Greene (1998).

20 Sharrock (2002d).

21 *Et multi, quae sit nostra Corinna, rogant*, *Ars Amatoria* 3.538. *Quae* can also
   mean 'what' here thus interrogating not just the relationship between Corinna
   and any 'real' Roman mistress, but also the figurative meaning of Corinna: see
   especially Wyke (2002).

22 See Skinner (2005) 168–9 on Laïs and her connections with Aphrodite;
   Propertius 2.6.1–6 also mentions Laïs of Corinth as a renowned Greek
   courtesan.

23 On the gaze in Roman culture, see Kaplan (1983), Fredrick (1995, 2002),
   Frontisi-Ducroux (1996), Barton (2000), Goldhill (2001), Salzman-Mitchell
   (2005), Elsner (2007a, 2007b).

24 Vout (2007).

25 *Quale fere silvae lumen habere solent,* | *qualia sublucent fugiente crepuscula
   Phoebo,* | *aut ubi non abiit, nec tamen orta dies* (1.5.4–6).

26 Papanghelis (1989) 54.

27 Du Quesnay (1973), Huntingford (1981), Greene (1998).

28 *Qualis Thesea iacuit cedente carina* | *languida desertis Cnosia litoribus;* | *qualis et
   accubuit primo Cepheia somno* | *libera iam duris cotibus Andromede;* | *Nec minus
   assiduis Edonis fessa choreis* | *qualis in herboso concidit Apidano*, 'like the maid of
   Cnossus as in a swoon she lay on the deserted shore when Theseus' ship sailed
   away; like Cepheus' daughter Andromeda as she rested in her first slumber on
   her release from the rugged cliff; no less like the Thracian bacchant, exhausted

after incessant dances, when she collapses on the grassy bank of the Apidanus',
Prop. 1.3.1–6.

29 Myerowitz (1992), Parker (1992), Fredrick (1995), Clarke (1998, 2003).

30 *Scilicet in domibus nostris ut prisca virorum | artificis fulgent corpora picta manu, | sic quae concubitus varios Venerisque figuras | exprimat, est aliquo parva tabella loco*, *Tr*. 2.521–4; *utque velis, Venerem iungunt per mille figuras: invenit plures nulla tabella modos*, 'according to your taste they will embrace you in a thousand ways; no picture could devise more modes than they', *Ars* 2.679–80.

31 Clarke (1998). E.g. *quae facie praesignis erit, resupina iaceto: | spectentur tergo, quis sua terga placent. | Milanion umeris Atalantes crura ferebat: | si bona sunt, hoc sunt accipienda modo*, 'Let her who is fair of face recline upon her back; let those whose backs please them be seen from behind. Milanion bore Atalanta's legs upon his shoulders; if they are comely, let them be taken thus', *Ars* 3.769–88. On classical 'sexual manuals' see Davidson (1988) and Parker (1992).

32 *Met*. 10.243–97; the seminal reading of Ovid's Pygmalion as a central myth of erotic elegy is Sharrock (1991); see also Fear (2000) and Sharrock (2002b).

33 See Myerowitz (1992), Vout (2007) on the 'slippage between flesh and marble'.

34 Nicoll (1977), Hinds (1987c), Papanghelis (1989), Keith (1994), Clauss (1995), Boyd (1997) 155, Hardie (2002) 42; Greene (1998) 79 argues against this interpretation.

35 See also Keith (1994), Sharrock (1995), Butrica (1999), Holzberg (2005), Hallett (2012).

36 *Quae nunc, ecce, vigent intempestiva valentque, | nunc opus exposcunt militiamque suam*, 3.7.67–8.

37 Keith (1994) 38, Holzberg (2005) 377.

38 Adams (1982).

39 Feinstein (1994).

40 Bate (1994) 62; *Symposium* 189a–193d.

41 Golding's *Metamorphoses* 4.352–481.

42 On anxiety and masculinity, Breitenberg (1996), Simons (2011).

43 Feinstein (1994) 66.

44 Of the six extant manuscript copies of Nashe's poem, one gives the title as *Nashes Dildo* (Folger MS Va 399, fols. 53v–57) and one *Nashe His Dildo* (Bodleian MS Rawl.poet.216): see Moulton (1997, 2000: 188). The first printed edition of Nashe's text in 1899 gave it the title *The Choice of Valentines or The Merie Ballad of Nashe His Dildo*: McKerrow (1958) 400.

45 All quotations from the *Choice of Valentines* are taken from McKerrow (1958).

46 One of the extant manuscripts seems to have been owned by a woman, Margaret Bellasys (BL.MS Add.10309, fols.135v–139v) and in this version Nashe's poem ends before the dildo appears so for that female reader the text is remade as a story about female sexual frustration rather than one which centres on male anxiety about phallic substitutes: see Moulton (2000) 190–2.

47 *Tr*. 2.207.

48 Lyne (2002), Hexter (2002).

49 On the political overtones of gender and authority in the 1590s, see Guibbory (1990), Frye (1993), Levin (1994), Montrose (1996, 2006), Betts (1998), Villeponteaux (1998), Walker (1998), Strong (1999), Moulton (2000) 178, Doran (2003), Brown (2004), Hackett (2008).

50 Riggs (1989), Shapiro (2005), Donaldson (2011), Potter (2012).

51 McKerrow (1958).

52 Moulton (2000) 168–71.

53 On Petrarchism at the Elizabethan court, see e.g. Marotti (1982), Berry (1989), Guibbory (1990), Frye (1993), Doran and Freeman (2003); on its transgression, Betts (1998), Walker (1998).

54 Hester (1987), Young (1987), Labriola (1996), Montrose (2006).

55 Habinek (2002), quotation from 46; also Davis (1999, 2006).

56 Sharrock (2002c) 102.

57 Sharrock (2002b), Hersey (2009); also Vout (2007).

58 Praxiteles was a fourth-century BCE Athenian artist and the story of his Aphrodite is recounted in Pliny's *Naturalis Historia* 7.127. See Havelock (1995) on the Aphrodite of Cnidos, also Sharrock (2002b), Skinner (2005) 172–6, Elsner (2007a, 2007b), Hersey (2009), Blanchard (2010) 22–4 on the Cnidia, 28–33 on Pygmalion and falling in love with statues, Squire (2011) ch.3 on the Cnidia and her legacy. The Christian writer Clement of Alexandria (c.150–216) wrote on the idolatry of men falling in love with pagan statues: see Blanchard (2010) 29. There is a medieval version of Venus's statue coming to life in William of Malmsebury's *Gesta Regum Anglorum* (1125): see Reid (1993) 159.

59 Philemon Holland's 1601 translation of this episode from Pliny is rather shyly circumspect: 'he [Praxiteles] devised his memorial by making one image of Venus, for the Gnidians, so lively, that a certain young man became so amorous of it, that he doted for love therof, and went beside himselfe'.

60 See Havelock (1995), Stewart (2003) 41, 91–110, Skinner (2005) 174. Titian's Venus of Urbino (c.1538), modelled on a courtesan, is shown in the same *pudica* pose. On the re-discovery of classical statuary in fifteenth- and sixteenth-century Rome, see Barkan (1999), also Rubin (2000) 30–1; Reid (1993) catalogues other appearances of Venus in Renaissance art.

61 Havelock (1995) 117–24 on elegiac mistresses and Venus statues as 'analogues' of each other (117); James (2001, 2003) on the elegiac mistress as courtesan.

62 Solodow (1988) 215–19 traces the story to Philostrephanus, a friend or pupil of Callimachus: now lost, this original had Pygmalion as the king of Cyprus having sex with a cult statue of Aphrodite.

63 See DeRose Evans (1992) on the Aeneas myth in Roman 'propaganda'; also Rose (1998) on the Roman political use of the Trojan legend: Augustus 'stressed his Trojan ancestry more forcefully than any other Roman before him' (409).

64 Weinstock (1971) 80–90 on Julius Caesar's appropriation of the cult of Venus, 82 on the dedication of the temple in the Forum, 84 on the epithet 'genetrix'.

65 On the civil wars and the victory of Augustus see Syme (1939), Galinsky (1996).

66 Zanker (1990), Galinsky (1996) 197–213, also Kellum (1997) on the Forum Augustum; for Augustus' own words on the forum, *Res Gestae* 21. On the complicated status of statues in Roman culture, Stewart (2003).

67 On the *Amores* as 'political' texts, see Davis (1999, 2006); Merriam (2006a) on Venus in love elegy generally; and Boyle (2003) on Ovid's engagement with the monuments of Augustan Rome.

68 Zanker (1990) 3, Galinsky (1996).

69 Kennedy (1992), Powell (1992).

70 On vision and ecphrases in the *Aeneid*, Bartsch (1998), Putnam (1998), Smith (2005); also Feeney (1990).

71 In 18 BCE the *lex Iulia de maritandis ordinibus* was put forward which regulated and encouraged marriage among the elite classes, and it was followed by the *lex Iulia de adulteriis coercendis* which criminalised adultery: see Treggiari (1991) on Roman marriage in general, 60–5. on Augustus' marriage legislation, and 277–80 on the adultery laws; also McGinn (1998) 140–215 on the adultery laws; and Skinner (2005) 206 on Augustus' moral legislation in general.

72 Reckford (1995), Leach (1997), Oliensis (1997b), Skinner (2005) 228–38.

73 Reckford (1995), Leach (1997), Oliensis (1997b).

74 'he went to look for the wood and found it close to the water | in a conspicuous place, and stopped underneath two bushes' (*Od.* 5.476–7). After spotting Nausicaa and her companions playing by the river, 'Great Odysseus came from under his thicket | and from the dense foliage with his heavy hand he broke off | a leafy branch to cover his body and hide the male parts' (6.127–9).

75 *Venetrix dederatque comam diffundere ventis, | nuda genu nodoque sinus collecta fluentis,* 1.319–20.

76 *Aen.* 4.129–72.

77 Cf. 'I am at your knees o queen. But are you mortal or goddess? | If indeed you are one of the gods who hold wide heaven | then I must find in you the nearest likeness to Artemis' (*Od.* 6.149–51).

78 Translations from the Homeric Hymn to Aphrodite are from West (2003).

79 *Multa tibi ante aras nostra cadet hostia dextra,* 1.334. In *Aen.* 12.411–22 when Venus heals the wounded Aeneas, she plucks the herb from Mount Ida, the scene of her seduction of Anchises, so that previous encounter re-appears as a subtext at various points throughout the poem.

5 'My Heart … with Love Did Inly Burn'

1 All quotations from Mary Sidney's works are from Hannay *et al.* (1998), with the English here modernised.

2 For an alternative, political reading of Sidney's *Triumph*, see Clarke (1997a, 1997b).

3 See also Duncan-Jones (1999) on Bess Carey's c.1594 translations of two of Petrarch's *canzoniere*.

4 E.g. Cat. 70, 72; the Fourth, Eighth and Eleventh songs in the *Astrophil and Stella*; Petrarch's *canzoniere* 250; Prop. 1.3.35–46; *Am.* 3.7.77–80 as well as

Propertius' fourth book and Ovid's *Heroides*. On 'transvestite ventriloquism', see Harvey (1992); on gender and elegy, Wyke (1994), Hallett (2002a), James (2010); on the *Heroides*, Verducci (1985), Desmond (1993), Rosati (1996), Gordon (1997), Lindheim (2003), Spentzou (2003), Fulkerson (2005); on Renaissance 'female persona poems', Coren (2001).

5 Mary Sidney, Countess of Pembroke (1561–1621), was the sister of Philip Sidney and was married to Henry Herbert, 2nd Earl of Pembroke; her sons William and Philip were the dedicatees of Shakespeare's First Folio: on Sidney's life, see Hannay (1990). Lady Mary Wroth (1587–1651/3) was Sidney's niece, the daughter of her brother Robert: see Hannay (2013) on her complicated life. She wrote a vast romance entitled *Urania* which included characters named Pamphilia and Amphilanthus: the sonnet sequence whose first poem we will read here was appended to the romance and is known as *Pamphilia to Amphilanthus*.

6 On female authored Petrarchan poetry, Travitsky (1989), Jones (1990), Lamb (1990), Dubrow (1995), Greer (1995), Heale (1995), Burke (2000), Clarke (2000, 2001), Moore (2000), Dunnigan (2002), Smith (2005).

7 This chapter assumes that Sulpicia is a female poet writing elegy sometime in the decade between 20 and 10 BCE: see also Hinds (1987a, 1987b, 1987c), Lowe (1988), Parker (1994, 2006), Keith (1997), Flaschenreim (1999), Holzberg (1999), Churchill *et al.* (2002), Hallett (2002a, 2002b, 2006, 2009), Hemelrijk (2002), Milnor (2002), Skoie (2002), Wyke (2002), Hubbard (2005), Keith (2006), Merriam (2006), Pearcy (2006).

8 On female authored closet drama, see Straznicky (1994, 2004), Raber (2001), Findley (2006), 27 on Sidney's *Antonie*; on English translations of Garnier, Oberth (2013).

9 Jones (1990) 1.

10 Latin quotations from Sulpicia are from Postgate (1924), translations from Postgate, revised by Goold (1988), lightly adapted as necessary.

11 The attribution of Sulpicia's poems remains problematic and since there is no evidence to support the various contentions beyond the texts themselves, the position taken here is that only [Tib.]3.13–18 are by Sulpicia, and that the *amicus* poems, [Tib.]3.8–17 are receptions of Sulpicia which respond to the outspoken nature of her texts and actively strive to re-place her into the more conventional position of the male-authored mistress. Keith (2006) summarises the state of Sulpician scholarship to that date; see also Fredericks (1976), Santirocco (1979), Hinds (1987a, 1987b, 1987c), Parker (1994), Hallett (2002a), Skoie (2002). Merriam (1990) re-orders the poems placing 3.13 at the end of the sequence which then becomes 3.18, 3.16, 3.17, 3.14, 3.15, 3.13 thus denying any programmatic role to 3.13.

12 *Cynthia prima suis miserum me cepit ocellis*, 1.1. Note, too, the Propertian echo in Petrarch's *canzoniere* 3: 'when I was captured, with my guard astray, | for your bright eyes, my lady, bound me then' (3.3–4).

13 *Tum mihi constantis deiecit lumina fastus | et caput impositis pressit Amor pedibus*, 'it was then that Love made me lower my looks of stubborn pride

and trod my head beneath his feet' (Prop. 1.1.3–4); *par erat inferior versus – risisse Cupido | dicitur atque unum surripuisse pedem*, 'the second verse was equal to the first – but Cupid, they say, with a laugh stole away one foot' (*Am.* 1.1.3–4).

14 On the general intertextual relationship of Sulpicia to Catullus see Lowe (1988), Hallett (2002a, 2002b, 2002c); on Propertius self-consciously drawing attention to the relationship between Catullus' Lesbia and his Cynthia, Prop. 2.31, 32: *haec eadem ante illam iam impune et Lesbia fecit: | quae sequitur, certest invidiosa minus*, 'Lesbia has already done all this before her with impunity: Lesbia's follower is surely less to blame' (45–6).

15 Catullus' Lesbia is an adulterous married woman; on the *puella* and Hellenised courtesans, James (2001, 2003).

16 *Qualem texisse pudori | quam nudasse alicui sit mihi fama magis*, 'and the rumour that I have concealed it would shame me more than disclosure', 3.13.1–2.

17 *Quod si pertendens animo vestita cubaris | scissa veste meas experiere manus*, Prop. 2.15.17–18. See also Cat. 64.60–70 for the eroticised description of Ariadne with all her clothes slipped off her body; and Corinna's unfastened tunic in *Am.* 1.5.

18 See Langlands (2006) on *pudor, pudicitia* and Roman sexual morality in general; Hardie (2012b) on *fama*.

19 See e.g. Flaschenreim (1999), Hemelrijk (2002), Langlands (2006).

20 *Este procul, vittae tenues, insigne pudoris, | quaeque tegis medios, instita longa, pedes*, *Ars Amatoria* 1.31–2.

21 Dixon (2001) 23.

22 *Indue me Cois, fiam non dura puella: | meque virum sumpta quis neget esse toga?*

23 On the toga, Hinds (1987a, 1987b, 1987c), Sebesta (1994). On Roman prostitutes and Augustan legislation see Gardner (1986), McGinn (1998), Skinner (2005) 206–7.

24 On Sappho 31 and Catullus 51 see Miller (1983), Greene (1985), Higgins (1996).

25 On female voices in Catullus see Hallett (2002c).

26 *Sapphica puella | musa doctior. Nam quo tempore legit incohatam | Dindymi dominam, ex eo misellae | ignes interiorem edunt medullam*, 'for since she read the beginning of his "Lady of Dindymus", ever since then, poor girl, the fires have been wasting her inmost marrow', 35.13–15.

27 *Me legat in sponsi facie non frigida virgo, | et rudis ignoto tactus amore puer*, 'for my readers I want the maid not cold at the sight of her promised lover's face and the untaught boy touched by passion till now unknown', *Am.* 2.1.5–6; *Per me decepto didicit custode Corinna | liminis adstricti sollicitare fidem, | delabique toro tunica velata soluta | atque inpercussos nocte movere pedes*, 'through me Corinna has learned to elude her guard and tamper with the faith of the tight-closed door, to slip away from her couch in tunic ungirdled and move in the night with unstumbling foot', *Am.* 3.1.49–52. *Ars Amatoria* 3 is purportedly written to and for the female reader.

28 See Churchill *et al.* (2002).

29 Cicero, *Brutus* 58.211. On Cornelia's letters see Santirocco (1979) 229; Parker (1994) 52; Hemelrijk (2002); also Hallett in Churchill *et al.* (2002) which publishes the fragments from the manuscripts of Cornelius Nepos (d.24 BCE).

30 From *Pompey* 55, quoted in Hemelrijk (2002) 17.

31 On dating, see Mackay (1962); on Sempronia, Boyd (1987); on Sallust's Catiline more generally, Levene (2000).

32 *Litteris Graecis et Latinis docta, psallere saltare elegantius quam necesse est probae, multa alia, quae instrumenta luxuriae sunt. Sed ei cariora semper omnia quam decus atque pudicitia fuit: pecuniae an famae minus parceret, haud facile discerneres: libido sic accensa, ut saepius peteret viros quam peterentur... verum ingenium eius haud absurdam: posse versus facere, iocum movere, sermone uti vel modesto vel proaci: prorsus multae facetiae multosque lepos inerat*, Cat. 25.

33 *Exorata meis illum Cytherea Camenis | attulit in nostrum deposuitque sinum*, 'Won over by my Muse's prayers, Cythera's queen has brought and placed him in my arms', 3.13.3–4.

34 Wyke (2002) 41.

35 *Non ego signatis quicquam mandare tabellis | ne legat id nemo quam meus ante, velim.*

36 See Roman (2006) on lost tablets in elegy; also *Amores* 1.11 and 1.12 for poems about writing tablets.

37 *Scribens versiculos uterque nostrum | ludebat numero modo hoc modo illoc | reddens mutua per iocum atque vinum*, c.50.4–6.

38 On Cerinthus, Boucher (1976), Roessel (1990).

39 *Tu loqueris, cum sis iam noto fabula libro | et tua sit toto Cynthia lecta foro?*.

40 See also *Amores* 3.12 which blurs the line between female body and text: *quae modo dicta mea est, quam coepi solus amare | cum multis vereor ne sit habenda mihi*, 'she who but now was called my own, whom I began alone to love, must now, I fear, be shared with many' (3.12.5–6).

41 Skinner (2005) 225 on *cum esse* as 'to make love with'.

42 e.g. *quaque patet domitis Romana potentia terris, | ore legar populi, perque omnia saecula fama, | siquid habent veri vatum praesagia, vivam*, 'wherever Rome's power extends over the conquered world, I shall have mention on men's lips, and, if the prophecies of bards have any truth, through all the ages shall I live in fame', *Met.* 15.877–9.

43 Hardie (2012a, 2012b).

44 Keith (1997).

45 Mary Wroth was the daughter of Robert Sidney and niece to his siblings Philip and Mary Sidney: on Mary Sidney's biography, Hannay (1990), on Mary Wroth's life, Hannay (2013).

46 Denny's letter dated 26 February 1621 is reproduced in Roberts (1983), English spellings here modernised.

47 On the Sidney psalms, see Trill (1996), Clark (2001); on Sidney's authorised editions of Philip Sidney's works, Duncan-Jones (1989), Lamb (1990), Hannay *et al.* (1998); on Mary Sidney's writing, Salzman (2006), Wynne-Davis (2007); on her role as a literary patron, Brennan (1988), Lamb (1990).

48 All quotations from Sidney's *Antonie* are from Hannay *et al.* (1998), spellings here modernised: quotation from Argument, 30–1.

49 On Daniel, see Rees (1964), his *Cleopatra* in Grosart (1896).

50 On *ars moriendi*, see Lamb (1990), Alexander (2006); on political commentary, Clarke (1997a, 1997b), Sanders (1998), Skretkowicz (1999), Prescott (2008a, 2008b), Kewes (2012).

51 All quotations from Garnier's *Marc Antoine* are from Lebègue (1974): translations are mine.

52 E.g. Wyke (1992, revised 2002); also Bono (1984).

53 *Hinc ope barbarica variisque Antonius armis ... sequiturque (nefas) Aegyptia coniunx.*

54 *Sequar atris ignibus absens | Et, cum frigida mors anima seducerit artus | Omnibus umbra locis adero*, 'Though far away, I will chase thee with murky brands and, when chill death has severed soul and body, everywhere my shade shall haunt thee', *Aen.* 4.384–6.

55 Hannay (1990), Knowles (2012).

56 Another explanation could be that Sidney adopted 'barking Anubis' from Thomas Phaer's 1558 English translation of *Aeneid* 8: 'all monstrous kinded gods, Anubys dog that barking slave' (8.745).

57 *Donec me docuit castas odisse puellas | improbus, et nullo vivere consilio.*

58 'Eut quelque imagination sur Cleopatre qu'elle s'entendist avec luy pour le ruiner, et par sa ruine moyenner son accord'.

59 Vickers (1981).

60 Burrow (2002) 105 dates sonnet 130 to c.1591–5, close to Sidney's translation date of 1590: the poem clearly draws on what were recognised as outworn formulas: 'My mistress' eyes are nothing like the sun, | coral is far more red than her lips' red; | if snow be white, why then her breasts are dun' (130.1–3).

61 E.g. *Astrophil and Stella* 82 where Astrophil promises 'I never more will bite' (82.14), and the Second Song which almost descends into rape, 'now will I invade the fort' (15).

62 E.g. 'I have my death wound' from 'that murth'ring boy' (20.1–2).

63 Apart from classical sources, Cleopatra appears in various medieval texts as a female examplar: strikingly, she is both celebrated for her love (e.g. Chaucer, Boccaccio) and condemned as a seductress (e.g. Dante's *Inferno* where she is *Cleopatras lussuriosa*, and condemned to the second circle of Hell amongst the lustful). In the *Faerie Queene*, she is both one of the 'proud wemen, vaine, forgetfull of their yoke' (1.5.50.2) and also 'high minded Cleopatra' (1.5.50.7) for her honourable death.

64 Cf. *Nunc te possideant aliae: mox sola tenebo: | mecum eris, et mixtis ossibus ossa teram*, 'other women may possess you now: soon I alone shall hold you: you will be with me, and my bones shall press yours in close entwining' (Propertius 4.7.93–4).

65 The poem-letter is available in Roberts (1983) 32–3, with Wroth's reply 34–5.

66 The 'casket sonnets', problematically attributed to Mary Queen of Scots, are written in French and are still subject to disputed authorship: see Travitsky (1989), Burke (2000), Dunnigan (2002), MacRobert (2002), Smith (2005).

67 Waller (1977), Roberts (1983), Masten (1991), Dubrow (2003).

68 2.1.13, quoted in Roberts (1983) 48.

69 All quotations of Wroth are from Roberts (1983) with spelling modernised and light punctuation added.

70 For dream-visions, see e.g. Propertius 4.7, *Amores* 1.2, possibly 1.5; Petrarch's *Triumph of Love* and *Triumph of Death*, *Astrophil and Stella* 32, 38, 39, 40.

71 *Perque leves auras iunctis invecta columbis; necte comam myrto, maternas iunge columbas.*

72 Estiénne published two volumes of Greek lyric in 1567 with Latin translations and ancient commentary which gave prominence to Sappho; this concluded with Ovid's *Heroides* 15, the letter from Sappho to Phaon which was adopted as the Renaissance 'authoritative' biography of the Greek poet: see DeJean (1989) 37–38, Revard (1993) 68. On fr.1 and 31 and Sappho generally in England during the early modern period Andreadis (1996). John Lyly's play *Sappho & Phao* was written in 1584, a few years before Wroth's birth, as a compliment to Elizabeth: Andreadis (1996) 110, and Donne had also written a *Sapho to Philaenis*. Christine de Pisan included Sappho in her *The Book of the City of Ladies*: 'this lady was placed and counted among the greatest and most famous poets' (1.30.2), her poems 'most remarkably constructed and composed, and they serve as illumination and models of consummate poetic craft and composition' (1.30.3): quotations from the Earl Jeffrey Richards translation (1982, revised 1988). Most recently on Sappho and Wroth, Cottegnies (2013).

73 Translations of Sappho are from Rayor (1991).

74 *Cur non matrisque tuumque imperium profers, Met.* 5.371–2.

75 *Aut puer aut longas compta puella comas.*

76 Propertius 1.1.1–9, 1.1.25.

77 As well as appearing in the Newberry manuscript of the second, unpublished, part of the *Urania*, this poem appears in four other manuscripts, three of which attribute it to Herbert. Tantalisingly, it does not appear in the 1660 selection of Herbert's verse edited by the younger John Donne: see Roberts (1983) for details and the full text of the poem, all quotations are from this version, spelling modernised. On Wroth's affair with Herbert, the son of Mary Sidney, see Hannay (2013).

Conclusion

1 Golding's 1567 translation of Ovid's *Metamorphoses*, 15.989–95.

2 *Nomenque erit indelebile nostrum, Met.* 15.876.

Bibliography

Primary Texts

Apollonius Rhodius. 2008. *Argonautica*, ed. and trans. William H. Race (Cambridge, Cambridge, MA and London: Harvard University Press)

Aretino, Pietro. 1988. *I Modi, The Sixteen Pleasures: An Erotic Album of the Italian Renaissance*, ed. and trans. Lynne Lawner (London: Owen)

Ascham, Roger. 1999. *The Schoolmaster* in *English Renaissance Literary Criticism*, ed. Brian Vickers (Oxford: Oxford University Press)

Aske, James. 1588. *Elizabetha Triumphans* (London: Printed by Thomas Orwin for Thomas Gubbin)

Castiglione, Baldesare. 1975. *The Book of the Courtier*, trans. Sir Thomas Hoby (1561) (London: JM Dent & Sons)

Catullus. 1958. *C. Valerii Catulli: Carmina*, ed. R.A.B. Mynors (Oxford: Oxford University Press)

1962. *Catullus, Tibullus, Pervigilium Veneris*, trans. F.W. Cornish, revised by G.P. Goold (Cambridge, Cambridge, MA and London: Harvard University Press)

1990. *The Complete Poems*, trans. Guy Lee (Oxford: Oxford University Press)

Chaucer, Geoffrey. 1957. *The Complete Works*, ed. F.N. Robinson, 2nd ed. (Oxford: Oxford University Press)

Cicero. 1905. *M. Tulli Ciceroni: Orationes*, ed. Albertus Curtis Clark (Oxford: Oxford University Press)

1974. *M. Tulli Ciceronis in M. Antonium Orationes Philippicae Prima et Secunda*, ed. J.D. Denniston (Oxford: Oxford University Press)

Crapelet, George-Adrian, ed. 1826. *Lettres de Henri VIIIième à Anne Boleyn avec la traduction* (Paris: Impr. de Crapelet)

Daniel, Samuel. 1896. *The Complete Works in Verse and Prose of Samuel Daniel*, ed. Alexander Balloch Grosart (London: Hazell, Watson, and Viney)

Deloney, Thomas. 1588. *The Queenes Visiting of the Campe at Tilsburie with her Entertainment There* (London: John Wolfe for Edward White)

De Lorris, Guillaume and Jean de Meun. 1994. *The Romance of the Rose*, trans. Frances Horgan (Oxford: Oxford University Press)

Donne, John. 1990, revised 2000. *The Major Works*, ed. John Carey (Oxford: Oxford University Press)

Elizabeth I. 2000. *Collected Works*, ed. Leah S. Marcus, Janel Mueller and Mary Beth Rose (Chicago and London: University of Chicago Press)

Elyot, Thomas. 1999. *The Boke Named the Governour* in *English Renaissance Literary Criticism*, ed. Brian Vickers (Oxford: Oxford University Press)

Garnier, Robert. 1974. *Marc Antoine, Hippolyte*, ed. Raymond Lebègue (Paris: Les Belles Lettres)

Gellius, Aulus. 1928. *The Attic Nights of Aulus Gellius*, trans. J.C. Rolfe, 3 vols. (London and New York: Harvard University Press)

Golding, Arthur. 2002. *The Metamorphoses*, ed. Madeleine Forey (London: Penguin)

Gosson, Stephen. 1579. *The Schoole of Abuse*, printed at London for Thomas VVoodcocke, STC (2nd ed.) | 12097.5, accessed via EEBO

Greville, Sir Fulke. 1907. *Life of Sir Philip Sidney*, introduction by Nowell Smith (Oxford: Clarendon Press)

Hall, Edward. 1809. *Chronicle, The Union of the Two Noble and Illustre Famelies of York and Lancaster*, ed. H. Ellis (London)

Henry VIII. 1826. *Lettres de Henri VIIIième à Anne Boleyn avec la traduction*, ed. and trans. George-Adrian Crapelet (Paris)

    1936. *The Letters of King Henry VIII*, ed. Muriel St. Clare Byrne (London: Cassell)

Hesiod. 2006. *Theogony, Works and Days, Testimonia*, ed. and trans. Glenn W. Most (Cambridge, Cambridge, MA and London: Harvard University Press)

Homer. 1951. *The Iliad of Homer*, trans. Richmond Lattimore (Chicago and London: University of Chicago Press)

    1965. *The Odyssey of Homer*, trans. Richmond Lattimore (New York: HarperCollins)

The Homeric Hymns. 2003. Ed. and trans. Martin L. West (Cambridge, Cambridge, MA and London: Harvard University Press)

Jonson, Ben. 1975, revised 1996. *Ben Jonson: The Complete Poems*, ed. George Parfitt (London: Penguin)

    2012. *The Cambridge Edition of the Works of Ben Jonson*, ed. David Bevington, Martin Butler and Ian Donaldson (Cambridge: Cambridge University Press)

Leland, John. Ed. and trans. Dana Sutton. www.philological.bham.ac.uk/lelandpoems/

Macchiavelli, Niccolò. 1996. *Machiavelli and His Friends: Their Personal Correspondence*, ed. James B Atkinson and David Sices (Northern Illinois University Press)

Marlowe, Christopher. 1979. *The Complete Poems and Translations*, ed. Stephen Orgel (London: Penguin)

Martial. 1963. *M. Val. Martialis: Epigrammata*, ed. W.M. Lindsay (Oxford: Clarendon Press)

Marvell, Andrew. 1990. *Andrew Marvell*, ed. Frank Kermode and Keith Walker (Oxford: Oxford University Press)

Nashe, Thomas. 1958. *The Works of Thomas Nashe*, ed. Ronald B. McKerrow (Oxford: Oxford University Press)

    1972. *The Unfortunate Traveller and Other Works*, ed. J.B. Steane (Harmondsworth: Penguin)

Ovid. 1961, 1994. *Amores, Ars Amatoria, Remedia Amoris*, ed. E.J. Kenney (Oxford: Oxford University Press)

    1963. *Tristia*, ed. S.G. Owen (Oxford: Clarendon Press)

    1977. *Metamorphoses*, trans. Frank Justus Miller, revised by G.P. Goold, 3rd ed., 2 vols. (Cambridge, Cambridge, MA and London: Harvard University Press)

    1988. *Tristia, Ex Ponto*, trans. Arthur Leslie Wheeler, revised by G.P. Goold, 2nd ed. (Cambridge, Cambridge, MA and London: Harvard University Press)

    2002. *Heroides, Amores*, trans. Grant Showerman, revised by G.P. Goold, 2nd ed. (Cambridge, Cambridge, MA and London: Harvard University Press)

    2004. *Metamorphoses*, ed. R.J. Tarrant (Oxford: Clarendon Press)

    2005. *The Poems of Exile: Tristia and the Black Sea Letters*, trans. Peter Green (Berkeley, Los Angeles and London: University of California Press)

    2013. *Fasti*, trans. Anne and Peter Wiseman (Oxford: Oxford University Press)

Petrarch. 1962. *The Triumphs of Petrarch*, trans. Ernest Hatch Wilkins (Chicago: Chicago University Press)

    1977. *Petrarch's Africa*, trans. Thomas G. Bergin and Alice S. Wilson (New Haven: Yale University Press)

    2002. *Canzoniere: Selected Poems*, trans. Anthony Mortimer (London: Penguin)

    2017. *Francesco Petrarca: Selected Letters*, ed. and trans. Elaine Fantham, The I Tatti Renaissance Library (Cambridge, MA and London: Harvard University Press)

Phaer, Thomas. 1987. *The Aeneid of Thomas Phaer and Thomas Twyne*, ed. Steven Lally (New York and London: Garland Publishing)

Plato. 1953. *Lysis, Symposium, Gorgias*, trans. W.R.M. Lamb (Cambridge, Cambridge, MA and London: Harvard University Press)

    2013. *Republic*, trans. Christopher Emlyn-Jones and William Preddy (Cambridge, Cambridge, MA and London: Harvard University Press)

Propertius. 1990. *Elegies*, trans. G.P. Goold (Cambridge, Cambridge, MA and London: Harvard University Press)

    1994. *The Poems*, trans. Guy Lee (Oxford: Oxford University Press)

    2007. *Sexti Properti: Elegos*, ed. S.J. Heyworth (Oxford: Oxford University Press)

Puttenham, George. 2004. *The Art of English Poesy* in *Sidney's 'The Defence of Poesy' and Selected Renaissance Literary Criticism*, ed. Gavin Alexander (London: Penguin)

Sallust. 1991. *C. Sallusti Crispi: Catilina*, ed. L.D. Reynolds (Oxford: Oxford University Press)

Sannazaro, Jacopo. 2009. *Latin Poetry*, ed. and trans. Michael Putnam (Cambridge, MA: Harvard University Press)

Sappho. 1955. *Poetarum Lesbiorum Fragmenta*, ed. Edgar Lobel and Denys Page (Oxford: Clarendon Press)

    1991. *Sappho's Lyre: Archaic Lyric and Women Poets of Ancient Greece*, trans. Diane J. Rayor (Berkeley, Los Angeles and London: University of California Press)

Secundus, Joannes. 1930. *The Love Poems of Joannes Secundus*, ed. and trans. F.A. Wright (London: Routledge)

1981. *Joannes Secundus: The Latin Love Elegy in the Renaissance*, ed. and trans. Clifford Endres (Connecticut: Archon Books)

Sidney, Mary. 1998. *The Collected Works of Mary Sidney Herbert, Countess of Pembroke: Poems, Translations, and Correspondence*, ed. Margaret Patterson Hannay, Noel J. Kinnamon and Michael G. Brennan (Oxford: Oxford University Press)

Sidney, Philip. 1962. *The Defence of Poesie, Political Discourses, Correspondance, Translation*, ed. Albert Feuillerat (Cambridge: Cambridge University Press)

1977. *The Countess of Pembroke's Arcadia*, ed. Maurice Evans (London: Penguin)

1985. *The Old Arcadia*, ed. Katherine Duncan-Jones (Oxford: Oxford University Press)

1989, revised 2002. *The Major Works*, ed. Katherine Duncan-Jones (Oxford: Oxford University Press)

Sidney, Robert. 1984. *The Poems of Robert Sidney, Edited from the Poet's Autograph Notebook*, ed. with introduction and commentary by P.J. Croft (Oxford: Oxford University Press)

Skelton, John. 1983. *The Complete English Poems*, ed. John Scattergood (New Haven and London: Yale University Press)

Spenser, Edmund. 1978. *The Faerie Queen*, ed. Thomas P. Roche (London: Penguin)

St. Clare Byrne, Muriel. 1936. *The Letters of King Henry VIII* (London: Cassell)

Sulpicia. 1924. *Tibulli Aliorumque Carminum Libri Tres*, ed. John Percival Postgate (Oxford: Clarendon Press)

1962. *Catullus, Tibullus, Pervirgilium Veneris*, trans. J.P. Postgate, revised by G.P. Goold (Cambridge, MA and London: Harvard University Press)

Tasso, Torquato. 2009. *The Liberation of Jerusalem*, trans. Max Wickert (Oxford: Oxford University Press)

Tottel's Miscellany. 1870. Collated by Edward Arber from the first and second editions of 5 June and 31 July 1557 (London: Edward Arber)

2011. Ed. Amanda Holton and Tom MacFaul (London: Penguin)

Virgil. 1916, revised 1935. *Eclogues, Georgics, Aeneid 1–6*, trans. H.R. Fairclough (Cambridge, MA and London: Harvard University Press)

1969. *P. Vergili Maronis: Opera*, ed. R.A.B. Mynors (Oxford: Oxford University Press)

2000. *Aeneid 7–12, Appendix Vergiliana*, trans. H.R. Fairclough, revised by G.P. Goold (Cambridge, MA and London: Harvard University Press)

Wyatt, Sir Thomas. 1978, revised 1997. *The Complete Poems*, ed. R.A. Rebholz (London: Penguin)

Secondary Literature

Acosta-Hughes, Benjamin and Susan A. Stephens. 2012. *Callimachus in Context: From Plato to the Augustan Poets* (Cambridge: Cambridge University Press)

Adams, J.N. 1982. *The Latin Sexual Vocabulary* (London: Duckworth)

Alexander, Gavin. 2006. *Writing After Sidney: The Literary Response to Sir Philip Sidney 1586–1640* (Oxford: Oxford University Press)

Allen, Graham. 2000. *Intertextuality* (London: Routledge)

Allen, Michael J.B., Valery Rees with Martin Davies, eds. 2002. *Marsilio Ficino: His Theology, His Philosophy, His Legacy* (Leiden: Brill)

Allen, Michael J.B., ed. and trans. 2008. *Marsilio Ficino, Commentaries on Plato vol 1: Phaedrus and Ion* (Cambridge, MA: Harvard University Press)

Allison, June W. 1980a. 'Virgilian Themes in Propertius 4.7 and 4.8', *Classical Philology* 75/4: 332–8

1980b. 'Propertius 4.7.94', *The American Journal of Philology* 101/2: 170–3

1984. 'The Cast of Characters in Propertius 4.7', *Classical World* 77/6: 355–8

Almasy, Rudolph P. 1993. 'Stella and the Songs: Questions about the Composition of "*Astrophil and Stella*"', *South Atlantic Review* 58/4: 1–17

Ancona, Ronnie and Ellen Greene, eds. 2005. *Gendered Dynamics in Latin Love Poetry* (Baltimore: Johns Hopkins University Press)

Anderson, Robert D., P.J. Parsons and R.G.M. Nisbet. 1979. 'Elegiacs by Gallus from Qaṣr Ibrîm', *Journal of Roman Studies* 69: 125–55

Anderson, William S. 1989. 'The Artist's Limits in Ovid: Orpheus, Pygmalion, and Daedalus', *Syllecta Classica* 1/1: 1–11

Andreadis, H. 1996. 'Sappho in Early Modern England: A Study in Sexual Reputation', in *Re-Reading Sappho: Receptions and Transmission*, ed. Ellen Greene (Berkeley: University of California Press)

Anglo, Sydney. 1969. *Spectacle, Pageantry and Early Tudor Policy* (Oxford: Clarendon Press)

Arkins, Brian. 2005. *An Interpretation of the Poetry of Propertius (c.50-15 BC)* (Lampeter: The Edwin Mellen Press)

Armstrong, A. 1977. 'The Apprenticeship of John Donne: Ovid and the "*Elegies*"', *English Literary History* 44/3: 419–42

Austin, R.G. 1977. *Aeneidos Liber Sextus with a Commentary* (Oxford: Oxford University Press)

Baca, Albert R. 1972. 'Propertian Elements in the "Cinthia" of Aeneas Silvius Piccolomini', *The Classical Journal* 67/3: 221–6

Baker, Moira P. 1991. ' "The Uncanny Stranger on Display": The Female Body in Sixteenth-and Seventeenth-Century Love Poetry', *South Atlantic Review* 56/2: 7–25

Bald, R.C. 1970. *John Donne: A Life* (Oxford: Clarendon Press)

Barchiesi, Alessandro. 1997. *The Poet and the Prince: Ovid and Augustan Discourse* (Berkeley, Los Angeles and London: University of California Press)

1999. 'Venus' Masterplot: Ovid and the Homeric Hymns', in Hardie *et al.* 1999

2002. 'Narrative Technique and Narratology in the Metamorphoses', in *The Cambridge Companion to Ovid*, ed. Philip Hardie (Cambridge: Cambridge University Press)

Barkan, Leonard. 1980. 'Diana and Actaeon: The Myth as Synthesis', *English Literary Renaissance* 10/3: 317–59

1986. *The Gods Made Flesh: Metamorphosis and the Pursuit of Paganism* (New Haven and London: Yale University Press)

1999. *Unearthing the Past: Archaeology and Aesthetics in the Making of Renaissance Culture* (New Haven and London: Yale University Press)

Barker, Duncan. 1996. "'The Golden Age is Proclaimed'? The *Carmen saeculae* and the Renascence of the Golden Race', *The Classical Quarterly* 46/2: 434–6

Barnard, M.E. 1987. *The Myth of Apollo and Daphne from Ovid to Quevedo: Love, Agon and the Grotesque* (Durham, NC: Duke University Press)

Barnes, Catherine. 1971. 'The Hidden Persuader: The Complex Speaking Voice of Sidney's Defence of Poetry', *Publications of the Modern Language Association of America* 86/3: 422–7

Barroll, Leeds. 2001. *Anna of Denmark, Queen of England: A Cultural Biography* (Philadelphia: University of Pennsylvania Press)

Barton, Carlin. 2000. 'Being in the Eyes: Shame and Sight in Ancient Rome', in Fredrick 2002

Barton, David and Nigel Hall, eds. 2000. *Letter Writing as a Social Practice* (Amserdam and Philadelphia: John Benjamins)

Bartsch, Shadi. 1998. '*Ars* and the Man: The Politics of Art in Virgil's *Aeneid*', *Classical Philology* 93/4: 322–42

Bassnett, Susan. 2014. *Translation* (London and New York: Routledge)

Bate, Jonathan. 1993. 'Sexual Perversity in "Venus and Adonis"', *The Yearbook of English Studies* 23: 80–92

1994. *Shakespeare and Ovid* (Oxford: Clarendon Press)

Bates, Catherine. 2007. *Masculinity, Gender and Identity in the English Renaissance* (Cambridge: Cambridge University Press)

2013. *Masculinity and the Hunt: Wyatt to Spenser* (Oxford: Oxford University Press)

Bath, Michael. 1979. 'The Legend of Caesar's Deer', *Medievalis et Humanistica* 9: 53–66

Batstone, William W. and Garth Tissol, eds. 2005. *Defining Genre and Gender in Latin Literature: Essays Presented to William S. Anderson on his 75th Birthday* (New York: Peter Lang)

2007. 'Catullus and the Programmatic Poem: The Origins, Scope, and Utility of a Concept', in Skinner 2007a

Beard, Mary. 2007. *The Roman Triumph* (Cambridge, MA and London: Harvard University Press)

Becker, Andrew S. 1995. *The Shield of Aeneas and the Poetics of Ekphrasis* (New York and Oxford: Rowman & Littlefield)

Behr, Francesca D'Allesandro. 2005. 'The Narrator's Voice: A Narratological Reappraisal of Apostrophe in Virgil's Aeneid', *Arethusa* 38/2: 189–221

Belsey, Andrew and Catherine Belsey. 1990. 'Icons of Divinity: Portraits of Elizabeth I', in *Renaissance Bodies: The Human Figure in English Culture c.1540–1660*, ed. Lucy Gent and Nigel Llewellyn (London: Reaktion Books)

Belsey, Catherine. 1994. *Desire: Love Stories in Western Culture* (Oxford: Blackwell)

Benediktson, D. Thomas. 1989. *Propertius: Modernist Poet of Antiquity* (Carbondale and Edwardsville: Southern Illinois University Press)

Berry, Philippa. 1989. *Of Chastity and Power: Elizabethan Literature and the Unmarried Queen* (London and New York: Routledge)

Berthoff, Ann. 1963. 'The Falconer's Dream of Trust: Wyatt's "They Flee From Me"', *The Swanee Review* 71/3: 477–94

Betts, Hannah. 1998. ' "The Image of this Queene so quaynt": The Pornographic Blazon 1588–1603', in Walker 1998

Blanchard, Alistair, J.L. 2010. *Sex: Vice and Love from Antiquity to Modernity* (Chichester: Wiley-Blackwell)

Blevins, J. 2004. *Catullan Consciousness and the Early Modern Lyric in England: From Wyatt to Donne* (Hampshire: Ashgate)

Bloom, Harold. 1973. *The Anxiety of Influence: A Theory of Poetry* (Oxford: Oxford University Press)

Boehrer, Bruce Thomas. 1989. 'Behn's "Disappointment" and Nashe's "Choice of Valentines": Pornographic Poetry and the Influence of Anxiety', *Essays in Literature* 16: 172–87

Bolgar, R.R. 1963. *The Classical Heritage and its Beneficiaries* (Cambridge: Cambridge University Press)

Bono, Barbara J. 1984. *Literary Transvaluation: From Vergilian Epic to Shakespearean Tragicomedy* (Berkeley: University of California Press)

Booth, Joan. 1995, revised 1999. *Catullus to Ovid: Reading Latin Love Elegy* (London: Bristol Classical Press)

1997. 'All in the Mind: Sickness in Cat.76', in *The Passions in Roman Thought and Literature*, ed. S.M. Braund and C. Gill (Cambridge: Cambridge University Press)

ed. 2007. *Cicero on the Attack: Invective and Subversion in the Orations and Beyond* (Swansea: The Classical Press of Wales)

Boucher, J.P. 1976. 'A Propos de Cérinthus et de quelques autres Pseudonyms dans la Poésie Augustiéene', *Latomus* 35/2: 504–19

Bowditch, P. Lowell. 2006. 'Propertius and the Gendered Rhetoric of Luxury and Empire: A Reading of 2.16', *Comparative Literature Studies* 43/3: 306–25

2009. 'Palatine Apollo and the Imperial Gaze: Propertius 2.31 and 2.32', *The American Journal of Philology* 130: 401–38

2012. 'Roman Love Elegy and the Eros of Empire', in Gold 2012

Boyd, Barbara Weiden. 1987. '*Virtus effeminata* and Sallust's Sempronia', *Transactions of the American Philological Association* 117: 183–201

1997. *Ovid's Literary Loves: Influence and Innovation in the Amores* (Ann Arbor: University of Michigan Press)

Boyle, A.J. 2003. *Ovid and the Monuments: A Poet's Rome* (Victoria: Aureal Publications)

Boyle, Marjorie O'Rourke. 1991. *Petrarch's Genius: Pentimento and Prophecy* (Berkeley, Los Angeles and Oxford: University of California Press)

Braden, Gordon. 1990. 'Unspeakable Love: Petrarch to Herbert', in *Soliciting Interpretation: Literary Theory and Seventeenth-Century English Poetry*, ed. Elizabeth D. Harvey and Katharine Eisaman Maus (Chicago: University of Chicago Press)

1996. 'Gaspara Stampa and the Gender of Petrarchism', *Texas Studies in Literature and Language* 38/2: 115–39

2000. 'Ovid, Petrarch, and Shakespeare's Sonnets', in *Shakespeare's Ovid: The Metamorphoses in the Plays and Poems*, ed. A.B. Taylor (Cambridge: Cambridge University Press)

Breitenberg, Mark. 1996. *Anxious Masculinity in Early Modern England* (Cambridge: Cambridge University Press)

Brennan, Michael. 1988. *Literary Patronage in the English Renaissance: The Pembroke Family* (London: Croom Helm)

Brigden, Susan. 2012. *Thomas Wyatt: The Heart's Forest* (London: Faber & Faber)

Brigden, Susan and Jonathan Woolfson. 2005. 'Thomas Wyatt in Italy', *Renaissance Quarterly* 58/2: 464–511

Brown, Georgia. 2004. *Redefining Elizabethan Literature* (Cambridge: Cambridge University Press)

Brulotte, Gaëtan and John Phillips, eds. 2006. *The Encyclopedia of Erotic Literature*, 2 vols. (New York and Oxford: Routledge)

Bull, Malcolm. 2005. *The Mirror of the Gods* (Oxford: Oxford University Press)

Burke, Mary. 2000. 'Queen, Lover, Poet: A Question of Balance in the Sonnets of Mary, Queen of Scots', in *Women, Writing, and the Reproduction of Culture in Tudor and Stuart Britain*, ed. Mary Elizabeth Burke, Jane Donawerth, Karen Nelson and Linda L. Dove (Syracuse: Syracuse University Press)

Burrow, Colin. 1988. 'Original Fictions: Metamorphoses in The Faerie Queene', in *Ovid Renewed: Ovidian Influences on Literature and Art from the Middle Ages to the Twentieth Century*, ed. Charles Martindale (Cambridge: Cambridge University Press)

1999. 'Full of the Maker's Guile: Ovid on Imitating and on the Imitation of Ovid', in Hardie *et al.* 1999

ed. 2002. *William Shakespeare: The Complete Sonnets and Poems* (Oxford: Oxford University Press)

2008. 'English Renaissance Readers and the Appendix Vergiliana', *Proceedings of the Virgil Society* 26: 1–16

Butrica, J.L. 1984. *The Manuscript Tradition of Propertius* (Toronto: University of Toronto Press)

1999. 'Using Water "Unchastely": Cicero "Pro Caelio" 34 Again', *Phoenix* 53: 136–9

2006. 'The Transmission of the Text of Propertius', in Günter 2006

2007. 'History and Transmission of the Text', in Skinner 2007a

Buxton, John. 1954. *Sir Philip Sidney and the English Renaissance* (London: Macmillan)

Cahoon, L. 1988. 'The Bed as Battlefield: Erotic Conquest and Military Metaphor in Ovid's Amores', *Transactions of the American Philological Association* 118: 293–307

1996. 'Calliope's Song: Shifting Narrators in Ovid's *Metamorphoses* 5', *Helios* 23: 43–66

Calame, Claude. 1999. *The Poetics of Eros in Ancient Greece*, trans. Janet Lloyd (New Jersey: Princeton University Press)

Camps, William Anthony. 1969. *An Introduction to Virgil's Aeneid* (Oxford: Oxford University Press)

Carey, John. 1981. *John Donne: Life, Mind, Art* (London and Boston: Faber & Faber)

ed. 1990, revised 2000. *John Donne: The Major Works* (Oxford: Oxford University Press)

Carley, James P. 1985. 'The Manuscript Remains of John Leland: "The king's anti-quary"', *Text: Transactions of the Society for Textual Scholarship* 2: 111–20

1986. 'John Leland in Paris: The Evidence of his Poetry', *Studies in Philology* 83/1: 1–50

Carley, James P. and Pierre Petitmengin. 2004. 'Pre-Conquest Manuscripts from Malmesbury Abbey and John Leland's Letter to Beatus Rhenanus Concerning a Lost Copy of Tertullian's Works', *Anglo-Saxon England* 33: 195–223

Carlson, David R. 1991. 'The Latin Writings of John Skelton', *Studies in Philology* 88/4: 1–125

Carr, John W. 1974. 'A Borrowing from Tibullus in Chaucer's *House of Fame*', *The Chaucer Review* 8: 191–7

Casali, Sergio. 1995. 'Aeneas and the Doors of the Temple of Apollo', *The Classical Journal* 91/1: 1–9

Cheney, Patrick. 2011. *Reading Sixteenth Century Poetry* (West Sussex: Wiley-Blackwell)

Churchill, Laurie J., Phyllis R. Brown and Jane E. Jeffrey, eds. 2002. *Women Writing Latin from Roman Antiquity to Early Modern Europe*, 3 vols. (New York and London: Routledge)

Clark, James G., Frank Coulson and Kathryn McKinley, eds. 2011. *Ovid in the Middle Ages* (Cambridge: Cambridge University Press)

Clark, Sandra. 1994. *Amorous Rites: Elizabethan Erotic Narrative Verse* (London: Everyman)

Clarke, Danielle. 1997a. 'The Politics of Translation and Gender in the Countess of Pembroke's *Antonie*', *Translation and Literature* 6/2: 149–66

1997b. '"Lovely Songs Shall Turne to Holy Psalmes": Mary Sidney and the Transformation of Petrarch', *The Modern Language Review* 92/2: 282–94.

2000. '"Formed into words by your divided lips": Women, Rhetoric and the Ovidian Tradition', in *'This Double Voice': Gendered Writing in Early Modern England*, ed. D. Clarke and E. Clarke (Hampshire and London: St. Martin's Press)

2001. *The Politics of Early Modern Women's Writing* (Harlow: Longman)

Clarke, John R. 1998. *Looking at Love-Making: Constructions of Sexuality in Roman Art 100 BC–AD 250* (Berkeley, Los Angeles and London: University of California Press)

2003. *Roman Sex: 100 BCE–AD 250* (New York: Harry N. Abrams)

Clauss, James J. 1995. 'A Delicate Foot on the Well-Worn Threshold: Paradoxical Imagery in Catullus 68B', *The American Journal of Philology* 116/2: 237–53

Cockburn, Gordon T. 1992. 'Aeneas and the Gates of Sleep: An Etymological Approach', *Phoenix* 46/4: 362–4

Conte, Gian Biagio. 1994. *Genres and Readers: Lucretius, Love Elegy, Pliny's Encyclopedia*, trans. Glenn W. Most (Baltimore and London: Johns Hopkins University Press)

— 2007. 'Poetic Memory and the Art of Allusion (On a Verse of Catullus and One of Vergil)', in Gaisser 2007

Copley, F.O. 1947. 'Servitium Amoris in the Roman Elegists', *Transactions and Proceedings of the American Philological Association* 78: 285–300

Corbeill, Antony. 1996. *Controlling Laughter: Political Humour in the Late Roman Republic* (New Jersey: Princeton University Press)

— 2005. 'The Topography of *Fides* in Propertius 1.16', in Batstone and Tissol 2005

Coren, P. 2001. 'In the Person of Womankind: Female Persona Poems by Campion, Donne, Jonson', *Studies in Philology* 98/2: 225–50

Cottegnies, Line. 2013. 'The Sapphic Context of Lady Mary Wroth's *Pamphilia to Amphilianthus*', in *Early Modern Women and the Poem*, ed. Susan Wiseman (Manchester: Manchester University Press)

Cotter, James Finn. 1970a. 'The Songs in Sidney's *"Astrophil and Stella"*', *Studies in Philology* 67/2: 178–200

— 1970b. 'The "Baiser" Group in Sidney's *"Astrophil and Stella"*', *Texas Studies in Literature and Language* 12/3: 381–403

Crewe, Jonathan. 1982. *Unredeemed Rhetoric: Thomas Nashe and the Scandal of Authorship* (Baltimore and London: Johns Hopkins University Press)

Cunnar, Eugene R. 1993. 'Fantasising a Sexual Golden Age in C17th Poetry', in Summers and Pebworth 1993

Cunningham, Valentine. 2007. 'Why Ekphrasis?', *Classical Philology* 102: 57–71

Dalby, A. 2000. *Empire of Pleasures: Luxury and Indulgence in the Roman World* (London: Psychology Press)

D'Ancona, Paolo. 1955. *The Farnesina Frescoes at Rome* (Milan: Edizioni del Milione)

D'Arms, John H. 1970. *Romans on the Bay of Naples: A Social and Cultural Study of the Villas and their Owners from 150 BC to AD 400* (Cambridge, MA: Harvard University Press)

Davidson, James. 1988. *Courtesans and Fishcakes: The Consuming Passions of Classical Athens* (London: HarperCollins)

Davies, Ceri. 1973. 'Poetry in the "Circle" of Messalla', *Greece & Rome* 20/1: 25–35

Davis, Alex. 'Revolution by Degrees: Philip Sidney and *Gradatio*', *Modern Philology* 108/4: 488–506

Davis, P.J. 1999. 'Ovid's *Amores*: A Political Reading', *Classical Philology* 94/4: 431–49

— 2006. *Ovid and Augustus: A Political Reading of Ovid's Erotic Poems* (London: Duckworth)

— 2012. 'Reception of Elegy in Augustan and Post-Augustan Poetry', in Gold 2012

De Grazia, Margreta. 1981. 'Lost Potential in Grammar and Nature: Sidney's Astrophil and Stella', *Studies in English Literature, 1500–1900* 21/1: 21–35

DeBrohun, Jeri Blair. 1994. 'Redressing Elegy's Puella: Propertius IV and the Rhetoric of Fashion', *The Journal of Roman Studies* 84: 41–63

— 2003. *Roman Propertius and the Reinvention of Elegy* (Ann Arbor: University of Michigan Press)

DeJean, Joan. 1989. *Fictions of Sappho, 1546–1937* (Chicago: University of Chicago Press)

DeRose Evans, Jane. 1992. *The Art of Persuasion: Political Propaganda from Aeneas to Brutus* (Ann Arbor: University of Michigan Press)

Desmond, Marilynn. 1993. 'When Dido Reads Vergil: Gender and Intertextuality in Ovid's Heroides' 7', *Helios* 20/1: 56–68

Dinter, Martin. 2005. 'Epic and Epigram: Minor Heroes in Virgil's Aeneid', *The Classical Quarterly* 55/1: 153–69

Dixon, Suzanne. 2001. *Reading Roman Women* (London: Duckworth)

Docherty, Thomas. 1986. *John Donne, Undone* (London and New York: Methuen)

Donaldson, Ian. 2011. *Ben Jonson: A Life* (Oxford: Oxford University Press)

Donaldson-Evans, Lance K. 1980. *Love's Fatal Glance: A Study of Eye Imagery in the Poets of the Ecole Lyonnaise* (Mississippi: Romance Monographs)

Doran, Susan. 2003. 'Virginity, Divinity and Power: The Portraits of Elizabeth', in Doran and Freeman 2003

Doran, Susan and Thomas S. Freeman, eds. 2003. *The Myth of Elizabeth* (Basingstoke: Palgrave Macmillan)

Du Quesnay, Ian M. Le M. 1973. 'The Amores', in *Ovid*, ed. J.W. Binns (London: Routledge)

Du Quesnay, Ian and Tony Woodman, eds. 2012. *Catullus: Poems, Books, Readers* (Cambridge: Cambridge University Press)

Dubrow, H. 1982. *Genre* (London and New York: Methuen)

    1995. *Echoes of Desire: English Petrarchism and its Counterdiscourses* (Ithaca and London: Cornell University Press)

    2003. '"And Thus Leave Off": Reevaluating Mary Wroth's Folger Manuscript, Va104', *Tulsa Studies in Women's Literature* 22: 273–91

Duckett, Eleanor Shipley. 1925. *Catullus in English Poetry* (Cambridge and Cambridge, MA: The Collegiate Press)

Dufallo, Basil. 2006. 'Propertius and the Blindness of Affect', in *Dead Lovers: Erotic Bonds and the Study of Premodern Europe*, ed. Basil Dufallo and Peggy McCraken (Ann Arbor: University of Michigan Press)

Duff, David, ed. 2000. *Modern Genre Theory* (Essex: Longman)

Duncan-Jones, Katherine. 1991. *Sir Philip Sidney: Courtier Poet* (London: Hamish Hamilton)

    1993. 'Much Ado with Red and White: The Earliest Readers of Shakespeare's Venus and Adonis (1593)', *The Review of English Studies* 44: 479–501

    1999. 'Bess Carey's Petrarch: Newly Discovered Elizabethan Sonnets', *The Review of English Studies* 50/199: 304–19

Dunnigan, Sarah. 2002. *Eros and Poetry at the Courts of Mary Queen of Scots and James I* (Basingstoke: Palgrave Macmillan)

Dyson, Julia, T. 2007. 'The Lesbia Poems', in Skinner 2007a

    2008. *Clodia: A Sourcebook* (Norman: University of Oklahoma Press)

Easthope, Antony. 1989. 'Foucault, Ovid and Donne: Versions of Sexuality, Ancient and Modern', in *Poetry and Phantasy* (Cambridge: Cambridge University Press)

Edmunds, Lowell. 2001. *Intertextuality and the Reading of Roman Poetry* (Baltimore and London: Johns Hopkins University Press)

Edwards, Catharine. 1993. *The Politics of Immorality in Ancient Rome* (Cambridge: Cambridge University Press)

1996. *Writing Rome: Textual Approaches to the City* (Cambridge: Cambridge University Press)

2007. *Death in Ancient Rome* (New Haven: Yale University Press)

El-Gabalawy, Saad. 1976. 'Aretino's Pornography and Renaissance Satire', *Rocky Mountain Review of Language and Literature* 30/2: 87–99

Elsner, Jas. 2007a *Roman Eyes: Visuality and Subjectivity in Art and Text* (Princeton and Oxford: Princeton University Press)

2007b. 'Viewing Ariadne: From Ekphrasis to Wall Painting in the Roman World', *Classical Philology* 102: 20–44

Elsner, John. 1996. 'Image and Ritual: Reflections on the Religious Appreciation of Classical Art', *CQ* 46/2: 515–31

Enterline, Lynn. 2000. *The Rhetoric of the Body from Ovid to Shakespeare* (Cambridge: Cambridge University Press)

Erasmo, Mario. 2008. *Reading Death in Ancient Rome* (Columbus: Ohio State University Press)

Estrin, Barbara L. 1984. 'Becoming the Other/the Other Becoming in Wyatt's Poetry', *ELH* 51/3: 431–45

1994. *Laura: Uncovering Gender and Genre in Wyatt, Donne and Marvell* (Durham, NC and London: Duke University Press)

Evans, Robert C. 1993. 'The Folger Text of Thomas Nashe's "Choise of Valentines"', *Bibliographical Society of America, Papers* 87: 363–75

Fabre-Serris, Jacqueline. 2009. 'Sulpicia: An/other Female Voice in Ovid's *Heroides*: A New Reading of *Heroides* 4 and 15', *Helios* 36/2: 149–73

Fairweather, Janet. 1984. 'The "Gallus Papyrus": A New Interpretation', *The Classical Quarterly* 34/1: 167–74

Falconer, Rachel. 2000. 'Wyatt's Who So List to Hunt', in *A Companion to English Renaissance Literature and Culture*, ed. Michael Hattaway (Oxford: Blackwell)

Fantham, Elaine. 2006. *Julia Augusti, The Emperor's Daughter* (London: Routledge)

Farmer, Norman Jr. 1984. 'Donne, Jonson and the Priority of Picture', in *Poets and the Visual Arts in Renaissance England* (Austin: University of Texas Press)

Fear, T. 2000. 'The Poet as Pimp: Elegiac Seduction in the Time of Augustus', *Arethusa* 33/2: 217–40.

2005. 'Propertian Closure: The Elegiac Inscription of the Liminal Male and Ideological Contestation in Augustan Rome', in Ancona and Greene 2005

Fedeli, Paolo. 2006. 'The History of Propertian Scholarship', in Günter 2006

2012. 'Propertius: Between the Cult of the Transmitted Text and the Hunt for Corruption', in *Propertius*, ed. Ellen Greene and Tara S. Welch (Oxford: Oxford University Press)

Feeney, Denis. 1990. 'The Taciturnity of Aeneas', in *Oxford Readings in Virgil's Aeneid*, ed. S.J. Harrison (Oxford: Oxford University Press)

Feinstein, Sandy. 1994. 'Donne's "Elegy 19": The Busk Between a Pair of Bodies', *Studies in English Literature 1500–1900* 34/1: 61–77

Feldherr, Andrew. 2007. 'The Intellectual Climate', in Skinner 2007a

Ferry, Anne. 1983. *The 'Inward' Language: Sonnets of Wyatt, Sidney, Shakespeare and Donne* (Chicago and London: University of Chicago Press)

Field, Arthur. 2002. 'The Platonic Academy of Florence', in Allen *et al.* 2002

Fienberg, Nona. 1985. 'The Emergence of Stella in *Astrophil and Stella*', *Studies in English Literature 1500–1900* 25/1: 5–19

Findlen, Paula. 1993. 'Humanism, Politics and Pornography in Renaissance Italy', in Hunt 1993

Findley, Alison. 2006. *Playing Spaces in Early Women's Drama* (Cambridge: Cambridge University Press)

Fisher, Will. 2006. *Materializing Gender in Early Modern English Literature and Culture* (Cambridge: Cambridge University Press)

Fitch, John, G., ed. 2008. *Seneca* (Oxford: Oxford University Press)

Fitzgerald, William. 1992. 'Catullus and the Reader: The Erotics of Poetry', *Arethusa* 25/3: 419–41

1995. *Catullan Provocations: Lyric Poetry and the Drama of Position* (Berkeley, Los Angeles and London: University of California Press)

2013. *How to Read a Latin Poem: If You Can't Read Latin Yet* (Oxford: Oxford University Press)

Flaschenreim, Barbara L. 1998. 'Speaking of Women: "Female Voice" in Propertius', *Helios* 25/1: 49–64

1999. 'Sulpicia and the Rhetoric of Disclosure', *Classical Philology* 94/1: 36–54

Forey, Madeleine, ed. 2002. *Ovid's Metamorphoses, Translated by Arthur Golding* (London: Penguin Books)

Fowler, Don. 1987. 'Vergil on Killing Virgins', in *Homo Viator: Classical Essays for John Bramble*, ed. Michael Whitby, Philip Hardie and Mary Whitby (Bristol: Bristol Classical Press)

1990. 'Deviant Focalisation in Virgil's Aeneid', *The Cambridge Classical Journal* 36: 42–63

2000. *Roman Constructions: Readings in Post-Modern Latin* (New York: Oxford University Press)

2002. 'Masculinity Under Threat? The Poetics and Politics of Inspiration in Latin Poetry', in Spentzou and Fowler 2002

Fox, Matthew. 1996. *Roman Historical Myths: The Regal Period in Augustan Literature* (Oxford: Clarendon)

Franz, David O. 1972. ' "Leud Priapians" and Renaissance Pornography', *Studies in English Literature 1500–1900* 12/1: 157–72

1989. *Festum Voluptatis: A Study of Renaissance Erotica* (Ohio: Ohio State University Press)

Fraser, Antonia. 1992. *The Six Wives of Henry VIII* (London: Weidenfeld & Nicolson)

Freccero, John. 1986. 'The Fig Tree and the Laurel: Petrarch's Poetics', in *Literary Theory/Renaissance Texts*, ed. Patricia Parker and David Quint (Baltimore and London: Johns Hopkins University Press)

Fredericks, S.C. 1976. 'A Poetic Experiment in the Garland of Sulpicia (Corpus Tibullianus, 3,10)', *Latomus* 35/2: 761–82

Fredrick, David. 1995. 'Beyond the Atrium to Ariadne: Erotic Painting and Visual Pleasure in the Roman House', *Classical Antiquity* 14/2: 266–88

1997. 'Reading Broken Skin: Violence in Roman Elegy', in Hallett and Skinner 1997

ed. 2002 *The Roman Gaze: Vision, Power and the Body* (Baltimore and London: Johns Hopkins University Press)

Freedman, Luba. 1995. *Titian's Portraits through Aretino's Lens* (Univeristy Park, PA: Penn State Press)

Friedman, Donald M. 1966. 'The "Thing" in Wyatt's Mind', *Essays in Criticism* 16/4: 375–81

1967. 'The Mind in the Poem: Wyatt's They Fle From Me', *Studies in English Literature 1500–1900* 7/1: 1–13

Frontisi-Ducroux, Françoise. 1996. 'Eros, Desire and the Gaze', in *Sexuality in Ancient Art*, ed. Natalie Boyel Kampen (Cambridge: Cambridge University Press)

Frow, John. 1990. 'Intertextuality and Ontology', in Worton and Still 1990

Frye, Susan. 1992. 'The Myth of Elizabeth at Tilbury', *Sixteenth Century Journal* 23: 95–114

1993. *Elizabeth I: The Competition for Representation* (New York: Oxford University Press)

Fulkerson, Laurel. 2005. *The Ovidian Heroine as Author: Reading, Writing and Community in the Heroides* (Cambridge: Cambridge University Press)

Fyler, John M. 2009. 'The Medieval Ovid', in *A Companion to Ovid*, ed. Peter E. Knox (Chichester: Blackwell)

Gaisser, Julia Haig. 1977. 'Mythological Exempla in Propertius 1.2 and 1.15', *The American Journal of Philology* 98/4: 381–91

1993. *Catullus and his Renaissance Readers* (Oxford: Clarendon Press)

ed. 2001. *Catullus in English* (Harmondsworth: Penguin)

ed. 2007. *Essays in Catullus* (Oxford: Oxford University Press)

2009. *Catullus* (West Sussex: Wiley-Blackwell)

Galinsky, Karl. 1996. *Augustan Culture: An Interpretative Introduction* (New Jersey: Princeton University Press)

Gardner, Helen. 1965. *The Elegies and The Songs and Sonnets* (Oxford: Clarendon Press)

Gardner, Jane F. 1986. *Women in Roman Law and Society* (London and Sydney: Croom Helm)

Gardner, R., trans. 1958. *The Speeches: Pro Caelio-De Provinciis Consularibus-Pro Balbo* (Cambridge, MA: Harvard University Press)

Gavinelli, Simona. 2006. 'The Reception of Propertius in Late Antiquity and Neolatin and Renaissance Literature', in Günter 2006

Geffcken, Katherine. 1973. *Comedy in the Pro Caelio* (Leiden: Brill)

Gibson, Bruce. 1999. 'Ovid on Reading: Reading Ovid. Reception in Ovid *Tristia* II', *Journal of the Roman Society* 89: 19–37

Gibson, Roy K. 2012. 'Gallus: The First Roman Love Elegist', in Gold 2012

Gildenhard, Ingo. 2007. 'Greek Auxiliaries: Tragedy and Philosophy in Ciceronian Invective', in *Cicero on the Attack: Invective and Subversion in the Orations and Beyond*, ed. J. Booth (Cerdigion: The University Press of Wales)

Gill, Daniel Juan. 2002. 'Before Intimacy: Modernity and Emotion in Early Modern Discourse of Sexuality', *English Literary History* 69/4: 861–87

Gill, Roma. 1972. '*Musa iocosa mea*: Thoughts on the *Elegies*', in *John Donne: Essays in Celebration*, ed. A.J. Smith (London: Methuen)

Gillespie, Stuart. 1992. 'A Checklist of Restoration English Translations and Adaptations of Classical Greek and Latin Poetry 1660–1800', *Translation and Literature* 1/1: 52–67

Ginzburg, Carlo. 1990. 'Titian, Ovid and Sixteenth Century Erotic Illustration', in *Myths, Emblems, Clues*, trans. John and Anne C. Tedeschi (London: Radius)

Golahny, Amy, ed. 1996. *The Eye of the Poet: Studies in the Reciprocity of the Visual and Literary Arts from the Renaissance to the Present* (New Jersey and London: Bucknell University Press)

Gold, Barbara, ed. 2012. *A Companion to Roman Love Elegy* (Malden and Oxford: Wiley-Blackwell)

Goldhill, Simon. 2001. 'The Erotic Eye: Visual Stimulation and Cultural Conflict', in *Being Greek Under Rome: Cultural Identity, the Second Sophistic and the Development of Empire*, ed. Simon Goldhill (Cambridge: Cambridge University Press)

2007. 'What is Ekphrasis For?' *Classical Philosophy* 102: 1–19

González, José M. 2000. 'Musai Hypophetores: Apollonius of Rhodes on Inspiration and Interpretation', *Harvard Studies in Classical Philology* 100: 269–92

Gordon, Pamela. 1997. 'The Lover's Voice in Heroides 15: Or, Why Is Sappho a Man?' in Hallett and Skinner 1997

2002. 'Some Unseen Monster: Rereading Lucretius on Sex', in Fredrick 2002

Gransden, K.W., ed. 1996. *Virgil in English* (London: Penguin)

Gratwick, A.S. 1991. 'Catullus XXXII', *The Classical Quarterly* 41/2: 547–51

Green, Ian. 2009. *Humanism and Protestantism in Early Modern English Education* (Farnham: Ashgate)

Green, Janet. 1997. ' "I My Self": Queen Elizabeth I's Oration at Tilbury Camp', *Sixteenth Century Journal* 28: 421–45

Greenblatt, Stephen. 1980. *Renaissance Self-Fashioning: From More to Shakespeare* (Chicago and London: University of Chicago Press)

2011. *The Swerve: How the World Became Modern* (New York and London: Norton & Co.)

Greene, Ellen. 1985. 'Reconfiguring the Feminine Voice: Catullus Translating Sappho', *Arethusa* 32: 1–18

1995a. 'The Catullan Ego: Fragmentation and the Erotic Self', *The American Journal of Philology* 116: 77–93

1995b. 'Elegiac Woman: Fantasy, *Materia* and Male Desire in Propertius 1.3 and 1.11', *The American Journal of Philology* 116/2: 303–18

1998. *The Erotics of Domination: Male Desire and the Mistress in Latin Love Poetry* (Baltimore: Johns Hopkins University Press)

2005a. 'Gender Identity and the Elegiac Hero in Propertius 2.1', in Ancona and Greene 2005

2005b. 'Gender and Genre in Propertius 2.8 and 2.9', in Batstone and Tissol 2005

Greene, T.M. 1982. *The Light in Troy: Imitation and Discovery in Renaissance Poetry* (New Haven and London: Yale University Press)

Greer, Germaine. 1995. *Slip-Shod Sibyls: Recognition, Rejection and the Woman Poet* (London: Viking Press)

Griffin, Jasper. 1977. 'Propertius and Antony', *Journal of the Roman Society* 67: 17–26

Guibbory, A. 1990. '"Oh let me not serve so": The Politics of Love in Donne's *Elegies*', *English Literary History* 57: 811–33

Günter, Hans-Christian, ed. 2006. *Brill's Companion to Propertius* (Leiden: Brill)

Gutting, Edward. 2006. 'Marriage in the *Aeneid*: Venus, Vulcan, and Dido', *Classical Philology* 101: 263–79

Gutzwiller, Kathryn. 2012. 'Catullus and the Garland of Meleager', in Du Quesnay and Woodman 2012

Guy-Bray, Stephen, Joan Pong Linton and Steve Mentz, eds. 2013. *The Age of Thomas Nashe* (Farnham: Ashgate)

Habinek, Thomas. 1997. 'The Invention of Sexuality in the World-City of Rome', in *The Roman Cultural Revolution*, ed. Thomas Habinek and Alessandro Schiesaro (Cambridge: Cambridge University Press)

　　1998. *The Politics of Latin Literature: Writing, Identity and Empire in Ancient Rome* (New Jersey: Princeton University Press)

　　2002. 'Ovid and Empire', in *The Cambridge Companion to Ovid*, ed. Philip Hardie (Cambridge: Cambridge University Press)

Hackett, Helen. 1995. *Virgin Mother, Maiden Queen: Elizabeth I and the Cult of the Virgin Mary* (Hampshire and London: Macmillan)

　　2000. *Women and Romance Fiction in the English Renaissance* (Cambridge: Cambridge University Press)

　　2008. 'Dream-visions of Elizabeth I', in *Reading the Early Modern Dream: The Terrors of the Night*, ed. Katharine Hodgkin, Michelle O'Callaghan and S.J. Wiseman (London: Routledge)

Hadfield, Andrew. 2003. 'Duessa's Trial and Elizabeth's Error – Judging Elizabeth in Spenser's *Faerie Queene*', in Doran and Freeman 2003

　　2006. 'Literary Contexts: Predecessors and Contemporaries', in *The Cambridge Companion to John Donne*, ed. Achsah Guibbory (Cambridge: Cambridge University Press)

　　2007. 'Donne's *Songs and Sonets* and Artistic Identity', in *Early Modern English Poetry: A Critical Companion*, ed. Patrick Cheney, Andrew Hadfield and Garrett A. Sullivan Jr. (Oxford: Oxford University Press)

Hager, Alan. 1991. *Dazzling Images: The Masks of Sir Philip Sidney* (London: Associated University Presses)

Hall, Edith. 2000. 'Female Figures and Metapoetry in Old Comedy', in *The Rivals of Aristophanes: Studies in Athenian Old Comedy*, ed. David Harvey and John Wilkins (London: Duckworth)

Hallett, Judith. 1977. '*Perusinae glandes* and the Changing Image of Augustus', *American Journal of Ancient History* 2: 151–71

　　1992. 'Martial's Sulpicia and Propertius' Cynthia', *Classical World* 86/2: 99–123

2002a. 'Women's Voices and Catullus' Poetry', *Classical World* 95/4: 421–4

2002b. 'Sulpicia and the Valerii: Family Ties and Poetic Unity', in *Noctes Atticae: 34 Articles on Graeco-Roman Antiquity and its Nachleben*, ed. Bettina Amden *et al.* (Copenhagen: Museum Tusculanum Press)

2002c. 'Women Writing in Rome and Cornelia, Mother of the Gracchi', in Churchill *et al.* 2002

2002d. 'The Eleven Elegies of the Augustan Poet Sulpicia', in Churchill *et al.* 2002

2006. 'Sulpicia and Her Fama: An Intertextual Approach to Recovering Her Latin Literary Image', *Classical World* 100/1: 37–42

2009. 'Sulpicia and Her Resistant Intertextuality', in *Jeux de Voix: Enonciation, Intertextualité et Intentionalité dans La Literature Antique*, ed. Danielle van Mal-Maeder, Alexandre Burnier and Loreto Núñez (Bern: Peter Lang)

2012. 'Authorial Identity in Latin Love Elegy: Literary Fictions and Erotic Failings', in Gold 2012

Hallett, Judith P. and Marilyn B. Skinner, eds. 1997. *Roman Sexualities* (New Jersey: Princeton University Press)

Hamer, Mary. 2008. *Signs of Cleopatra: Reading an Icon Historically* (Exeter: University of Exeter Press)

Hamrick, Stephen. 2003. 'Tottel's Miscellany and the English Reformation', *Criticism* 44/4: 329–61

ed. 2013. *Tottel's Songes and Sonettes in Context* (Farnham: Ashgate)

Hannay, Margaret P. 1985. *Silent But for the Word: Tudor Women as Patrons, Translators and Writers of Religious Works* (Ohio: Kent State University Press)

1990. *Philip's Phoenix: Mary Sidney, Countess of Pembroke* (Oxford: Oxford University Press)

2002. 'The Countess of Pembroke's Agency in Print and Scribal Culture', in Justice and Tinker 2002

2013. *Mary Sidney, Lady Wroth* (Farnham: Ashgate)

Hannen, Thomas A. 1974. 'The Humanism of Sir Thomas Wyatt', in *The Rhetoric of Renaissance Poetry: From Wyatt to Milton*, ed. Thomas O. Sloan and Raymond B. Waddington (Berkeley, Los Angeles and London: University of California Press)

Hardie, Philip. 1997. 'Questions of Authority: The Invention of Tradition in Ovid Metamorphoses 15', in *The Roman Cultural Revolution*, ed. Thomas Habinek and Alessandro Schiesaro (Cambridge: Cambridge University Press)

1999. 'Ovid as Laura: Absent Presences in the *Metamorphoses* and Petrarch's *Rime Sparse*', in Hardie *et al.* 1999

2002. *Ovid's Poetics of Illusion* (Cambridge: Cambridge University Press)

2012a. 'Virgil's Catullan Plots', in Du Quesnay and Woodman 2012

2012b. *Rumour and Renown: Representations of Fama in Western Literature* (Cambridge: Cambridge University Press)

2013. '*Redeeming the Text*, Reception Studies, and the Renaissance', *Classical Receptions Journal* 5/2: 190–8

Hardie, Philip, Alessandro Barchiesi and Stephen Hinds, eds. 1999. *Ovidian Transformations: Essays on the Metamorphoses and its Reception* (Cambridge: Cambridge University Press)

Harmon, Daniel P. 1974. 'Myth and Fantasy in Propertius 1.3', *Transactions of the American Philological Society* 104: 151–65

Harper, Kyle. 2013. *From Shame to Sin: The Christian Transformation of Sexual Morality in Late Antiquity* (Cambridge, MA: Harvard University Press)

Harries, Byron. 1990. 'The Spinner and the Poet: Arachne in Ovid's Metamorphoses', *Proceedings of the Cambridge Philological Society* 36: 64–82

2007. 'Acting the Part', in *Cicero on the Attack: Invective and Subversion in the Orations and Beyond*, ed. J. Booth (Cerdigion: The University Press of Wales)

Harrison, Stephen. 2002. 'Ovid and Genre: Evolutions of an Elegist', in *The Cambridge Companion to Ovid*, ed. Philip Hardie (Cambridge: Cambridge University Press)

Harvey, Elizabeth D. 1992. *Ventriloquized Voices: Feminist Theory and English Renaissance Texts* (London and New York: Routledge)

1999. 'Matrix as Metaphor: Midwifery and the Conception of Voice', in *John Donne, Contemporary Critical Essays*, ed. Andrew Mousley (Basingstoke: Palgrave)

2007. 'Spenser, Virginity and Sexuality', in *Early Modern English Poetry: A Critical Companion*, ed. Patrick Cheney, Andrew Hatfield and Garrett A. Sullivan Jr. (New York and Oxford: Oxford University Press)

Havelock, Christine Mitchell. 1995. *The Aphrodite of Knidos and her Successors: A Historical Review of the Female Nude in Greek Art* (Ann Arbor: University of Michigan Press)

Heale, Elizabeth. 1995. 'Women and the Courtly Love Lyric: The Devonshire MS (BL Additional 17492)', *The Modern Language Review* 90/2: 296–313

1998. *Wyatt, Surrey and Early Tudor Poetry* (Essex: Longman)

Heath, John. 1996. 'The Stupor of Orpheus: Ovid's "Metamorphoses" 10.64–71', *The Classical Journal* 91/4: 353–70

Helgerson, Richard. 1976. *The Elizabethan Prodigals* (Berkeley, Los Angeles and London: University of California Press)

Hemelrijk, Emily A. 2002. *Matrona Docta: Educated Women in the Roman élite from Cornelia to Julia Domna* (Abingdon: Routledge)

Hentschell, Roze. 2009. 'Moralizing Apparel in Early Modern Literature, Sermons and Sartorial Display', *Journal of Medieval and Early Modern Studies* 39/3: 571–95

Herman, Peter C., ed. 1994. *Re-Thinking the Henrician Era: Essays on Early Tudor Texts and Contexts* (Urbana and Chicago: University of Illinois Press)

1996. *Squitter-Wits and Muse-Haters: Sidney, Spenser, Milton and Renaissance Anti-Poetic Sentiment* (Detroit: Wayne State University Press)

2009. 'Early English Protestantism and Renaissance Poetics: The Charge is Committing Fiction in the Matter of Rastell v. Frith', *Renaissance and Reformation* 18/1: 5–18

2010. *Royal Poetrie: Monarchic Verse and the Political Imaginary of Early Modern England* (Ithaca and London: Cornell University Press)

Herrera, Gregorio Rodriguez. 1999. 'Propertius 2.1.71-78 and the Latin Epitaphs', *Mnemosyne* 52/2: 194–7

Hersey, George L. 2009. *Falling in Love with Statues: Artificial Humans from Pygmalion to the Present* (Chicago and London: University of Chicago Press)

Hester, M. Thomas. 1987. 'Donne's (Re)Annunciation of the Virgin(ia Colony) in *Elegy XIX*', *South Central Review* 4/2: 49–64

Hexter, Ralph. 2002. 'Ovid in the Middle Ages: Exile, Mythographer, Lover', in *Brill's Companion to Ovid*, ed. Barbara Weiden Boyd (Leiden: Brill)

Heyworth, Gregory. 2009. *Desiring Bodies: Ovidian Romance and the Cult of Form* (Indiana: University of Notre Dame Press)

Heyworth, S.J. 2007. *Cynthia: A Companion to the Text of Propertius* (Oxford: Oxford University Press)

2012. 'The Elegiac Book: Patterns and Problems', in Gold 2012

Hibbard, G.R. 1962. *Thomas Nashe: A Critical Introduction* (London: Routledge)

Higgins, D. 1996. 'Sappho's Splintered Tongue: Silence in Sappho 31 and Catullus 51', in *Re-Reading Sappho: Reception and Transmission*, ed. Elaine Greene (California: University of California Press)

Hill, Christine M. and Mary G. Morrison, eds. 1975. *Robert Garnier, Two Tragedies: Hippolyte and Marc Antoine* (London: Athlone Press)

Hilliard, Stephen. 1986. *The Singularity of Thomas Nashe* (Lincoln and London: University of Nebraska Press)

Hillman, David and Carla Mazzio, eds. 1997. *The Body in Parts: Fantasies of Corporeality in Early Modern Europe* (New York and London: Psychology Press)

Hillman, Richard. 2012. 'The French Accent of Seneca on the Tudor Stage', in *New Perspectives on Tudor Cultures*, ed. Mike Pincombe and Zsolt Almási (Newcastle upon Tyne: Cambridge Scholars Publishing)

Hinds, Stephen. 1987a. *The Metamorphoses of Persephone: Ovid and the Self-Conscious Muse* (Cambridge: Cambridge University Press)

1987b. 'The Poetess and the Reader: Further Steps Towards Sulpicia', *Hermathena* 143: 29–46

1987c. 'Generalising about Ovid', *Ramus* 16: 4–31

1998. *Allusion and Intertext: Dynamics of Appropriation in Roman Poetry* (Cambridge: Cambridge University Press)

Holzberg, Niklas. 1999. 'Four Poets and a Poetess or a Portrait of the Poet as a Young Man? Thoughts on Book 3 of the Corpus Tibullianum', *The Classical Journal* 94/2: 169–91

2005. 'Impotence? It Happened to the Best of Them! A Linear Reading of the "Corpus Priapeorum"', *Hermes* 133/3: 368–81

Hooper, Richard W. 1985. 'In Defence of Catullus' Dirty Sparrow', *Greece and Rome* 32/2: 162–78.

Houghton, Luke. 2011. 'Death Ritual and Burial Practice in the Latin Love Elegists', in *Memory and Mourning: Studies on Roman Death*, ed. Valerie Hope and Janet Huskinson (Oxford: Oxbow Books)

2013. 'Renaissance Latin Love Elegy', in *The Cambridge Companion to Latin Love Elegy*, ed. Thea S. Thorsen (Cambridge: Cambridge University Press)

Howard, Skiles. 1994. '"Ascending the Riche Mount": Performing Hierarchy and Gender in the Henrician Masque', in Herman 1994

Hubbard, Thomas K. 1984. 'Art and Vision in Propertius 2.31/2.32', *Transactions of the American Philological Association* 114: 281–97

2005. 'The Invention of Sulpicia', *The Classical Journal* 100/2: 177–94

Hull, Elizabeth M. 1996. 'All My Deed But Copying Is: The Erotics of Identity in Astrophil and Stella', *Texas Studies in Literature and Language* 38/2: 175–90

Hulse, S. Clark. 1978. 'Shakespeare's *Venus and Adonis*', *Proceedings of the Modern Languages Association* 93/1: 95–105

1986. 'Stella's Wit: Penelope Rich as Reader of Sidney's Sonnets', in *Rewriting the Renaissance: The Discourse of Sexual Difference in Early Modern Europe*, ed. Margaret W. Ferguson, Maureen Quilligan and Nancy Vickers (Chicago and London: University of Chicago Press)

Hunt, Lynn, ed. 1993. *The Invention of Pornography: Obscenity and the Origins of Modernity, 1500–1800* (New York: Zone Books)

Hunter, Richard. 1993. *The Argonautica of Apollonius: Literary Studies* (Cambridge: Cambridge University Press)

2006. *The Shadow of Callimachus: Studies in the Reception of Hellenistic Poetry at Rome* (Cambridge: Cambridge University Press)

Huntingford, N.P.C. 1981. 'Ovid Amores 1.5', *Acta Classica* 24: 107–17

Hutchinson, G.O. 1984. 'Propertius and the Unity of the Book', *The Journal of Roman Studies* 74: 99–106

2012. 'Booking Lovers: Desire and Design in Catullus', in Du Quesnay and Woodman 2012

Hutson, Lorna. 1989. *Thomas Nashe in Context* (Oxford: Clarendon Press)

Irish, Bradley J. 2011. 'Gender and Politics in the Henrician Court: The Douglas-Howard Lyrics in the Devonshire Manuscript (BL Add 17492)', *Renaissance Quarterly* 64/1: 79–114

Irving, Singer. 2009. 'Neoplatonism and the Renaissance', in *The Nature of Love: Courtly and Romantic* (Chicago: University of Chicago Press)

Ives, Eric. 2004. *The Life and Death of Anne Boleyn* (Cambridge, Cambridge, MA and Oxford: Blackwell)

James, Sharon. 1998. 'Constructions of Gender and Genre in Roman Comedy and Elegy', *Helios* 25/1: 3–16

2001. 'The Economics of Roman Elegy: Voluntary Poverty, the Recusatio, and the Greedy Girl', *The American Journal of Philology* 122/2: 223–53

2003. *Learned Girls and Male Persuasion: Gender and Reading in Roman Love Elegy* (Berkeley: University of California Press)

2010. 'Ipsa Dixerat: Women's Words in Roman Love Elegy', *Phoenix* 64: 314–44

Janan, Michaela. 2001. *The Politics of Desire: Propertius IV* (Berkeley, Los Angeles and London: University of California Press)

Javitch, Daniel. 1984. 'The Orlando Furioso and Ovid's Revision of the Aeneid', *MLN* 99/5: 1023–36

Jayne, Sears. 1995. *Plato in Renaissance England* (Netherlands: Springer)

Jocelyn, H.D. 1980. 'On Some Unnecessarily Indecent Interpretations of Catullus 2 and 3', *The American Journal of Philology* 101/4: 421–41

Johnson, Patricia J. 1996. 'Constructions of Venus in Ovid's *Metamorphoses* 5', *Arethusa*: 125–49

Johnson, Patricia and Martha Malamud. 1988. 'Ovid's "Musomachia"', *Pacific Coast Philology* 23/1–2: 30–8

Johnson, W.R. 1996. 'The Rapes of Callisto', *The Classical Journal* 92/1: 9–24

2007. 'Neoteric Poets', in Skinner 2007a

2009. *A Latin Lover in Ancient Rome: Readings in Propertius and his Genre* (Columbus: Ohio State University Press)

2012. 'Propertius', in Gold 2012

Jones, Anne Rosalind. 1990. *The Currency of Eros: Women's Love Lyric in Europe 1540–1620* (Bloomington: Indiana University Press)

Jones, Anne Rosalind and Peter Stallybrass. 1984. 'The Politics of *Astrophil and Stella*', *Studies in English Literature, 1500–1900* 24: 53–68

Jones, Julian Ward Jr. 1998. 'Catullus' "Passer" as "Passer"', *Greece & Rome* 45/2: 188–94

Justice, George L. and Nathan Tinker, eds. 2002. *Women's Writing and the Circulation of Ideas: Manuscript Publication in England, 1550–1800* (Cambridge: Cambridge University Press)

Kallendorf, Craig. 1999. *Virgil and the Myth of Venice: Books and Readers in the Italian Renaissance* (Oxford: Oxford University Press)

ed. and trans. 2002. *Humanist Educational Treatises* (Cambridge and Cambridge, MA: Harvard University Press)

2007a. *The Virgilian Tradition: Book History and the History of Reading in Early Modern Europe* (Aldershot: Ashgate)

2007b. *The Other Virgil: 'Pessimistic' Readings of the Aeneid in Early Modern Culture* (Oxford: Oxford University Press)

Kamholtz, Jonathan Z. 1978. 'Thomas Wyatt's Poetry: The Politics of Love', *Criticism* 20/4: 349–65

Kaplan, E. Ann. 1983. 'Is the Gaze Male?', in *Powers of Desire*, ed. Anne Snitow, Christine Stansell and Sharon Thompson (New York: Monthly Review)

Kay, Dennis, ed. 1987. *Sir Philip Sidney: An Anthology of Modern Criticism* (Oxford: Oxford University Press)

Keach, William. 1977. *Elizabethan Erotic Narratives: Irony and Pathos in the Ovidian Poetry of Shakespeare, Marlowe and Their Contemporaries* (New Jersey: Rutgers University Press)

Keith, Alison. 1994. 'Corpus Eroticum: Elegiac Poetics and Elegiac Puellae in Ovid's "Amores"', *Classical World* 88/1: 27–40

1997. 'Tandem Venit Amor: A Roman Woman Speaks of Love', in Hallett and Skinner 1997

1999. 'Versions of Epic Masculinity', in Hardie *et al.* 1999

2000. *Engendering Rome: Women in Latin Epic* (Cambridge: Cambridge University Press)

2006. 'Critical Trends in Interpreting Sulpicia', *Classical World* 100/1: 3–10

2008. *Propertius: Poet of Love and Leisure* (London: Duckworth)

2012. 'The Domina in Roman Elegy', in Gold 2012

Kellum, Barbara. 1997. 'Concealing/Revealing: Gender and the Play of Meaning in the Monuments of Augustan Rome', in *The Roman Cultural Revolution*, ed. Thomas Habinek and Alessandro Schiesaro (Cambridge: Cambridge University Press)

Kennedy, Duncan F. 1992. '"Augustan" and "Anti-Augustan": Reflections on Terms of Reference', in Powell 1992

1993. *The Arts of Love: Five Studies in the Discourses of Roman Love Elegy* (Cambridge: Cambridge University Press)

2002. 'Epistolarity: The Heroides', in *The Cambridge Companion to Ovid*, ed. Philip Hardie (Cambridge: Cambridge University Press)

2008. 'Elegy and the Erotics of Narratology', in Liveley and Salzman-Mitchell 2008

2012. 'Love's Tropes and Figures', in Gold 2012

Kennedy, William J. 1994. *Authorizing Petrarch* (Ithaca and London: Cornell University Press)

Kewes, Paulina. 2012. '"A Fit Memorial for the Times to Come": Admonition and Topical Application in Mary Sidney's Antonius and Samuel Daniel's Cleopatra', *The Review of English Studies* 63: 243–64

Kilgour, Maggie. 2012. *Milton and the Metamorphosis of Ovid* (Oxford: Oxford University Press)

Kinney, Arthur F. 1972. 'Parody and its Implications in Sidney's *Defence of Poesy*', *Studies in English Literature* 12: 1–19

Klein, Lisa M. 1992. 'The Petrarchism of Sir Thomas Wyatt Reconsidered', in *The Work of Dissimilitude: Essays from the Citadel Conference on Medieval and Renaissance Literature*, ed. David G. Allen and Robert A. White (New Jersey and London: Associated University Presses)

Knowles, Melody D. 2012. '"Now English denizend, though Hebrue borne": Did Mary Sidney Herbert, Countess of Pembroke, Read Hebrew?', *Studies in Philology* 109/3: 279–89

Knox, Peter E. 1985. 'Wine, Water, and Callimachean Polemics', *Harvard Studies in Classical Philology* 89: 107–19

2007. 'Catullus and Callimachus', in Skinner 2007a

Kohn, Thomas D. 2013. *The Dramaturgy of Senecan Tragedy* (Ann Arbor: University of Michigan Press)

Kragelund, Patrick. 2008. 'Senecan Tragedy: Back on Stage?', in Fitch 2008

Krostenko, Brian A. 2001. *Cicero, Catullus and the Language of Social Performance* (Chicago and London: University of Chicago Press)

2007. 'Catullus and Elite Republican Social Discourse', in Skinner 2007a

Kuin, Roger and Anne Lake Prescott. 2000. 'The Wrath of Priapus: Rémy Belleau's "Jean qui ne peult" and its Tradition', *Comparative Literature Studies* 37/1: 1–17

LaBranche, A. 1966. '"Blanda Elegeia": The Background to Donne's "Elegies"', *The Modern Language Review* 61/3: 357–68

Labriola, Albert C. 1996. 'Painting and Poetry of the Cult of Elizabeth I: The Ditchley Portrait and Donne's "Elegie: Going to Bed" ', *Studies in Philology*, 93/1: 42–63

Laird, Andrew. 1993. 'Sounding Out Ecphrasis: Art and Text in Catullus 64', *Journal of the Roman Society* 83: 18–30

2002. 'Authority and Ontology of the Muses in Epic Receptions', in Spentzou and Fowler 2002

Lamb, Mary Ellen. 1990. *Gender and Authorship in the Sidney Circle* (Madison: University of Wisconsin Press)

Langlands, Rebecca. 2006. *Sexual Morality in Ancient Rome* (Cambridge: Cambridge University Press)

Lateiner, Donald. 1977. 'Obscenity in Catullus', in Gaisser 2007

1984. 'Mythic and Non-Mythic Artists in Ovid's Metamorphoses', *Ramus* 13/ 1: 1–30

Lawner, Lynn. 1988. 'I modi', in *The Sixteenth Pleasures (1527)* (London: Peter Owen Publishers)

Leach, Eleanor Winsor. 1997. 'Venus, Thetis and the Social Construction of Maternal Behaviour', *The Classical Journal* 92/4: 347–71

Leen, Anne. 2000. 'Clodia Oppugnatrix: The Domus Motif in Cicero's *Pro Caelio*', *The Classical Journal* 96/2: 141–62

Lehnhof, Kent Russell. 2008. 'Profeminism in Philip Sidney's *Apologie for Poetrie*', *Studies in English Literature 1500–1900* 48/1: 23–43

Leigh, M. 2004. 'The Pro Caelio and Comedy', *Classical Philology* 99: 300–35

Leishman, J.B. 1951. *The Monarch of Wit: An Analytical and Comparative Study of the Poetry of John Donne* (London: Hutchinson University Library)

Lerer, Seth. 1997. *Courtly Letters in the Age of Henry VIII* (Cambridge: Cambridge University Press)

Lerner, Laurence. 1988. 'Ovid and the Elizabethans', in Martindale 1988

Levene, D.S. 2000. 'Sallust's Catiline and Cato the Censor', *The Classical Quarterly* 50/1: 170–91

Lever, J.W. 1956. *The Elizabethan Love Sonnet* (London: Methuen)

Levin, Carole. 1994. *'The Heart and Stomach of a King': Elizabeth I and the Politics of Sex and Power* (Philadelphia: University of Pennsylvania Press)

Levin, Harry. 1969. *The Myth of the Golden Age in the Renaissance* (Bloomington and London: Indiana University Press)

Levy, Charles S. 1984. 'Sidneian Indirection: The Ethical Irony of *Astrophil and Stella*', in *Sir Philip Sidney and the Interpretation of Renaissance Culture*, ed. Gary F. Waller and Michael D. Moore (London: Croom Helm)

Lewalski, B.K. 1993. *Writing Women in Jacobean England* (Cambridge, Cambridge, MA and London: Harvard University Press)

Lindheim, Sara H. 2003. *Mail and Female: Episolary Narrative and Desire in Ovid's Heroides* (Wisconsin: University of Wisconsin Press)

Liveley, Genevieve and Patricia Salzman-Mitchell, eds. 2008. *Latin Elegy and Narratology: Fragments of a Story* (Columbus: Ohio State University Press)

Lobanov-Rostovsky, Sergei. 1997. 'Taming the Basilisk', in Hillman and Mazzio 1997

Low, Anthony. 1990. 'Donne and the Reinvention of Love', *English Literary Renaissance* 20: 465–86

Lowe, N.J. 1988. 'Sulpicia's Syntax', *Classical Quarterly* 38/1: 193–205

Lowrie, Michèle. 2009. *Writing, Performance and Authority in Augustan Rome* (Oxford: Oxford University Press)

Lyne, Raphael. 2001. *Ovid's Changing Worlds: English Metamorphoses, 1567–1632* (Oxford: Oxford University Press)

  2002. 'Love and Exile After Ovid', in *The Cambridge Companion to Ovid*, ed. Philip Hardie (Cambridge: Cambridge University Press)

Lyne, R.O.A.M. 1978. 'The Neoteric Poets', in Gaisser 2007

  1979. 'Servitium Amoris', *The Classical Quarterly* 29/1: 117–30

  1980. *Latin Love Poets: From Catullus to Horace* (Oxford: Oxford University Press)

  1987. *Further Voices in Vergil's Aeneid* (Oxford: Oxford University Press)

  1998. 'Love and Death: Laodamia and Protesilaus in Catullus, Propertius, and Others', *The Classical Quarterly* 48/1: 200–12

Mackay, L.A. 1962. 'Sallust's Catiline: Date and Purpose', *Phoenix* 16/3: 181–94

MacRobert, A.E. 2002. *Mary, Queen of Scots and the Casket Sonnets* (London: I.B. Tauris)

Mahon, Alyce. 2005. *Eroticism and Art* (Oxford: Oxford University Press)

Maltby, Robert. 2002. *Tibullus: Elegies – Text, Introduction, and Commentary* (Cambridge: Francis Cairns)

Manuwald, Gesine. 2012. 'Thomas Campion: A Poet Between The Two Worlds of Classical and English Literature', in *Neo-Latin Poetry in the British Isles*, ed. L.B.T. Houghton and Gesine Manuwald (London: Bristol Classical Press)

Marotti, A. 1982. ' "Love is not love": Elizabethan Sonnet Sequences and the Social Order', *English Literary History* 49/2: 396–428

  1986. *John Donne: Coterie Poet* (Madison: University of Wisconsin Press)

  1995. *Manuscript, Print, and the English Renaissance Lyric* (Ithaca and London: Cornell University Press)

  1999. *Catholicism and Anti-Catholicism in Early Modern English Texts*, ed. Arthur F. Marotti (Hampshire: Macmillan)

Martindale, Charles, ed. 1988. *Ovid Renewed: Ovidian Influences on Literature and Art from the Middle Ages to the C20th* (Cambridge: Cambridge University Press)

  1993. *Redeeming the Text: Latin Poetry and the Hermeneutics of Reception* (Cambridge: Cambridge University Press)

  2006. 'Thinking Through Reception', in Martindale and Thomas 2006

  2013. 'Reception: A New Humanism? Receptivity, Pedagogy, the Transhistorical', *Classical Receptions Journal* 5/2: 169–83

Martindale, Charles and Michelle Martindale. 1990. *Shakespeare and the Uses of Antiquity: An Introductory Essay* (London: Routledge)

Martindale, Charles and Richard F. Thomas, eds. 2006. *Classics and the Uses of Reception* (Oxford: Blackwell)

Mason, H.A. 1986. *Sir Thomas Wyatt: A Literary Portrait* (Bristol: Bristol Classical Press)

Masten, Jeffrey. 1991. '"Shall I turne blabb?": Circulation, Gender, and Subjectivity in Wroth's Sonnets', *Reading Mary Wroth: Representing Alternatives in Early Modern England*, ed. Naomi J. Miller and Gary Fredric Waller (Knoxville: University of Tennessee Press)

Matz, Robert. 2000. *Defending Literature in Early Modern England: Renaissance Literary Theory in Social Context* (Cambridge: Cambridge University Press)

Maus, K.E. 1993. 'A Womb of His Own: Male Renaissance Poets in the Female Body', in *Sexuality and Gender in Early Modern Europe: Institutions, Texts, Images*, ed. J.G. Turner (Cambridge: Cambridge University Press)

McCabe, Richard A. 1981. 'Elizabethan Satire and the Bishops' Ban of 1599', *Yearbook of English Studies* 1: 188–93

McCarthy, K. 1998. 'Servitium Amoris: Amor Servitii', in *Women and Slaves in Greco-Roman Culture*, ed. Sandra R. Joshel and Sheila Murnaghan (London and New York: Routlege)

McCrea, Adriana. 1995. 'Whose Life is it, Anyway? Subject and Subjection in Fulke Greville's Life of Sidney', in *The Rhetorics of Life-Writing in Early Modern Europe: Form of Biography from Cassandra Fedele to Louis XIV*, ed. Thomas F. Myer and D.R. Woolf (Michigan: University of Michigan Press)

McDonnell, Miles. 2006. *Roman Manliness: Virtus and the Roman Republic* (Cambridge: Cambridge University Press)

McGinn, Thomas J.J. 1998. *Prostitution, Sexuality and the Law in Ancient Rome* (Oxford: Oxford University Press)

McIntyre, John P. 1962. 'Sidney's Golden World', *Comparative Literature* 14/4: 356–65

McKeown, J.C. 1995. '*Militat omnis amans*', *The Classical Journal* 90/3: 295–304

McNamee, Kathleen. 1993. 'Propertius, Poetry and Love', in *Woman's Power, Man's Game*, ed. Mary DeForest (Illinois: Bolchazy-Carducci)

McPeek, James A.S. 1939. *Catullus in Strange and Distant Britain* (Cambridge and Cambridge, MA: Harvard University Press)

Merriam, Carol U. 1990. 'Some Notes on the Sulpicia Elegies', *Latomus* 49: 95–8

2006a. *Love and Propaganda: Augustan Venus and the Latin Love Elegists* (Brussels: Editions Latomus)

2006b. 'Sulpicia: Just Another Roman Poet', *Classical World* 100/1: 11–15

Merrix, Robert P. 1986. 'The Vale of Lillies and the Bower of Bliss: Soft-Core Pornography in Elizabethan Poetry', *The Journal of Popular Culture* 19/4: 3–16

Miller, John F. 1995. 'Reading Cupid's Triumph', *The Classical Journal* 90/3: 287–94

Miller, Paul Allen. 1983. 'Sappho 31 and Catullus 51: The Dialogism of Lyric', *Arethusa* 26: 183–99.

1991. 'Sidney, Petrarch and Ovid, or Imitation as Subversion', *English Literary History* 58/3: 499–522

1994. *Lyric Texts and Lyric Consciousness: The Birth of a Genre from Archaic Greece to Augustan Rome* (London and New York: Routledge)

2007. 'Catullus and Roman Love Elegy', in Skinner 2007a

Milnor, Kristina. 2002. 'Sulpicia's (Corpo)reality: Elegy, Authorship, and the Body in [Tibullus] 3.13', *Classical Antiquity* 21/2: 259–82

Mitsi, Efterpi. 2011. 'Myth and Metamorphosis in Stephen Gosson's *Schoole of Abuse*', *English* 60: 108–23

Monti, Richard. 1981. *The Dido Episode and the Aeneid: Roman Social and Political Values in the Epic* (Leiden: Brill)

Montrose, Louis. 1996. '"Shaping Fantasies": Figurations of Gender and Power in Elizabethan Culture', in *New Casebooks: A Midsummer Night's Dream*, ed. Richard Dutton (Basingstoke and London: Palgrave Macmillan)

    2006. *The Subject of Elizabeth: Authority, Gender and Representation* (Chicago and London: University of Chicago Press)

Moore, M.B. 2000. *Desiring Voices: Women Sonneteers and Petrarchism* (Carbondale and Edwardsville: Southern Illinois University Press)

Morales, Helen. 2011. 'Fantasising Phryne: The Psychology and Ethics of Ekphrasis', *The Cambridge Classical Journal (New Series)* 57: 71–104

Morgan, Llewelyn. 2012. 'Elegiac Metre: Opposites Attract', in Gold 2012.

Mortimer, Anthony, ed. 2005. *Petrarch's Canzoniere in the English Renaissance* (Amsterdam and New York: Editions Rodopi)

Moss, Ann. 1982. *Ovid in Renaissance France: A Survey of the Latin Editions of Ovid and Commentaries Printed in France Before 1600* (London: The Warburg Institute)

    1996. *Printed Common-Place Books and the Structures of Renaissance Thought* (Oxford: Clarendon Press)

Moulton, Ian Frederick. 1997. 'Transmuted into a Woman or Worse: Masculine Gender Identity and Thomas Nashe's "Choice of Valentines"', *English Literary Renaissance* 27/1: 57–88

    2000. *Before Pornography: Erotic Writing in Early Modern England* (Oxford: Oxford University Press)

Muecke, Frances. 1974. 'Nobilis Historia? Incongruity in Propertius 4.7', *Bulletin of the Institute of Classical Studies* 21/1: 124–32

Mulvihill, James D. 1982. 'Jonson's Poetaster and the Ovidian Debate', *Studies in English Literature, 1500–1900* 22/2: 239–55

Murgatroyd, P. 1975. '*Militia Amoris* and the Roman Elegists', *Latomus* 34: 59–79

Murray, Penelope. 1981. 'Poetic Inspiration in Early Greece', *The Journal of Hellenic Studies* 101: 87–100

    2002. 'Plato's Muses: The Goddesses that Endure', in Spentzou and Fowler 2002

Myerowitz, Molly. 1992. 'The Domestication of Desire: Ovid's *parva tabella* and the Theater of Love', in Richlin 1992

Myers, Sara K. 1996. 'The Poet and the Procuress: The *lena* in Latin Love Elegy', *The Journal of Roman Studies* 86/1: 1–21

    2012. 'Catullan Contexts in Ovid's *Metamorphoses*', in Du Quesnay and Woodman 2012

Nadeau, Yvan. 1980. 'O passer nequam (Catullus 2, 3)', *Latomus Bruxelles* 39/4: 879–80

1984. 'Catullus' Sparrow, Martial, Juvenal and Ovid', *Latomus* 43/4: 861–8.

Nappa, Christopher. 2007a. 'Catullus and Vergil', in Skinner 2007a

2007b. 'Elegy on the Threshold: Generic Self-Consciousness in Propertius 1.16', *Classical World* 101/1: 57–73

Nash, Ralph. 1996. *The Major Latin Poems of Jacopo Sannazaro* (Michigan: University of Michigan Press)

Nead, Lynda. 1992. *The Female Nude: Art, Obscenity and Sexuality* (London and New York: Routledge)

Nelis, Damien P. 2012. 'Callimachus in Verona: Catullus and Alexandrian Poetry', in Du Quesnay and Woodman 2012

Nelson, C.E. 1963. 'A Note on Wyatt and Ovid', *Modern Language Review* 58: 60–3

Newman, John. 1984. 'The New Gallus and the Origins of Latin Love Elegy', *Illinois Classical Studies* 9/1: 19–29

Newton, Francis L. 1962. 'Tibullus in Two Grammatical Florilegia of the Middle Ages', *Transactions and Proceedings of the American Philological Association* 93: 253–86

Nicholl, Charles. 1984. *The Cup of News: The Life of Thomas Nashe* (London: Routledge & Kegan Paul)

Nicoll, W.S.M. 1977. 'Ovid's Amores 1.5', *Mnemosyne* 30: 40–9

1980. 'Cupid, Apollo, and Daphne (Ovid *Met.* 1.452ff)', *Classical Quarterly* 30/1: 174–82

Norbrook, David. 1984. *Poetry and Politics in the English Renaissance* (London and Boston: Routledge and Kegan Paul)

Oberth, Iris. 2013. 'English Translations of Robert Garnier's Plays', *Elizabethan Translation and Literary Culture* 36: 275–7

O'Hara, James. 1989. 'The New Gallus and the *alternae voces* of Propertius 1.10.10', *The Classical Quarterly* 39/2: 561–2

1996. 'An Unconvincing Etymological Argument About Aeneas and the Gates of Sleep', *Phoenix* 50/3–4: 331–34

2007. *Inconsistency in Roman Epic: Studies in Catullus, Lucretius, Vergil, Ovid and Lucan* (Cambridge: Cambridge University Press)

Oliensis, Ellen. 1997a. 'The Erotics of *amicitia*: Readings in Tibullus, Propertius and Horace', in Hallett and Skinner 1997

1997b. 'Sons and Lovers: Sexuality and Gender in Virgil's Poetry', in *The Cambridge Companion to Virgil*, ed. Charles Martindale (Cambridge: Cambridge University Press)

O'Rourke, Donncha. 2012. 'Intertextuality', in Gold 2012

Orr, Mary. 2003. *Intertextuality: Debates and Contexts* (Cambridge: Polity Press)

Pach, Wilhelm Michelle. 1987. 'Venus, Diana, Dido and Camilla in the *Aeneid*', *Vergilius* 33: 43–8

Papaioannou, Sophia. 2005. *Epic Succession and Dissension: Ovid, Metamorphoses 13.623–14.582 and the Reinvention of the Aeneid* (Berlin: Walter de Gruyter)

Papanghelis, Theodore D. 1987. *Propertius: A Hellenistic Poet on Love and Death* (Cambridge: Cambridge University Press)

1989. 'About the Hour of Noon: Ovid, Amores 1.5', *Mnemosyne* 42: 54–61

Parker, Holt N. 1992. 'Love's Body Anatomized: The Ancient Erotic Handbooks and the Rhetoric of Sexuality', in Richlin 1992

    1994. 'Sulpicia, the *auctor de Sulpicia* and the Authorship of 3.9 and 3.11 of the Corpus Tibullianum', *Helios* 21/1: 39–62

    1997. 'The Teratogenic Grid', in Hallett and Skinner 1997

    2006. 'Catullus and the Amicus Catulli: The Text of a Learned Talk', *Classical World* 100/1: 17–29

    2012. 'Renaissance Latin Elegy', in Gold 2012

Parry, Adam. 1966. 'The Two Voices of Virgil's *Aeneid*', in *Virgil: A Collection of Critical Essays*, ed. Steele Commager (New Jersey: Prentice Hall)

Pearcy, Lee T. 2006. 'Erasing Cerinthus: Sulpicia and Her Audience', *Classical World* 100/1: 31–6

Perkell, Christine. 1997. 'The Lament of Juturna: Pathos and Interpretation in the Aeneid', *Transactions of the American Philological Association* 127: 257–86

    2002. 'The Golden Age and its Contradictions in the Poetry of Vergil', *Vergilius* 48: 3–39

Perkins, Caroline. 2011. 'The Figure of Elegy in *Amores* 3.1: Elegy as Puella, Puella as Poeta', *Classical World* 104/3: 313–31

Petrie, Jennifer. 1983. *Petrarch: The Augustan Poets, the Italian Tradition, and the Canzoniere* (Dublin: Irish Academic)

Pfeiffer, Rudolf. 1976. *History of Classical Scholarship from 1300–1850* (Oxford: Oxford University Press)

Pigman, George. 1985. *Grief and English Renaissance Elegy* (Cambridge: Cambridge University Press)

Pincus, Matthew. 2004. 'Propertius, Gallus and the Erotics of Influence', *Arethusa* 37/4: 165–96

Platter, Charles. 1995. '*Officium* in Catullus and Propertius: A Foucauldian Reading', *Classical Philology* 90/3: 211–24

Pomeroy, Arthur John. 2003. 'Heavy Petting in Catullus', *Arethusa* 36/1: 49–60

Potter, Lois. 2012. *The Life of William Shakespeare: A Critical Biography* (Chichester: Wiley-Blackwell)

Powell, A., ed. 1992. *Roman Poetry and Propaganda in the Age of Augustus* (London: Bristol Classical Press)

Prendergast, Maria Teresa Micaela. 1995. 'The Unauthorised Orpheus of *Astrophil and Stella*', *Studies in English Literature 1500–1900* 35/1: 19–34

    1999. *Renaissance Fantasies: The Gendering of Aesthetics in Early Modern Fiction* (Ohio and London: Kent State University Press)

Prescott, Anne Lake. 2008a. 'Mary Sidney's French Sophocles: The Countess of Pembroke Reads Robert Garnier', in *Representing France and the French in Early Modern English Drama*, ed. Jean-Christophe Mayer (Newark: Associated University Press)

    2008b. 'Mary Sidney's *Antonius* and the Ambiguities of French History', *Yearbook of English Studies* 38: 216–33

Pugh, Syrithe. 2005. *Spenser and Ovid* (Aldershot: Ashgate)

Putnam, Michael. 1980. 'Propertius and the New Gallus Fragment', *Zeitschrift Für Papyrologie und Epigraphik* 39:49–56

1998. *Virgil's Epic Designs: Ekphrasis in the Aeneid* (New Haven and London: Yale University Press)

ed. and trans. 2009. *Jacopo Sannazaro: Latin Poetry* (Cambridge and Cambridge, MA: Harvard University Press)

Quinn, Kenneth. 1968. *Virgil's Aeneid: A Critical Description* (London: Routlege & Kegan Paul)

Quint, David. 1983. *Origin and Originality in Renaissance Literature: Versions of the Source* (New Haven and London: Yale University Press)

1993. *Epic and Empire: Politics and Generic Form from Virgil to Milton* (Princeton: Princeton University Press)

Raber, Karen. 2001. *Dramatic Difference: Gender, Class and Genre in the Early Modern Closet Drama* (Delaware: University of Delaware Press)

Reckford, Kenneth. 1995. 'Recognising Venus (1): Aeneas Meets his Mother', *Arion* 3/2: 1–42

Reed, Nicholas. 1973. 'The Gates of Sleep in *Aeneid 6*', *Classical Quarterly* 23/2: 311–15

Rees, Joan. 1964. *Samuel Daniel: A Critical and Biographical Study* (Liverpool: Liverpool University Press)

Reid, Jane Davidson. 1993. *The Oxford Guide to Classical Mythology in the Arts, 1300–1990s*, 2 vols. (Oxford: Oxford University Press)

Revard, Stella P. 1986. 'Donne and Propertius: Love and Death in London and Rome', in *The Eagle and the Dove: Reassessing John Donne*, ed. Claude J. Summers and Ted-Larry Pebworth (Columbia: University of Missouri Press)

1993. 'The Sapphic Voice in Donne's Sapho to Philaenis' in Summers and Pebworth 1993

Reynolds, L.D., ed. 1983. *Texts and Transmission: A Survey of the Latin Classics* (Oxford: Clarendon Press)

Reynolds, L.D. and N.G. Wilson. 1968, revised 1991. *Scribes and Scholars: A Guide to the Transmission of Greek and Latin Literature* (Oxford: Oxford University Press)

Richardson, L. Jr. 2006. *Propertius Elegies I–IV with Introduction and Commentary* (Oklahoma: University of Oklahoma Press)

Richlin, Amy. 1983, revised 1992. *The Garden of Priapus: Sexuality and Aggression in Roman Humour* (Oxford: Oxford University Press)

ed. 1992. *Pornography and Representation in Ancient Greece and Rome* (Oxford: Oxford University Press)

Richmond, John. 2002. 'Manuscript Traditions and the Transmission of Ovid's Works', in *Brill's Companion to Ovid*, ed. Barbara Weiden Boyd (Leiden: Brill)

Riggs, David. 1989. *Ben Jonson: A Life* (London, Cambridge and Cambridge, MA: Harvard University Press)

Roberts, Josephine. 1983. Introduction to *The Poems of Lady Mary Wroth* (Baton Rouge: Louisiana State University Press)

Roche, Thomas Jr. 1989. *Petrarch and the English Sonnet Sequences* (New York: AMS Press)

    1997. '*Astrophil and Stella*: A Radical Reading', in *Sir Philip Sidney: An Anthology of Modern Criticism*, ed. Dennis Kay (Oxford: Oxford University Press)

Roessel, David. 1990. 'The Significance of the Name Cerinthus in the Poems of Sulpicia', *Transactions of the American Philological Association* 120: 243–50

Rogerson, Anne. 2002. 'Dazzling Likeness: Seeing Ekphrasis in *Aeneid* 10', *Ramus* 31: 51–72

Roman, L. 2006. 'A History of Lost Tablets', *Classical Antiquity* 25/2: 351–88

Rosati, Gianpiero. 1996. 'Sabinus, the Heroides and the Poetnightingale: Some Observations on the Authenticity of the Epistula Sapphus', *The Classical Quarterly* 46/1: 207–16

Rose, C.B. 1998. 'Troy and the Historical Imagination', *Classical World* 91/5: 405–13

Rose, H.J. 1924. 'Anchises and Aphrodite', *Classical Quarterly* 18/1: 11–16

Rosenthal, Margaret F. 1992. *The Honest Courtesan: Veronica Franco, Citizen and Writer in Sixteenth-Century Venice* (Chicago and London: University of Chicago Press)

Rouse, Richard H. 1979. 'Florilegia and Latin Classical Authors in Twelfth- and Thirteenth-Century Orleans', *Viator* 10/1: 131–60

Rouse, R. and M. Reeve. 1983. '*Tibullus*', in Reynolds 1983

Rowse, A.L. 1974. *Simon Forman: Sex and Society in Shakespeare's Age* (London: Weidenfeld & Nicolson)

Rubin, Patricia. 2000. 'The Seductions of Antiquity', in *Manifestations of Venus: Art and Sexuality*, ed. Caroline Arscott and Katie Scott (Manchester: Manchester University Press)

Rudd, Niall. 1990. 'Dido's *culpa*', in *Oxford Readings in Virgil's Aeneid*, ed. S.J. Harrison (Oxford: Oxford University Press)

Ruvoldt, Maris. 2004. *The Italian Renaissance Imagery of Inspiration: Metaphors of Sex, Sleep, and Dreams* (Cambridge: Cambridge University Press)

Salzman, Michele Renee. 1982. 'Cicero, the Megalenses and the Defence of Caelius', *The American Journal of Philology* 103/3: 299–304

Salzman, Paul. 2006. *Reading Early Modern Women's Writing* (Oxford: Oxford University Press)

Salzman-Mitchell, Patricia B. 2005. *A Web of Fantasies: Gaze, Image and Gender in Ovid's Metamorphoses* (Columbus: Ohio State University Press)

    2008. 'Snapshots of a Love Affair: *Amores* 1.5 and the Program of Elegiac Narrative', in Liveley and Salzman-Mitchell 2008

Sanchez, Melissa E. 2013. '"In My Selfe the Smart I Try": Female Promiscuity in *Astrophil and Stella*', *English Literary History* 80/1: 1–27

Sanders, Rachele. 1988. *Gender and Literary on Stage in Early Modern England* (Cambridge: Cambridge University Press)

Santirocco, Matthew S. 1979. 'Sulpicia Reconsidered', *The Classical Journal* 74/3: 229–39

Scanlon, James J. 1976. 'Sidney's Astrophil and Stella: "See What It Is to Love" Sensually!' *Studies in English Literature, 1500–1900* 16/1: 65–74

Schneider, Gary. 2005. *The Culture Of Epistolarity: Vernacular Letters And Letter Writing In Early Modern England, 1500–1700* (New Jersey: Rosemount Publishing)

Schurink, Fred. 2010. 'Manuscript Commonplace Books, Literature and Reading in Early Modern England', *Huntingdon Library Quarterly* 73/3: 453–69

Schwarz, Kathryn. 2000. *Tough Love: Amazon Encounters in the English Renaissance* (Durham, NC and London: Duke University Press)

Scott-Baumann, Elizabeth. 2013. 'Early Modern Women's Writing and the Rhetoric of Modesty', *The Review of English Studies* 64: 344–5

Sebesta, Judith Lynn. 1994. *Weavers of Fate: Symbolism in the Costume of Roman Women* (College of Arts & Sciences, Vermillion: University of South Dakota)

Sessions, W.A. 1994. 'Surrey's Wyatt: Autumn 1542 and the New Poet', in *Rethinking the Henrician Era: Essays on Early Tudor Texts and Contexts*, ed. Peter Herman (Urbana: University of Illinois Press)

Seznec, Jean. 1995. *The Survival of the Pagan Gods: The Mythological Tradition and its Place in Renaissance Humanism and Art*, trans. Barbara F. Sessions (New Jersey: Princeton University Press)

Shapiro, James. 2005. *1599: A Year in the Life of William Shakespeare* (London: Faber & Faber)

Sharrock, Alison. 1991. 'Womanufacture', *The Journal of Roman Studies* 81: 36–49

1995. 'The Drooping Rose: Elegiac Failure in *Amores* 3.7', *Ramus* 24/2: 152–80

2002a. 'An A-musing Tale: Gender, Genre and Ovid's Battles with Inspiration in the *Metamorphoses*', in Spentzou and Fowler 2002

2002b. 'Looking at Looking: Can You Risk a Reading?', in Fredrick 2002

2002c. 'Gender and Sexuality', in *The Cambridge Companion to Ovid*, ed. Philip Hardie (Cambridge: Cambridge University Press)

2002d. 'Ovid and the Discourse of Love: the Amatory Works', in *The Cambridge Companion to Ovid*, ed. Philip Hardie (Cambridge: Cambridge University Press)

Simon, Margaret. 2012. 'Refraining Songs: The Dynamics of Form in Sidney's *Astrophil and Stella*', *Studies in Philology* 109/1: 86–102

Simons, Patricia. 2011. *The Sex of Men in Premodern Europe: A Cultural History* (Cambridge: Cambridge University Press)

Sinfield, Alan. 1980. 'Sidney and Astrophil', *Studies in English Literature 1500–1900* 20/1: 25–41

Singer, Irving. 2009. *The Nature of Love* (Cambridge, MA: MIT Press)

Sitterson, Joseph C. 1992. 'Allusive and Elusive Meanings: Reading Ariosto's Vergilian Ending', *Renaissance Quarterly* 45/1: 1–19

Skinner, Marilyn. 1981. *Catullus' Passer: The Arrangement of the Book of Polymetric Poems* (New Hampshire: Arno Press)

1983. 'Clodia Metelli', *Transactions of the American Philological Association* 113: 273–87

1993. '*Ego mulier*: The Construction of Male Sexuality in Catullus', in Gaisser 2007

2003. *Catullus in Verona: A Reading of the Elegiac Bibellus, Poems 65–116* (Columbus: The Ohio State University Press)

2005. *Sexuality in Greek and Roman Culture* (Cambridge, Cambridge, MA and Oxford: Blackwell)

ed. 2007a. *A Companion to Catullus* (Cambridge, Cambridge, MA and Oxford: Blackwell)

2007b. 'Authorial Arrangement of the Collection: Debate Past and Present', in Skinner 2007a

2011. *Clodia Metelli: The Tribune's Sister* (Oxford: Oxford University Press)

Skoie, Mathilde. 2002. *Reading Sulpicia: Commentaries 1475–1990* (Oxford: Oxford University Press)

2006. 'Passing on the Panpipes: Genre and Reception', in *Classics and the Uses of Reception*, ed. C. Martindale and R. Thomas (Malden and Oxford: Blackwell)

2008. 'Telling Sulpicia's Joys: Narrativity at the Receiving End', in Liveley and Salzman-Mitchell 2008

2012. 'Corpus Tibullianorum, Book 3', in Gold 2012

Skretkowicz, Victor. 1999. 'Mary Sidney Herbert's *Antonius*, English Philhellenism and the Protestant Cause', *Women's Writing* 6: 7–25

Skulsky, Susan. 1985. '"Invitus, Regina…": Aeneas and the Love of Rome', *The American Journal of Philology* 106/4: 447–55

Smith, C.J. and R. Corvino, eds. 2011. *Praise and Blame in Roman Oratory* (Swansea: Classical Press of Wales)

Smith, Riggs Alden. 2005. *The Primacy of Vision in Virgil's Aeneid* (Austin: University of Texas Press)

Smith, Rosalind. 2005. *Sonnets and the English Woman Writer, 1560–1621: The Politics of Absence* (Hampshire and New York: Palgrave Macmillan)

Solodow, Joseph B. 1988. *The World of Ovid's Metamorphoses* (Chapel Hill: University of North Carolina Press)

Southall, Raymond. 1964. *The Courtly Maker: An Essay on the Poetry of Wyatt and his Contemporaries* (Oxford: Blackwell)

Spentzou, Efrossina. 2002a. 'Secularizing the Muse', in Spentzou and Fowler 2002

2002b. 'Stealing Apollo's Lyre', in Spentzou and Fowler 2002

2003. *Readers and Writers in Ovid's Heroides: Transgressions of Genre and Gender* (Oxford: Oxford University Press)

Spentzou, Efrossina and Don Fowler, eds. 2002. *Cultivating the Muse: Struggles for Power and Inspiration in Classical Literature* (Oxford: Oxford University Press)

Spiller, Michael. 2001. *Early Modern Sonneteers: From Wyatt to Milton* (Devon: Northcote House Publishers)

Squire, Michael. 2011. *The Art of the Body: Antiquity and Its Legacy* (London: I.B. Tauris)

St. Clare Byrne, Clare. 1936. *The Letters of King Henry VIII* (London, Toronto and Melbourne: Cassell and Company)

Stallybrass, Peter. 1992. 'Transvestism and the "Body Beneath": Speculating on the Boy Actor', in *Erotic Politics: Desire on the Renaissance Stage*, ed. Susan Zimmerman (New York and London: Routledge)

Stapleton, M.L. 1991. 'Nashe and the Poetics of Obscenity: The Choise of Valentines', *Classical and Modern Literature* 12: 29–48

1995. 'A New Source for Thomas Nashe's The Choise of Valentines', *English Language Notes* 31: 15–18

1996. *Harmful Eloquence: Ovid's Amores from Antiquity to Shakespeare* (Ann Arbor: University of Michigan Press)

1999. '"Thou idle wanderer, about my heart": Rochester and Ovid', *Restoration: Studies in English Literary Culture 1660–1700* 23: 15–18

2001. 'Ovid the Rakehell: The Case of Wycherley', *Restoration: Studies in English Literary Culture 1660–1700* 25/2: 85–102

2014. 'Marlovian Residue in Jonson's *Poetaster*', *Early Modern Literary Studies*, 2014

Starkey, David. 2008. *Henry: Virtuous Prince* (London: HarperPress)

Stevens, John. 1961, reprinted with corrections 1979. *Music and Poetry in the Early Tudor Court* (Cambridge: Cambridge University Press)

Stewart, Alan. 2000. *Philip Sidney: A Double Life* (London: Chatto & Windus)

Stewart, Peter. 2003. *Statues in Roman Society: Representations and Response* (Oxford: Oxford University Press)

Straznicky, Marla. 1994. '"Profane Stoical Paradoxes": The Tragedie of Mariam and Sidnean Closet Drama', *English Literary Renaissance* 24/1: 104–34.

2004. *Women's Closet Drama, 1550–1700* (Cambridge: Cambridge University Press)

Strong, Roy. 1973. *Splendour at Court: Renaissance Spectacle and Illusion* (London: Weidenfeld & Nicolson)

1987. *Gloriana: The Portraits of Elizabeth I* (London and New York: Thames & Hudson)

1999. *The Cult of Elizabeth: Elizabethan Portraiture and Pageantry* (London: Pimlico)

Stroup, Sarah Culpepper. 2010. *Catullus, Cicero, and a Society of Patrons: The Generation of the Text* (Cambridge: Cambridge University Press)

Strout, Nathaniel. 1984. 'Reading "A Celebration of Charis" and the Nature of Jonson's Art', *Texas Studies in Literature and Language* 26/1: 128–43

Stubbs, John. 2007. *John Donne: The Reformed Soul* (London: Penguin)

Suleiman, Susan Rubin. 1986. *The Female Body in Western Culture: Contemporary Perspectives* (Cambridge, Cambridge, MA and London: Harvard University Press)

Sullivan, J.P. 1976. *Propertius: A Critical Introduction* (Cambridge: Cambridge University Press)

Summers, C.J. and T.-L. Pebworth, eds. 1993. *Renaissance Discourses of Desire* (Columbia and London: University of Missouri Press)

Sutton, Dana. 1986. *Seneca on the Stage* (Leiden: Brill)

Swann, Bruce W. 1994. *Martial's Catullus: The Reception of an Epigrammatic Rival* (Hildesheim: Georg Olms)

Syme, Ronald. 1939. *The Roman Revolution* (Oxford: Oxford University Press)

Talvacchia, Bette. 1999. *Taking Positions: On the Erotic in Renaissance Culture* (Princeton: Princeton University Press)

Tarrant, R.J. 1982. 'Aeneas and the Gates of Sleep', *Classical Philology* 77/1: 51–5
  2002. 'Ovid and Ancient Literary History', in *The Cambridge Companion to Ovid*, ed. Philip Hardie (Cambridge: Cambridge University Press)
Tatum, W. Jeffrey. 2011. 'Invective Identities in *Pro Caelio*', in *Praise and Blame in Roman Republican Rhetoric*, ed. Christopher Smith and Ralph Corvino (Swansea: The Classical Press of Wales)
Taylor, A.B., ed. 2000. *Shakespeare's Ovid: The Metamorphoses in the Plays and Poems* (Cambridge: Cambridge University Press)
Thibault, John C. 1964. *The Mystery of Ovid's Exile* (Berkeley and Los Angeles: University of California Press)
Thomson, Patricia. 1964. *Sir Thomas Wyatt and His Background* (London: Routledge and Kegan Paul)
Todd, F.A. 1931. 'Virgil's Evocation of Erato', *The Classical Review* 45/6: 216–18
Toll, Katherine. 1989. 'What's Love Got To Do With It? The Invocation to Erato and Patriotism in the *Aeneid*', *Quaderni Urbanati di Cultura Classica* 33/3: 107–18
Tonry, Kathleen. 2008. 'John Skelton and the New Fifteenth Century', *Literature Compass* 5/4: 721–39.
Travitsky, Betty, ed. 1989. *The Paradise of Women: Writings by Englishwomen of the Renaissance* (New York: Columbia University Press)
Treggiari, Susan. 1991. *Roman Marriage: iusti coniuges From the Time of Cicero to the Time of Ulpian* (Oxford: Oxford University Press)
Trill, Suzanne. 1996. 'Sixteenth-Century Women's Writing: Mary Sidney's Psalmes and the "Femininity" of Translating', in *Writing and the English Renaissance*, ed. William Zunder and Suzanne Trill (London and New York: Longman)
Turner, James Grantham, ed. 1993. *Sexuality and Gender in Early Modern Europe: Institutions, Texts, Images* (Cambridge: Cambridge University Press)
Uden, James and Ian Fielding. 2010. 'Latin Elegy in the Old Age of the World: The Elegiac Corpus of Maximinius', *Arethus* 43/3: 439–60
Uhlfelder, Myra L. 1955. 'Medea, Ariadne and Dido', *The Classical Journal* 50/7: 310–12
Ullman, Berthold Louis. 1928. 'Tibullus in the Mediaeval florilegia', *Classical Philology* 23/2: 128–74
Valladares, Hérica. 2012. 'Elegy, Art and the Viewer', in Gold 2012
van Eck, Caroline, Stijn Bussels, Maarten Delbeke and Jürgen Pieters, eds. 2012. *Translations of the Sublime: The Early Modern Reception and Dissemination of Longinus' Peri Hupsous in Rhetoric, the Visual Arts, Architecture and the Theatre* (Leiden: Brill)
Verducci, Florence. 1985. *Ovid's Toyshop of the Heart: Epistulae Heroidum* (New Jersey: Princeton University Press)
Veyne, Paul. 1988. *Roman Erotic Elegy: Love, Poetry and the West* (Chicago and London: University of Chicago Press)
Vickers, Brian, ed. 1999. *English Renaissance Literary Criticism* (Oxford: Oxford University Press)
Vickers, N.J. 1981. 'Diana Described: Scattered Woman and Scattered Rhyme', *Critical Enquiry* 8/2: 265–79

Villeponteaux, Mary. 1998. '"Not as women wonted be": Spenser's Amazon Queen', in Walker 1998

Vout, Caroline. 2007. *Power and Eroticism in Imperial Rome* (Cambridge: Cambridge University Press)

Walker, Greg. 2000. 'John Skelton and the Royal Court', in *Vernacular Literature and Current Affairs: France, England and Scotland*, ed. Jennifer Britnell and Richard Britnell (Aldershot: Ashgate)

Walker, Julia M., ed. 1998. *Dissing Elizabeth: Negative Representations of Gloriana* (Durham, NC and London: Duke University Press)

Wall, Wendy. 1993. *The Imprint of Gender: Authorship and Publication in the English Renaissance* (Ithaca and London: Cornell University Press)

Wallace, Andrew. 2010. *Virgil's Schoolboys: The Poetics of Pedagogy in Renaissance England* (Oxford: Oxford University Press)

Wallace, Marina, Martin Kemp and Joanna Bernstein. 2007. *Seduced: Art and Sex from Antiquity to Now* (London and New York: Merrell)

Wallace-Hadrill, Andrew. 1982. 'The Golden Age and Sin in Augustan Ideology', *Past and Present* 95: 19–36

Waller, Gary Fredric. 1977. *Pamphilia to Amphilanthus* (Vienna: University of Salzburg Press)

Warden, John. 1980. *Fallax Opus: Poet and Reader in the Elegies of Propertius* (Toronto, Buffalo and London: University of Toronto Press)

   1996. 'The Dead and the Quick: Structural Correspondances and Thematic Relationships in Propertius 4.7 and 4.8', *Phoenix* 50/2: 118–29

Weiner, Andrew D. 1974. 'Structure and Fore Conceit in Astrophil and Stella', *Texas Studies in Literature and Language* 16.1: 1–25

Weinstock, Stefan. 1971. *Divus Julius* (Oxford: Oxford University Press)

Welch, Tara S. 2005. *The Elegiac Cityscape: Propertius and the Meaning of Roman Monuments* (Columbus: The Ohio State University Press)

   2012. 'Elegy and the Monuments', in Gold 2012

Wells, Robin Headwell. 1983. *Spenser's Faerie Queene and the Cult of Elizabeth* (London: Croom Helm)

West, David A. 1990. 'The Bough and the Gate', in *Oxford Readings in Virgil's Aeneid*, ed. S.J. Harrison (Oxford: Oxford University Press)

Wheeler, Bonnie, ed. 2000. *Listening To Heloise: The Voice of a Twelfth-Century Woman* (New York: Palgrave Macmillan)

Wheeler, Stephen Michael. 1999. *A Discourse of Wonders: Audience and Performance in Ovid's Metamorphoses* (Pennsylvania: University of Pennsylvania Press)

Whigham, Frank. 1981. 'The Rhetoric of Elizabeth Suitors' Letters', *Proceedings of the Modern Languages Association* 96/5: 864–82

Wiggers, Nancy. 1977. 'Reconsideration of Propertius II.1', *The Classical Journal* 72/4: 334–41

Wilkinson, Lancelot Patrick. 1955, new ed. 2015. *Ovid Recalled* (Cambridge: Cambridge University Press)

Williams, Craig. 2010. *Roman Homosexuality*, 2nd ed. (Oxford: Oxford University Press)

   2012. *Reading Roman Friendship* (Cambridge: Cambridge University Press)

Williams, Gareth. 1994. *Banished Voices: Readings in Ovid's Exile Poetry* (Cambridge: Cambridge University Press)

Williams, James A. 2009. 'Erected Wit and Effeminate Repose: Philip Sidney's Postures of Reader-Response', *The Modern Language Review* 104/3: 640–58

Wills, Jeffrey. 1996. *Repetition in Latin Poetry: Figures of Allusion* (Oxford: Clarendon Press)

Wilson-Okamura, David Scott. 2010. *Virgil in the Renaissance* (Cambridge: Cambridge University Press)

Wiseman, S. 2008. '"Romes Wanton Ovid": Reading and Writing Ovid's Heroides 1590–1712', *Renaissance Studies* 22/3: 295–306

Wiseman, T.P. 1985. *Catullus and his World: A Reappraisal* (Cambridge: Cambridge University Press)

Witherspoon, Alexander Maclaren. 1924. *The Influence of Robert Garnier on Elizabethan Drama* (Connecticut: Archon Books)

Woodcock, B. 1996. '"Anxious to Amuse": Metaphysical Poetry and the Discourse of Renaissance Masculinity', in *Writing and the English Renaissance*, ed. William Zunder and Suzanne Trill (London and New York: Longman)

Worton, Michael and Judith Still, eds. 1990. *Intertextuality: Theories and Practices* (Manchester: Manchester University Press)

Woudhuysen, Henry. 1996. *Sir Philip Sidney and the Circulation of Manuscripts 1558–1640* (Oxford: Clarendon Press)

Wray, D. 2001. *Catullus and the Poetics of Roman Manhood* (Cambridge: Cambridge University Press)

——— 2012. 'Catullus the Roman Love Elegist?', in Gold 2012

Wyke, Maria. 1992. 'Augustan Cleopatras: Female Power and Poetic Authority', in *Roman Poetry and Propaganda in the Age of Augustus*, ed. A. Powell (London: Bristol Classical Press)

——— 1994. 'Taking the Woman's Part: Engendering Roman Love Elegy', *Ramus* 23/1: 110–28

——— 2002. *The Roman Mistress: Ancient and Modern Representations* (Oxford: Oxford University Press)

Wynne-Davis, Marion. 2007. *Women Writers and Familial Discourse in the English Renaissance* (Basingstoke and New York: Palgrave Macmillan)

Yardley, Y.C. 1977. 'Cynthia's Ghost: Propertius 4.7 Again', *Bulletin of the Institute of Classical Studies* 24/1: 83–7

——— 1978. 'The Elegiac Paraclausithyron', *Eranos* 76: 19–34

——— 1983. 'Propertius 4.7.94 Yet Again', *The American Journal of Philology* 104/3: 281–2

Young, R.V. 1987. '"O my America, my new-found land": Pornography and Imperial Politics in Donne's *Elegies*', *South Central Review* 4/2: 35–48

Zanker, Paul. 1990. *The Power of Images in the Age of Augustus* (Michigan: University of Michigan Press)

Ziolkowski, Jan M. and Michael C.J. Putnam, eds. 2008. *The Virgilian Tradition: The First Fifteen Hundred Years* (New Haven and London: Yale University Press)

Zissos, Andrew. 1999. 'The Rape of Proserpina in Ovid "Met." 5.341–661: Internal Audience and Narrative Distortion', *The Phoenix* 53: 97–113

Index